UTSA DT LIBRARY RENEWALS 458-2440

DATE DUE

D0786620

UTSA DT LIBRARY RENEWALS 458-2440

D0786620

WITHDRAWN
UTSA LIBRARIES

The Polycentric Metropolis

The Polycentric Metropolis
Learning from Mega-City Regions in Europe

Written and Edited by

Peter Hall and Kathy Pain

This project has received European Regional Development Funding through the INTERREG III B Community Initiative

nwe eno
INTERREG IIIB
NORTH WEST EUROPE

EARTHSCAN
London • Sterling, VA

First published by Earthscan in the UK and USA in 2006

Copyright © Selection and editorial matter: Peter Hall and Kathy Pain on behalf of the POLYNET Partners; individual chapters: the contributors, 2006

All rights reserved

ISBN-13: 978-1-84407-329-0 hardback
ISBN-10: 1-84407-329-7 hardback

Typesetting by MapSet Ltd, Gateshead, UK
Printed and bound by Gutenberg Press Ltd, Malta
Cover design by Yvonne Booth

For a full list of publications please contact:

Earthscan
8–12 Camden High Street
London, NW1 0JH, UK
Tel: +44 (0)20 7387 8558
Fax: +44 (0)20 7387 8998
Email: earthinfo@earthscan.co.uk
Web: **www.earthscan.co.uk**

22883 Quicksilver Drive, Sterling, VA 20166-2012, USA

Earthscan is an imprint of James & James (Science Publishers) Ltd and publishes in association with the International Institute for Environment and Development

A catalogue record for this book is available from the British Library

Library of Congress Cataloging-in-Publication Data

Hall, Peter Geoffrey.
  The Polycentric Metropolis : learning from mega-city regions in Europe / by Peter Hall and Kathy Pain
    p. cm.
  Includes bibliographical references and index.
  ISBN-13: 978-1-84407-329-0
  ISBN-10: 1-84407-329-7
  1. Metropolitan area–Europe. 2. Regional planning–Europe. 3. City planning–Europe. I. Pain, Kathy. II. Title.
  HT334.E85H32 2006
  307.76'4094–dc22

                                                              2005034646

Library
University of Texas
at San Antonio

Printed on totally chlorine-free paper

Contents

Part 1 The Polycentric Metropolis: Emerging Mega-City Regions

Part 2 Analysing the Polycentric Metropolis: Quantifying the Mega-City Region

Part 3 Understanding the Polycentric Metropolis: Actors, Networks, Regions

Part 4 Visiting the Polycentric Metropolis: Regional Identities, Regional Policies

Part 5 Planning Europolis: The Effectiveness of Policy

List of Figures and Tables

Figures

Tables

List of Contributors

Laurent Aujean is a researcher in IGEAT (Institut de Gestion de l'Environnement et d'Aménagement du Territoire) at the Free University (Université Libre) of Brussels.

Etienne Castiau is a researcher in IGEAT at the Free University (Université Libre) of Brussels.

David Evans is a Research Associate at the Department of Geography, Loughborough.

Christian Fischer is Lecturer in Human Geography at the University of Trier and was Research Associate in the Heidelberg research team.

Tim Freytag is Lecturer in Human Geography at the University of Heidelberg.

Simone Gabi is Research Assistant in IRL (Institut für Raum- und Landschaftsentwicklung), Netzwerk Stadt und Landschaft, at ETH (Swiss Federal Institute of Technology) Zürich.

Lars Glanzmann is Research Assistant with IRL, Netzwerk Stadt und Landschaft, at ETH Zürich.

Nick Green is a freelance consultant specializing in cartography for planners. He was formerly Fellow of the Institute of Community Studies, now the Young Foundation.

Nathalie Grillon is with IRL, Netzwerk Stadt und Landschaft, at ETH Zürich.

Ludovic Halbert is an Economic Geography Researcher with the French National Scientific Research Centre (CNRS) working at the Laboratoire Techniques, Territoires, Sociétés based at the Ecole Nationale des Ponts et Chaussées.

Peter Hall is Bartlett Professor of Planning and Regeneration at University College London (UCL) and Senior Research Fellow at the Young Foundation, and was Director of the Institute of Community Studies and Project Manager of POLYNET.

Michael Hoyler is Lecturer in Human Geography at Loughborough University and was Associate Team Leader of the Heidelberg research team.

Loek Kapoen is a Senior Lecturer at AMIDSt (Amsterdam Institute for Metropolitan and International Development Studies), University of Amsterdam.

Robert Kloosterman is Professor of Economic Geography and Planning at AMIDSt, University of Amsterdam.

Wolfgang Knapp is Senior Economist and Spatial Planner at ILS NRW (Institut für Landes- und Stadtentwicklungsforschung und Bauwesen des Landes Nordrhein-Westfalen) in Dortmund.

Christian Kruse is Research Assistant in ORL (Institut für Orts-, Regional- und Landesplanung) at ETH Zürich.

Bart Lambregts is a Senior Researcher at AMIDSt, University of Amsterdam.

Christoph Mager is Research Associate at the Department of Geography, University of Heidelberg.

Kathy Pain is a Research Fellow of the Young Foundation (formerly the Institute of Community Studies) and was Project Coordinator of POLYNET.

Gareth Potts is with the Young Foundation (formerly the Institute of Community Studies).

Marcel Roelandts is a Researcher in IGEAT at the Free University (Université Libre) of Brussels.

Robert Röling is a Junior Researcher at AMIDSt, University of Amsterdam.

Daniela Scherhag is an employee of the Chamber of Industry and Commerce in Cologne and was a geographer in the ILS NRW research team.

Peter Schmitt is a Geographer at the University of Dortmund and was involved in the ILS NRW research team.

Martin Sokol is Lecturer at the Department of Geography, Queen Mary, University of London. He was formerly Research Fellow at the Urban Institute Ireland, University College Dublin.

Peter Stafford is Research and Policy Development Executive at the Construction Industry Federation, Ireland. He was formerly Research Fellow at the Urban Institute Ireland, University College Dublin.

Peter Taylor is Professor of Geography and Co-Director of the GaWCT (Globalization and World Cities) Study Group and Network at Loughborough University.

Alain Thierstein is Professor for Raumentwicklung (Spatial Development) at the Technical University Munich. He was formerly Professor for Raumordnung (Spatial Planning) at ETH Zürich.

Christian Vandermotten is Professor of Geography and Vice-President of IGEAT at the Free University (Université Libre) of Brussels.

Chris van Egeraat is Research Fellow at the National Institute for Regional and Spatial Analysis, National University of Ireland, Maynooth. He was formerly Research Fellow at the Urban Institute Ireland, University College Dublin.

Merijn van der Werff is a Junior Researcher at AMIDSt, University of Amsterdam.

David Walker is a Visiting Fellow at GaWC in the Department of Geography at Loughborough and was a research consultant for POLYNET.

Acknowledgements

We want first to thank the funding bodies that made this study possible: the European Union Interreg IIIB North West Europe office in Lille and the Office of the Deputy Prime Minister (ODPM) in London, which provided the main co-funding; and also the South East England Development Agency, the South East Regional Planning Body, the South West Regional Planning Body and the Balzan Foundation, which provided additional funding.

Thanks are also due to the Corporation of London and the ODPM Urban Policy Directorate, which acted as host organizations for the Focus Group meetings in Action 3 of the study.

We would like specifically to acknowledge the help of the following individuals:

In Lille:
Interreg IIIB Secretariat: Philippe Doucet, Claire Colomb, Jacqueline Archer, Nicola Barrett, Monica Tanaka, Jean-Christophe Charlier.

In London and Guildford:
Office of the Deputy Prime Minister, London: Paul Hildreth.
South East Economic Development Agency: Pam Alexander, Paul Hudson, Detlef Golletz, Arno Schmickler.
South East Regional Planning Body: Michael Gwilliam, John Pounder.
South West Regional Planning Body: Keith Woodhead.
Corporation of London: John Watson. Particular thanks are also due to the Corporation of London Economic Development Unit for permission to incorporate data from an earlier study into the South East England interview record reported in Chapters 6–8.
Institute of Community Studies/Young Foundation: Geoff Mulgan, John Stevens, Jill McComish, Teresa Nunes, Nick Green, Gareth Potts, David Walker, Ron Hoyle, Aye Aye San, Thet-Su Naing, Nigel Prentis.
Effusion: Andrew Pain and Richard Dickinson. We owe a particular debt to Andrew Pain for completing an extremely complex job of editing and fine-tuning the illustrations against a sometimes impossibly tight timetable.
Earthscan: Camille Adamson, who worked with us to shape and reshape the design of the book.
London School of Economics: Paul Cheshire, for help with data in the early stages.

In the Randstad:
The *Dutch Ministry of Housing, Spatial Planning and the Environment* for their generous financial support.
The *Amsterdam Institute for Metropolitan and International Development Studies* for additional financial and general assistance. Anna Korteweg, Pieter Preijde and Eva Stegmeijer for performing a variety of supporting activities during the course of the project; Fleur Boulogne for having shown that it does not always have to be that way; and the numerous representatives of both public and private organizations that were so kind to share their valuable knowledge with us during the policy Focus Group meetings and the interviews.

In Heidelberg:
University of Heidelberg, Department of Geography: Professor Peter Meusburger and Stefan Berwing.
The *Ministry of Science, Research and the Arts of the State of Baden-Württemberg* for additional financial support.

In Paris:

Paris-1 Panthéon-Sorbonne University: Professor Pierre Beckouche, Maude Sainteville, Renan Combreau, Flavien Cros, Lucie Déjouhanet, Charles-Henri Froment, Frédérique Delatorre, Frédérique Baudier, for their assistance in researching and writing Chapter 15.
IAURIF: Anne-Marie Roméra, Renaud Diziain, Dominique Lecomte, Catherine Valdérama.
DATAR: Vincent Fouchier.

In Dublin:

Urban Institute Ireland, University College Dublin: Professor Frank Convery, Professor John Yarwood, Frank McGennis for his valuable assistance during the web survey, Daniel McInerney for his cartographic support, and Seán Morrish.
Compass Informatics, Dublin: Gearoid O'Riain, Aidan Power.

All the interviewees and Focus Group participants (business people, sectoral and local experts alike) who generously offered their time and shared their knowledge; and all those managers who took the trouble and time to complete the web survey.

We wish to acknowledge the sources of the following figures: Figures 1.1 and 1.2, ESPON 1.1.1; Figure 9.1, NWMA Spatial Vision Group; Figure 9.2, ODPM; Figure 9.3, Mayor of London; Figure 9.4, SEERA; Figure 9.5, ODPM/GOSE/GOEM/GOEE; Figure 10.3, LISA, 2002.

Finally, the research teams owe a profound debt of gratitude to Ann Rudkin of Alexandrine Press, who copy-edited an exceptionally complex manuscript with exemplary professional skill and efficiency. She went far beyond the narrow definition of her task by making many suggestions that have greatly improved the overall quality of the book, above all by clarifying difficult academic and professional issues for the general reader. We are equally delighted that she is also copy-editing and publishing the special issue of the journal *Built Environment* (Vol. 32, Number 2) which is being published simultaneously with this book and which will illustrate some of these issues in greater detail.

List of Acronyms and Abbreviations

AMIDSt	Amsterdam Institute for Metropolitan and International Development Studies
APS	advanced producer services
CASI	computer-assisted self-interview
CATI	computer-assisted telephone interviews
CBD	central business district
CBS	Central Bureau of Statistics (*Centraal Bureau voor de Statistiek*)
CBSA	core-based statistical area
CEO	chief executive officer
CERN	*Conseil Européen pour la Recherche Nucléaire*
CHF	Swiss francs
CMSA	Combined (formerly Consolidated) Metropolitan Statistical Area
CNRS	*Centre National de la Recherche Scientifique*
CPER	*Contrat de Plan Etat-Région*
CPIBP	*Contrat de Plan Interrégional du Bassin Parisien*
CTRL	Channel Tunnel Rail Link
DATAR	*Délégation à l'Aménagement du Territoire et l'Action Régionale*
DB	Deutsche Bahn
DDR	Deutsche Democratische Republik
DELG	Department of Environment, Heritage and Local Government
DETR	Department of the Environment, Transport and the Regions
DRA	Dublin Regional Authority
EC	European Commission
EERA	East of England Regional Assembly
EMR	European Metropolitan Region
EMRA	East Midlands Regional Assembly
ESDP	European Spatial Development Perspective
ESPON	European Spatial Planning Observation Network
ETCI	European Territorial Cohesion Index
ETH	Swiss Federal Institute of Technology
EU	European Union
EU25	the enlarged European Union
FDI	foreign direct investment
FUR	functional urban region
GaWC	Globalization and World Cities
GDP	gross domestic product
GEMACA	Group for European Metropolitan Areas Comparative Analysis
GOEE	Government Office for the East of England

GOEM	Government Office for the East Midlands
GOSE	Government Office for the South East
Hbf	*Hauptbaunhof* (main station)
HQ	headquarters
IAURIF	*Institut d'Aménagement et d'Urbanisme de la Région Île de France*
ICE	InterCity Express
ICT	information and communication technology
IDA	Industrial Development Agency
IFSC	International Financial Services Centre
IGEAT	*Institut de Gestion de l'Environnement et d'Aménagement du Territoire*
IJ	*IJ-Devers*
ILS NRW	*Institut für Landes- und Stadtentwicklungsforschung und Bauwesen des Landes Nordrhein-Westfalen*
INSEE	*Institut National de la Statistique et des Études Économiques*
INTERREG	EC Community initiative promoting cross-border, transnational and inter-regional cooperation
IRL	*Institut für Raum- und Landschaftsentwicklung*
ISP	Internet Service Provider
IT	information technology
KIS	knowledge-intensive services
KVR	*Kommunalverband Ruhrgebiet*
MCR	mega-city region
MERA	Mid-East Regional Authority
MIPIM	*Marché International des Professionnels d'Immobilier*
MKRO	*Ministerkonferenz für Raumordnung*
MNC	multi-national company
MSA	Metropolitan Statistical Area
MST	micro-systems technology
MURL	*Ministerium für Umwelt, Raumordnung und Landwirtschaft des Landes NRW*
NFA	*Neuer Finanzausgleich*
NSS	National Spatial Strategy
NUTS	Nomenclature of Territorial Units for Statistics
NWE/ERDF	North West Europe European Regional Development Fund
NWMA	North West Metropolitan Area
ODPM	Office of the Deputy Prime Minister (UK)
OECD	Organisation for Economic Co-operation and Development
OMB	United States Office of Management and Budget
ONSS	*Office National de la Sécurité Sociale*
OPODO	Opportunity To Do (a web-based Pan-European travel company)
ORL	*Institut für Orts-, Regional- und Landesplanung*
PA	personal assistant
PAPI	paper-and-pencil interview
PASER	*Projet d'Action Stratégique de l'Etat*
PAT	*Politique d'aménagement du territoire*
PBKAL	Paris–Brussels–Köln-Amsterdam–London high-speed rail network
PN8	the eight POLYNET mega-city regions
PRD	*Plan Régional de Développement*
PUA	Principal Urban Area
R&D	research and development
RER	*Réseau Express Régional*
RPB	Regional Planning Body
RSS	Regional Spatial Strategy
RSV	*Ruimtelijke Structuurplan Vlaanderen*
RVR	*Regionalverband Ruhr*
SDER	*Schéma de Développement de l'Espace Régional Wallon*

SDRIF	*Schéma Directeur de la Région Île-de-France*
SEERA	South East England Regional Assembly
SMEs	small and medium size enterprises
SPF	*Service Public Fédéral*
SPV	Special Purpose Vehicle
SRADT	*Schéma Régional d'Aménagement et de Développement du Territoire*
SVR	*Siedlungsverband Ruhrkohlenbezirk*
TAK	*Tripartite Agglomerationskonferenz*
TEN	trans-European network
TGV	*Train à Grande Vitesse*
UCL	University College London
UNCTAD	United Nations Conference on Trade and Development
UNESCO	United Nations Educational, Scientific and Cultural Organization
VROM	*Ministerie van Volkshuisvesting, Ruimtelijke Ordening en Milieu*
WAN	wide area network
ZDF	*Zweites Deutsches Fernsehen*

PART 1

The Polycentric Metropolis:
Emerging Mega-City Regions

From Metropolis to Polyopolis

Peter Hall and Kathy Pain

The mega-city region: A new phenomenon

A new phenomenon is emerging in the most highly urbanized parts of the world: the *polycentric mega-city region* (MCR). It arises through a long process of very extended decentralization from big central cities to adjacent smaller ones, old and new. Though Jean Gottmann originally identified it as long ago as 1961 in his pioneering study of *Megalopolis: The Urbanized Northeastern Seaboard of the United States*, and Martin Mogridge and John Parr (1997) recognized a similar development around London, its recent rediscovery has been in Eastern Asia, in areas like the Pearl River Delta and Yangtze River Delta regions of China, the Tokaido (Tokyo–Osaka) corridor in Japan, and Greater Jakarta (Gottmann, 1961; Xu and Li, 1990; McGee, 1995; Yeung, 1996; Sit and Yang, 1997; Mogridge and Parr, 1997; Hall, 1999; Scott, 2001; Yeh, 2001). It is a new form: a series of anything between 10 and 50 cities and towns, physically separate but functionally networked, clustered around one or more larger central cities, and drawing enormous economic strength from a new functional division of labour. These places exist both as separate entities, in which most residents work locally and most workers are local residents, and as parts of a wider functional urban region (FUR) connected by dense flows of people and information carried along motorways, high-speed rail lines and telecommunications cables: the 'space of flows' (Castells, 1996, pp376–428) with major implications for sustainable development (Blowers and Pain, 1999). It is no exaggeration to say that this is the emerging urban form at the start of the 21st century.

But MCRs are not exclusively an Asian phenomenon. Recent American work has identified ten 'megalopolitan areas' housing 197 million people, almost 68 per cent of the entire US population (Lang and Dhavale, 2005). And they are a reality in Europe – where this book is the end product of an ambitious attempt to analyse them and understand their significance. Funded by a €2.4 million grant from the European Commission (EC) under the Interreg IIIB (North West Europe) project, in the POLYNET study eight research teams[1] came together, under the leadership of Professor Sir Peter Hall and Dr Kathy Pain in London, to analyse and compare the functioning of eight such regions: *South East England*, the *Randstad (The Netherlands)*, *Central Belgium*, *RhineRuhr*, *Rhine-Main*, the *European Metropolitan Region (EMR) Northern Switzerland*, the *Paris Region* and *Greater Dublin*.

A key feature of these regions is that in different degrees they are polycentric. POLYNET adopts a basic hypothesis that they are becoming more so over time, as an increasing share of population and employment locates outside the largest central city or cities, and as other smaller cities and towns become increasingly networked with each other, exchanging information which bypasses the large central city altogether. But, it needs stressing at the outset, this was simply a hypothesis to be tested in the course of the study.

Polycentricity: Geographical phenomenon or Holy Grail?

This reservation is significant because, in a European context, there is increasing stress on the active encouragement of polycentricity as a policy objective. The European Spatial Development Perspective (ESDP), finally agreed by European Union (EU) Ministers of Planning in Potsdam in 1999, proposed a central policy objective of *polycentrism*: promoting greater polycentricity in the European urban system (European Commission,

1999). But this central term, polycentricity, needs defining.

At the EU level, in the ESDP, *polycentricism* means promoting alternative centres, outside the so-called 'Pentagon' (Figure 1.1) bounded by Birmingham, Paris, Milan, Hamburg and Amsterdam – into 'gateway' cities outside North West Europe, many of which are national political or commercial capitals, serving broad but sometimes thinly populated territories such as the Iberian peninsula, Scandinavia and East Central Europe (Hall, 1993, 1995a, 1995b, 1996, 1999, 2003). But at a finer-grained or regional level, polycentricity refers to outward diffusion from major cities to smaller cities within MCRs, reconfiguring different levels of the urban hierarchy (Christaller, 1966 (1933)): lower-level service functions are dispersed out from higher-order central cities to lower-order cities (Llewelyn Davies, 1996), thus altering not only Manuel Castells's celebrated 'space of places' but also his 'space of flows'. Recent research (Kloosterman and Musterd, 2001; Ipenburg and Lambregts, 2001; Taylor et al, 2003) suggests that indeed, polycentric urban regions in North West Europe may exhibit features that conflict with ESDP sustainability objectives. And this may occur in parallel with increasing *monocentricity* in the developing peripheral regions of the EU (especially the accession countries joined in May 2004) as capital and labour increasingly migrate to a few leading cities and so create regional imbalances between core and periphery within each country. Thus, the entire concept of polycentricity proves highly scale-dependent: polycentricity at one scale may be monocentricity at another (Nadin and Duhr, 2005, p82).

Underlying mechanisms: Globalization and the shift to the advanced service economy

Underlying these spatial processes are two basic and parallel shifts, independent but closely and complexly related: the *globalization* of the world economy, and what can only be called (in an ugly but necessary word) its 'informationalization', the shift in advanced economies away from manufacturing and goods-handling and towards service production, particularly into advanced services that handle information (Castells, 1989, 1996; Hall, 1988, 1995b).

Globalization is not of course new (Cochrane and Pain, 2000; Taylor, 2004a, p815). Ancient Athens and Renaissance Florence were global cities in their respective worlds; so was London from the 16th century onward (Hall, 1998). Thirty foreign banks were already established in London before 1914, a further 19 were added between the two world wars, another 87 by 1969. Then the pace

accelerated: 183 in the 1970s, 115 in the first half of the 1980s; in all, between 1914 and the end of 1985 the number of foreign banks in the City grew more than 14-fold, from 30 to 434. Both London and New York now had more foreign than domestic banks (Thrift, 1987, p210; King, 1990, pp89–90, 113; Moran, 1991, p4; Coakley, 1992, pp57–61; Kynaston, 1994, 1995, passim).

The shift to the informational economy, likewise, is by no means new. It was already recognized over half a century ago (Clark, 1940); by 1991, in typical advanced countries, between three-fifths and three-quarters of all employment was already in services, while between one-third and one-half was in information handling: for information, the proportions were 48 per cent for the USA, 46 per cent for the UK, 45 per cent for France, 39 per cent for Germany and 33 per cent for Japan. Typically these proportions have doubled since the 1920s (Castells, 2000, pp304–324). The trends are very strong and consistent, so there can be little doubt that the proportions will continue to rise, thus by 2025 80–90 per cent of employment will be in services, and up to 60–70 per cent will be in information production and exchange. Thus the shift already appears to be a fundamental long-term economic process, as momentous as the transition from an agrarian to a manufacturing economy in the 18th and 19th centuries; Castells terms it the shift from a manufacturing to an informational mode of development (Castells, 1989, p17, 19).

Its most significant expression is the emergence of the so-called *advanced producer services* (APS): a cluster of activities that provide specialized services, embodying professional knowledge and processing specialized information, to other service sectors. Such knowledge-intensive services, provided by specialist consultancies, are a central feature of the new post-industrial economy, reflecting an acceleration of technological change based especially on micro-electronics, information and computer technology, new materials and biotechnology. Peter Wood describes them:

> … they consist of new and growing types of services, promoting new ways of doing things. These include such diverse activities as television production companies, new types of financial intermediary, contract cleaning corporations and 'bucket-shop' travel agencies. Where the provision of knowledge about change is their purpose, these activities may generally be described as 'knowledge-intensive services' (Wood, 2002, p3).

They offer expertise in a wide range of areas: management and administration, production, research, human resources, information and communication, and marketing (Wood, 2002, p56). Key consultancy companies and networks are becoming increasingly internationalized. Wood and his colleagues have analysed their structure and location in eight EU countries: France,

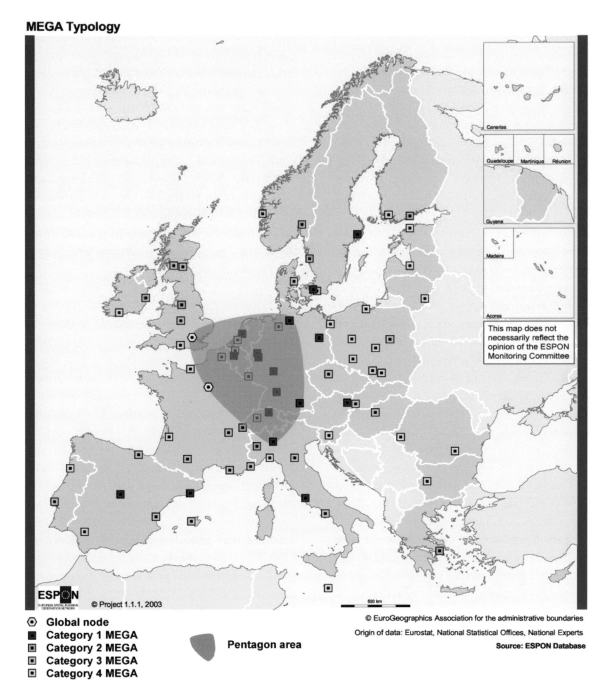

MEGA Typology

⊙ **Global node**
■ **Category 1 MEGA**
▣ **Category 2 MEGA**
▣ **Category 3 MEGA**
▣ **Category 4 MEGA**

Pentagon area

© EuroGeographics Association for the administrative boundaries
Origin of data: Eurostat, National Statistical Offices, National Experts
Source: ESPON Database

Source: ESPON, 2005, Map 5.3, p119

Figure 1.1 The ESDP 'Pentagon'

Germany, The Netherlands, the UK, Italy, Greece, Portugal and Spain. APS are a major focus of the POLYNET study.

A new urban hierarchy: The rise of the world cities[2]

In 1933 Walter Christaller published a famous study of central places in Southern Germany. Later discredited by reason of its use by the Nazi administration in the planning of occupied territory in Europe, it was nevertheless a pioneering attempt to apply spatial modelling in geography. Yet, re-examined, the world it sought to analyse has profoundly changed, almost out of existence.

Christaller's model analysed a town or city's capacity to supply retail services to a surrounding rural area. It identified a seven-level urban hierarchy (Table 1.1) ranging down from the *Landstadt* with a population of 500,000 and a catchment population of 3.5 million, represented by centres such as Munich, Nürnberg, Stuttgart and Frankfurt, and immediately below this the *Provinzstadt* with 100,000 and a regional population of 1 million, represented by places like Augsburg, Ulm, Würzburg and

Regensburg, all the way down to the tiny *Marktorte* with a typical population of 1000 and a catchment area of 3500 people (Christaller, 1966 (1933); Dickinson, 1967). Even then his system failed to capture higher levels in the hierarchy, in particular national capitals. Today, it has been profoundly affected by the globalization of the economy and the progressive shift of advanced economies to information handling, whereby the great majority of the workforce no longer deals with material outputs. Peter Taylor has specifically criticized the Christaller tradition for its obsession with national hierarchies and internal relationships (Taylor, 2004a, p2).

Globalization and informationalization together result in the increasing importance of cities at the very top of the hierarchy, the so-called *world cities* or *global cities*. These, too, are not a new phenomenon: as already seen, they can be traced back for centuries, even millennia (Taylor, 2004a, p815). Patrick Geddes recognized world cities and defined them as early as 1915, in *Cities in Evolution* (Geddes, 1915). In *The World Cities*, first published in 1966, Hall defined them in terms of multiple roles (Hall, 1966). They were centres of political power, both national and international, and of the organizations related to government; centres of national and international trade, acting as entrepôts for their countries and sometimes for neighbouring countries also; hence, centres of banking, insurance and related financial services; centres of advanced professional activity of all kinds, in medicine, law, higher education, and the application of scientific knowledge to technology; centres of information gathering and diffusion, through publishing and the mass media; centres of conspicuous consumption, both of luxury goods for the minority and mass-produced goods for the multitude; centres of arts, culture and entertainment, and of the ancillary activities that catered for them. And it was already evident that these kinds of activities tended to grow in importance; so, in the 20th Century, the world cities went from strength to strength: even as they shed some kinds of activity, from routine manufacturing to routine paper-processing, so they took on new functions and added to existing ones (Hall, 1984).

In the 1980s John Friedmann began to deepen this analysis, suggesting that globalization was resulting in a global hierarchy, in which London, New York and Tokyo were 'global financial articulations', while Miami, Los Angeles, Frankfurt, Amsterdam and Singapore were 'multinational articulations', and Paris, Zürich, Madrid, Mexico City, São Paulo, Seoul and Sydney were 'important national articulations', all forming a 'network' (Friedmann and Wolff, 1982; Friedmann, 1986; Smith and Timberlake, 1995, p294). True, there was a continuing process of goods production and exchange (Gershuny and Miles, 1983; Cohen and Zysman, 1987); the significant development was that the locus of production of APS was becoming increasingly disarticulated from that of production. As Saskia Sassen put it:

The spatial dispersion of production, including its internationalization, has contributed to the growth of centralized service nodes for the management and regulation of the new space economy... To a considerable extent, the weight of economic activity over the last fifteen years has shifted from production places such as Detroit and Manchester, to centers of finance and highly specialized services (*Sassen, 1991, p325*).

Thus there are contradictory trends: as production disperses worldwide, services increasingly concentrate into a relatively few trading cities, both the well-known 'global cities' and a second rung of about 20 cities immediately below these, which we can distinguish as 'sub-global'. These are centres for financial services (banking, insurance) and headquarters of major production companies; most are also seats of major world-power governments (King, 1990; Sassen, 1991). A study of four world cities (Llewelyn-Davies, 1996) distinguished four key groups of advanced service activity:

1 *finance and business services*: including banking and insurance, commercial business services such as law, accountancy, advertising and public relations, and design services including architecture, civil engineering, industrial design and fashion;

Table 1.1 The Christaller central place system (1933)

Type	Market area radius km	Population of town	Population of market area
M (Marktort)	4.0	1000	3500
A (Amtsort)	6.9	2000	11,000
K (Kreisstadt)	12.0	4000	35,000
B (Bezirkstadt)	20.7	10,000	100,000
G (Gaustadt)	36.0	30,000	350,000
P (Provinzstadt)	62.1	100,000	1,000,000
L (Landstadt)	108.0	500,000	3,500,000

Sources: Christaller (1966 (1933)), p67; Dickinson (1967), p51

2 *'power and influence'* (or *'command and control'*): national government, supra-national organizations like the United Nations Educational, Scientific and Cultural Organization (UNESCO) or the Organisation for Economic Co-operation and Development (OECD), and headquarters of major organizations including transnational corporations;

3 *creative and cultural industries*: including live performing arts (theatre, opera, ballet, concerts), museums and galleries and exhibitions, print and electronic media;

4 *tourism*: including both business and leisure tourism, and embracing hotels, restaurants, bars, entertainment, and transportation services.

All these are service industries processing information in a variety of different ways; all demand a high degree of immediacy and face-to-face exchange of information, so that strong agglomeration forces operate. Further, they tend to be highly synergistic, and many key activities fit into interstices between them: hotels, conference centres and exhibition centres are simultaneously business services and part of tourism; museums and galleries are creative/cultural but also parts of tourism; advertising is both creative and a business service. And so strong agglomeration tendencies apply not only within each sector, but also between them.

Understanding world cities: The work of the Loughborough Group

The most important advance in our understanding of the new global hierarchy has come from the *Globalization and World Cities* (GaWC) Study Group and Network at Loughborough University, led by Peter Taylor. Building on the insights of Castells, their thesis represents a fundamental criticism of previous urban research: they argue that in contradistinction, future work should be based on *flows* rather than *attributes*, and that it should take a global rather than a national perspective.

Their argument is that many previous approaches – even in such key contributions as those of Friedmann (1986, 1995) and Sassen (1991, 1994) – concentrate simply on measuring data on global city *attributes*, while ignoring the critical importance of understanding the mutual relationships, the *interdependencies*, between individual members of an entire system of cities: we have to infer for instance that, because of a concentration of high-level service activities such as international banks, a city is exceptionally well-connected (Taylor, 2004a, p8). To some degree, this emphasis is simply due to the abundance of data on attributes and the relative paucity of data on

relationships (Taylor, 2004a, p18) – though the pioneering work of Allan Pred (1973, 1977) on American urban networks was a major exception (van Houtum and Lagendijk, 2001, p749). There are exceptions: for instance, air traffic data and telecommunications traffic data. But they suffer from lack of differentiation: air traffic figures for Miami, for instance, are distorted by the huge tourist traffic into and out of Florida – and similarly, though perhaps to a lesser degree, with the figures for London as compared with other major cities.

There are two major problems with such relational data. First, the fact that London (for instance) is the first international airport system in traffic terms reflects the fact that it is simultaneously a major business centre, a major cultural centre and a major tourist centre, and that all these are synergistic; likewise with competitor cities like Paris, Amsterdam or Rome (Government Office for London, 1996; Association of London Government, 1997). So the degree of interrelationship among cities is a reflection of the concentration of advanced services within them; but, conversely, this concentration reflects the degree of actual and potential connectivity between them; the process is circular and cumulative. Second, the analysis is complicated by the existence of national boundaries – which Taylor and his group seek to ignore. Despite major advances in integration, Europe is still a system of separate nation states, with separate languages and cultures, in a way that the United States and Canada and Australia (and other continental-scale nations, like China, Brazil and Argentina) are not. This helps to protect small capital cities like Brussels, Copenhagen, Stockholm, Helsinki, Vienna and Lisbon, which command their national territories – in terms of governmental systems, legal systems, and the mass media – that are quite disproportionate to their size. And, of course, international boundaries distort comparisons of international air traffic: it is no accident that European airports figure so prominently in Figure 1.2.

This poses basic questions: as Beaverstock et al (2000a, p46) comment, on most indicators London is the most important city in Europe, but how in relational terms is it connected to other European cities? And does that place it at the apex of a hierarchy, or is the relationship more complex and non-hierarchical? Attribute data alone will not answer these questions, nor, indeed, will relational data. Figure 1.2 shows particularly strong intercontinental linkages between London, New York and Tokyo but also intercontinental linkages between these cities and other cities in their parts of the world, but how far these relationships are symmetrical, suggesting equality between the centres, or how far asymmetrical, suggesting a hierarchy, cannot be read from the map.

The Loughborough analysis does not attempt to measure relationships between cities directly, in terms of

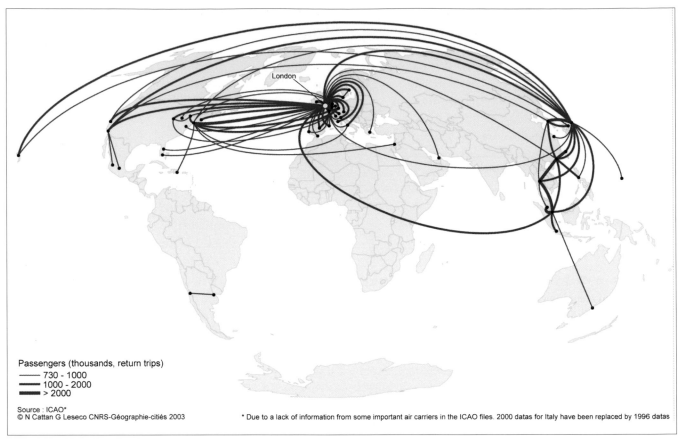

Passengers (thousands, return trips)
——— 730 - 1000
——— 1000 - 2000
▬▬▬ > 2000

Source : ICAO*
© N Cattan G Leseco CNRS-Géographie-citiés 2003   * Due to a lack of information from some important air carriers in the ICAO files. 2000 datas for Italy have been replaced by 1996 datas

Source: ESPON, 2003, Map 22, p252

Figure 1.2 Main world air traffic corridors

Table 1.2 The Loughborough Group 'GaWC' inventory of world cities[a]

A Alpha world cities

12 *London*, *Paris*, New York, Tokyo
10 Chicago, *Frankfurt*, Hong Kong, Los Angeles, *Milan*, Singapore

---

B Beta world cities

9 San Francisco, Sydney, Toronto, *Zürich*
8 *Brussels*, *Madrid*, Mexico City, São Paulo
7 *Moscow*, Seoul

C Gamma world cities

6 *Amsterdam*, Boston, Caracas, Dallas, *Düsseldorf*, *Geneva*, Houston, Jakarta, Johannesburg, Melbourne, Osaka, *Prague*, Santiago, Taipei, Washington
5 Bangkok, Beijing, *Rome*, *Stockholm*, *Warsaw*
4 Atlanta, *Barcelona*, *Berlin*, Buenos Aires, *Budapest*, *Copenhagen*, *Hamburg*, Istanbul, Kuala Lumpur, Manila, Miami, Minneapolis, Montreal, *Munich*, Shanghai

---

D Evidence of world city formation

Di Relatively strong evidence
3 Auckland, *Dublin*, *Helsinki*, *Luxembourg*, *Lyon*, Mumbai, New Delhi, Philadelphia, Rio de Janeiro, Tel Aviv, *Vienna*

Dii Some evidence
2 Abu Dhabi, Almaty, *Athens*, *Birmingham*, Bogotá, *Bratislava*, Brisbane, *Bucharest*, Cairo, Cleveland, *Cologne*, Detroit, Dubai, Ho Chi Minh City, *Kiev*, Lima, *Lisbon*, *Manchester*, Montevideo, *Oslo*, *Rotterdam*, Riyadh, Seattle, *Stuttgart*, *The Hague*, Vancouver

Diii Minimal evidence
1 Adelaide, *Antwerp*, *Århus*, *Athens*, Baltimore, Bangalore, *Bologna*, Brasilia, Calgary, Cape Town, Colombo, Columbus, *Dresden*, *Edinburgh*, *Genoa*, *Glasgow*, *Göteborg*, Guangzhou, Hanoi, Kansas City, *Leeds*, *Lille*, *Marseille*, Richmond, *St Petersburg*, Tashkent, Tehran, Tijuana, *Turin*, *Utrecht*, Wellington

---

Note: a Cities are ordered in terms of world city-ness values ranging from 1 to 12. European cities are italicized.

Sources: Beaverstock et al (1999a); Taylor et al (2002a); Taylor, (2004a)

actual flows of information. Instead, it uses a proxy: the internal structures of large APS firms, expressed by the relationship between head office and other office locations.[3] The outcome (Table 1.2) shows that about half the so-called global cities are in Europe and that a high proportion of these are in the central part of the North West Europe region, the focus of the POLYNET study.

Looking at individual APS sectors, London ranks as first global city for banking/finance, insurance, law and accountancy and second global city to New York for advertising and management consultancy. Paris ranks third global city for accountancy and management consultancy and in its network connectivity, fifth global city for insurance. Frankfurt is third global city for law in terms of global connectivity and fifth in terms of nodal size while Amsterdam ranks fourth global city for advertising in terms of nodal size (Taylor, 2004a, pp134–137).

Applying the same methodology in a separate study of architectural practices reveals rather different results. For this sector, London ranks top global city by far, scoring 51 as against second-ranking city New York which scores only 26. But in this case, no other European cities feature as significant architectural practice cities (Knox and Taylor, 2004). Yet it is clear from this work that the eight POLYNET regions are globally connected through their First Cities, as shown by their high connectivity rankings among all European cities (Taylor, 2003, Table 1). London (1.00) and Paris (0.70) are first, Amsterdam fourth (0.59), Frankfurt fifth (0.57), Brussels sixth (0.56), Zürich seventh (0.48), Dublin equal ninth (0.43) and Düsseldorf equal twelfth (0.39).[4] For banking and finance the order changes and all eight POLYNET First Cities rank in the top 14 European cities. After London and Paris (first and second European cities) comes Frankfurt third (0.70), Brussels sixth (0.59), Amsterdam eighth (0.54), Düsseldorf tenth (0.51), Dublin thirteenth (0.48) and Zürich fourteenth (0.46).

Working independently, Kyonung Ho-Shin and Michael Timberlake (2000) have measured world cities in terms of air connections. The technique they use is a rather complex one called equivalence analysis. They say:

> by measuring the role of each city in the exchange matrix on the basis of the similarities in the pattern of air passenger flows to all other cities, we identify each city's location on a continuum of something like 'centrality' to the overall system of cities (Ho-Shin and Timberlake, 2000, p2277).

Table 1.3 shows the results, which present some similarities to the Loughborough analysis, though they are not the same. In this system, of the top six cities, four are in North West Europe, and London stands at the top, as it has for the last quarter century.

Table 1.3 World city hierarchy based on air connections, 1997[a]

1	*London*	11	Tokyo
2	*Frankfurt*	12	Seoul
3	*Paris*	13	Bangkok
4	New York	14	*Madrid*
5	*Amsterdam*	15	*Vienna*
6	*Zürich*	16	San Francisco
7	Miami	17	Chicago
8	Los Angeles	18	Dubai
9	Hong Kong	19	Osaka
10	Singapore	20	*Brussels*

Note: a European cities are italicized.

Source: Ho-Shin and Timberlake (2000)

It is clear that the Christaller hierarchy now needs to be supplemented by at least two or even three additional levels, producing a hierarchy of perhaps six or seven ranks – though effectively, his two bottom levels have ceased to perform roles as service centres in the intervening 70 years, while the next two lowest have lost significance as their functions have been taken over by higher-order centres; thus the whole system has effectively shifted upwards and has lost its original hexagonal regularity. At the very top are *global cities* (in the Loughborough terminology, 'alpha' global cities) typically with 5 million and more people within their administrative boundaries and up to 20 million within their hinterlands, but effectively serving very large global territories: London, Paris, New York, Tokyo. Immediately below are *sub-global cities* (in the Loughborough terminology, 'beta' or 'gamma' global cities), typically with 1–5 million people and up to perhaps 10 million in their hinterlands, performing an almost complete range of similar functions for more restricted national or regional territories, as well as certain specialized global service functions (banking, fashion, culture, media): in this category come all European capitals apart from the global cities, together with 'commercial capitals' in nations that divide top political and commercial functions (Milan, Barcelona) as well as major provincial cities in large nation states (Glasgow, Manchester, Lyon, Marseille, Hamburg). Below this come regional cities (Christaller's *Landstadt*) (population 250,000–1,000,000), some of which fall into the Loughborough group's 'Showing evidence of world city formation' and provincial cities (Christaller's *Provinzstadt*) (population 100,000–250,000) (Hall, 2002).

This last group of cities has a particular significance, because they play a key role in the formation of MCRs. They are the typical county market towns of rural Europe, found across much of southern England, southern Germany, and most of France. They have grown because they provide the local services for their populations – including services once provided by smaller lower-order places, as mobility has increased Christaller's 'range of a good' – and sometimes national services (such as universities) also. In Europe's more prosperous and densely-populated regions – including, critically, the eight MCRs considered – they have attracted out-migration of people and employment from major cities at the higher levels of the hierarchy, especially within the transport-rich sectors radiating out from those cities, as illustrated long ago by Lösch (1954) in his theoretical development of the Christaller scheme. In a few cases this has resulted in the formation of discontinuous corridors or axes of urbanization, most notably in the so-called 'Blue Banana' connecting Birmingham, London, Brussels, Amsterdam, Cologne, Frankfurt, Basel, Zürich and Milan (Brunet, 1989). But the process is not universal: Paris, for instance, has deliberately concentrated its own dispersal into the five large *cités nouvelles* proposed in the 1965 *Schéma Directeur*, so that – in sharp contrast to London – there has been only minimal dispersal beyond their limits.

From global cities to global city regions[5]

If global cities are defined – directly or indirectly – in terms of their *external* information exchanges, logic suggests that polycentric global MCRs should be defined in terms of corresponding *internal* linkages. These linkages, accordingly, form the main research focus of the POLYNET study. The first need is to conceptualize how information is transmitted along these links, and how that transmission impacts on the urban nodes that connect them into a network.

Information can move in two ways: electronically, and inside people's heads for face-to-face exchange (Hall, 1991). The latter movements may occur daily on a regular basis (commuting, which brings people's brains into a workplace) or less frequently and/or more irregularly (business meetings, where participants bring their brains to a common exchange). We have good data on commuting for most cities, but very little information on other movements. A few pioneering attempts have been made to record all information exchanges through diaries (Goddard, 1973; Carlstein et al, 1978); these suggest that electronic exchanges tend to be more routine in character (using what Goddard calls 'programmed' information) and serve as a prelude to face-to-face meetings where 'unprogrammed' information is exchanged, a point underlined by more recent studies (Mitchell, 1995, 1999; Graham and Marvin, 1996). Because of this basic distinction, traditional dense central business districts (CBDs) still offer massive agglomeration economies, as first argued long ago (Haig, 1926).

Crucial here is the recent interest of economists in business clustering. Michael Porter's work on clusters,

defined as 'geographic concentrations of interconnected companies, specialized suppliers, service providers, firms in related industries, and associated institutions … in particular fields that compete but also co-operate' (Porter, 1998, p197), has been highly influential in European economic and spatial policy. The concept is a venerable one in economics, albeit only recently rediscovered (Marshall, 1890), but specific studies on APS clustering have been sparse.[6] The recent study of clustering in London, based on large postal questionnaire and in-depth interview studies in central London (Taylor et al, 2003), reinforces the Porter thesis but also confirms the pioneer findings of Goddard (1973). For knowledge transfer and innovation a balance between competition and cooperation is vital; both are accentuated when firms are located close together. Innovation is more likely there because it depends on market trading of codified or tacit knowledge, where face-to-face interaction is critical to establish and maintain personal relationships of trust and cooperation. Cooperation comes not only through 'institutional thickness' provided by closely located trade and professional institutions but also through increasingly complex interdependencies between firms and between service providers and their customers. Paradoxically, there is close cooperation with competitors in client project teams and through cross-servicing relations, for example, in financial and legal services. Further, for the most clustered firms access to skilled labour – the core of APS business – is equally or more important than proximity to customers. Consequently, such clusters develop a depth of infrastructure, advantageous to all firms but essential to those operating globally. Clustering is important for new firm formation; very small offices (as well as large offices of major global firms) are a feature of such concentrated clusters. Thus, while 'back-office' functions and staff may leave (or be outsourced to distant locations), the overall scale of clustering may be little affected. The vital need to keep key staff, coupled with customized operational requirements, keeps the most centralized office locations remarkably resilient over time.

The critical question here, much discussed, is the impact of technology: sophisticated systems of electronic exchange potentially permit highly flexible mixtures of the two kinds of exchange. Specialized consultants seem to be able to operate effectively up to about two hours' travel time from metropolitan cores (or from the major airports associated with those cores), in semi-rural locations like the Cotswold Hills outside London, or the Odenwald outside Frankfurt MCR, conducting many exchanges electronically, but travelling to meetings in those cores – or, via air or rail connections, in other cores. High-quality transportation networks, in the form of highways or high-speed rail links, are crucial here.

Further, these meeting places may no longer be located in traditional CBDs. Increasingly, professional and managerial workers function effectively in a variety of geographical spaces: they may process electronic information in home offices in suburbs or the remote countryside, in airplanes and trains and hotels and airport lounges; they may meet face-to-face in all these places as well as in convention centres (which may be purpose-built, or in adapted hotels, or in converted country houses), or in new-style offices such as IBM's UK headquarters at Bedfont Lakes outside London Heathrow airport, which features a central cafeteria-type atrium surrounded by hot-desk cubicles. Some of these face-to-face meeting places may be scattered; others however will be clustered, for the good reason that they are located close to transport nodes such as airports or train stations.

Perhaps because of this, such face-to-face functions requiring agglomeration appear to be undergoing a complex process of what Dutch planners have called concentrated deconcentration: they disperse over the scale of a wide city region, but simultaneously reconcentrate at particular nodes within it, limited only by continuing time-distance constraints. Traditional central city locations still matter, but increasingly they are not the sole clustering points for economic activity; they form merely a part of a wider spatial division of labour within the urban area, with other significant clusterings (Kloosterman and Musterd, 2001, p626). The result in many large cities, observable over many decades, is an increasingly polycentric urban structure. The traditional CBD, based on walking distances and served by a radial public transportation structure, is still attractive to old-established informational services (banking, insurance, government) as in the City of London, Downtown Manhattan, Marunouchi/ Otemachi in Tokyo. But from the 1930s and above all from the 1960s, it came to be supplemented by a secondary CBD, often developing in a prestigious residential quarter, and attracting newer services such as corporate headquarters, the media, advertising, public relations and design, as in London's West End, the 16ᵉ *arrondissement* of Paris, Midtown Manhattan or the Akasaki/Roppongi districts of Tokyo. Even more recently, since 1960, a tertiary CBD or 'internal edge city' has developed through speculative development on old industrial or transport land, now redundant: London Docklands, La Défense in Paris, New York's World Trade Center and World Financial Center, and Tokyo's Shinjuku.

All these clusters are usually close together in terms of distance (typically 3 to 4 miles, 5 to 8km) and in time (15 to 20 minutes) and are connected by high-quality urban public transport; secondary centres invariably developed on the basis of new connections developed a few years earlier (the London tube, the Paris metro, the New York subway and the Penn and Grand Central Stations, the Tokyo metro), tertiary centres sometimes developed on the same basis (Shinjuku on Tokyo's Yamanote ring railway; the World Trade Center and World Financial Center on the PATH system), but more often required new investment (the Paris Réseau Express Régional (RER) Line A serving La Défense; London's Jubilee Line extension serving Canary Wharf).

But there are also more distant manifestations. Many cities have recently come to demonstrate also an 'external' edge city, often on the axis of the main airport, sometimes (very recently) a high-speed train station: London Heathrow; Paris Charles de Gaulle; Brussels Zaventem; Amsterdam Schiphol and its extension, the so-called Zuidas (Southern Axis) next to the city's new Zuid (South) station; Stockholm Arlanda and the adjacent E4 corridor; and the corridor connecting Washington's Reagan and Dulles airports through the city's Virginia suburbs, with new 'edge cities' at Rosslyn, Ballston and Tysons Corner. In Europe the most notable examples, like the tertiary CBDs, take a special form: they result from conscious strategic planning, albeit in reaction to market forces, and they depend on considerable public investment in transport infrastructure (Bontje and Burdack, 2005). And these overlap with even more distant 'outermost' edge city complexes attracting back office and R&D functions, typically at major train stations 20–40 miles (35–65km) from the main core: Reading 40 miles (70km) west of London; the planned *Ville Nouvelle* of St Quentin-en-Yvelines only 15.5 miles (25km) south-west of Paris; Kista at the terminus of the Stockholm *Tunnelbana* close to the E4 corridor; Greenwich in Connecticut; and Shin-Yokohama in Kanagawa prefecture west of Tokyo. Finally, specialized subcentres may develop for certain functions like education, entertainment and sport, exhibition and convention centres: London's Royal Docks; the Open University in Milton Keynes 55 miles (90km) north of London; or the Tokyo Waterfront. These take various forms and have equally varied locations: reclaimed or recycled land close to the traditional core, older university cities that have become progressively embedded in a wider metropolitan area (Oxford and Cambridge in the UK, Uppsala in Sweden, and New Haven in the US), relocated universities (Université de Paris-XI, Amsterdam's Vrije Universiteit, Tsukuba University outside Tokyo). And some may acquire new functions, as with the emergence of Cambridge as a major high-technology centre ('Silicon Fen') since 1970.

Within this increasingly polycentric structure, there is increasing specialization: many functions – back offices, logistics management, new-style headquarters complexes, media centres, and large-scale entertainment and sport – relocate over time to decentralized locations, albeit at different speeds and with different effects. The result is that increasingly, the relevant focus is no longer the city: it is the region (Kloosterman and Musterd, 2001, p627). And here, two key concepts that often appear to be contraposed – the Christallerian hierarchy and the concept of urban networks – make an uneasy reunion (van Houtum and Lagendijk, 2001, p751): the resulting city region is highly networked through its multiple nodes and links, but there is a recognizable urban hierarchy that operates at a regional scale. In the extreme case, the Asian mega-city, this is mediated by state planning, but in a highly flexible way: in the Pearl River Delta region of China core command-and-control functions are concentrated in Hong Kong, other service functions in Guangzhou, while other routine manufacturing and service functions are scattered across the cities of the delta, but the entire region is by definition highly centralized on a global scale (Xu and Li, 1990; Yeung, 1996; Sit and Yang, 1997; Hall, 1999); the same pattern can be recognized in the Yangtze delta, in the relationships between Shanghai as centre for advanced services as against Suzhou for R&D and high-technology manufacturing (Hall, 2005).

The form bears some similarities to Gottmann's megalopolis (see p3); but it is infinitely more complex, because more highly interconnected; besides, it differs fundamentally from Gottmann's formulation because it is based on Castells's 'space of flows' connecting the individual urban elements, and consciously seeks to measure these flows (Taylor, 2004a, p20). Here, as around Shanghai, around Jakarta and around Singapore, we see the beginnings of a new urban form that in some cases even transcends national boundaries: a city region on a vast scale, networked externally on a global scale and internally over thousands of square kilometres: the precursor of a new scale of urban organization. Allen Scott has titled the largest such areas the 'global city-region' (Scott, 2001); the POLYNET study builds on his pioneering work.

Introducing POLYNET

The starting point of the POLYNET study, as stressed earlier in this chapter, is that polycentricity, a central objective of the ESDP, needs more closely defining. At the European level, it would promote global economic and knowledge flows from global (and sub-global) cities within the European 'Pentagon', like London, Paris and Frankfurt, to benefit cities in other more peripheral parts of Europe (Hall, 1993, 1996) – especially 'gateway' cities outside North West Europe, and smaller cities within it through cooperation and improved high-speed transport links between cities (Taylor et al, 2003). But at a finer geographical scale, *polycentricity* refers to outward diffusion

from major cities to smaller cities within their spheres of influence, sometimes over wide areas, as found in the eight MCRs in North West Europe that are the focus of the study:

1 *South East England*, where London is now the centre of a system of some 30–40 centres within a 100 mile (160km) radius from Central London, extending as far as Bournemouth and Swindon in South West England, Northampton in the East Midlands and Peterborough in the East of England.
2 *The Randstad* in The Netherlands, encompassing the Randstad cities of Amsterdam, The Hague, Rotterdam and Utrecht, but now extending outwards to include the new city of Almere in the reclaimed polders east of Amsterdam.
3 *Central Belgium*, comprising Brussels and a surrounding ring of large and medium size cities, with a high degree of interdependence and a total population of some 7.8 million.
4 *RhineRuhr*, one of the world's largest polycentric MCRs, embracing 90 towns and cities, among them 11 high-order centres more or less on the same level with a total population of some 12 million people, in this case with no obvious 'core city'.
5 The *Rhine-Main Region* of Germany, encompassing the core cities of Frankfurt am Main (including Offenbach), Wiesbaden, Mainz, Darmstadt, Hanau and Aschaffenburg.
6 The *EMR of Northern Switzerland*, an incipient MCR extending in a discontinuous linear pattern across East Central Switzerland from Zürich in the east to Basel in the west;
7 The *Paris Region*, a special case: through the 1965 *Schéma Directeur*, outward decentralization pressures have been accommodated in new city concentrations forming extensions of the agglomeration, with little impact on surrounding rural areas. But recent research shows that the region's economic core is no longer within the historic *Ville de Paris*, but in a 'Golden Triangle' bounded by the city's western arrondissements, La Défense and the suburbs of Boulogne-Billancourt and Issy-les-Moulineaux (Beckouche, 1999; Halbert, 2002);
8 *Greater Dublin*, within a 30–40 mile (50–70km) radius of the city, but particularly northward along the Dublin-Belfast corridor; here decentralization appears to extend as far as Newry, crossing national boundaries.

A long-continued process of concentrated deconcentration in these areas (though much less noticeably in Paris or Dublin) has thus produced clusters of up to 50 cities constituting networked urban regions with up to 20 million people, drawing enormous economic strength from a new functional division of labour and connected by dense flows of people and information along motorways, high-speed rail lines and telecommunications systems. Recent work in fact suggests that the so-called Central Area of North West Europe – the area centred upon Paris, Brussels, Cologne, Amsterdam and London – is an incipient MCR of 37 million people (Anon, 2002), characterized by functional divisions of labour between city units in a highly networked region and by intensive development along transportation corridors (Ipenburg et al, 2001). As Chapter 2 will show, the eight POLYNET MCRs together make up a much bigger (though discontinuous) mass of no less than 72 million people, and while not contiguous they are sufficiently close and highly linked as to form a super MCR: *Europolis*, fully comparable with the largest such regions in Eastern Asia.

Within such MCRs, people relate to cities in increasingly multiple ways (Kloosterman and Musterd, 2001); the 'space of flows' becomes extremely complex. POLYNET has sought to fill a major gap by studying systematically the actual operation of such regions – and their potential fusion – including material and virtual information flows within and outside them and their implications for North West European spatial planning and related policies.

Our starting-point has been the relations, earlier discussed, between electronic and face-to-face information exchange. These are complex and even apparently contradictory: diminishing transport and communication costs may bring the 'Death of Distance' (Cairncross, 1995, 1997), but telecommunications may also complement and stimulate face-to-face contact (Goddard, 1973; Graham and Marvin, 1996; Hall, 1998; Beaverstock et al, 2001). A recent study of business clustering in London by the GaWC group has emphasized the importance of face-to-face contact as a key agglomeration factor (Taylor et al, 2003): central London firms exhibited interdependencies across a wide South East city region, but many so-called back offices have dispersed to the wider region. Specialized business services, such as law and accountancy, establish themselves there to serve local clients (Breheny, 1999).

Our initial premise, then, was that falling costs of transportation and (more particularly) communication, combined with new informational agglomeration economies, lead to the emergence of a highly complex 'space of flows' (Castells, 1989) within such global MCRs, reconfiguring previous geographical relationships. Yet this reconfiguration follows a 'Christaller rule': lower-level service functions tend to decentralize and reconcentrate at lower levels of the urban hierarchy (Christaller, 1966 (1933)). These new urban regions thus achieve major agglomeration economies through clustering of activities, not in any one centre, but in a complex of centres, with a degree of functional differentiation between them which leads to increasing flows of information along multiple channels.

Important also, in the research formulation, were the implications for regional spatial development strategies. At the city region scale the principle of 'sustainable concentrated deconcentration' suggests that growth should be guided on to selected development corridors along strong public transport links, including high-speed 'regional metros' such as proposed for London, or even along true high-speed lines such as London–Ashford, Amsterdam–Antwerp or Frankfurt–Limburg (Ipenburg et al, 2001). These would not represent continuous urbanization, but clusters of urban developments around train stations and key motorway interchanges up to 100 miles (160km) from the central city, thus reducing the probability of long-distance commuting and assisting remoter areas. And this could help reduce the danger that European polycentric urban regions may come to conflict with ESDP sustainability objectives (Kloosterman and Musterd, 2001; Ipenburg and Lambregts, 2001; Taylor et al, 2003).

POLYNET: Developing theory, formulating hypotheses

To provide a foundation for the study, we first need to summarize – at the risk of repetition – some of the theoretical formulations discussed in this chapter. There are four key elements which underpin the study (Knox and Taylor, 1995).

The first is the notion of a *world city hierarchy* (Friedmann, 1986, 1995) or global city (Sassen, 1991, 2001). Friedmann emphasized the command-and-control functions of major cities – the locations of corporate headquarters running global businesses. Sassen emphasized the concentration of APS (financial, professional, and creative) in major cities that facilitate production and distribution across the global economy. Both identified New York, London and Tokyo as the leading cities in the world economy; neither was quite clear about the cities below that level.

The second is the notion of a *world city network* (Taylor, 2001, 2004a). This analyses inter-city relations in terms of the organizational structure of the global economy; it views world cities as 'global service centres' connected into a single worldwide network. This emphasis on networks implies that cities in a globalized world do not merely compete with each other, as so often argued; crucially, they also have cooperative relations – a feature that is strongly encouraged in the ESDP. A network requires mutuality between its members in order to operate and survive. This approach is not just theoretically interesting: it has important practical policy implications. 'Connectivities' within multiple business networks located in global cities confer cooperative relations on world city networks. Work within this framework by the GaWC Group at Loughborough has already demonstrated in complementary quantitative and interview studies that London and Frankfurt, often viewed as competitor financial centres since the establishment of the Eurozone (excluding London) and the establishment of the European Central Bank in Frankfurt, in fact have mutually cooperative relationships as well (Beaverstock et al, 2001, 2003a, b, 2005; Hoyler and Pain, 2002; Pain, 2005).

The third is the recognition of *global city regions* (Scott, 2001). This treats world cities as more than simply centre-cores; they are viewed as more complex urban regions, encompassing several cities, networked in a *polycentric* structure. The starting-point of the Polynet project uniquely combines these two research strategies: it studies the internal network structures of global city regions within a worldwide network of regions. To paraphrase a long-ago formulation of the geographer Brian Berry (Berry, 1964), it aims to study 'City Regions as Systems within Systems of City Regions'.

The fourth is Manuel Castells's immensely influential concept of a *space of flows* in the network society (Castells, 1996). He contrasts our traditional concern for 'spaces of places' (such as countries or cities) with contemporary transnational movements of people, commodities, and – especially – information, which he calls 'spaces of flows'. This space of flows is today found at a range of different geographical scales up to and including the global scale. Cities within networks and as city regions are the critical *hubs and nodes* of the space of flows.

Methodologically, the study builds on established GaWC techniques (Beaverstock et al, 1999a, b, 2000a, b; Taylor et al, 2002a, b), but extends its techniques, and with a quite new intra-regional focus, to study patterns of information flows within the eight North West Europe global MCRs. The study would integrate the most recently available data on traffic, commuting and tele-communications flows with unique primary research on cross-border financial and business services operations.

In it, we undertook to address new interrelated research questions. First, how are virtual and material flows of information and people reconfiguring intra-regional relationships? Are functional relationships between top-level and other centres in these regions changing? To what extent are other urban centres dependent on, or independent of, concentrations of service industries in core cities? (Here the focus of inquiry would be largely intra-regional.) Second, in what ways are changes in regional functional relations affecting the cross-border

connectivities of these regions within Europe and globally? To what extent will changes contribute to, or damage, transnational service business connectivity? (Here the focus would be on cross-border relations.) Third, in what ways are these flows different between the four polycentric MCRs and the much more 'monocentric' Paris and Greater Dublin regions? Can it be said that one or the other pattern is more sustainable, and if so in what ways and to what degree?

At the outset, we need to set out certain key hypotheses which provided the starting-point of the entire POLYNET study, and which animated the research throughout.

The first and central POLYNET hypothesis is that APS knowledge flows extend beyond the global city network to create interlinkages between other cities and towns in North West Europe at a city region scale, leading to a new spatial phenomenon: the global 'mega-city region'. But the GaWC methodologies, adapted for use in this research, are not concerned with geographical or administrative boundaries. Global cities are conceptualized as 'processes' (Castells, 1996) and as hubs or nodes in globalizing APS network servicing strategies (Sassen, 2001). Firms and their networks thus become the subjects of investigation, and relations within and between 'global cities' are examined through their business connectivities in the global city network. Hence a first overarching research question for POLYNET has been *how to define the area for study – the MCR*.

Preliminary MCR boundaries were defined at the outset, using data on inter-urban commuting patterns, and are presented in Chapter 2. But the process of data collection and definition has necessarily been iterative: later stages of the research, in particular interviews with key economic actors, have sought to examine regional functional relations, using different methods and data, in order finally to re-evaluate these initial definitions. In the first of these, reported in Chapter 3, inter-urban functional linkages associated with APS business operations in each city region were studied, using established GaWC methodologies but adapting them to the intra-regional scale: connectivities within firms were calculated and significant regional locations for APS functions identified. Intra-firm networks operating at different geographical scopes (regional, national, European and global) were analysed and mapped to reveal potential functional relations. In the second, reported in Chapter 5, an attempt was made to measure directly the 'space of flows' in terms of business travel and virtual information exchanges. In the third, reported in Chapters 6–8, an alternative qualitative approach was used: through interviews with senior decision-makers in firms and organizations, the research teams sought to gauge their own understanding of the strength and quality of the relationships. Thus it was possible to reconsider the relevance and value of the original MCR definitions in the light of the evidence from these different empirical studies.

A second, related hypothesis is that knowledge-intensive APS business operations and flows are associated with a polycentric pattern of urban development in each MCR. Since the ESDP seeks to promote polycentric regional development as an antidote to problems associated with uneven economic development within the European Union, a key concern is to understand how major informational and skills flows associated with leading European global cities London and Paris can benefit other European cities and regions. While the POLYNET study regions differ in their internal regional urban structures, they all contain important business services centres. A second overarching question for the research has therefore been *to what extent flows associated with concentration of services in primary business services centres in each region are associated with polycentric development at the regional scale?*

The analysis of urban hierarchies and of business organizational structures, reported in Chapters 2 and 3, reveals that the concept of polycentricity is both process-sensitive and scale-sensitive, reflecting the complexity of functional interdependencies between the contemporary space of flows and the space of places in a 'knowledge economy'. While analysis of commuting flows suggests a low degree of regional polycentricity in all the MCRs, specific APS inter-urban linkages, based on intra-firm connectivities, suggest a potentially higher degree of polycentricity for most regions. The nature of polycentricity associated with different sectors, functions and scales of APS activity is examined in each MCR.

The logic of POLYNET and the structure of this book

Testing the central hypothesis – that these regions are polycentric and becoming increasingly so – was the central objective of POLYNET and the central theme of this book. It is analysed at progressively deeper and more complex levels.

First, in Part 2 of the book, we make several successive attempts to measure polycentricity quantitatively, by numbers. Chapter 2 is the first sweep: here we present basic Census and other data for the eight regions, culminating in an attempt to measure their degree of polycentricity in three ways – through a rank-size analysis of constituent FURs, through measuring their degree of self-containment, and finally by analysing commuter flows to measure their degree of daily connectivity.

But these measure only what we call *geographical* or *morphological* connectivity; they tell us nothing (except for the notion that commuters take their brains with them each day) about *actual flows of information*, which are our central concern. The remaining chapters of Part 2 seek to analyse these flows, or in other words functional polycentricity: a key POLYNET distinction.

Chapter 4 seeks to analyse information exchanges between the eight MCRs, using typical weekday airline and train timetables as a proxy for business travel. This shows remarkable differences, with London overwhelmingly the most highly connected.

In Chapter 4, however, MCRs are presented as aggregates: the analysis does not try to penetrate the internal structure of information flows. Chapter 3 is a first attempt to do this. It approaches the problem indirectly, by applying the Loughborough GaWC analysis for the first time at a regional scale: it analyses the internal structure of business linkages within each of the eight regions, through the organizational structures of multi-locational firms in the APS industries, in a selection of key centres within each region. It enables the study of their connectivity at four different scales: global, European, national and regional and the potential inter-city functional linkages within each MCR that follow from these. This quantitative analysis shows that the cities in these eight regions display very different patterns of connectivity, depending on the scale in question though the presence of actual functional interactions between the cities has to be established by other complementary methods that are described next.

Chapter 5 goes more directly to the question, in what was always intended as the heart of the research: it tries directly to measure the flows of information between executives and managers in each region, by analysing the patterns of business travel, telephone calls, conference calls and e-mails that connect them. Unfortunately, as reported here, it proved extremely difficult to win the cooperation of respondents in completing the survey, thus limiting its scope and utility; nonetheless, it revealed evidence of important barriers to virtual information flows. Although the results cannot be regarded as in any sense statistically representative, they are remarkably suggestive both in the commonalities and the differences they reveal.

So Part 3 of the book attacks the problem in a different way. Now, rather than quantifying, the study seeks to probe qualitative information gleaned by several hundred interviews with executives and senior managers in the eight key APS sectors in the eight regions. These chapters present and overview the most important results that emerge from the interviews across all the regions, with some flavour of the local variations.

In Chapter 6 we investigate the location of offices in the APS sectors, in particular their clustering. We relate this to their geographical scopes, from global to local and examine the connectivities within and between firms and cities. We briefly consider globalization and its impact on the regional geography of APS.

In Chapter 7 we focus on the role of information, seeking to understand processes of knowledge production, transfer and innovation. We consider the different roles and varying importance of virtual communications and face-to-face contact, including the importance of travel and transport for direct business contact.

Finally, in Chapter 8, we focus on the relations between the space of places and the space of flows. We consider the significance of skilled labour and of labour markets, and the importance of 'place' – in particular the role of what we call the 'First Cities' of each MCR – in knowledge production. We reconsider two basic assumptions of the study: that MCRs exist and can be defined, and that polycentricity is a growing reality. From this discussion, we go on to identify key issues for sustainable regional management, to which we return later in the book.

Then, in Part 4, Chapters 9–16, members of the research teams in the eight regions seek to emphasize some of their special characteristics. Anticipating and feeding into the final section of the book, they then introduce the policy responses that have been developed in their regions in recent years, asking how well they deal with the challenge of strategic planning and delivery for such complex polycentric entities.

Chapter 17 constitutes Part 5, the final section of the book, which turns to focus on questions of policy. It sums up the key general conclusions that emerge from Chapters 9–16 before setting the policy responses, reported there, in a common framework. Finally it sets out some key conclusions from the entire study, and an agenda of continuing research questions that have emerged from it.

Notes

1 Active membership of the eight teams is shown in the List of Contributors (pxi). Professor John Yarwood, who initially led the Dublin team, left the study after the first year.
2 This section is based in part on Hall (2002).
3 The method is described in more detail in Chapter 3.
4 These rankings apply to the original six POLYNET sectors.
5 This section draws on Hall (2001).
6 For a review see Taylor et al (2003).

PART 2

Analysing the Polycentric Metropolis:
Quantifying the Mega-City Region

Anatomy of the Polycentric Metropolis: Eight Mega-City Regions in Overview

Peter Hall, Kathy Pain and Nick Green

The first task, before starting to analyse the eight mega-city regions (MCRs), is to understand them more fully. To that end, the eight regional study teams needed to achieve three preliminary objectives.

First, to establish preliminary definitions of the eight areas. These might well change as the research proceeded and we developed deeper and subtler understanding of the 'space of flows' within each region, but there had to be a geographical basis for collecting data. Second, on this basis, to present a statistical overview of each area, based on available Census and other statistical material, with a comparative concluding summary comparing the results. Third, to present preliminary conclusions, based on this evidence, about the degree to which each area could be said to be polycentric and/or was moving in that direction.

In this chapter, we present results for each of these objectives. But a health warning is needed at the outset: this exercise was always conceived as an introduction to the research, using readily available secondary materials to present a preliminary portrait and analysis. In this sense, it is necessarily superficial. That particularly applies to the third objective, the measurement of polycentricity.

Basic building blocks: Functional urban regions and mega-city regions

The comparative analysis of cities has to begin by addressing basic problems of definition, so as to allow systematic comparison of urban areas from one country to another. Administrative city units will not serve, because cities may be overbounded or (a much more common phenomenon) underbounded, as suburbs develop outside city limits. Physical or morphological definitions are better, helping to define limits in terms of urban land uses; but

even they fail to unpick the functional relationships that may tie physically separate towns and villages to a central city. The problem here is twofold: different systems of national land use regulation mean that built-up areas of cities relate very differently to their functional reality; while increasing commuting distances and increasingly complex cross-commuting patterns mean that built-up areas no longer describe the functional reality. So, comparable boundary definitions using functional, not morphological, criteria are essential for comparative analysis of urban systems and urban development patterns.

The *functional urban region* (FUR): to overcome these problems, American urban analysts have long employed the concept of the Metropolitan Statistical Area (MSA):[1] a functionally defined urban region that goes out beyond the physically built-up area to encompass all the areas that have regular daily relationships with a core city. Essentially the MSA comprises a central core (usually, the county containing the central city) defined in terms of a minimum level of population, together with a suburban ring defined in terms of a minimum level of daily commuter movements into the core. Because the POLYNET study is centrally interested in information flows, such a statistical base provides the necessary basic building block.

Already in 1980, Hall and Hay defined and analysed data for a set of 539 uniform FURs in Western Europe, and a decade later a larger follow-up study by Cheshire and Hay, funded by the European Commission (EC), updated and deepened the work for a set of 229 larger FURs in the then 12-member EC area, and conducted a further detailed analysis of a subset of 53 FURs (Hall and Hay, 1980; Cheshire and Hay, 1989). This and subsequent work (Cheshire, 1995, 1999; Cheshire and Carbonaro, 1996; Magrini, 1999), though updating the database from the 1990 Census round, had to rely on the original FUR definitions based on data from the 1970 Census round or nearest equivalent. In consequence the definitions became in some cases out of date and misleading. (In the USA, MSAs are regularly redefined on the basis of the latest Census and other data.) This was demonstrated in the work of the Group for European Metropolitan Areas Comparative Analysis (GEMACA) (IAURIF, 1996) which showed, for example, that, while the boundaries of the Paris urban region had remained relatively stable down to 1991, the boundaries of London had expanded substantially.

It was therefore essential for the POLYNET study to review and update the basic European database, updating the basic definitions of functionally defined city regions, using where possible the 2000 Census round, extending it to smaller regions than in the GEMACA database, and providing an extended analysis of basic data, including population, employment, income, unemployment and other key socio-economic variables. After examination of various possible models, POLYNET adopted a variant of the GEMACA criteria for defining FURs in our eight study areas:

- *FURs*: comprise a core defined in terms of employment size and density, and a ring defined in terms of regular daily journeys (commuting) to the core:
  1 *Cores*: using Nomenclature of Territorial Units for Statistics (NUTS) 5 units (the smallest units for which published data are generally available), define cores on the basis of 7 or more workers per hectare, and minimum 20,000 workers in either single NUTS 5 units or in contiguous NUTS 5 units.
  2 *Rings*: using NUTS 5 units, where possible, define rings on the basis of 10 per cent or more of the residentially based workforce commuting daily to the core. Where they commute to more than one core, allocate to the core to which most commuters go.
- The *MCR*: having defined FURs that were uniform, as far as possible, within and also between our eight study areas, the POLYNET study then needed to aggregate them into the basic units for comparative study: the eight MCRs. In a sense, there is a significant element of circularity here: since the objective was to study functional polycentricity, the study could logically only seek to define MCRs when the research was complete; but it was necessary to start with a working definition. Bearing in mind that this could only be rough and approximate, the research teams agreed that the basic criteria for the initial mapping of the MCRs should be one of contiguity:
  1 *MCR*: defined in terms of contiguous FURs, and thus similar to the so-called Combined (formerly Consolidated) Metropolitan Statistical Areas (CMSAs), used in the US.[2] Contiguity is the sole criterion. There may be functional relations (cross-commuting) between the constituent FURs, or there may not; this could not form a basis for the definition, since it has emerged only in the course of the analysis.
  2 *Basic data*: for both individual FURs (and, by definition, for aggregate MCRs), each study team assembled basic data on population, employment and commuting (including cross-commuting between FURs in MCRs). They then went on to develop a uniform analysis of polycentricity within their regions, using three alternative and complementary methods.

Finally, each separate regional study produced uniform analyses of polycentricity within the region, using three alternative and complementary methods. This chapter again compares the results. It is important, before starting, to emphasize again the health warning: these are strictly provisional and essentially somewhat superficial analyses – albeit interesting in themselves in giving an introductory overview and comparison of the eight study regions.

Eight mega-city regions compared: People and jobs

The eight MCRs differ greatly both in size and internal structure. Basic data are set out in Table 2.1.

Area, population, employment

In *area* the regions vary from 3017 miles^2 (7800km^2) (Dublin) to 11,268 miles^2 (29,184km^2) (South East England) and 16,609 miles^2 (43,019km^2) (Paris Region), which however represents an exceptional case (see p21, note c). In *population*, the variation is similar: from 1,637,267 (Dublin) to 15,691,730 (Paris Region) and 18,984,000 (South East England). But five of the eight MCRs are between 8000 and 16,000km^2 in area and between 8 million and 11 million in population (Figure 2.1).

The regions also differ in their *internal structure*: in particular, the size and separation of their constituent urban areas. Figure 2.2 shows the composition in terms of numbers of constituent FURs: they range from 51 in the case of South East England to only one in the case of Dublin, which thus – at least on this measure – is not polycentric at all; here, rules had to be broken to allow the inclusion of the nine additional proto-FURs within this larger FUR, which would certainly not have qualified on the criteria used elsewhere, and the contiguity criterion does not apply. Figure 2.3 shows the relative importance of the

Table 2.1 Eight MCRs: Basic data

MCR	Area km²	Population 2000/2001	Population change % 1990/1991– 2000/2001	Employment 2000/2001	Employment change % 1990/1991– 2000/2001	Number of FURs
South East England	29,184	18,984,298	+13.5	9,040,000	+32.9	51
The Randstad	8757	8,575,712	+7.1	4,031,900	+29.0	25
Central Belgium	16,000	7,800,000	+2.6	3,320,000	+10.0	8
RhineRuhr	11,536	11,700,000	+1.1	5,4000,000	+3.4	47 (6)[a]
Rhine-Main	8211	4,200,000	+5.7	1,695,000	+1.7	6
EMR Northern Switzerland	13,700	3,500,000	+7.6	2,200,000	+6.7	8
Paris Region[b,c]	43,019	15,691,730	+2.9	7,660,880	+3.2	30
Greater Dublin	7814	1,637,267[d]	+9.3[e]	798,515[f]	+62.9[g]	1[h] (10?)[i]

Notes: a See the text comment on the problem of defining the MCR RhineRuhr.

b Based on National Census Data: 1990 and 1999 (not 2000).

c Total values for the 30 FURs, not including rural interstitial spaces between FURs. In this regard, the Paris Region is not conventionally defined. A softer contiguity criterion was applied here because of statistical uncertainty resulting from the very low-density rural municipalities. But for the total area, most data do not differ considerably when applying the stricter contiguity hypothesis.

d POLYNET definition of the 'Greater Dublin region': Dublin City, Dublin County (Fingal, South Dublin, Dun Laoghaire-Rathdown), Co. Louth, Co. Meath, Co. Kildare, Co. Wicklow.

e Census 2002.

f The figure represents the number of 'persons employed' from Census 2002 (i.e. the number of economically active persons residing in the region, but not necessarily the number of jobs located in the region).

g Calculation based on 1991 and 2002 Census figures.

h Calculation based on 1991 and 2002 Census figures ('persons employed').

i Within the Greater Dublin region, there may be a number of smaller FURs emerging in the long run.

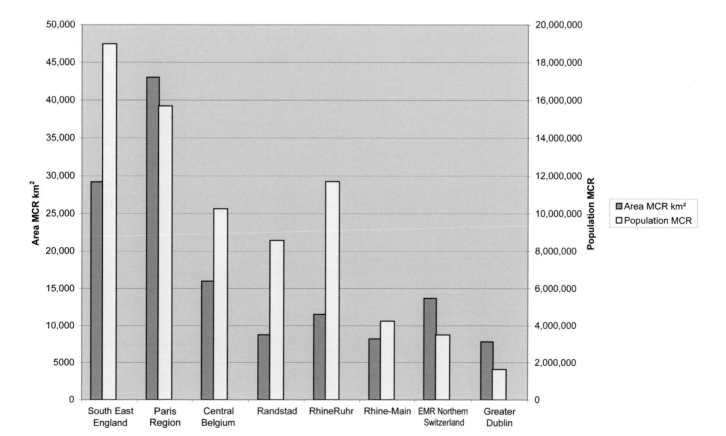

Figure 2.1 Comparative areas and populations c. 2000

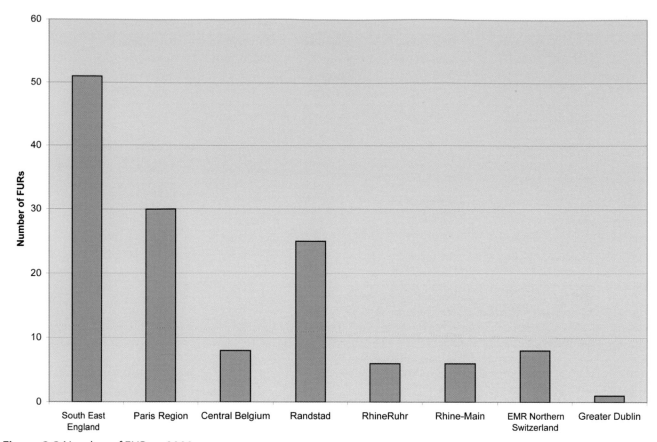

Figure 2.2 Number of FURs c. 2000

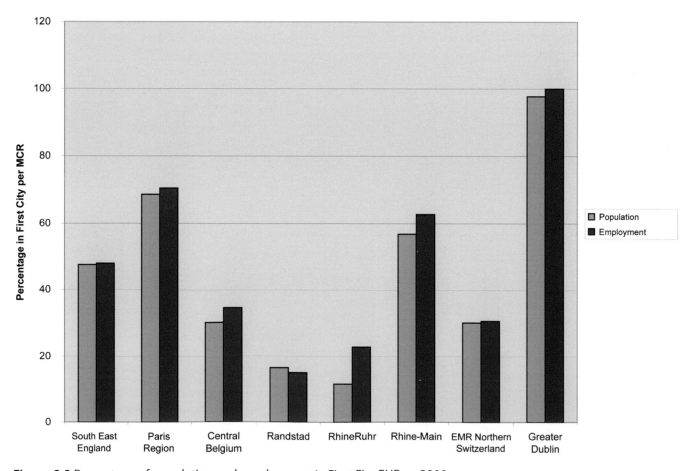

Figure 2.3 Percentage of population and employment in First City FURs c. 2000

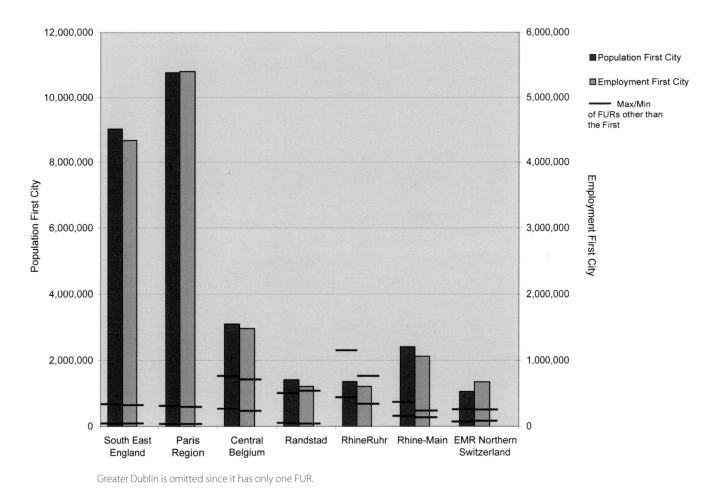

Greater Dublin is omitted since it has only one FUR.

Figure 2.4 Population and employment in the First City FUR, largest other FUR and smallest FUR c. 2000

first FUR, in terms of population and employment; and Figure 2.4 develops this comparison, demonstrating the structure in terms of the relationship between the first FUR, measured in terms of population and employment, and the extremes of the remaining range. Six MCRs prove to be relatively monocentric, dominated by one central FUR: London (where the central core has 9.0 million), Brussels (3.1 million), Frankfurt (2.4 million), Zürich (1.1 million), Paris (10.7 million) and Dublin (1.0 million). Two are strictly polycentric, with no dominant city: the Randstad and RhineRuhr. But the majority have between five and 25 constituent FURs, and are less monocentric than 'semi-polycentric': with the exception of RhineRuhr, the pattern tends to be dominated by the FURs of one (or sometimes two) major business and trading cities: Amsterdam–Rotterdam, Brussels, Frankfurt, Zürich, Paris. A key question for analysis, in these FURs, is to discover how far – through outward migration of people and employment – an older monocentric (or part-monocentric) urban system adapts into a partially polycentric one.

Comparative maps showing constituent FURs bring out these contrasts between the eight regions even more strikingly (Figures 2.5a–h). *South East England* (Figure 2.5a) occupies a huge area, more than one-fifth of

England, and contains nearly two-fifths (38.6 per cent) of its population. Stretching northwards for some 80 miles (130km) from London and south-westwards as far as 110 miles (180km) from the capital, it is dominated by the huge built-up mass – about 15 miles (25km) in radius – of Greater London, bounded by the green belt that was placed around it after World War II as the result of the Greater London Plan of 1944 and by the M25 orbital motorway, also part of that plan but completed only in 1986. London's FUR dominates the region with 9,025,960 people, just under half the total population. Most significantly, though, outside this are no less than 50 other FURs, ranging in size from 79,000 to 600,000, which have shown consistent and strong growth in the last half century; almost half of these are contiguous with the London FUR, which in some cases almost surrounds them. And further FURs could almost without doubt have been defined using the standard criteria, which would have had contiguous boundaries and so would have extended the MCR further into the English Midlands. Strong land use planning policies have kept their urban cores physically separate, but they have become functionally interdependent. These policies have also progressively restrained growth nearer to London, effectively diverting it

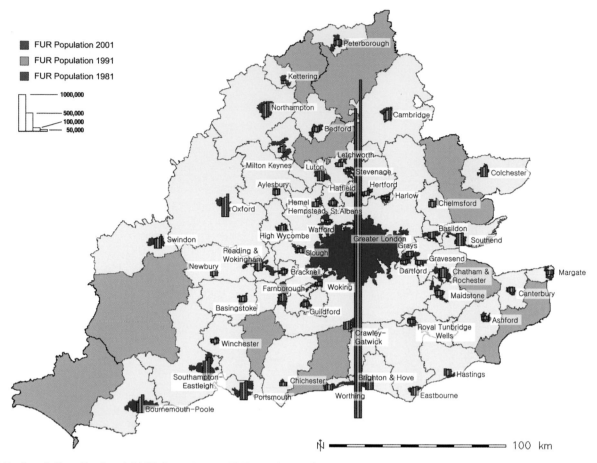

Figure 2.5a South East England: MCR Constituent FURs and populations 1981–1991–2001

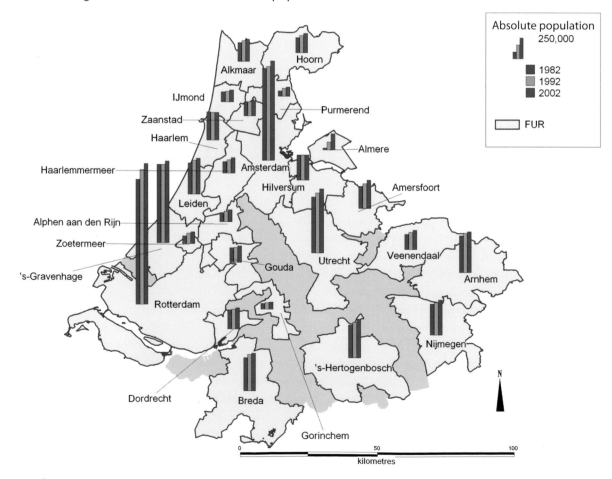

Figure 2.5b The Randstad MCR: Constituent FURs and populations 1982–1992–2002

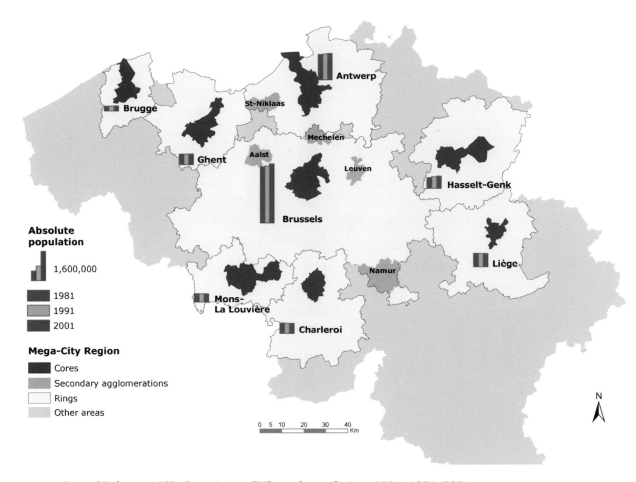

Figure 2.5c Central Belgium MCR: Constituent FURs and populations 1981–1991–2001

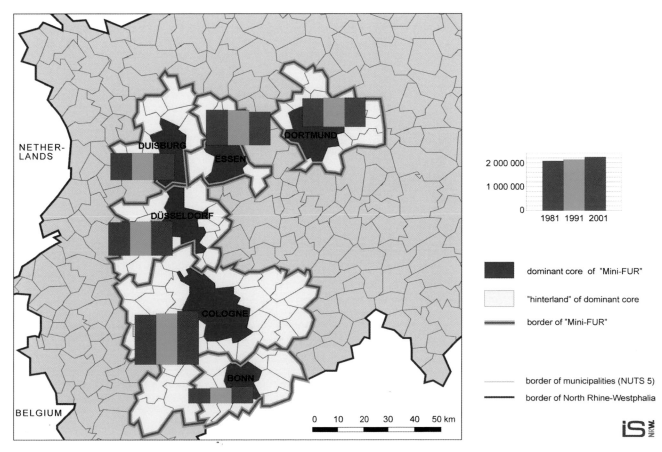

Figure 2.5d RhineRuhr MCR: Constituent FURs and populations 1981–1991–2001

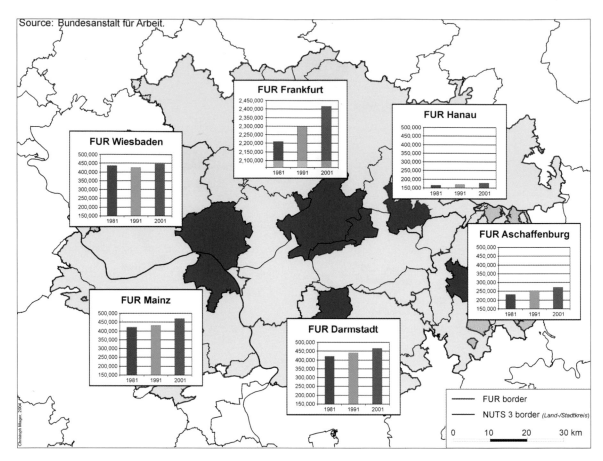

Figure 2.5e Rhine-Main MCR: Constituent FURs and populations 1981–1991–2001

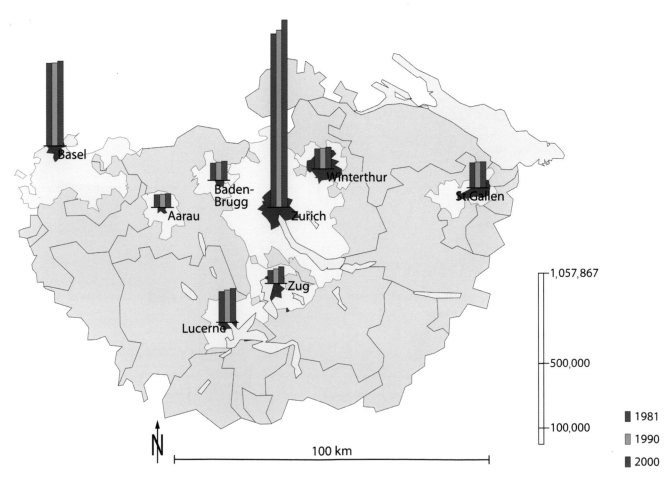

Figure 2.5f EMR Northern Switzerland MCR: Constituent FURs and populations 1981–1990–2000

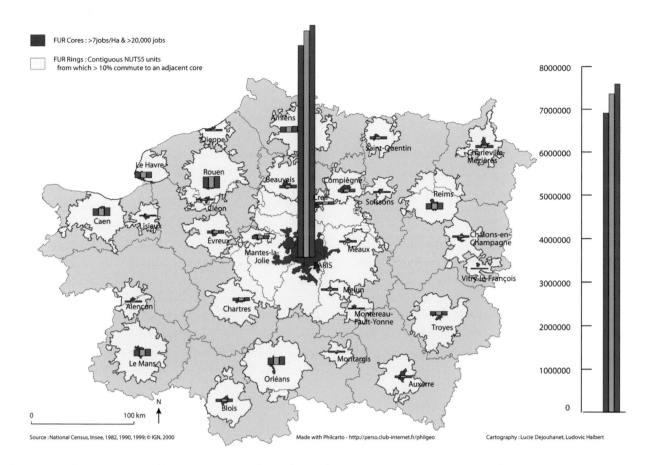

FUR Cores : >7jobs/Ha & >20,000 jobs

FUR Rings : Contiguous NUTS5 units
from which > 10% commute to an adjacent core

Source : National Census, Insee, 1982, 1990, 1999; © IGN, 2000   Made with Philcarto - http://perso.club-internet.fr/philgeo   Cartography : Lucie Dejouhanet, Ludovic Halbert

Figure 2.5g Paris Region MCR: Constituent FURs and populations 1982–1990–1999

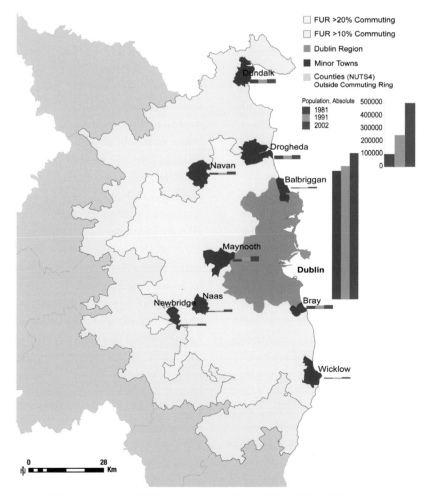

FUR >20% Commuting

FUR >10% Commuting

Dublin Region

Minor Towns

Counties (NUTS4)
Outside Commuting Ring

Population, Absolute
1981
1991
2002

Figure 2.5h Greater Dublin MCR: Constituent FURs and populations 1981–1991–2002

to more distant towns and cities. The original eight London new towns, started in 1946–1950 and completed some 20 years later, are 20–35 miles (35–55km) from London; their three successors, started in the 1960s, are 50–80 miles (80–130km) distant. The UK government's most recent spatial development strategy, published in 2003 (ODPM, 2003a), aims to concentrate growth in discrete towns along three major development corridors running north-north west, north-north east and east from London, and following new or upgraded high-speed train links and motorways.

The Randstad (Figure 2.5b), though a textbook case of strategic planning, has a very different structure. The polycentric Randstad ('Ring City') is a horseshoe-shaped complex around a protected 'green heart', dominated by the 'big four' cities of Amsterdam, The Hague, Rotterdam and Utrecht, but including also important medium-sized towns such as Haarlem, Leiden, Delft, Dordrecht and Amersfoort, as well as an important and fast-growing new town from the 1960s, Almere, and many even smaller towns and villages that together produce a complex physical structure. Like South East England, the Randstad is the country's economic powerhouse, containing its major port (Rotterdam) and airport (Amsterdam Schiphol) and intersected by numerous motorways and railways, about to be supplemented by the new high-speed line under construction from Brussels. Successive strategic reports from 1958 onwards have sought to preserve the green heart and to divert growth pressures first outwards, to urban extensions and new towns in the newly drained polders, but then – after 1980, as de-industrialization caused contraction of the major cities – back into them, the so-called 'compact city' policy. Here there is a clear parallel with contemporary British attempts to divert growth back into London, through the Docklands regeneration project from 1981, and the larger Thames Gateway project from 1991 onwards.

Central Belgium (Figure 2.5c) has a partially polycentric spatial structure that is in some ways intermediate between those of South East England and the Randstad. Straddling the linguistic boundary between Flemish and French-speaking Belgians (which also runs through Brussels), it is dominated by Brussels, capital of the European Union (EU) and a major provider of advanced services. Nearby Antwerp, a great port and manufacturing city, is under-represented in command-and-control services (banking and finance, headquarters), as are a number of smaller Flemish towns close by, as well as Ghent, the region's third city, and Hasselt–Genk near the Dutch border; the sole exception is Leuven, an important university city. Finally, there is a distinctive belt of old industrial towns on the region's southern French-speaking margin: Mons–La Louvière, Charleroi, Liège.

RhineRuhr (Figure 2.5d), like the Randstad, has a classic polycentric structure: a set of strong medium-sized cities, one (Cologne) nearing 1 million people and four others (Duisburg, Essen, Dortmund and Düsseldorf) with over half a million each. These and other cities are relatively very close together, especially in the Ruhr area in the northern half of the region, reflecting their location along an old European trade route and as the heart of 19th Century industrialization; they have been kept physically separate only by land use planning. Towards the south, along the Rhine axis, and on the left (west) bank of the Rhine the cities are more widely spaced, with broad green areas sometimes disfigured by old opencast coal workings.[3]

Rhine-Main (Figure 2.5e) is a very different kind of region, somewhat resembling Central Belgium in its structure: Germany's second polycentric city region (after RhineRuhr), it is dominated by Frankfurt, one of Europe's great banking and business service cities and a major transport hub (a role it developed in the Middle Ages, and seized back from Berlin after 1945). However, it also contains two other cities (Mainz and Wiesbaden) that are Land (state) capitals (of Rheinland-Pfalz and Hessen respectively) and four further medium-sized cities (Darmstadt, Offenbach, Hanau, in Hessen and Aschaffenburg in Bavaria), thus unusually extending into three Länder. These cities and towns, strung out along the axes of the Rhine and Main rivers, remain physically separate, although extensive suburbanization sometimes makes it difficult to distinguish them.

European Metropolitan Region Northern Switzerland (Figure 2.5f) has a rather similar spatial structure to Central Belgium and Rhine-Main, albeit extending over a wider area that stretches for some 80 miles (130km) from west to east: it is semi-polycentric, including a number of other cities, both medium-sized (Basel, Lucerne) and smaller (Aarau, Baden-Brugg, Winterthur, St Gallen, Zug), but dominated by Zürich and its suburbs. And the parallel with Frankfurt is of course even closer, for Zürich is a banking, business service and transportation hub of global importance.

The *Paris Region* (Figure 2.5g) in contrast has a spatial structure that is unique, though it offers some similarities to South East England: it is very large in area, extending for some 186 miles (300km) from west to east and 155 miles (250km) from north to south, and almost equals RhineRuhr in population (10.7 against 11.7 million). At the centre of this region is the relatively compact Île-de-France agglomeration, centred on an economic core straddling the historic city of Paris and the neighbouring Hauts-de-Seine *département*. This also includes important decentralized activity nodes (Charles de Gaulle airport, the five new towns) which, unlike London, are still located within the agglomeration itself. The Île-de-France

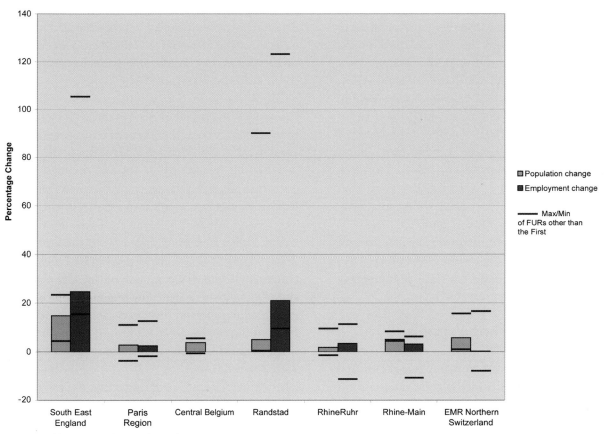

Note: Greater Dublin is omitted since it has only one FUR.

Figure 2.6 Population and employment change in the First City FUR, largest other FUR and smallest FUR 1990–2000

therefore lacks a zone of nearby medium-sized towns such as is found in South East England. It has a few such places (Évreux, Chartres, Beauvais, Compiègne, Meaux), but the really significant urban development is found at much greater distances, outside the Île-de-France in the wider Paris Region, in the so-called 'Cathedral Cities' forming a distinct ring at distances of about 93 miles (150km) from Paris: Rouen, Amiens, Reims, Troyes, Orléans, Le Mans. Current strategic planning policies aim to allow these cities to share from the region's general growth, but historically – ever since the famous *Schéma Directeur* of 1965 – the main emphasis has been first on promoting short-distance decentralization, then short-distance inner-city recentralization, within the agglomeration itself. Construction of urban motorways and the RER (*Réseau Express Régional*) in the 1970s and 1980s, and of the Orbitale light rail-busway system in course of realization in the 1990s, have all been devoted to promoting this objective. As a result, this region represents a special case: the analysis produced one very large central FUR (Paris) and seven smaller contiguous FURs (with four others displaying marginal contiguity), but with no less than 18 non-contiguous FURs at distances up to 62 miles (100km) from Paris; here, therefore, the MCR definition was produced by bending the contiguity rule.

Greater Dublin (Figure 2.5h) is without doubt the most distinctive of all the eight MCRs in its urban settlement structure. Totally dominated by the city of Dublin and its suburbs, it is hardly polycentric at all by the standards of the other regions. What it does have is a series of relatively small country towns at distances of 18.5–37 miles (30–60km) from Dublin: Wicklow, Bray, Newbridge, Naas, Maynooth, Navan, Balbriggan, Drogheda, Dundalk. Five of these are located along the main coastal road, two south and three north of Dublin, and these last three form part of a corridor of such small towns leading across the border to Belfast. This corridor is currently of great planning interest, both because Balbriggan is regarded as an official growth centre and because growth pressures from Dublin are now extending out here, aided by impending completion of a new motorway, to impact as far as Newry just across the border.

Employment distributions closely follow population distributions, as might be expected. But in general, employment remains more concentrated in larger FURs than does population (Figure 2.8, p35). Thus in South East England, out of a 2001 total of 9,040,000 jobs, the London FUR alone had 4,336,000, or 48 per cent; the next largest employment centre was Oxford with 307,000 jobs, followed by Southampton with 286,000. In the Randstad, out of some 4 million jobs, Rotterdam alone had 606,000, Amsterdam 578,000, The Hague 416,000 and Utrecht 391,000 – almost exactly half. In Central Belgium, Brussels alone had 1,250,000 jobs, far ahead of Antwerp with 510,000, and almost one-third of the regional total. In RhineRuhr, though the Cologne FUR was well ahead of the rest, the distribution of employment was far more polycentric than in Belgium. Rhine-Main in contrast is dominated by Frankfurt, which accounts for 487,000 of a regional total of 1.7 million, about 28 per cent; six core areas have 58 per cent of employment against only 37 per cent of population. EMR Northern Switzerland is again not very polycentric: the Zürich FUR with 676,000 employees, 31 per cent of the regional total, dominates the region. In the Paris Region, the Paris FUR accounts for no less than 5.4 million workers, 70 per cent of the total, out-numbering the totality of the other FURs. In Greater Dublin, the central Dublin FUR completely dominates the picture.

Dynamics of change: Population and employment

All eight MCRs have recorded growth of population and employment over the last decade, but the variation was great (Figure 2.6): in population growth it ranged from only 1.1 per cent (RhineRuhr) to as high as 13.5 per cent (South East England); for employment the variation was even greater, from 1.7 per cent (Rhine-Main) to 62.9 per cent (Greater Dublin). This figure also demonstrates the strength of decentralization both of people and jobs, in less polycentric and more polycentric MCRs alike: smaller and more peripheral FURs in general have recently tended to grow faster than larger and more central ones, sometimes by a considerable margin.

Population changes for the decades 1980–1990 and 1990–2000 are mapped in Figures 2.7a–h. In South East England, after generally overall sluggish growth in the 1980s (with decline in the London FUR and some others), exceptionally strong regional growth in the 1990s has ensured that every one of the 51 constituent FURs has grown to some degree, but the percentage growth has ranged from under 6 per cent (Southend) to over 22 per cent (Milton Keynes); here, quite unusually, the central FUR (London) has reversed the previous decline to show strong growth, by nearly 15 per cent (Figure 2.7a). In the Randstad, the four large core cities have declined (though recovering in the 1990s, because of migration from abroad and the fashion for urban living), as have some smaller core cities in the western core of the area; older cities farther out have shown some growth, but have lost through suburbanization; suburban areas around the cities have gained (Figure 2.7b). In Central Belgium, there is a notable contrast between growth in the Brussels FUR (including, latterly, the core city) and the Flemish FURs, versus decline in the Walloon FURs in the southern strip

of the country, which were affected negatively by deindustrialization (Figure 2.7c). In RhineRuhr, core cities have lost populations to their suburban hinterlands, while smaller cities like Bonn and Mönchengladbach have continued to grow (Figure 2.7d).

In Rhine-Main more complex trends are evident: the Frankfurt FUR actually showed the largest absolute growth in the 1990s, because of migration from the so-called Neue Länder (the old Deutsche Demokratische Republik (DDR)), but smaller FURs showed the highest relative growth, while the Wiesbaden FUR showed loss due to local out-migration (Figure 2.7e). In EMR Northern Switzerland, there has been notable suburbanization within FURs, from core cities to suburban rings (Figure 2.7f). The Paris Region has experienced a more complex pattern still, with strong growth of the central Paris FUR and of some more distant medium-sized FURs (Orléans, Caen), while others in this latter category have stagnated (Amiens, Le Havre); there is thus no relationship between size and growth; rather, the relationship is geographical, with nearer fast-growing FURs to the north and west of Paris, more distant slower-growing FURs to the east (Figure 2.7g). In the case of Greater Dublin, likewise, the central Dublin FUR has continued to grow strongly (though with some slowing in the 1990s), but some smaller and more distant centres have shown sharply accelerated growth (Figure 2.7h).

Very much the same trends can be found for employment as for population change, as might be expected (Figures 2.8 and 2.9). In South East England, where total employment shrank in the 1980s (with especially sharp decline in the London FUR), it rebounded in the 1990s, growing by 2,237,000 (33 per cent); the London FUR accounted for an increase of 860,000, or nearly 25 per cent, representing nearly two-fifths the regional total and slightly above the regional percentage growth. In the Randstad, where employment grew by almost 30 per cent between 1993 and 2002, growth in Amsterdam and Utrecht was significantly stronger than in Rotterdam and The Hague. But suburban areas around the cities grew even more rapidly, and dormitory towns like Almere, Zoetermeer, Alphen aan den Rijn, Gorinchem and Schiphol-Haarlemmermeer grew rapidly to become significant employment centres. In Central Belgium, employment has grown robustly in Brussels and the Flemish FURs, but much less strongly in the Walloon ones where the impact of de-industrialization has been less strongly countered by the growth of business services.

In RhineRuhr, likewise, there is a clear distinction between the Ruhr cities of Duisburg, Essen and Dortmund, which lost employment in the 1980s and 1990s, and the Rhine cities of Bonn, Cologne and Düsseldorf, which gained from service industry growth –

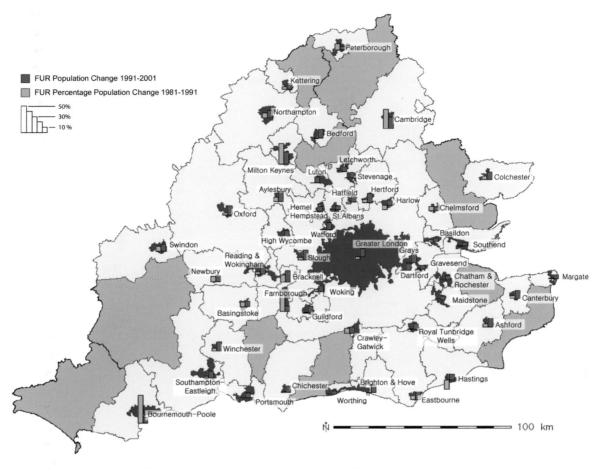

Figure 2.7a South East England MCR population change 1981–1991–2001

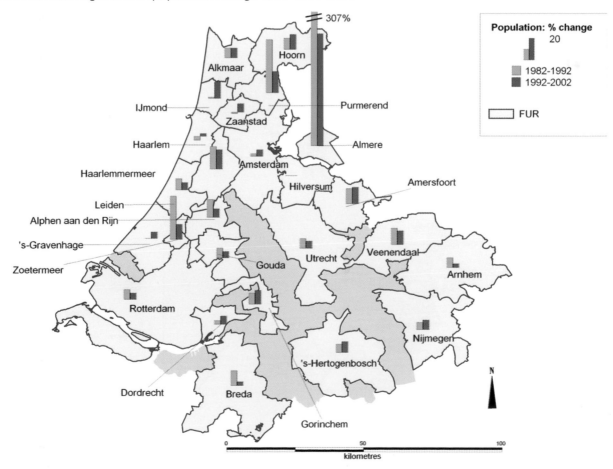

Figure 2.7b The Randstad MCR population change 1982–1992–2002

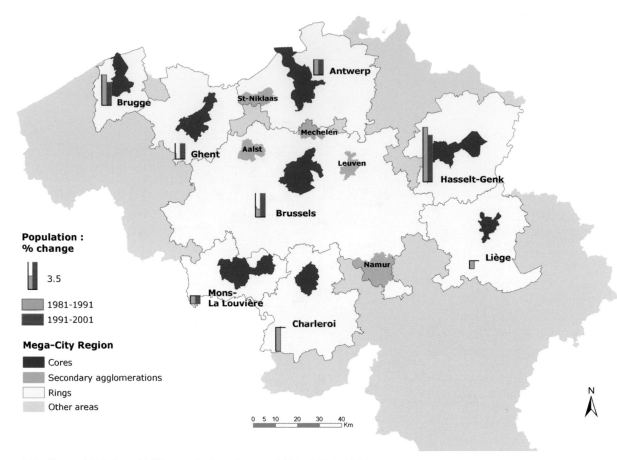

Figure 2.7c Central Belgium MCR population change 1981–1991–2001

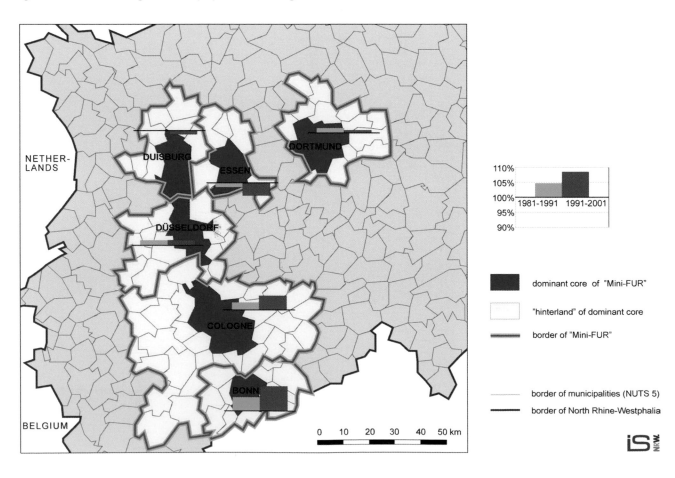

Figure 2.7d RhineRuhr MCR population change 1981–1991–2001

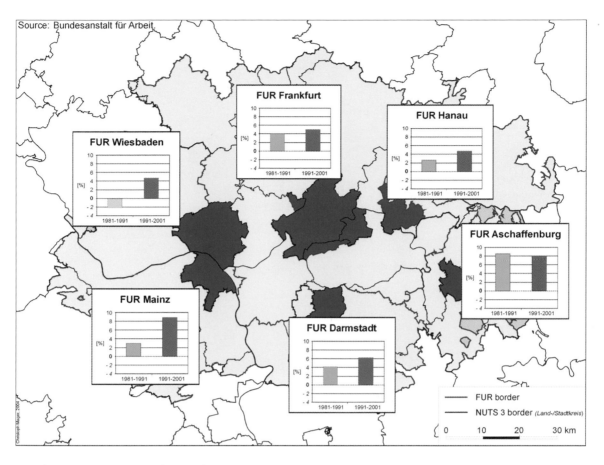

Figure 2.7e Rhine-Main MCR population change 1981–1991–2001

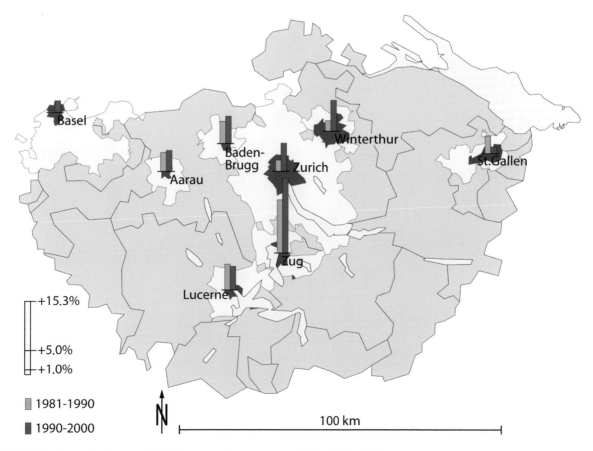

Figure 2.7f EMR Northern Switzerland MCR population change 1981–1990–2000

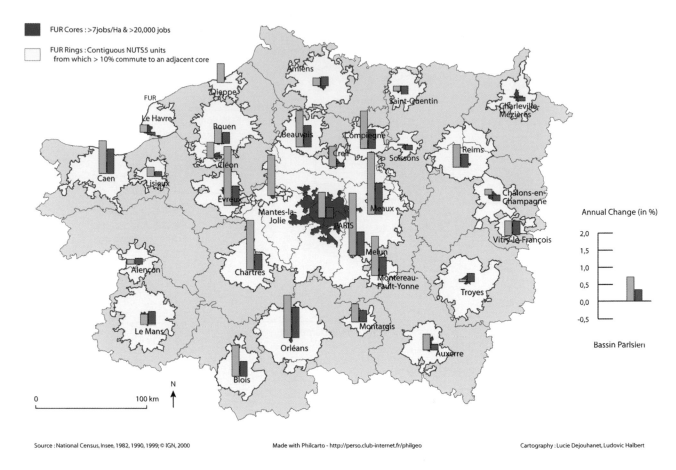

Figure 2.7g Paris Region MCR population change 1982–1990–1999

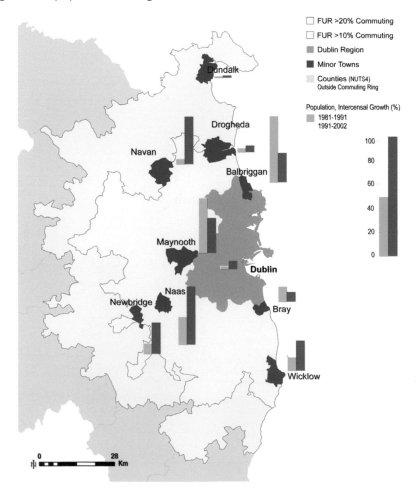

Figure 2.7h Greater Dublin MCR population change 1981–1991–2002

though less strongly than might be thought. In Rhine-Main, there was a sharp contrast between the decade from 1980 to 1990 with considerable growth in the entire MCR, and the decade from 1990 to 2000 when all FURs (except Frankfurt) stagnated or suffered a moderate loss of jobs. EMR Northern Switzerland grew overall through the expansion of service sector employment, but with a sharp contrast: Zug, a suburban area close to Zürich, grew sharply, Zürich and St Gallen grew weakly, while other FURs – Winterthur, Baden, Basel – contracted because of losses in manufacturing employment. In the Paris Region, the dominant Paris FUR grew relatively slowly while a number of smaller FURs on the edge of the Île-de-France – Meaux, Melun, Compiègne, Évreux, Chartres, Beauvais – grew rapidly, while others (especially east of Paris and in the lower Seine valley) declined relatively or absolutely. For Greater Dublin, reliable figures are lacking.

Population density

The MCRs also differ significantly in population density (Figure 2.8). But in all, there has been a tendency for higher densities in the cities to fall while lower rural densities have risen through progressive suburbanization of the population. (This simply reflects the pattern of population change, since the areas are fixed.) South East England's overall density in 2001 was close on 1800 per mile^2 (700/km^2), one of the densest of the MCRs, but densities of individual FURs ranged from 340/mile^2 (131/km^2) (Chichester) to 9640/mile^2 (3721/km^2)

(Watford); London, unexpectedly, came somewhere above the middle of the range at 4290/mile^2 (1655/km^2), because it is so large and extends over rural areas, while the highest values belonged to relatively small FURs overlapping with the London FUR ring, like Dartford, Hemel Hempstead, Slough and Watford. As populations have everywhere grown, so have densities – and some of the higher-density FURs (like Slough and Watford) have shared in this strong growth, because they were in areas of exceptionally strong population pressure just outside London. In the Randstad, The Hague stands out as the most densely populated FUR (2500/km^2 in 2002); Amsterdam is second (2000/km^2), Rotterdam and Utrecht respectively ninth (1100/km^2) and 13th (1000/km^2) – Rotterdam because of its large harbour area, while Utrecht has a large open area within its boundaries. Here, densities have fallen in the core cities while increasing in the suburban areas around them. In Central Belgium, densities have declined in the old Walloon industrial towns while they have increased in the suburban areas around the 'Flemish diamond' of Brussels–Ghent–Antwerp–Leuven – but large low-density rural areas survive south of Brussels. In RhineRuhr, FUR densities have shown little change in recent decades, though there have been shifts as between cores and rings, while in Rhine-Main they have shown notable increases, largely due to strong increases in the suburban rings. The same process is evident in EMR Northern Switzerland, though again it arises from rapid suburban development in the rings around the cities. The

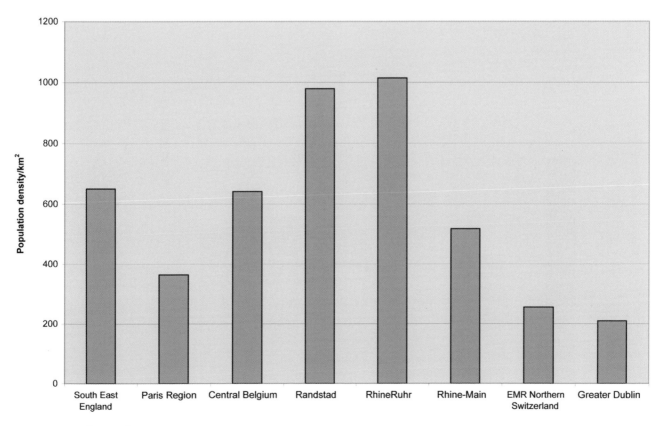

Figure 2.8 Population density c. 2000

Paris Region has always been characterized by exceptionally high urban density in the Central Paris FUR and this has actually increased in the last decades with the development of the outer fringe of the agglomeration. In contrast the FURs in the surrounding ring demonstrate very low rural densities, with intermediate (and relatively stable) values in the outer ring of medium size cities. Greater Dublin stands in sharp contrast to most other MCRs, with high densities in the Dublin and neighbouring Bray FURs and much lower densities outside; however, in these latter densities are rising sharply because of a very rapid rate of house construction.

Employment is invariably more concentrated than residential population, and so tends to show sharper peaks in core FURs (Figure 2.7). In South East England, as with population, London itself does not dominate simply because this FUR is so large and extends over rural areas; as with population, the highest densities are recorded by relatively small FURs which overlap with the London ring and are therefore artificially truncated, such as Slough or Watford. In the Randstad, employment density is highest in The Hague, followed by Amsterdam; generally, densities are higher in smaller central FURs, lower in peripheral FURs (Breda, 's Hertogenbosch, Nijmegen, Arnhem) containing large areas of undeveloped land. In RhineRuhr employment densities are generally moderate and quite uniform, reflecting the highly polycentric structure. In Rhine-Main, by way of contrast, they are relatively much higher in Frankfurt (where they have risen) and the

relatively small FUR of Hanau than elsewhere. In EMR Northern Switzerland, interestingly, they are much more even as between the major FURs of Zürich and Basel and the others. The Paris Region, as might be expected, displays a sharp contrast between high densities in the central Paris FUR and all the others, persisting over time. As mentioned earlier, unfortunately data are lacking for Greater Dublin.

Employment structure

Throughout Europe in the decades since 1970, urban employment structures have been moving steadily away from manufacturing and goods-handling activities towards services, especially advanced services. This is very evident in the eight MCR study areas. South East England is heavily geared towards the service sector and above all to business services: almost exactly 80 per cent of all employment is in services, of which banking and financial services employ over 22 per cent, public services nearly 27 per cent, and distribution 22 per cent. Financial services are strongly represented in South Coast FURs and in a cluster of FURs south-west and west of London; public services are well represented in university cities like Oxford and Cambridge and in some coastal resorts, but also more generally in major county towns; manufacturing remains significant with over 15 per cent of overall employment, and rises higher in some FURs toward the fringes of the MCR, especially north and west of London. In the Randstad business service jobs rose by no less than

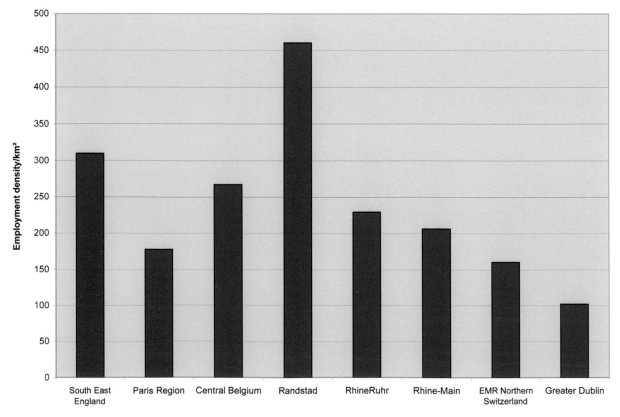

Figure 2.9 Employment density c. 2000

41 per cent between 1996 and 2002, and this was evident both in large core FURs (Amsterdam, Rotterdam, The Hague and Schiphol-Haarlemmermeer) and more peripheral FURs like Almere, 's Hertogenbosch and Hilversum. In Central Belgium, likewise, financial services play a prominent role, especially in Brussels, with insurance important in Liège and logistics in Antwerp and Brugge, while accountancy is more widely distributed. RhineRuhr has a weaker representation of advanced services than other MCRs because of its surviving strong industrial base, but even here de-industrialization is evident; in fact the service sector in general and knowledge-intensive business services in particular are more strongly represented here than in the remainder of the Land Nordrhein-Westfalen, particularly in Düsseldorf, Cologne and Bonn, though weakly in Duisburg. Rhine-Main is exceptionally service-industry dependent, with 73 per cent of total employment in 2001 and even higher shares in Frankfurt, Wiesbaden and Mainz, rising higher than this in the cores; here, a marked loss in manufacturing jobs has been only partially absorbed by new service employment. EMR Northern Switzerland, likewise, is very service-oriented, especially towards advanced producer services (APS). These services, with strong value creation, are highly concentrated in the biggest FUR cores of Zürich and Basel. As elsewhere, employment in the Paris Region is characterized by declines in manufacturing and growth in services – here, especially, personal services to households. Business service employment is more uneven, with losses in banking and insurance and gains in law, accountancy and design consultancy. Some such services, such as research and development (R&D), are now beginning to decentralize to some degree from Paris to smaller peripheral FURs, or at least to more peripheral suburbs such as the area of Saint-Quentin-en-Yvelines and Plateau de Saclay. Again, data are lacking for Greater Dublin.

The journey to work: Commuting as a measure of polycentricity

As population decentralizes within MCRs more rapidly than does employment, it can be postulated that both the number and average length of commuter journeys will increase, and also that an increasing proportion of such trips will no longer be 'core'-oriented (i.e. to the cores of the big central FUR or FURs within each MCR) but rather 'edge'-oriented (i.e. between peripheral FURs). This proves to be the case (Figure 2.10a–h). But there are some surprises.

In South East England, the pattern is dominated by strong radial flows into and out of London, some of them long distance, and especially evident along strong transport corridors representing parallel motorways and rail main lines. But notably, many centres along these corridors, located between 40 and 100 miles (65–160km) from London, also have complex and increasingly important cross-links with other centres. This is particularly noticeable in a wide crescent north-west, west and south-west of London, from Northampton and Milton Keynes round to Bournemouth-Poole, Southampton, Portsmouth, Brighton-Hove and Eastbourne, which almost seems to be developing as a networked MCR within the larger MCR – confirming a hypothesis of much stronger independent economic growth on that side of London. In the Randstad, most commuter journeys are short, and there are two main concentrations: in the northern part of the Randstad, towards Amsterdam as the major employment core, with a subsidiary flow to Haarlemmermeer (Schiphol Airport), and in the southern part, where there is a two-way exchange between Rotterdam and The Hague. The only other significant flow is two-way on the eastern periphery, between Nijmegen and Arnhem. Significantly, there seem to be no major flows between the south-eastern periphery (Veenendaal, Arnhem, Nijmegen, 's Hertogenbosch and Breda) and the central Randstad FURs. And, most surprisingly, major flows cannot be found between the core Randstad cities, in particular between the northern and southern 'wings'; in this sense, an integrated Randstad does not exist. In Central Belgium Brussels is by far the dominant direction of commuter flows: nearby FURs like Charleroi, Mons-La Louvière and Ghent send appreciable numbers; more distant ones like Brugge, Liège and Hasselt-Genk far fewer. In the core 'Flemish diamond' there is extensive short-distance commuting between FURs, especially from one ring to a neighbouring ring; here, there are strong reverse flows from larger FURs like Brussels and Antwerp towards nearby smaller ones; commuting between more peripheral FURs is more limited.

In RhineRuhr, as might be expected from its polycentric structure, closely-neighbouring FURs show strong commuting relationships. However, Düsseldorf is very much the dominant commuter destination, receiving big flows from neighbouring FURs such as Duisburg, Essen, Mönchengladbach, Cologne, Krefeld and Wuppertal. Also evident is a major two-way flow between Cologne and Bonn and similar two-way flows between the major Ruhr cities of Essen, Bochum and Dortmund. Rhine-Main in contrast is dominated by flows into the Frankfurt FUR which employs some 1 million people, 200,000 of whom commute from the ring and another 72,000 commute from other FURs into the employment core. Here, as elsewhere, distance is significant: there are big flows between neighbouring FURs, relatively little between peripheral ones such as Wiesbaden–Hanau or

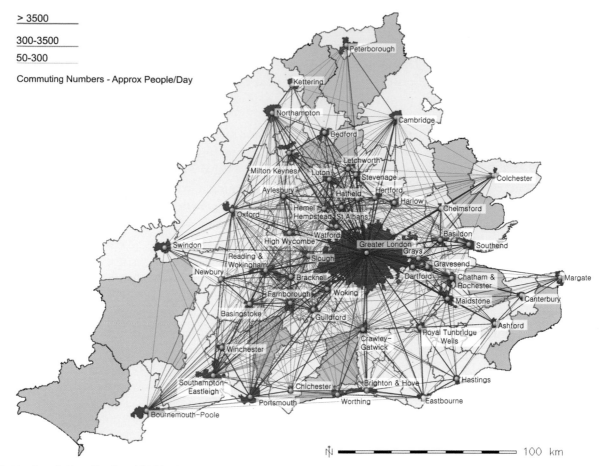

> 3500

300-3500

50-300

Commuting Numbers - Approx People/Day

Figure 2.10a South East England MCR: Commuting 2001

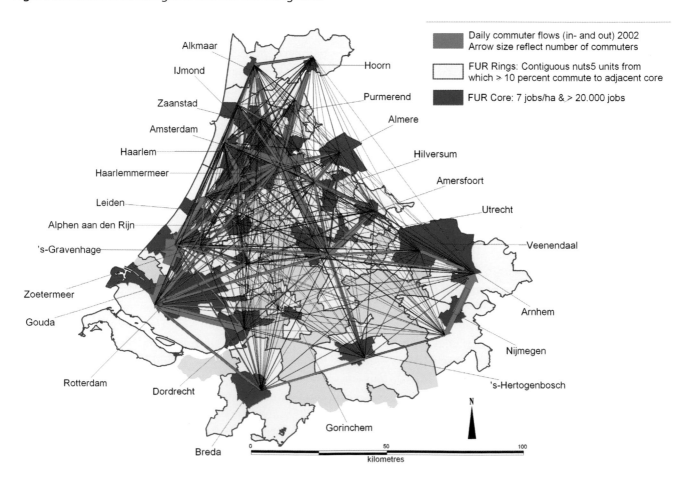

Daily commuter flows (in- and out) 2002
Arrow size reflect number of commuters

FUR Rings: Contiguous nuts5 units from
which > 10 percent commute to adjacent core

FUR Core: 7 jobs/ha & > 20.000 jobs

Figure 2.10b The Randstad MCR: Commuting 2002

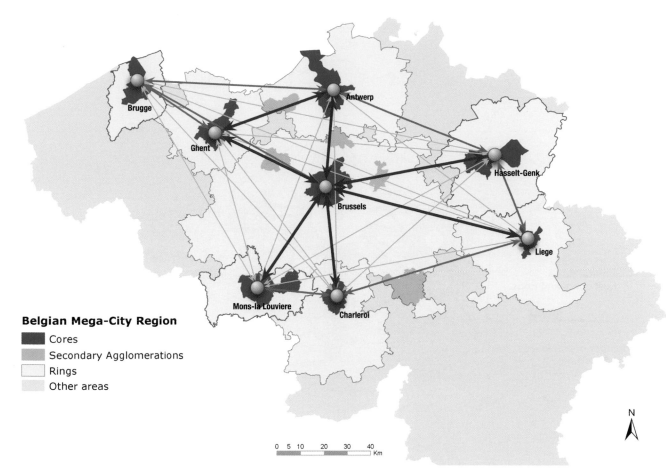

Note: Arrows are proportionate in width to number of commuters.

Figure 2.10c Central Belgium MCR: Commuting 2001

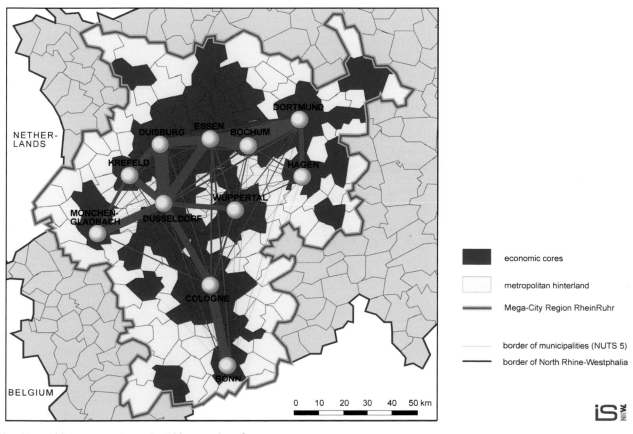

Note: Line widths are proportionate in width to number of commuters.

Figure 2.10d RhineRuhr MCR: Commuting 2001

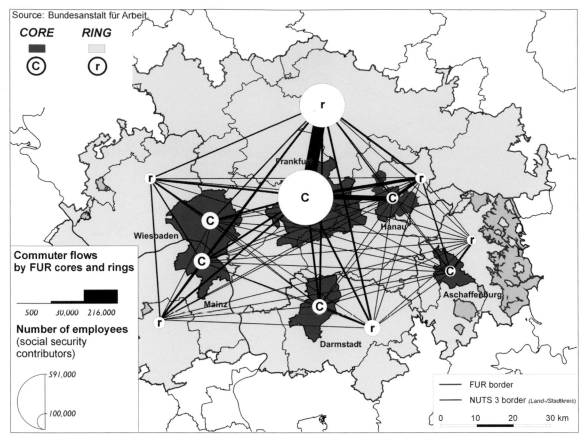

Figure 2.10e Rhine-Main MCR: Commuting 2001

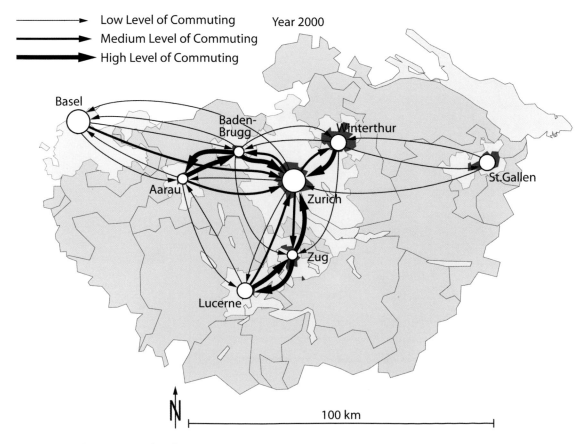

Figure 2.10f EMR Northern Switzerland MCR: Commuting 2000

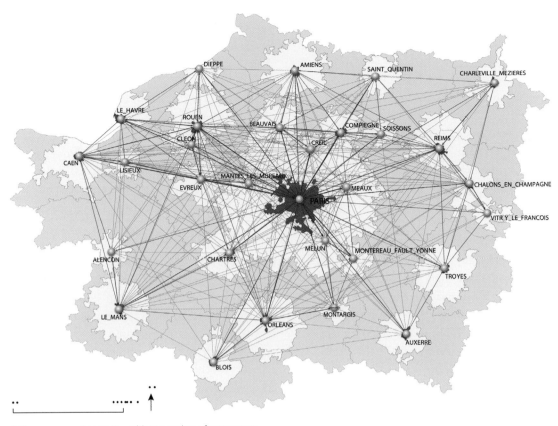

Note: Line widths are proportionate in width to number of commuters.

Figure 2.10g Paris Region MCR: Commuting 1999

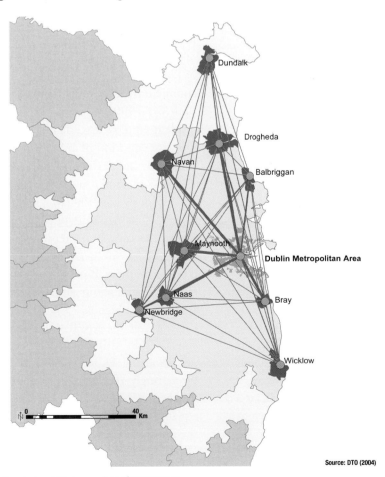

Source: DTO (2004)

Note: Line widths are proportionate in width to number of commuters.

Figure 2.10h Greater Dublin MCR: Commuting 2002

Mainz–Aschaffenburg. Interestingly, here, both rivers and land boundaries prove significant impediments to commuting.

In EMR Northern Switzerland, likewise, Zürich itself is the dominant commuter destination, attracting significant and increasing flows from other FURs as distant as Basel and St Gallen as well as even bigger numbers from nearby areas like Winterthur, Zug and Baden-Brugg. But there are also significant movements between neighbouring FURs in the region, as between Aarau and Baden-Brugg. The Paris Region, as might be expected, demonstrates an extremely monocentric commuter pattern, dominated by the huge flows into the Paris FUR, yet these are primarily from the smaller and nearer FURs such as Mantes-la-Jolie, Meaux, Melun, Creil, Chartres, Compiègne and Beauvais. But there are also significant localized commuter fields around the larger and more peripheral centres, constituting virtually sub-regional networks. Finally, the Greater Dublin MCR has a highly unusual pattern dominated by flows within the central Dublin FUR, with relatively weak flows into Dublin from outside and negligible reverse flows: a pattern of extreme monocentricity.

Measuring polycentricity

In this preliminary deck-clearing analysis the eight POLYNET teams also sought to make preliminary comparative measurements of polycentricity for each of the eight MCRs, derived from available Census data for population and commuting. Here, it is again important to stress that these were necessarily preliminary and tentative, to be checked and verified (or otherwise) in later stages of the research.

Rank-size indices

Population size can be used to generate a first and admittedly crude measure of relative polycentricity: the rank-size index. This has been a staple measuring tool of urban geography since the 1960s (Haggett, 1965; Chorley and Haggett, 1967), and is still regularly used – normally at a national scale, but equally applicable at a regional scale as represented by the MCR. When FURs within a nation or region are arrayed by size on double-log graph paper, the 'log-normal' distribution takes the form of a straight line at a 45-degree angle from the vertical; divergences towards a more concave pattern (a tendency to 'primacy') indicate a hierarchical system dominated by one or maybe two or three leading cities, as Hall and Hay (1980) showed for different European countries: France and the UK have a strongly primate distribution dominated by a capital city, while The Netherlands and the former West Germany had a different distribution dominated by a number of top

cities of roughly equal rank. Berry, analysing distributions for 38 countries, found no simple relationship with explanatory variables such as economic development, but there is a suggestion that primate distributions are characteristic of countries that are small, have a short urbanization history, and are economically or politically simple (Haggett, 1965, pp104–106; Berry, 1961; Berry and Horton, 1970, pp67–75).

Applied at regional scale, a primate distribution is more likely because of the absence of 'balancing' second-order cities; Stewart (1959) found that the ratio between second and first city was much higher at provincial than at national level.

The rank-size plots (Figure 2.11a–h) confirm the division of MCRs into two groups: South East England, Central Belgium, Rhine-Main, EMR Northern Switzerland, Paris Region and Greater Dublin are quite strongly primate, though in many of them a single primate city seems to be superimposed on a rank-size relationship at lower levels, and in all of them smaller FURs are gaining relative to the large central FUR; the Randstad and RhineRuhr are strongly non-primate and there is no tendency to greater primacy; in the latter, smaller FURs have somewhat gained recently at the expense of larger ones.

Measures of self-containment

It is also possible to develop a simple standardized index of self-containment of a FUR, following the pioneering work of Ray Thomas in the 1960s and Michael Breheny's later commentary on it (Thomas, 1969; Hall et al, 1973; Breheny, 1990). Thomas's measure showed how many resident employed workers were employed in that urban unit; for this kind of analysis, FURs are the logical units since they are defined in terms of a degree of 'closure'. Thomas's method is used here (Figure 2.12a–h).

In South East England at the Census date 2001, no less than 70 per cent of all workers lived and worked within the same FUR, representing a high degree of self-containment for a region with such a high degree of interconnectivity. But this proportion varied considerably, from as low as about 30 per cent in some FURs close to London to as high as 75–85 per cent for some FURs near the edges of the MCR. Even here, however, there were considerable differences, reflecting the closeness of neighbouring FURs and the potential for commuting. Interestingly, there does not seem to be a strong west–east distinction here: strong self-containment seems to be equally evident in the extreme west and extreme east. In the Randstad, the larger FURs (Rotterdam, Amsterdam, Utrecht and The Hague) are quite strongly self-contained with more than 50 per cent of commuter movements staying within the same FUR; these also have the smallest proportions of out-commuters. In Central Belgium, all

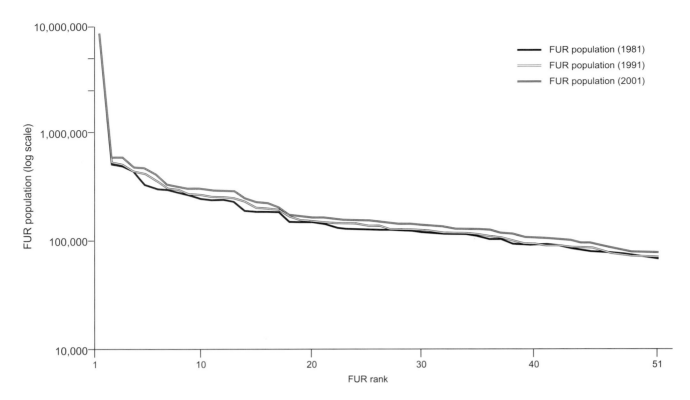

Figure 2.11a South East England MCR: Rank-size population plot 1981, 1991, 2001

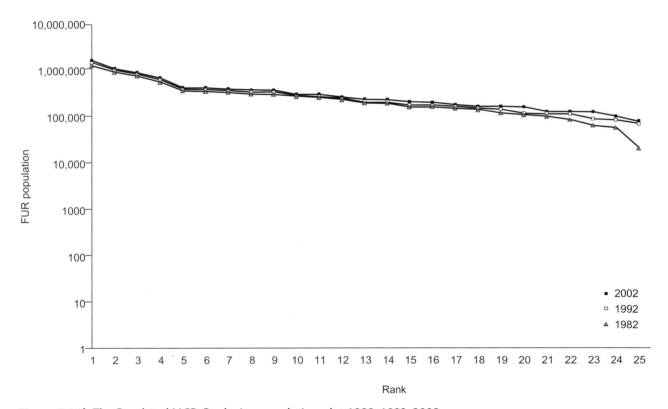

Figure 2.11b The Randstad MCR: Rank-size population plot 1982, 1992, 2002

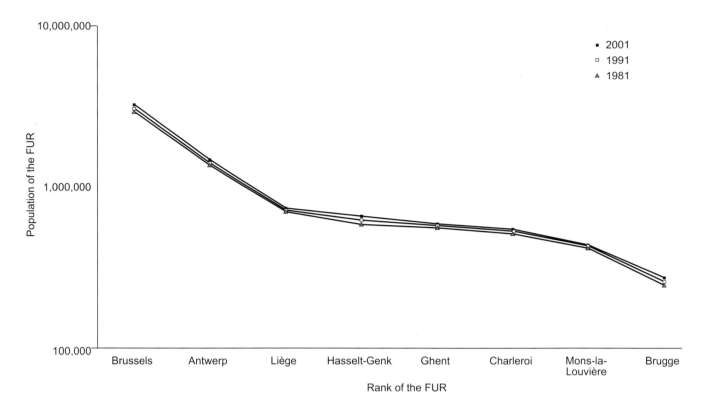

Figure 2.11c Central Belgium MCR: Rank-size population plot 1981, 1991, 2001

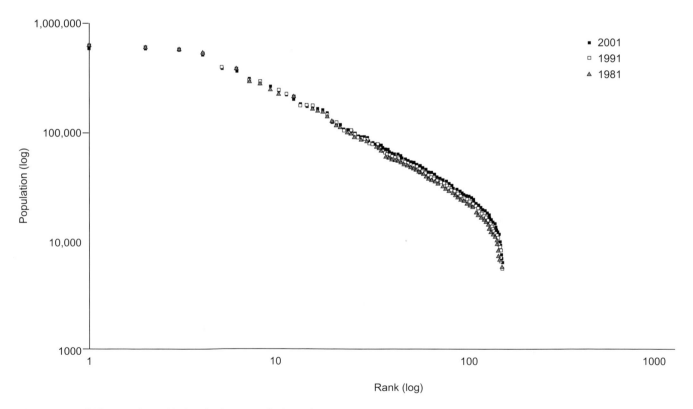

Figure 2.11d RhineRuhr MCR: Rank-size population plot 1981, 1991, 2001

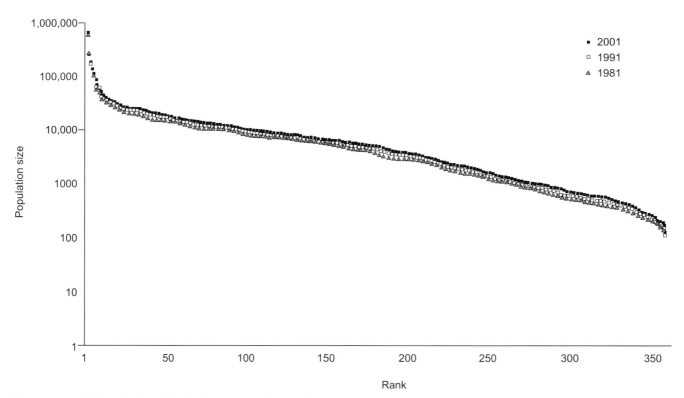

Figure 2.11e Rhine-Main MCR: Rank-size population plot 1981, 1991, 2001

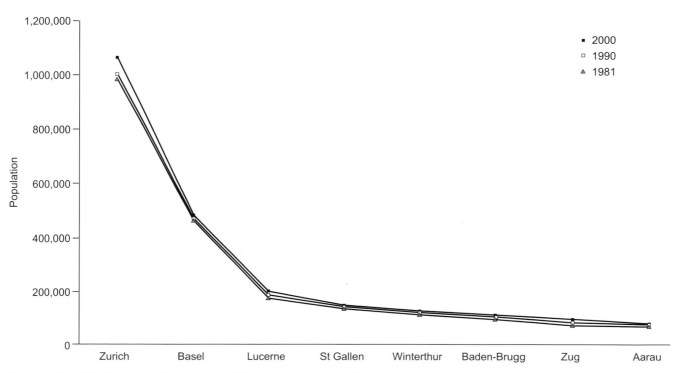

Figure 2.11f EMR Northern Switzerland MCR: Rank-size population plot 1981, 1990, 2000

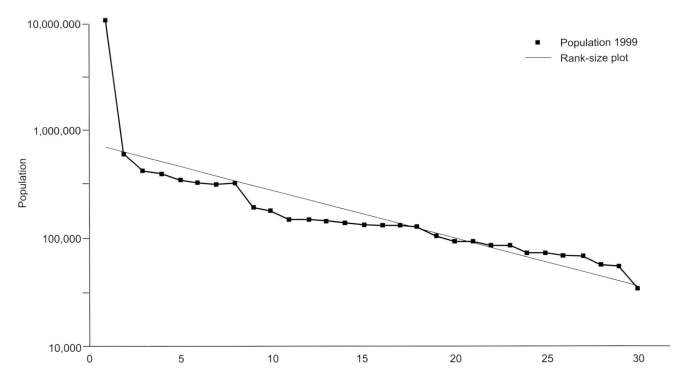

Figure 2.11g Paris Region MCR: Rank-size population plot 1999

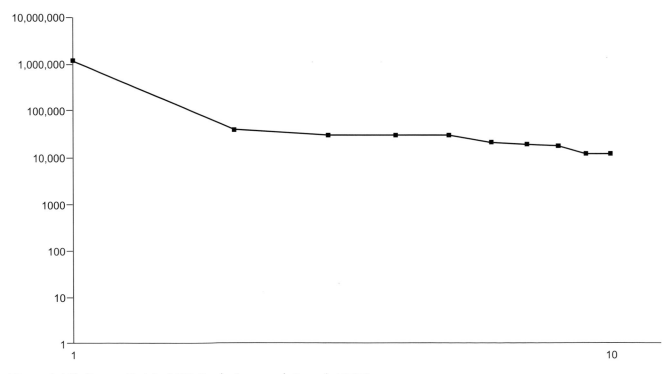

Figure 2.11h Greater Dublin MCR: Rank-size population plot 2002

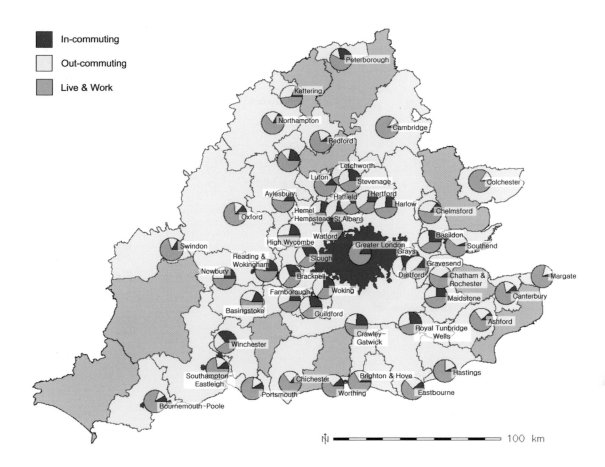

Figure 2.12a South East England MCR: Self-containment 2001

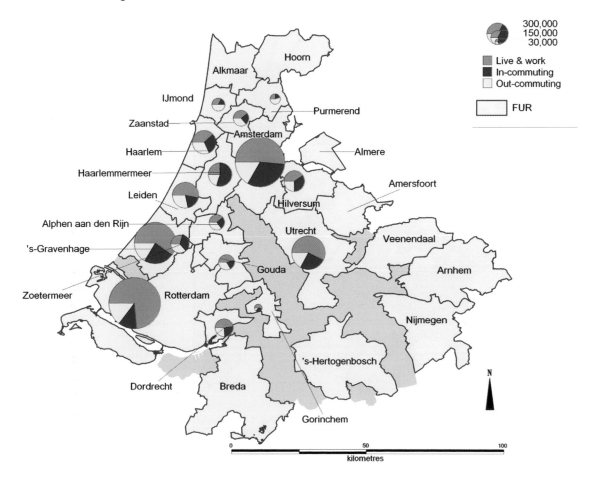

Figure 2.12b The Randstad MCR: Self-containment 2002

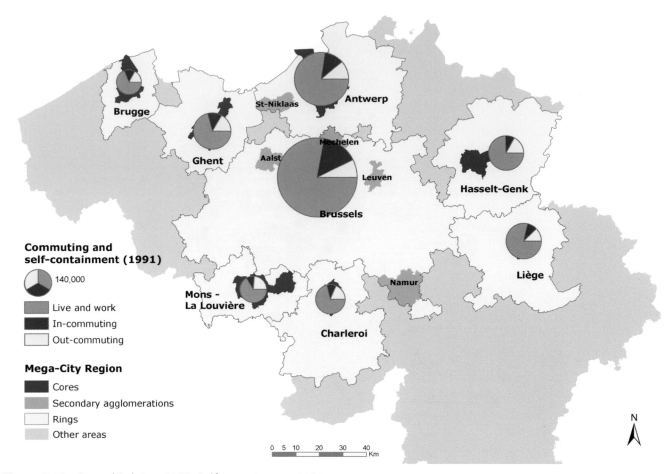

Figure 2.12c Central Belgium MCR: Self-containment 2001

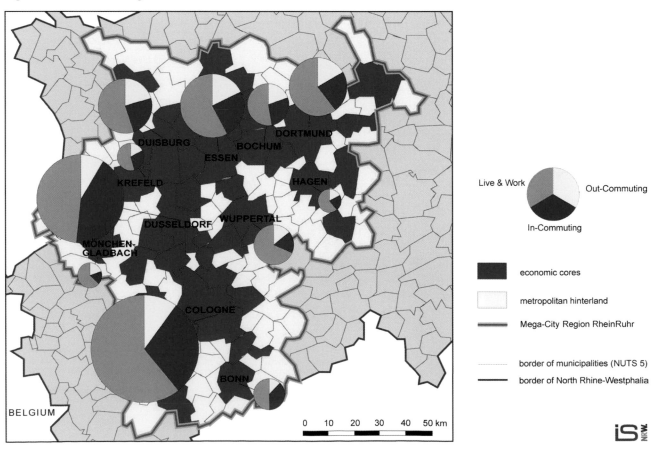

Figure 2.12d RhineRuhr MCR: Self-containment 2001

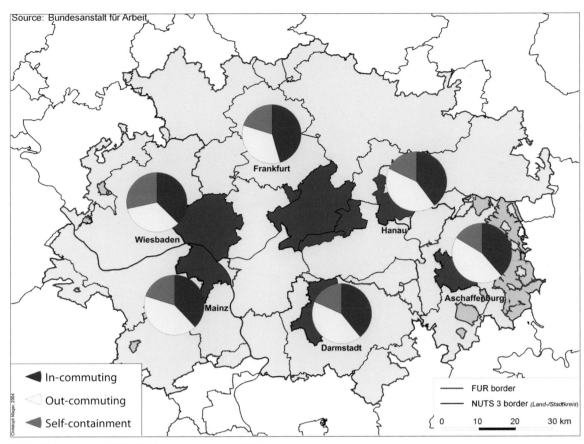

Figure 2.12e Rhine-Main MCR: Self-containment 2001

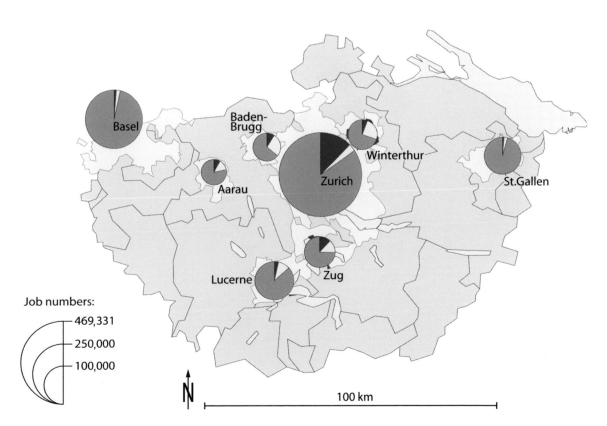

Figure 2.12f EMR Northern Switzerland MCR: Self-containment 2000

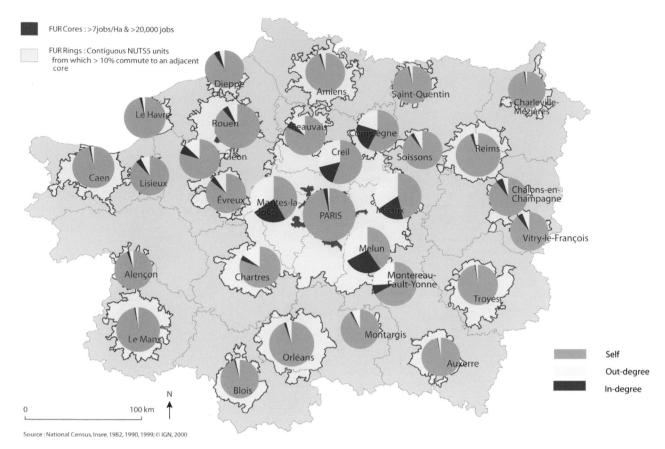

FUR Cores : >7jobs/Ha & >20,000 jobs

FUR Rings : Contiguous NUTS5 units from which > 10% commute to an adjacent core

Self

Out-degree

In-degree

0   100 km

N

Source : National Census, Insee, 1982, 1990, 1999; © IGN, 2000

Figure 2.12g Paris Region MCR: Self-containment 1999

In-Commuting

Out-Commuting

Live & Work

Circle Size is log of Commuting Numbers

Source: DTO (2004)

Figure 2.12h Greater Dublin MCR: Self-containment 2002

constituent FURs demonstrate high self-containment. In RhineRuhr, in contrast, classical commuter flows from the peripheries to the dominant FUR cores still play a major role, but one that is modified by the emergence of flows between cores and even between secondary centres. However, even here, the labour markets of all the 11 FURs showed a self-containment of over 50 per cent in 1991, though with declines by 2001.

Rhine-Main shows the highest rates of self-containment in Wiesbaden (46 per cent) and Frankfurt (37 per cent); Aschaffenburg, Darmstadt, Hanau and Mainz in contrast demonstrate considerable out-commuting. In EMR Northern Switzerland, Zürich itself is very self-contained (about 80 per cent) and Basel even more so; all FURs are 70 per cent or more self-contained. The Paris Region presents a similar picture because of the almost complete self-containment (98 per cent) of the dominant Paris FUR, modified by strong outflows and relatively weak self-containment (between 50 and 65 per cent) of the nearby small FURs having close links to Paris – Mantes-la-Jolie, Melun, Montereau, Creil and Meaux. The more distant medium-sized centres of the region occupy an intermediate position with between 80 and 90 per cent closure.

Graph-theory-derived analyses: Special and general polycentricity indices

These too have been employed in geographical analysis since the early 1960s (Haggett, 1965, pp251–253; Chorley and Haggett, 1967, pp634–642; Tinkler, 1977). The Alpha Index is one of the most useful measures of the connectivity of a network: it is the ratio of the observed number of fundamental circuits to the maximum number of circuits that may exist in a network (Garrison and Marble, 1962, p24). The method used here, derived from Social Network Analysis, fits firmly within this tradition. Its merit is that it allows 'mapping' of the flows with a system of cities in a way the other two measures do not. It is therefore a vital supplement to them, with the additional merit that it can be used to derive yet further numerical measures of connectivity such as the Alpha Index.

In a paper, Green (2004) has developed concepts of Special Functional Polycentricity and General Functional Polycentricity. The first is generated from separate observations of in-commuting and out-commuting to and from all individual FURs within the MCR. The second is generated from aggregate observations of both sets of commuter movements.

Specifically, the formula for special functional polycentricity is:

$$P_{SF}(N) = (1 - \sigma_\delta / \sigma_{\delta max}) \Delta$$

where:

P_{SF} is special functional polycentricity for a function F within network N;
σ_δ is the standard deviation of nodal degree;
$\sigma_{\delta max}$ is the standard deviation of the nodal degree of a 2-node network (n_1, n_2) derived from N where $d_{n1} = 0$ and d_{n2} = value of the node with highest value in N.
Δ is the density of the network.

The expression for general functional polycentricity is:

$$P_{GF}(N) = \left[(1 - \sigma_\delta \sigma_{\delta max}) \Delta \right] / n$$

where:
$P_{GF}(N_1, N_2 \ldots N_n)$ is general functional polycentricity for functional networks $N_1, N_2, \ldots N_n$;
and the sum is taken over all P_{SF}
n is the number of networks.

Both special and general functional polycentricity indices are summarized for the eight case study MCRs in Table 2.2.

Considering that the maximum possible value in any of the three cases is 1.00, it is seen that all the observed values for all regions are very low, suggesting a very weak degree of polycentricity. The lowest value, for the traditionally 'monocentric' region of Paris Region, is as low as 0.02; the highest values, for the traditionally 'polycentric' regions of the Randstad and RhineRuhr, are only in the range 0.15–0.20. But the comment of the Randstad team is relevant here:

A value of 1.0 would mean that all FURs in the greater Randstad area are equally well connected to each other in terms of commuter flows and that the entire working population works in a place different from their place of residence. Next to being a polycentric utopia, it would also be a clear recipe for traffic chaos and environmental degradation (van der Werff et al, 2005, p19).

Also relevant is the comment of the Belgian team, who emphasize that:

The Belgian mega-city region, characterized by important phenomena of sub- and counter-urbanization to the detriment of most of its cores, is an area of intense commuting toward Brussels, the major employment centre. Yet, it is above all within the FURs of these cities that commuting flows dominate, not only due to the very definition of the FURs (cores and their employment area), but also to the particularly weak commuting flows between cores, most of the flows coming from populated border municipalities… The functional polycentricity measured between FURs, from the commuting flows of 1991, appears then quite weak. The Belgian mega-city region is above all an area made up of a group of 'self-centred' FURs, undergoing in addition the attraction of Brussels and to a lower level Antwerp (Aujean et al, 2005a, p13).

Table 2.2 Eight MCRs: Special and general functional polycentricity indices, c. 2000

MCR	Special functional polycentricity index (in-commuting)	Special functional polycentricity index (out-commuting)	General functional polycentricity index
South East England	0.14[a]	0.16[a]	0.15[a]
The Randstad	0.16	0.15	0.16
Central Belgium	0.04	0.04	0.04
RhineRuhr	0.20[b]	0.17[b]	0.19[b]
Rhine-Main	0.07	0.09	0.08
EMR Northern Switzerland	0.03	0.03	0.03
Paris Region	0.02	0.02	0.02
Greater Dublin	0.06	0.06	0.06

Notes: a Calculation based on 2001 data with rings at NUTS 4.
b Calculation based on 151 NUTS 5 units, not on FURs.

In other words: an MCR like Central Belgium may appear physically quite polycentric but in functional terms is not polycentric at all, either because it consists of a set of functionally quite self-contained FURs, or because the dominant commuter flows are to one or two of these multiple centres, or both. And this may prove to be a general conclusion regarding the phenomenon of polycentricity, at least so far as that concept is measured by daily commuter journeys. How far it is modified by further and deeper analysis must be a central concern for the following chapters of this book.

Notes

1 The United States Office of Management and Budget (OMB) defines metropolitan and micropolitan statistical areas according to published standards that are applied to Census Bureau data. The general concept of a metropolitan or micropolitan statistical area is that of a core area containing a substantial population nucleus, together with adjacent communities having a high degree of economic and social integration with that core. Similar definitions were first used in the 1950 US Census. The county (or counties) in which at least 50 per cent of the population resides within urban areas of 10,000 or more population, or that contain at least 5000 people residing within a single urban area of 10,000 or more population, is identified as a 'central county' (counties).

2 Any two adjacent core-based statistical areas (CBSAs) form a combined statistical area if the employment interchange measure between the two areas is at least 25.

3 RhineRuhr presented a special problem of definition: it has a total of 47 FURs, but because of the large number and spatial extent of the cores meeting the POLYNET criteria, these coalesce to produce an almost 'monocentric' MCR. The RhineRuhr team therefore defined six contiguous FURs by neglecting their contiguous economic cores, and these represent the MCR.

3

Organization of the Polycentric Metropolis: Corporate Structures and Networks

Peter Taylor, David Evans and Kathy Pain

We now start to tackle the central research question: how to capture and measure the 'space of flows' in an economy based on knowledge-intensive advanced producer services (APS)? How exactly does information flow from individual to individual, within businesses or organizations, and between those businesses and organizations? How do these flows operate at different geographical scales – within functional urban regions (FURs), between FURs within a mega-city region (MCR), between a group of MCRs such as the eight we have identified for study in North West Europe, and between those MCRs and the rest of the world?

Chapter 2 ended by establishing some preliminary comparative measurements for each region of its polycentricity, as measured by daily commuting patterns. But these, it explained, were in some important sense inadequate: they failed to capture a key element, which was the exchange of information within regions and also between them. In Part 2, we successively seek to establish better ways of measuring these linkages.

This is no easy task. Ideally, we would try to capture the flows directly: by measuring the location of face-to-face business meetings, the origins and destinations of telephone calls and e-mail traffic. But, as explained in Chapter 1, data on these flows are sparse and difficult to obtain. In order to approach the problem, we need to reinforce these thin pickings, by going a different way via a less direct route.

As explained in Chapter 1, POLYNET was designed to bring together four sets of conceptual insights: Friedmann's 'global city hierarchy', Taylor's 'world city network', Scott's 'global city regions' and Castells's 'space of flows'. The research reported in this chapter brings together these four theoretical approaches. Using methodologies developed by the Loughborough Globalization and World Cities (GaWC) group, we describe and analyse global, European, national and regional spaces of flows through measures of inter-city relations.

Introducing the analysis

We wish to understand how cities and MCRs are knitted together through business practices. In particular, we are interested in business projects that require information and knowledge in several places to achieve their goals. For instance, a law firm may use partners and junior lawyers in several offices to draw up a particularly complex contract for a major client. Such use of a geographical spread of professional expertise is quite common in advanced financial, professional and creative services for large business clients. Thus providers of such services invariably have large office networks in cities and throughout MCRs. Such services are quintessentially city-based economic activities: therefore one important way in which the cities and MCRs are integrated into 'economic wholes' is through advanced service provision by firms that are simultaneously local, national and global.

However, one of the most frustrating problems for understanding how businesses use cities and MCRs is the lack of data. In the production of advanced services for business we know that there are numerous communications – face-to-face, telephone, fax and e-mail – but there is no readily available information on these practices. Collecting such information is costly, time-

Table 3.1 The office networks of two law firms

City	Law firm A: Number of partners	Law firm B: Number of partners	Nodal size[a]	Network connectivity[b]
Frankfurt	1	2	3	11
London	3	2	5	15
Paris	2	1	3	12

Notes: a Number of partners in the city.
b Number of inter-city partner dyads involving the city (counted on Figure 3.1).

consuming, and rarely very comprehensive. Is there a simpler way to estimate such connections through which service firms link cities and MCRs? We need a surrogate measure using information that is readily available. Well, we can easily find out where offices of service firms are located (e.g. from their websites) and, in addition, the functions and importance of different offices can be gleaned from the available information. With a little simple modelling based upon plausible assumptions, such information allows us to estimate links between cities and the importance of a city in terms of links, which we term its 'network connectivity'.

A basic example will clarify the method. The office networks of two hypothetical law firms are shown in Table 3.1. Both have just three offices, one each in Frankfurt, London and Paris. The importance of the office is given by the number of partners located in an office – partners are the basic cost centres of legal work. The law firms are similar in size – Law Firm A has six partners and Law Firm B has five partners – but the distributions of partners across the three cities are very different. The largest office is Law Firm A's in London. We will assume that each partner generates approximately the same amount of business: thus summing the rows for each city measures the amount of law business done in each city. We call this a city's 'nodal

size' in Table 3.1 and we can see that London is the leading 'law city' in this example, with Frankfurt and Paris ranked second equal.

We can go a crucial stage further through the reasonable surmise that links between offices are a simple function of the amount of business done in offices (i.e. the number of partners located there). This is illustrated in Figure 3.1. In Law Firm A, Paris has two partners and Frankfurt only one, therefore there are only two potential inter-partner links. In contrast, London has three partners and therefore there are six potential inter-partner links with Paris and three with Frankfurt. Law Firm B is similarly depicted in Figure 3.1; this time it is Paris that is weakly linked to the other two cities. The key point is that by adding up the links between cities estimates of inter-city connections are derived: Figure 3.1c shows that London–Paris is the strongest link and Frankfurt–Paris the weakest. In addition, all of a city's links can be added together to indicate the total inter-city connectivity of the city. In this case, London is again ranked first (Table 3.1). However, notice that with this measure Paris is more important (has more links) than Frankfurt. It is this latter measure – inter-city network connectivity – that is preferred over simple nodal size as an index of a city's importance because it tells us how significant the city is across the network.

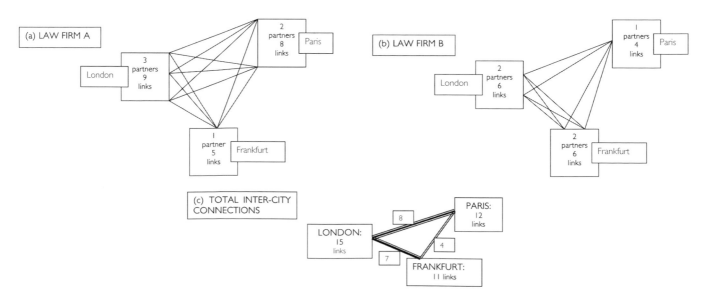

Figure 3.1 Illustration of inter-partner connections of two law firms

Table 3.2 Distribution of firms studied in MCRs by sector

MCR	Accountancy	Advertising	Banking/ finance	Design consultancy	Insurance	Law	Logistical services	Management consultancy/IT
South East England	20	20	20	25	8	16	11	23
The Randstad	23	20	22	23	17	23	18	30
Central Belgium	26	38	35	30	18	34	47	96
RhineRuhr	21	27	73	18	27	21	19	91
Rhine-Main	26	56	148	47	55	28	22	76
EMR Northern Switzerland	10	25	15	17	11	10	31	16
Paris Region	55	27	24	22	24	26	32	37
Greater Dublin	23	18	21	22	23	34	22	20

Note: EMR, European Metropolitan Region.

All the results reported in this chapter involve inter-city connections of pairs of cities and the network connectivities of cities. The only practical difference is that we use many more firms and cities. It is particularly important to use large numbers of firms so that the idiosyncrasies of individual firms are ironed out in the aggregate results to provide stable, replicable estimates of linkages and connectivities. While these are based on information about connectivities within individual firms, the inclusion of a large number of firms operating across the cities – as in the very complex Figure 3.1c – can provide vital evidence of potential inter-city network connectivities that are conferred on cities by networks of firms.

Collecting the data

The data collection for this analysis is the largest of its kind ever attempted. Eight service sectors were selected for study: accountancy, advertising, banking/finance, design consultancy, insurance, law, logistics services and management consultancy/IT. Data were collected for the office networks of a total of 1963 firms within the eight MCRs. Sources used varied between countries and included:

- National databases, e.g. Trends-Tendance in Belgium, Hoppenstedt in Germany;
- Other directories, Yellow Pages and similar.

There were many examples of firms offering services in more than one sector; in each case the firm's core activity was identified and it was allocated accordingly. Although not necessarily comprehensive for all city regions, this exercise produced a *universe of firms* representing a wide range of business services for each region that was in every case large enough for the study.

Each regional team selected firms from their universe of firms for inclusion in the analysis. Firms were chosen both on the basis of local knowledge and for pragmatic reasons. First, firms had to be multi-locational, in the sense of having offices in at least two cities. Firms were also chosen on the basis of the quality of information available about them, and ease of obtaining it (e.g. whether a firm had an informative website). Overall the choice of firms had to correspond roughly to the relative importance of different sectors in that particular city region. All these were regional team decisions because each case study is about a distinctive, particular city region. Table 3.2 shows the different numbers of firms sampled by sectors and selected by each team. Each team carried out checks to ensure that variations in the sample shares broadly matched the structure of the sectors in each city region. In cases of a large sample in a specific sector there are no implications for the connectivity and linkage scores obtained.

The office networks extended to national, European and global scales but here we concentrate on cities and towns within the MCRs. Table 3.3 shows the numbers of firms and cities/towns studied in each MCR. Each regional team selected the urban centres that they thought were important to an understanding of the operation of their

Table 3.3 Data production: Service firms and cities/towns across the MCRs

MCR	Number of service firms	Number of cities/towns
The Randstad	176	12
Central Belgium	324	6
Greater Dublin	183	9
Rhine-Main	458	6
South East England	143	9
Paris Region	247	18
RhineRuhr	297	6
EMR Northern Switzerland	135	8

Table 3.4 Cities chosen for study by mega-city region

MCR	Regional cities	National cities	
The Randstad	Amsterdam	Eindhoven	
	Rotterdam	Groningen	
	The Hague	Tilburg	
	Utrecht	Arnhem	
	Amersfoort	's Hertogenbosch	
	Haarlemmermeer	Breda	
	Amstelveen	Nijmegen	
	Alkmaar	Apeldoorn	
	Almere	Zwolle	
	Haarlem	Maastricht	
	Hilversum	Enschede	
	Zaanstad	Leeuwarden	
Central Belgium	Brussels		
	Antwerp		
	Ghent		
	Liège		
	Mechelen		
	Hasselt-Genk	-	
Greater Dublin	Dublin	Limerick Shannon	
	Balbriggan	Cork	
	Bray	Galway	
	Drogheda	Waterford	
	Dundalk	Sligo	
	Navan	Belfast	
	Maynooth	Newry	
	Naas Newbridge	Derry	
	Wicklow		
Rhine-Main	Frankfurt	Aachen	Essen
	Mainz	Augsburg	Halle
	Wiesbaden	Berlin	Hamburg
	Darmstadt	Bielefeld	Hannover
	Aschaffenburg	Bonn	Karlsruhe
	Hanau	Bochum	Kiel
		Braunschweig	Leipzig
		Bremen	Magdeburg
		Chemnitz	Mannheim
		Cologne	Munich
		Dortmund	Münster
		Dresden	Nürnberg
		Duisburg	Saarbrucken
		Düsseldorf	Stuttgart
		Erfurt	Wuppertal
South East England	London	Birmingham	Belfast
	Cambridge	Manchester	Cardiff
	Reading	Sheffield	Edinburgh
	Milton Keynes	Bristol	Glasgow
	St Albans	Newcastle	Leeds
	Southampton	Nottingham	Liverpool
	Crawley-Gatwick		
	Swindon		
	Bournemouth		
Paris Region	Paris	Lyon	
	Cergy-Pontoise	Lille	
	Marne-la-Vallée	Marseille	
	Saint-Quentin-en-	Toulouse	
	Yvelines	Bordeaux	
	Evry/Melun-Sénart	Strasbourg	

MCR	Regional cities	National cities	
	Roissy	Nantes	
	Meaux		
	Mantes-la-Jolie/		
	Les Mureaux		
	Compiègne		
	Beauvais		
	Evreux		
	Rouen		
	Reims		
	Amiens		
	Orléans		
	Chartres		
	Le Mans		
	Troyes		
RhineRuhr	Dortmund	*Outer Region*	Horne
	Essen	Krefeld	Hamm
	Duisburg	Mönchengladbach	Herten
	Düsseldorf	Remscheid	Marl
	Cologne	Solingen	Recklinghausen
	Bonn	Wuppertal	Bochum
	National – as for	Velbert	Hagen
	Frankfurt	Menden	Witten
		Viersen	Iserlohn
		Wesel	Lüdenscheid
		Dorsten	
EMR Northern	Zürich	Bern	
Switzerland	Aarau	Chur	
	Baden-Brugg	Geneva	
	Basel	Lausanne	
	Lucerne	Lugano	
	St Gallen		
	Winterthur		
	Zug		

city region – it is these cities that are the focus of the research. Again this relied upon local knowledge. Table 3.4 shows details for the regional cities selected by each team. These cities were used to define city-regional servicing strategies by firms and the *regional connectivities for regional cities.*

In addition each team selected major national cities beyond their region that they thought were important for understanding their city region. The two German teams coordinated their national city selections to produce a common set. The Belgian team did not select a separate national set of cities because the Central Belgium city region included all major Belgian cities. Table 3.4 also shows the different numbers of national cities selected by each team. These cities were used to define national servicing strategies by firms and the *national connectivities for regional cities.*

At the European and global scales, the cities selected were necessarily the same for all teams. Based upon previous GaWC analyses of global connectivities (Taylor,

2004a), 25 European top cities were identified: London, Paris, Milan, Madrid, Amsterdam, Frankfurt, Brussels, Zürich, plus Stockholm, Prague, Dublin, Barcelona, Moscow, Istanbul, Vienna, Warsaw, Lisbon, Copenhagen, Budapest, Hamburg, Munich, Düsseldorf, Berlin, Rome, and Athens. These cities were used to define European servicing strategies by firms and the *European connectivities for regional cities.*

Global-level cities were similarly selected. Based upon previous GaWC analyses of global connectivities (Taylor, 2004a), 25 top world cities were chosen: London, New York, Hong Kong, Paris, Tokyo, Singapore, Chicago, Milan, Los Angeles, Toronto, Madrid, Amsterdam, Sydney, Frankfurt, Brussels, São Paulo, San Francisco, Mexico City, Zürich, Taipei, Mumbai, Jakarta, Buenos Aires, Melbourne, Miami. These cities were used to define global servicing strategies and the *global connectivities for regional cities.*

Unsurprisingly, eight of the global level cities also appear in the European list. Likewise, some European cities will appear in national city lists, and some major national cities in regional city lists. Thus analyses at each different scale will not produce independent measures. This is not a problem because cities by their very nature are multi-scalar in their reach: London, Paris and other cities are simultaneously regional, national, European, and global service centres. However, it is useful that overlaps between scales generally involve less than one-third of cities in any list, allowing distinctive differences across scales to be measured.

Analysing the data: The services activity matrix

These selected firms and cities set the dimensions of the services activity matrix that must be constructed. Because cities are related to four different geographical scales, the overall matrix can be divided into four service activity sub-matrices for the computation of connectivities at different scales. The same rules for allocating service values were adopted across all scales.

To define service values, only two types of information were gathered:

- indications of size of a presence in a city (e.g. number of practitioners or partners working in an office);
- any indications that an office carries out extra-local functions for the firm (e.g. headquarters, research).

Because the form of the information gathered is unique to each firm, it had to be converted into a common data matrix to make comparisons of service values across firms (and therefore all analyses) possible.

The data collected consisted of estimates of the importance of each city or town to the office network of a given firm. The scale ranged from 3 indicating the headquarter location of the firm, to 0 for a city/town where the firm had no office at all. From these data four matrices arraying firms against cities/towns at different scales were produced for each MCR. For instance, for the Randstad the four matrices arrayed the 176 firms as follows: at the city region scale the matrix was 176 firms × 12 cities/towns (see Table 3.3); at the national scale an additional 12 cities were added (see Table 3.4) to produce a 176 × 24 matrix; at the European scale 24 cities (not 25 because Amsterdam was already in the matrix from the regional level) were added for the regional scale) to produce a 176 × 36 matrix; and, at the global scale 24 cities were similarly added (again without double counting Amsterdam) to produce the final 176 × 36 matrix. Each of these matrices is the equivalent to the simple 2 law firms 3 × cities matrix of Table 3.1, except they are very much larger! However, the same

principles apply for calculating inter-city/town links and city/town network connectivities although they can no longer all be shown as was the case in Figure 3.1. Here it is assumed that the more important the office, the more business will be conducted in that city/town and therefore more information will flow to and from other cities/towns. In other words we can compute the network connectivity of each city/town within its respective MCR. These are the results we now report upon.

Connectivities within North West European mega-city regions

The findings reported in this section are *network connectivities*, showing connectivity *within* each MCR as in the final column of Table 3.1. However, because of the large numbers of links involved due to the quantity of data used, all connectivities have been converted into percentages of the most linked city in the respective regions. This also facilitates easy comparison between regions. The results for the top six cities/towns in each of the eight MCRs are shown in Table 3.5. The percentages in this table can be interpreted as follows. Taking the first case as the example, it is clear that in the Randstad MCR, Amsterdam and Rotterdam are by far the most connected cities: very many service firms do important business in both cities thereby connecting them to the rest of the region. Utrecht and The Hague are quite well connected, whereas the network connectivities of Alkmaar and Amersfoort are relatively low. Thus, a clear pattern of network connectivities is shown, dividing the cities/towns into three pairs.

The eight MCRs fall into two groups: four 'primate' regions and four regions with more complex patterns. Clearly Dublin, Frankfurt, London and Paris strongly dominate the intra-regional linkages in their respective regions. Three regions show a duopoly of linkage dominance with Rotterdam rivalling Amsterdam, Antwerp rivalling Brussels, and Basel rivalling Zürich. In the first we have previously noted that Utrecht and The Hague are also relatively important but there are no equivalent 'medium-high' linked cities in the other two regions. However, in the final region, RhineRuhr, the situation is an enhanced version of the Amsterdam situation with all six cities showing relatively high levels of connectivity and Düsseldorf and Cologne almost tying for first place.

These initial results show a clear ordering of multi-nodality in North West European MCRs: RhineRuhr, the Randstad, Central Belgium, EMR Northern Switzerland, Rhine-Main, Paris Region, Greater Dublin, South East England.

Table 3.5 Network connectivities within MCRs

City/town	%	City/town	%	City/town	%
The Randstad		*Rhine-Main*		*RhineRuhr*	
Amsterdam	100	Frankfurt	100	Düsseldorf	100
Rotterdam	91	Wiesbaden	61	Cologne	99
Utrecht	72	Mainz	57	Dortmund	90
The Hague	71	Darmstadt	44	Essen	89
Alkmaar	40	Aschaffenburg	27	Bonn	79
Amersfoort	39	Hanau	25	Duisburg	77
Central Belgium		*South East England*		*EMR Northern Switzerland*	
Brussels	100	London	100	Zürich	100
Antwerp	94	Reading	52	Basel	80
Ghent	66	Southampton	47	St Gallen	53
Hasselt-Genk	48	Cambridge	39	Zug	49
Liège	48	Milton Keynes	34	Lucerne	36
Mechelen	25	Crawley-Gatwick	33	Aarau	33
Greater Dublin		*Paris Region*			
Dublin	100	Paris	100		
Naas Newbridge	61	Rouen	61		
Dundalk	53	Orléans	53		
Drogheda	43	Reims	45		
Navan	31	Amiens	41		
Bray	31	Chartres	36		

Table 3.6 Global connectivities within MCRs

City/town	%	City/town	%	City/town	%
The Randstad		*Rhine-Main*		*RhineRuhr*	
Amsterdam	100	Frankfurt	100	Düsseldorf	100
Rotterdam	68	Wiesbaden	12	Cologne	58
Utrecht	37	Mainz	8	Essen	39
The Hague	36	Darmstadt	7	Dortmund	34
Amstelveen	23	Aschaffenburg	3	Bonn	26
Haarlemmermeer	18	Hanau	3	Duisburg	22
Central Belgium		*South East England*		*EMR Northern Switzerland*	
Brussels	100	London	100	Zürich	100
Antwerp	38	Reading	24	Basel	41
Ghent	20	Cambridge	17	Zug	13
Hasselt-Genk	14	St Albans	15	St Gallen	11
Liège	13	Southampton	11	Aarau	10
Mechelen	9	Crawley-Gatwick	11	Lucerne	8
Greater Dublin		*Paris Region*			
Dublin	100	Paris	100		
Naas Newbridge	3	Rouen	37		
Dundalk	3	Orléans	32		
Drogheda	2	Reims	25		
Navan	2	Marne-la-Vallée	20		
Bray	1	Amiens	19		

Table 3.7 Areas under the curve for connectivity gradients for different geographical scales by MCR

MCR	Regional scale	National scale	European scale	Global scale
South East England	205	204	133	78
The Randstad	313	346	181	182
Central Belgium	281	281[a]	99	94
RhineRuhr	434	374	193	179
Rhine-Main	214	76	37	33
EMR Northern Switzerland	251	193	87	83
Paris Region	236	190	125	133
Greater Dublin	219	106	15	11

Note: a The Belgium national scale was conflated with the Brussels regional scale.

Global connectivities of North West European mega-city regions

As well as coding the service firms' offices within the MCRs, we also searched out their offices in the 25 leading world cities and estimated the importance of these cities to the firms' business. These data allow us to calculate new network connectivities for the cities and towns of North West European MCRs within the wider global economy via leading world cities. The results are shown in Table 3.6. Looking again at the first MCR in the table, we can interpret these results as follows. Amsterdam is clearly more connected worldwide in terms of services than is Rotterdam – the service firms in Amsterdam have office networks that do more business in, and therefore have more links to, major cities across the world economy. In this case, Utrecht and The Hague have relatively low service links to the world economy, and the final two cities, in this table Amstelveen and Haarlemmermeer, have even fewer connections. Clearly, for global service connections it is Amsterdam that is the 'gateway' for the Dutch MCR.

The major interest in Table 3.6 is its contrast with Table 3.5. It is not the minor changes of towns with low connectivities that is important, rather it is the consistent pattern of a lessening of multi-nodality for global connections: in other words, increasing primacy. In every one of the eight regions, the city ranked first for intra-regional connections (Table 3.5) increases its dominance markedly over the second ranked city in Table 3.6. Thus Cologne declines from 99 per cent of Düsseldorf's local connectivity to only 58 per cent of its global connectivity: when it comes to global servicing it is Düsseldorf that is outstandingly the main city in RhineRuhr. Rotterdam is the 'second city' that maintains most connectivity in terms of global links while, in the other direction, primacy is most enhanced with global links for Dublin: other cities/towns in this MCR are effectively unconnected directly by services to the rest of the world economy.

Clearly these results show that service network connectivities vary with the geographical scale of services, with global services producing a concentration of provision in the leading cities of each MCR.

Comparing connectivity gradients

These variations can be further analysed by bringing in the national and European scales to measure the *gradients* of connectivities from the highest- to the lowest-linked city. These vary consistently by geographical scale. As we would expect, smaller cities have relatively more connections at lower scales of service provision – so that in all regions, gradients are shallowest at the intra-regional scale and get steeper up through the scales, so that the global scale has the steepest gradient (because, as shown above, at this scale smaller cities provide least service provision).

But the rise in gradient differs across city regions, and this produces a very significant comparison. To make it, we have to concentrate on just the top six cities for all gradients, because the gradient is sensitive to the number of cities and three regions only deal with six regional cities. By using six cities for every comparison, we can measure the area under the curve (gradient) to show the degree of fall-off of connectivity from the most connected city. Since, for all cases, this most connected city is scored at 100 per cent, we use just the connectivity scores for the remaining five cities: their sums of scores for all eight MCRs across different geographical scales are shown in Table 3.7. These values can be understood through their limiting values: if all five cities have the same connectivity as the 'leading' city, then the sum is 500; conversely, if all five cities have zero connectivity, then the sum is zero. Thus the values can range from 500, representing 'perfect' polycentricity of equal cities, to 0, representing extreme primacy with all connections to one city. Interpreting Table 3.7 by rows we can see that the gradient gets steeper (less area under the curve) with increasing scale. The columns are more interesting because they show differences in polycentricity by scale.

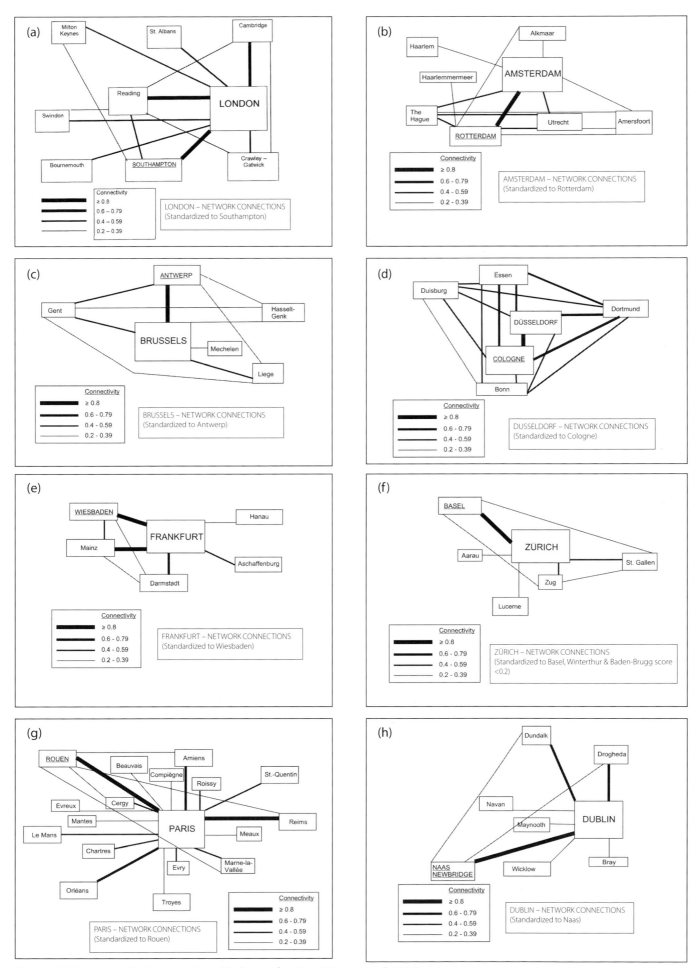

Figure 3.2 Comparative intra-regional linkages for First Cities in each MCR

Table 3.8 Major intra-regional linkages

a Major linkages to the First City

Prime links [All 100]	Other First City links ≥ 60	
Amsterdam – Rotterdam	London – Reading	93
Brussels – Antwerp	Frankfurt – Mainz	91
Dublin – Naas-Newbridge	Paris – Reims	80
Düsseldorf – Cologne	Paris – Amiens	79
Frankfurt – Wiesbaden	Paris – Orléans	79
London – Southampton	Dublin – Dundalk	77
Paris – Rouen	Düsseldorf – Dortmund	75
Zürich – Basel	London – Cambridge	70
	Frankfurt – Darmstadt	65
	Dublin – Drogheda	64
	Paris – Chartres	62

b Major linkages that bypass the First City

Links not including First Cities (≥ 40)	
Cologne – Essen	76
Cologne – Dortmund	73
Antwerp – Ghent	59
Bonn – Cologne	58
Dortmund – Essen	57
Mainz – Wiesbaden	51
Rotterdam – The Hague	48
Rotterdam – Utrecht	47
Duisburg – Essen	47
Bonn – Dortmund	45
Bonn – Essen	45
Dortmund – Duisburg	44
Cologne – Duisburg	44
The Hague – Utrecht	42
Reading – Southampton	40

We can see that the Randstad and RhineRuhr are the most polycentric regions (i.e. with values closest to 500) for all scales and, generally, Greater Dublin and Rhine-Main are the least polycentric. However, anticipating the conclusions from the complementary interview analysis reported on in Part 3, a point of interest looking across the scales is that South East England is more regionally polycentric in its connectivity to global than to regional scale business networks. With a ratio of 2.63:1 South East England appears less primate than Central Belgium 2.99:1, Northern Switzerland 3.02:1, Rhine-Main 6.48:1 and Dublin 19.91:1.

Comparing intra-regional linkages

We can take this analysis deeper by looking at individual connections within each of the eight MCRs. In Figure 3.2 the connectivities between the cities in each MCR are measured as a ratio of the value awarded to the strongest pair of city links in that region. The connectivity values between individual MCR cities are standardized as ratios to 1.00. Table 3.8 presents a summary of the larger MCR linkages. The pair of cities in the region with the largest link is termed the MCR 'prime link'. To aid comparison between the MCRs, here each prime link is scored as 100 and the values of all other links are computed as proportions of this.

The eight prime links are shown in the first column of Table 3.8a. Each involves the First City of each region and one other major city. First Cities are identified as the city in each region with the highest global connectivity, as

measured in previous GaWC research (Taylor, 2004b). It is particularly important to stress that the methodology used here analyses each region separately, so *it is not possible to say that one prime link is larger than any other*: they are each simply the largest in their respective regions. But it is possible to look at relative patterns of links and their sizes across regions – and it is this that makes the analyses useful in understanding comparative levels of polycentricity.

The second column of Table 3.8a shows the 11 other highest links to the First City of each MCR. This list has to be interpreted with care. Links to Paris are conspicuous, totalling four in all. What this shows is that in this MCR the prime link (Paris–Rouen) is not particularly dominant. This implies that Paris is at the centre of a region with a number of similar links, possibly indicating the primacy of Paris. South East England, Greater Dublin and Rhine-Main each have two major First City links, again implying that the prime link is not particularly dominant in their respective regions. Again, this might indicate primacy in these three regions. The other link in the table features Düsseldorf and it will be shown in the analysis below that in this case a rather different situation prevails.

Table 3.8b shows the highest 15 links that do not include the First City. There is one remarkable feature of this list: the majority, nine, of the links are from just one MCR, RhineRuhr. This is undoubtedly an indication of the polycentricity of this region. Clearly in this region not all major links are to Düsseldorf: five other RhineRuhr cities feature here. The Randstad is the only other MCR to feature prominently in Table 3.8b with three links other than to Amsterdam listed. Again this implies a degree of polycentricity. Of the other six MCRs, three (Central Belgium, Rhine-Main and South East England) have just one link each listed and three (Greater Dublin, Paris Region and EMR Northern Switzerland) are not represented at all. This further suggests primacy for the latter three and note also that the South East England link (Reading–Southampton) only qualifies for the list at the threshold level.

What can be said comparatively about the intra-regional linkages? From this evidence, three statements appear to be reasonable summaries:

- Paris Region, Rhine-Main, Greater Dublin and perhaps South East England appear to be relatively primate MCRs.
- RhineRuhr appears the most polycentric MCR, and the Randstad region also appears to be polycentric.
- It is not clear whether the Central Belgium and EMR Northern Switzerland are primate or polycentric.

Conclusion

The results reported above for North West European MCRs are unique for both Europe and the world. Business practice – office network location decisions – has been used to estimate inter-city links based on a very large sample of firms (almost 2000) for the first time for MCRs. The findings consolidate and give specificity to our understanding of the regions under study.

The basic findings on service network connectivities are as follows:

1 *South East England* is a strongly single-node region serviced through London. With global links London dominates further but other cities, notably Reading and Cambridge, do have moderate global connections.
2 *The Randstad* ranks second in multi-nodality. The MCR is interconnected through two major cities, Amsterdam and Rotterdam, supplemented by the medium-level connectivity of Utrecht and The Hague. For global links Amsterdam dominates but Rotterdam remains important, with Utrecht and The Hague being moderately connected.
3 *Central Belgium* is largely a dual-nodality region serviced through Brussels and Antwerp. However, global links are very strongly dominated by just Brussels, with Antwerp and Ghent being only moderately connected.
4 *RhineRuhr* is the most polycentric MCR. At the local scale Düsseldorf and Cologne dominate approximately equally but this is not a dual-nodality pattern: there are six importantly connected nodes in the region. At the global level, Düsseldorf dominates in service linkages but Cologne remains important, and Dortmund, Essen, Bonn and Duisburg drop to moderate levels of connectivity.
5 *Rhine-Main* is a strongly single-node region serviced through Frankfurt. This is appreciably accentuated with global links.
6 *EMR Northern Switzerland* is a dual-nodality region serviced through Zürich and Basel, although the latter city is relatively less important than other 'second cities' in duality patterns. At the global level Zürich's connectivity dominates, but with Basel maintaining a high moderate level of service connectivity.
7 The *Paris Region* is a strongly single-node region serviced through Paris. With global links Paris's dominance increases but less so than for other such regions: Rouen, Orléans and Reims all have moderate global connections.
8 *Greater Dublin* is a strongly single-node region serviced through Dublin. With global links Dublin dominates to a remarkably extreme degree.

These results are significant in modifying the preliminary and tentative conclusions about polycentricity that we were able to reach, on the limited evidence of commuter flows, at the end of Chapter 2. But some caveats, which will emerge from the interview results in Part 3, should be noted because they prove to be of vital importance. The quantitative analysis of MCR connectivities cannot take into account the intensity or quality of actual interactions between the cities. Although RhineRuhr has the most even distribution of regional scale connectivities of the eight MCRs studied, it is only by examining actual flows and knowledge transfers that we can evaluate the strength of inter-city functional relationships and their contribution to regional polycentricity.

Further analysis is especially important because, in order to measure polycentricity quantitatively, it is necessary to calculate the regional linkages between cities for each MCR individually; thus it is not possible to compare connectivity values *between* the regions. Taking the example of RhineRuhr again, First City Düsseldorf is shown by GaWC global city network analysis as having the lowest overall global APS connectivity of any of the POLYNET First Cities (Taylor, 2003, Table 1). The intensity of its actual intra-regional connectivities could therefore be weaker than those of the other regions; this cannot be evaluated from the comparative analysis presented thus far. The strength of the quantitative study is that it maps *potential* inter-city connectivities, generated by knowledge-based APS, which cannot be revealed from analysis of official statistics. These potential connectivities, of key relevance for the ESDP (European Spatial Development Perspective) priorities to promote balanced development through cooperation between cities, must then be explored using other methods.

In Chapters 4 and 5, we go on to tackle the central but difficult task of seeking to quantify the actual flows of information between individuals and firms, for which the analysis in this chapter has provided such a vital surrogate.

The Connectivity of the European Heartland

Peter Hall, Kathy Pain and Loek Kapoen

In this and the following chapter, we turn to a central challenge of the POLYNET study: how directly to measure flows of information, within and between the eight mega-city regions (MCRs). Chapter 3 has delivered what it promised: a sophisticated analysis of such linkages, as revealed by the structures of business firms. But this remains an indirect measure, a proxy, for the flows themselves. How is it possible then to capture such flows between the MCRs, and also out to the wider world?

There is a first and obvious way of measuring them: by analysing business travel movements. Ideally we should do this in two ways: by measuring first business travel, and then telecommunications traffic. But because data on telecommunications traffic appear to be completely lacking due to commercial confidentiality, the analysis has to be restricted to personal travel by air or train, taken as a proxy for face-to-face business travel.

Nor, for reasons of confidentiality, were we able to obtain direct measures of business travel movements.[1] As a proxy, we therefore used timetabled flights and trains. These provide a measure, albeit an indirect one, of business travel flows between the eight MCRs, and each of them and the rest of the world. (They are of little use for measuring flows within each region: here flights become irrelevant and train traffic becomes dominated by commuter flows.) We measured these flows:

- between the eight POLYNET MCRs (PN8); and
- between these 8 and the 25 capital cities/commercial cities of the enlarged European Union (EU25).

This required designation of a key 'core' city for each MCR or country. It clearly should be the core travel site: the location of either the leading airport (or airports) or the leading train station (or stations). In most cases, this gave no problem because the core city effectively defined itself, and contained both the leading airport or airports and train station or stations. But it soon became evident that in the larger MCRs, particularly the more polycentric ones, it would be necessary to choose more than one airport in order to avoid distortion. In South East England, all the London airports were selected, even though some (Gatwick, Luton and Stansted) were 30 miles (50km) and more from the city. Likewise, in other MCRs low-cost airports like Frankfurt (Hahn) needed to be included for completeness. For RhineRuhr, all commercial airports within the region were used; here, Cologne Central station (Hbf) was selected in preference to Düsseldorf because, though not central to the region, it was the logical rail core. Generally, for the EU25, the capital city was chosen: Berlin was used in addition to Cologne and Frankfurt on this criterion. The sole exception was Italy, where Milan was chosen in preference to Rome as the leading commercial city.

The resulting list of airports and train stations is set out in Table 4.1.

The analysis

Air flight movements

The analysis of flights was made from the OPODO (Opportunity To Do) web timetable, supplemented by Ryanair and easyJet web timetables since low-cost carriers do not appear on the OPODO site. OPODO shows many duplicate flights because of airline code-sharing, but these are easily recognized and eliminated. All direct non-stop flights starting and ending within an extended business day (05:00–02:30) on a typical autumn midweek business day were analysed. It was assumed that business travellers

Table 4.1 The connectivity survey: Choice of centres

	Air	Rail
PN8		
South East England	London airports: Heathrow (LHR), Gatwick (LGW), City (LCY), Stansted (STN), Luton (LTN)	Waterloo International
The Randstad	Amsterdam (AMS) Rotterdam (RTM)	Amsterdam Centraal
Central Belgium	Brussels (BRU) Brussels (Charleroi) (CRL)	Bruxelles Midi/ Brussel Zuid
RhineRuhr	Cologne-Bonn (CGN) Düsseldorf (DUS) Düsseldorf-Weeze (NLN) Dortmund (DOR)	Köln Hbf
Rhine-Main	Frankfurt airports: Frankfurt (FRA), Hahn (HHN)	Frankfurt Hbf
EMR Northern Switzerland	Zürich (ZRH) Basel (BSL)	Zürich HB
Paris Region	Paris airports: Charles de Gaulle (CDG), Orly (ORY)	Paris stations (Nord, Est, Lyon)
Greater Dublin	Dublin (DUB)	
EU25		
Athens	Athens (ATH)	
Berlin	Berlin airports: Tegel (TXL), Tempelhof (THF), Schönefeld (SXF)	Berlin Zoo
Bratislava	Bratislava (BTS)	
Budapest	Budapest (BUD)	
Copenhagen	Copenhagen (CPH)	
Helsinki	Helsinki (HEL)	
Nicosia	Larnaca (LCA)	
Lisbon	Lisbon (LIS)	
Ljubljana	Ljubljana (LJU)	
Madrid	Madrid (MAD)	
Malta	Malta (MLA)	
Milan	Milan airports: Linate (LIN), Malpensa (MXP), Bergamo (BGY)	Milano Centrale
Prague	Prague (PRG)	
Riga	Riga (RIX)	
Stockholm	Stockholm airports: Arlanda (ARN), Skavta (NYO), Linköping-Malmen (LPI)[a]	
Tallinn	Tallinn (TLL)	
Vienna	Vienna (VIE)	Wien West Bf
Vilnius	Vilnius (VNO)	
Warsaw	Warsaw (WAW)	

Note: a Linköping-Malmen airport (LPI) is not recognized as a Stockholm airport in World Airport Codes, but is included because Ryanair describes it thus in its timetables.
EMR, European Metropolitan Region.

would not choose non-direct flights, involving a change, on relatively short European journeys when direct flights were available. This had the effect that zero flights were entered into some cells in the data matrix to some smaller and more remote European capitals.

Train movements

The analysis was derived from the DB (*Deutsche Bahn*) European Timetable website to which was added the Eurostar website when it became evident that the DB site failed to list all Eurostar services. It is not known whether it fails to list other services, but it appears reasonably complete. Wherever the DB site showed an alternative that was irrational, because it involved a longer journey than an alternative, it was eliminated from the analysis. As for air, the analysis covered trains leaving after 05:00 and arriving by 02:30 on a typical midweek autumn business day.

To maintain consistency with the air analysis, the rail analysis covered only direct trains (involving no change). These are not necessarily faster than trains involving a change, because of the operating characteristics of different types of train. (Between Frankfurt and Berlin, direct trains via Eisenach-Erfurt take the same time as trains on the less direct route involving a change at Hannover, both segments of which are high speed.) Unlike air travel, where frequent direct non-stop services are available between all major centres, many pairs of centres lack direct rail connections, even when they are quite close together (as for instance Brussels–Düsseldorf).[2]

The results

Detailed air and rail analyses are in Figures 4.1 and 4.2. The overall connectivity indices are set out in Table 4.2. They are derived in slightly different ways.

The maps use a formula which normalizes both number of connections (flights, trains) and time:

$$c^s_{ij} = (c_{ij} - c_{min})/(c_{max} - c_{min})tt^s_{ij}$$
$$= 1 - (tt_{ij} - tt_{min})/(tt_{max} - tt_{min})$$

in which:
c^s_{ij} = standardized number of connections between city i and city j;
c_{ij} = number of connections between city i and city j;
tt^s_{ij} = standardized travel time in minutes from city i to city j;
tt_{ij} = travel time in minutes from city i to city j;
c_{min}, tt_{min} = minimum number of connections, travel time;
c_{max}, tt_{max} = maximum number of connections, travel time.

All values for any pair of cities lie between 0 and 1. The highest value (1) indicates the highest number of connections and/or the least travel time.

Table 4.2 uses indices which are obtained by dividing the total number of trips by a weighted average of time of each trip. Thus a single value is obtained for every city for each mode and for the two modes combined.

Air

Figure 4.1 shows a pattern of very dense interconnections within the eight MCRs of North West Europe, save only where they are affected by rail competition (as discussed below). It also demonstrates the degree to which connectivity of all these regions and other European capitals diminishes very sharply towards the EU periphery, especially towards the new accession countries of East Central Europe, which can presently be characterized as only very partially integrated into the European system of face-to-face information exchange. This may change as a result of new services from low-cost airlines like easyJet and Ryanair, both of which were actively developing new links as this study was being conducted in autumn 2003.

The overall index of air connectivity (Table 4.2) shows that South East England is overwhelmingly the best-connected of the eight MCRs because of the huge range of direct services from the five London airports, currently being supplemented almost on a weekly basis by the low-cost carriers. The Paris Region and Rhine-Main follow, reflecting the international status of their airports, closely followed in turn by the Randstad, EMR Northern Switzerland and RhineRuhr; Central Belgium and Greater Dublin follow with considerable gaps.

Rail

Rail connectivity (Figure 4.2) is quite skeletal, dominated by a handful of major city–city connections. Within the eight MCRs, these are London–Paris, London–Brussels, Paris–Brussels, Brussels–Amsterdam and Amsterdam–Düsseldorf–Frankfurt. These reflect existing high-speed connections, soon to be augmented by completion of the PBKAL (Paris–Brussels–Köln–Amsterdam–London) high-speed network in 2007–2008. Outside this geographical frame, there are only three strong connections: Cologne–Berlin, Frankfurt–Berlin, and Zürich–Milan. The first two are internal connections within Germany between two of the eight MCRs and the capital city. The third is an interesting cross-Alpine link where an efficient rail link successfully competes with air over a relatively short distance.

Overall, the table illustrates an important point: rail competes successfully with air only over relatively well-defined distances, typically less than 300 miles (500km)

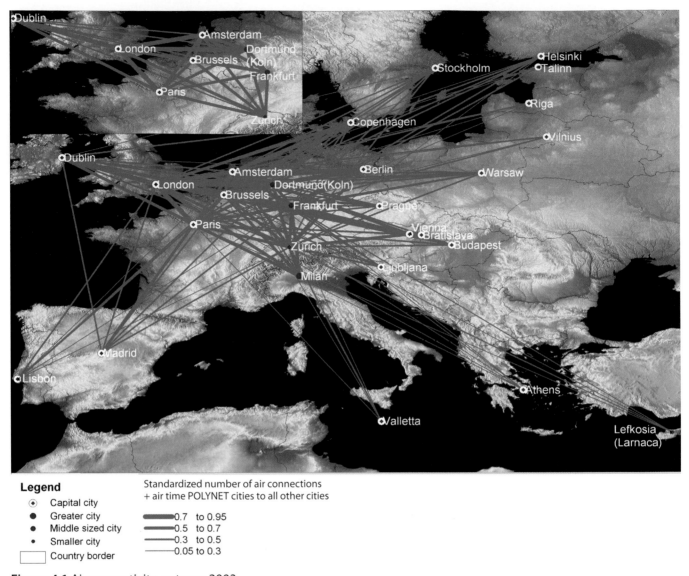

Legend

- ⊙ Capital city
- ● Greater city
- ● Middle sized city
- · Smaller city
- ☐ Country border

Standardized number of air connections
+ air time POLYNET cities to all other cities

- ▬▬ 0.7 to 0.95
- ▬▬ 0.5 to 0.7
- ▬▬ 0.3 to 0.5
- ─── 0.05 to 0.3

Figure 4.1 Air connectivity, autumn 2003

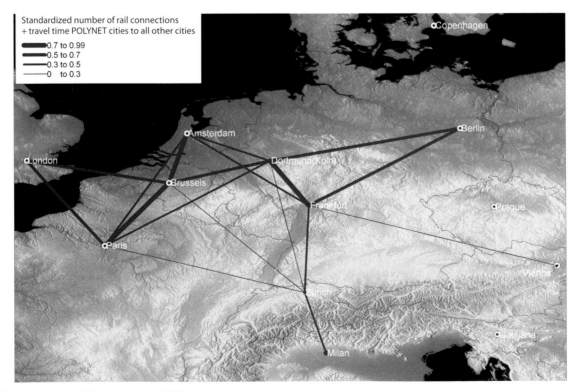

Standardized number of rail connections
+ travel time POLYNET cities to all other cities

- ▬▬ 0.7 to 0.99
- ▬▬ 0.5 to 0.7
- ▬▬ 0.3 to 0.5
- ─── 0 to 0.3

Figure 4.2 Rail connectivity, autumn 2003

and in some cases less than 185 miles (300km), separating major city regions; consequently, it is most successful when such regions are found closely clustered within such distance ranges, which are found especially but not exclusively within the North West European core, the former 'Central Capitals region', forming the heart of the ESDP (European Spatial Development Perspective) 'Pentagon'.

The index of rail connectivity (Table 4.2) puts Central Belgium at the head, followed by the Paris Region and RhineRuhr. This is primarily a result of geographical centrality. Brussels stands at the core of the PBKAL network, even before completion of the final high-speed links; Paris has excellent connections by the completed part of this network to both London and Brussels, with onward travel to Amsterdam and Cologne; and Cologne forms the critical junction between this network and the German internal high-speed InterCity Express (ICE) network onward to Frankfurt and to Berlin. The other five regions are considerably farther behind, primarily because of their peripheral position to this network, either at its edges or completely outside it.

Overall

Indices of overall connectivity, by air and by rail and by both modes combined, are set out in Table 4.2. These indices are obtained by dividing the total number of trips by a weighted average of time of each trip. Overall, South East England is outstandingly the best-connected MCR, a product of the very high number of trips which compensates for slightly longer average trip times. This is primarily a result of its superb air connections through no less than five airports. Its rail connectivity is distinctly poorer because it remains unconnected beyond Brussels and Paris, though this may improve after completion of PBKAL if direct services to Amsterdam and Cologne are introduced. It is followed by the Paris Region and (after an interval) Rhine-Main, which combine good air connectivity with a rail connectivity that is better than South East England's. The Randstad, RhineRuhr, Central Belgium and EMR Northern Switzerland follow in a close bunch, all characterized by weaker air connectivity (especially low for Central Belgium) compensated by excellent rail connectivity for Central Belgium (in particular) and RhineRuhr. Greater Dublin shows much

Table 4.2 Connectivity indices, air, rail, combined, autumn 2003

	Air	Rail	Combined
South East England	6.87	0.27	7.08
The Randstad	3.72	0.36	3.87
Central Belgium	2.69	0.99	3.64
RhineRuhr	4.52	0.63	4.68
Rhine-Main	4.96	0.49	4.08
EMR Northern Switzerland	4.68	0.14	4.31
Paris Region	4.37	0.72	5.01
Greater Dublin	1.87	0.00	1.87

lower connectivity, zero by rail, but also, somewhat surprisingly, very low by air.

Overall, it appears that six regions in the former Central Capitals region, the heart of the 'Pentagon' and perhaps of the EU, benefit outstandingly from their proximity and the excellence of both their air and rail connections – but that, at the very core, rail accessibility becomes much more significant in relationship to air accessibility. These findings would seem to suggest further research and analysis. But this analysis is sufficient for the purpose of the POLYNET study. We next return to the difficult task of probing the internal flows of information within each MCR.

Notes

1 Since the research was completed, a most interesting research report has been published, based on actual airport traffic (passenger flows) rather than flight movements (Derudder et al, 2004). The general conclusions, which are restricted to major European airports, appear however to be in line with those reported here.

2 Direct Thalys high-speed service from Paris and Brussels to Düsseldorf was abandoned in early September 2004, apparently on the grounds of poor profitability, though the high-speed line through Belgium is still under construction for completion in 2006. It was partly for this reason that Cologne was substituted in the final rail analysis.

5

The Informational Geography of Europolis: Mapping the Flow of Information

Peter Hall, Kathy Pain and Nick Green

In this chapter we move into the core of the POLYNET study. Following the limited survey of business movements between the eight regions, reported in Chapter 4, we now go into these regions and begin direct first-hand investigation into the actual linkages and flows within and between firms and organizations in advanced producer services (APS) and their individual members. We approach this central task through two very different but linked methods: first, we *quantify* the flows, taking a sample of key actors in these organizations and making a precise quantified survey of their business journeys and their information exchanges; second, we make a parallel *qualitative* study of these same individuals, through detailed and discursive interviews, to tease out patterns of both flows of information and also more subtle and less measurable linkages. This chapter reports on the quantitative travel and communication diary survey; Part 3 of the book, Chapters 6–8, will introduce the detailed and discursive interviews.

POLYNET aimed to achieve these two central objectives through a common research strategy: in each of the mega-city regions (MCRs), research teams conducted a relatively small number of in-depth face-to-face interviews with a carefully chosen sample of senior executives and managers in eight sectors and eight cities, already selected and surveyed in the study of business organization reported in Chapter 3. This was essential in order to investigate the *actual* interactions taking place within and between firms and thus within, between and beyond the MCR cities. Simultaneously, interviewees were asked to participate in a travel and communication diary survey to *quantify* their business journeys and information exchanges, allowing the research team to 'map the space of

informational flows' for a sample of key actors within regional, national, European and global scale organizations.

The travel diary, a survey instrument designed to record all movements of a person over a given period of time with all relevant details for the modelling time horizons, has long been a fundamental and essential basis for transport planners in their development of travel demand models. It consists of the diary proper, recording all movements sequentially during a specific period of time, supplemented by person-specific information, relevant household-based information, and details of household vehicle ownership and similar data.

Surveys approximating to travel diaries were used as early as the mid-1940s in origin-destination transportation studies in a number of American cities, and their methods and content have remained remarkably constant over half a century. Recently, however, researchers have reported that respondents are increasingly reluctant to give up time for any type of survey (Axhausen, 1995). Perhaps because of this, but also because of rapid advances in technology, early surveys, using paper-and-pencil interview (PAPI) methods in the form of mail-out and mail-back surveys supplemented by in-home interviews, were replaced during the 1980s and 1990s by computer-assisted telephone interviews (CATI) and then by computer-assisted self-interview (CASI) methods, in which respondents record their responses directly into a computer (desktop, laptop or handheld) (Wolf et al, 2001). Researchers have extended the principle to communication diaries (Mokhtarian and Meenakshisundaram, 1999). However, John Goddard employed this principle in his pioneering study of communication in the City of London as early as 1970 (Goddard, 1973). A further remarkable development of the approach came from a group of researchers in the Department of Social and Economic Geography at Lund University under the direction of Torsten Hägerstrand (Tommy Carlstein, Solveig Mårtensson, Sture Öberg and Bo Lenntorp) in their remarkable work on time-space geography during the 1960s and early 1970s, which influenced a great deal of work abroad (Carlstein et al, 1978; Jones et al, 1983). This work commonly tracked the movement of individuals between points of location, or stations – residences, workplaces, schools or other places – over time.

Designing the research

The research proposal for POLYNET stipulated that 'Travel diaries and a sample of telephone, e-mail and video-conferencing traffic would be used to map respondents' in-work journeys and virtual communication over a time period to be agreed. Dependent on the cooperation of participants, we hoped to collect data on business journeys for a minimum period of one month and on virtual communication for a minimum period of one week. This, we suggested, would result in 'maps' of telephone and e-mail traffic for respondents in selected firms in the eight study areas, distinguishing intra-regional and extra-regional (national, European-wide and global) traffic. An especially important outcome would be to understand how far organizations outside the core cities communicate directly with other organizations both within and outside the relevant region. This information would be likely to have important implications for regional policy and investment in relation to information and communication technology (ICT), particularly skills development.

At this stage, prior to the widespread use of portable miniature devices such as 'Blackberries', it was planned to use a paper format for the diary so that respondents could easily record their in-work journeys, meetings and communications whenever and wherever convenient. However it was later agreed to adopt a web survey method which (it was hoped) would increase the sample size by allowing senior managers, additional to those interviewed, to participate.

At an earlier stage of the research design it had been hoped that it would be possible to analyse all telephone traffic, with the assistance of telephone companies, and e-mail data from sent-mail and in-boxes. We sought the advice of a number of experts, including Martin Dodge (Centre for Advanced Spatial Analysis, University College London), and we investigated using a commercial database which identifies the geographical location of firms using their Internet Service Provider (ISP) address. But we encountered two major problems.

First, we were advised that tracing ISP locations of 'in' and 'sent-mail' boxes would contravene the UK Data Protection Act and its equivalents in other EU countries, particularly because of the problem of forwarded e-mail and multiple addresses which meant we would be recording addresses of people who had not given consent for this to happen. Second, we found that in many cases there is no automatic and direct correlation between ISP address and the geographical location of offices. (We conducted a pilot survey on a small number of addresses known to us, and found that a substantial minority were located at servers distant, sometimes far distant, from the locations of the actual respondents.) We were also advised that non-work-related e-mails constitute 40 per cent on average of e-mail traffic in the private sector and substantially higher in the public sector; this would need to be deleted, together with the rapidly rising proportion of spam and junk mail and traffic that is not directly business-related – for example, news, updates from mailing services, and subscriptions. For the same reasons we rejected the idea of a multiple survey approach whereby respondents could opt to provide more or less complete information.

Third, though data from France Télécom have been successfully used in research by a member of the Paris team to map telephone traffic in the Paris Region (Halbert, 2004a) (Figure 5.1), such data are not available elsewhere – or indeed any longer in the Île-de-France itself (Jean-Louis Piquepé, personal communication, December 2004). We looked at the potential for using commercially available databases such as the one produced by Telegeography, but they only give data for international traffic and, in any case, important high volume traffic within business networks and mobile calls would not be identifiable. We concluded therefore that the only way to collect the information we specifically needed (directly business-related and place-specific traffic) was by asking respondents themselves to analyse their telephone calls (separately distinguishing conference calls) and e-mail traffic for one week, and to report to us the top five locations for sent and received messages, discounting spam and other irrelevant mail.

We also investigated, through the Swiss team, the possible availability of credit card data on travel patterns, but determined that such data would not be freely available; in any case, the problem is that in many cases (for instance, travel by car) the payment does not distinguish the individual journey.

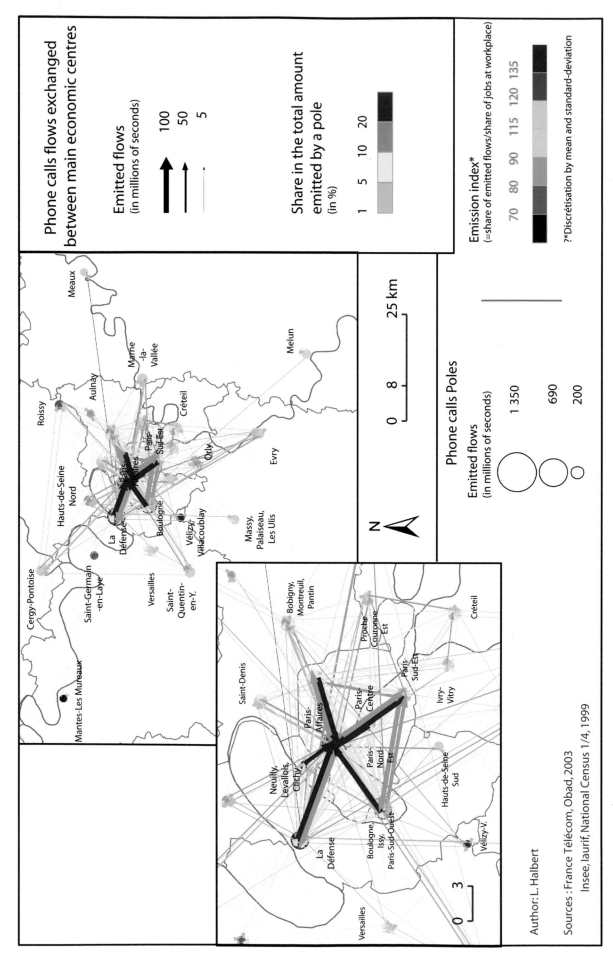

Figure 5.1 Telephone traffic, Île-de-France, 2003

Table 5.1 Response to the web survey

Region	Percentage
South East England	4.3
The Randstad	23.5
Central Belgium	12.0
RhineRuhr	8.6
Rhine-Main	4.5
EMR Northern Switzerland	16.1
Paris Region	24.2
Greater Dublin	6.8
Total	100.0
Number	442

Table 5.2 Main line of business

Business	Percentage
Accounting	7.2
Banking/finance	12.9
Insurance	5.0
Legal services	13.5
Logistics	6.5
Management consulting/IT	14.0
Advertising	5.2
Design consultancy	12.6
Other	23.0
Total	100.0
Number	442

Developing the web survey

We finally determined therefore to ask respondents taking part in the face-to-face interviews whether they would be willing to complete a travel and communication diary later on. Once the web survey mode had been decided upon, these individuals would subsequently be contacted by e-mail, offering them the choice of participating in the virtual web survey or printing this for completion as a 'paper diary' to be returned by post or fax. All addressees were to be asked to cooperate by forwarding the survey to a selection of other senior staff within their office or network.

To increase the sample size further, while guaranteeing consistency with the other quantitative and qualitative research elements, we then decided that teams should further extend the survey, this time by inviting the senior managers of all firms on the APS database (described in Chapter 3) to participate. The diary was limited to a one-week record and many simplifications were introduced to encourage these other recipients, having had no previous contact with the researchers, to participate.

Since the survey anonymized the firms (which senior managers strongly advised us to do in order to obtain potentially sensitive information about the locations of key business contacts), it would not be possible to identify individual respondents; thus details of the project website (where the results would eventually be posted) would have to be sent to all firms with the survey. There were concerns that this would reduce the response rate, and these unfortunately proved only too justified: to what extent it was responsible will never be known, because a number of other factors, discussed in the conclusion to this chapter, were finally identified as limiting the response. Attempts to secure the backing of business groups and policy-making bodies in support of the survey and follow-up e-mails, so as to boost participation, proved only partially successful.

The London, Zürich and Amsterdam teams worked closely together in the first half of 2004 on developing the survey – the Swiss team developing and refining the web

form interface, above all seeking to simplify it,[1] the Dutch team implementing the survey and managing the responses. The final version of the form, produced in July 2004 in English, was translated into French, German and Dutch. This also made it possible to develop slightly different conventions for the response categories to take account of different linguistic/cultural preferences though such adaptations were centralized and coordinated by the London team to ensure consistency between the regional interpretations. The survey went online in ten versions for a one-week pilot. Several dozen changes had to be implemented, not in one standard version but in ten different versions divided between four different languages – a rather complex and time-consuming activity. The survey was simplified and made more visually attractive and user-friendly, and questions were rephrased to rule out ambiguities; sometimes the page design was adjusted to make responses easier. Finally adapted for the different languages, the survey was simultaneously launched by all eight teams for a three-week period in September 2004, allowing for slightly different holiday ending times in different countries and regions, but was subsequently extended for a further five weeks into November 2004 to try to achieve a higher response rate.

The Amsterdam team, who managed the process, measured and reported responses each week. Their reports,

Table 5.3 Total number of meetings in the same firm and in other firms or organizations

Day	Total meetings[a]			
	In same firm	N =	In other firms	N =
Monday	2.0	160	1.0	122
Tuesday	1.9	174	1.0	120
Wednesday	1.9	142	1.2	116
Thursday	1.8	137	1.3	120
Friday	1.8	147	1.1	113

Note: a Without extreme values (outliers).

which revealed a disappointingly low response rate, were responsible for the decision to extend the period of the survey. On completion the results (save for business travel profiles) were handed over to the London team for centralized analysis.

The web survey: Structure and content

The final version of the web-based survey concentrated on two main categories:

- *Personal travel*: commuting and in-work for face-to-face meetings.
- *Virtual communication*: e-mail/web-based; telephone; telephone/video-conferencing.

It consisted of ten web pages or steps (see Appendix 1). It was originally agreed that the diaries should cover a seven-day week because of increasingly undifferentiated work and personal leisure patterns (e.g. weekend conferences and travel to and from business meetings). But, in order to keep the survey manageable, we eventually had to reduce business travel to a standard five-day week and reduce other communication modes (paper mail and faxes having been deleted) to the 'top five' locations in a seven-day week for each. We added a two-page 'business location factor' element to the survey to allow some basic cross-referencing to the parallel interview results, hopefully with a larger sample size.

Geographical coding was a point of difficulty, particularly for very big cities like London and Paris: should we treat them as a single unit or seek to analyse them by sub-units (London boroughs, Paris *arrondissements*, postcodes)? A particular problem arose with areas like La Défense in the Paris Region, outside the city but inside the agglomeration. Likewise, there was a problem with telephone calls: was the appropriate unit of analysis the main area code (020 London, 01 Île-de-France), or the individual exchange, which respondents might not know? We asked respondents to give as much detail as possible, down to postcode and telephone code but completion of these details proved very varied: much more precise for instance in Switzerland, where most respondents gave postcodes, than in other places.

In practice, however, locating each journey end proved to be relatively easy. We used the excellent and widely-known Multimap program, freely available on the World Wide Web, which gives a choice of locating a place either by area code or by place name. In practice this gave an almost instant and unambiguous location, easily placed by varying the geographical map scale (the default is the large scale 1:10,000, but a scale of 1:500,000 or even

1:1,000,000 is necessary to locate the place on a national scale). The sole exception was the Republic of Ireland, where the Multimap base seems to be much less well developed than in the other countries.

The research results

The output

The original plan was to produce quite elaborate output, consisting of:

1 Mapped flows (in and out) for each communication mode for each region over all eight business sectors and for each sector separately and across all eight study areas.
2 Analysis of differences in the use of the modes for communications within the same business network and with other firms/organizations (for example, is teleconferencing mainly used for internal communications? Are web-based communications overtaking e-mail for internal communications?).
3 Travel for business: here, a range of questions was to be answered (for example, which are the most used terminals in each region? Which are the most popular city locations for business meetings?).
4 Business location factors: responses by region, for all eight business sectors and for each sector, likewise across all eight areas.

In the event, as we progressively tested the survey, these plans proved to be over-optimistic. The final response results are shown in Figure 5.2 and tabulated in Tables 5.1 and 5.2. Even after the time extension into early November, they remained disappointing – so much so, that some parts of the planned analysis proved simply impossible to undertake. Although the survey website was visited by 633 people, only 442 filled in enough variables (that is at least their personal background variables) to enable analysis. These 442 respondents represent less than 10 per cent of the several thousand individuals who were approached. The best results were obtained by the Randstad and Paris Region teams, with over 100 results each. (In the French case this was the result of a sustained effort of publicity to attract further responses beyond the original POLYNET database.) The EMR (European Metropolitan Region) Northern Switzerland (over 70) and Central Belgium (over 50) results were also highly satisfactory. The RhineRuhr and Greater Dublin teams achieved adequate returns (in the 25–40 range), but Rhine-Main and South East England lagged with 20 results or less. And for business travel, in particular, not all these results proved to be usable; some returns were started

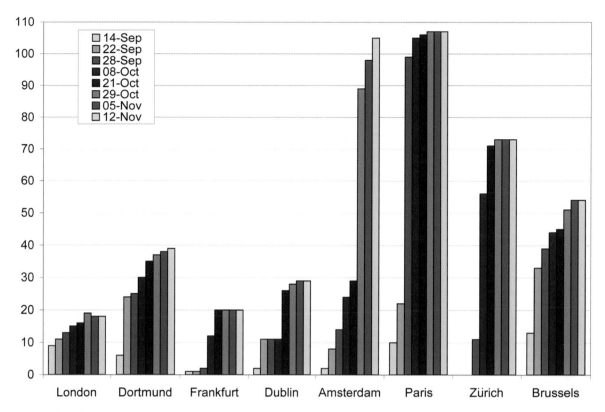

Figure 5.2 Final web survey responses, November 2004

but were never completed, while others appeared implausible. Finally, the relevant returns ranged from 64 in the case of the Randstad, to only 7 in South East England (not all of which gave a full week's analysis). To compound matters, these correspondents in many cases failed to give an indication of telephone or e-mail traffic; overall, there were no more than 46 complete records showing all kinds of contact for all the eight centres in aggregate – and even then, some respondents failed to complete all the cells.

Analysing the results

The results were therefore finally presented in three different ways:

1 *Business travel*: these results were originally mapped (in rough draft form) in aggregate for each study area, but the results proved so complex as to be effectively incomprehensible. Therefore, it was decided that each of the eight teams should choose between three and five apparently representative cases, which would be centrally mapped in purely diagrammatic fashion (not to geographical scale), centred on the respondent's office, to show the pattern of all movements during the week. The teams would each then write short explanatory commentaries to accompany the maps, since they had conducted the original interviews and had the necessary local knowledge. The maps with commentaries are shown in Figures 5.3–5.10.

2 *Telephone/conference call/e-mail traffic*: the five top locations were plotted on maps showing responses in all eight regions (Figures 5.11–5.13), thus allowing an immediate graphical impression of traffic both within each region, and also between them and outside them to the rest of the world.

3 *Location factors*: these results were presented for all eight regions, in aggregate, in the form of a combined graph (Figure 5.14).

Business travel: Case studies

Respondents were asked to complete their travel patterns for business trips during the survey week. The sample proved too small to yield detailed information. The survey also asked for a record of total meetings in the same firm and in other firms. Table 5.3 gives an overview of the meetings during a week. Outliers (two cases with more than 50 meetings a day) are omitted. Meetings in the same firm prove to be relatively stable during the week with an average of around 1.9 a day. Meetings in other firms or organizations are somewhat less frequent or regular than meetings in the same firm, with the highest score occurring on a Thursday.

Most business trips are made by car, about 60 to 65 per cent during the week. The high rate of taxi use chiefly occurs in Dublin and London.

Altogether, 31 cases were analysed: 4 for each study centre except London, where only 4 usable studies could

Table 5.4 Primary travel mode for business travel for day of the week

Mode	Monday	Tuesday	Wednesday	Thursday	Friday
Air	5.1	4.3	4.1	0.5	3.9
Train	11.1	9.7	10.4	13.0	9.0
Bus	3.7	5.3	4.1	4.9	5.1
Car	59.4	60.9	64.8	64.3	59.6
Taxi	9.2	10.6	8.3	9.2	10.7
Foot	6.5	5.3	4.7	5.4	6.2
Other	5.1	3.9	3.6	2.7	5.6
Total	100%	100%	100%	100%	100%
N =	217	207	193	185	178

be identified, and RhineRuhr where there proved to be only 2 such cases.

South East England: the patterns for South East England (Figure 5.3b–d) show a great deal of travelling between centres outside London, much of it regular commuting, but also including business trips. One, a management communications consultant (764), lives in Northampton and works in nearby Milton Keynes – both new towns developed from the 1960s – also making a business trip to the Swindon headquarters and to Oxford. The second, an accountant (833), shuttles between his office in Cambridge and a head office in London, with one business trip into Surrey on the other side of London. The third case (1343) is an international banker who makes trips to Paris and Brussels and also has his main telephone and e-

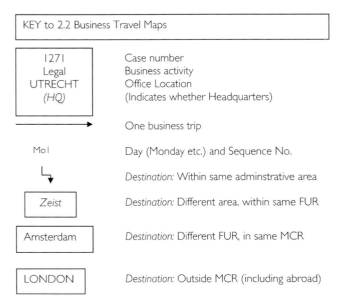

Figure 5.3a Key to business trip maps (Figures 5.3–5.10)

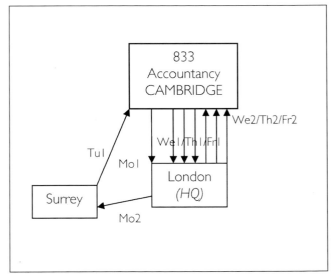

Figure 5.3c Business travel, South East England, case 833

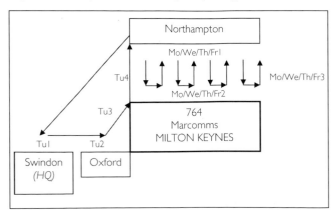

Figure 5.3b Business travel, South East England, case 764

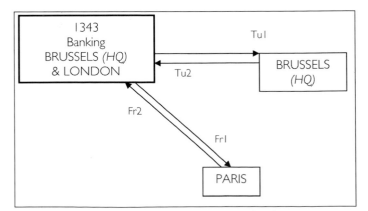

Figure 5.3d Business travel, South East England, case 1343

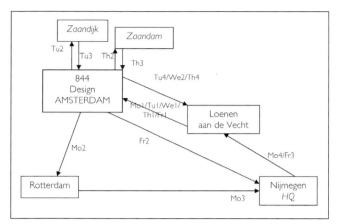

Figure 5.4a Business travel, the Randstad, case 844

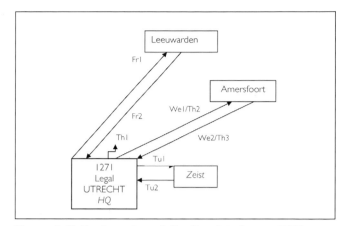

Figure 5.4b Business travel, the Randstad, case 1271

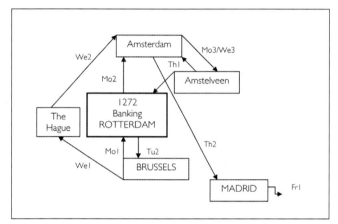

Figure 5.4c Business travel, the Randstad, case 1272

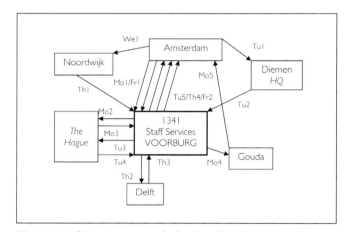

Figure 5.4d Business travel, the Randstad, case 1341

mail contacts with these cities.

The Randstad: the first Randstad case (1341) shows the travel pattern of a person whose business travel remains confined to the western part of the MCR. He or she travels frequently, sometimes visiting four destinations on a day, and occasionally has some business to take care of in smaller places as well (e.g. Noordwijk, Gouda). The Rotterdam-based bank employee (1272) makes fewer trips, covers larger distances and tends to meet in larger cities only. He or she travels as easily to nearby cities such as The Hague and Amsterdam as to 'far away' places such as Brussels and Madrid. For the trip to Madrid the business traveller depends on the connections offered by Schiphol Airport. The design consultant (844), who lives strategically in a small village between Amsterdam and Utrecht near the A2 motorway, does not travel on a daily basis but is not afraid of spending a day on the road. Monday's trip, which runs from home to the person's office in Amsterdam, then to a meeting in Rotterdam and another one at the firm's headquarters in Nijmegen before going home, covers more than 185 miles (300km) and must be considered close to what can maximally be done in a day, given the traffic situation on Dutch motorways. The

legal consultant, finally, who works from the firm's headquarters in Utrecht (1271) in this particular week had no business in the western part of the Randstad but focused on Utrecht's easterly 'hinterland' (Zeist, Amersfoort) and also made a longer trip to provincial capital Leeuwarden in the far north of the country. The cases are too few in number to allow for generalization. However, they do give us an intriguing insight into the many different faces of business travel in the Randstad, ranging from the regionally oriented staff services consultant to the internationally operating bank employee.

Central Belgium: the first case here (805) is also a banker who makes few trips in Belgium outside Brussels, notably to Namur (business centre of the Walloon district), but also travels to Paris. The second (840), an ICT consultant with headquarters in Utrecht (Holland) and an office in Antwerp, visits clients directly by car because of its flexibility in reaching remote destinations in the west of Flanders. The third (896), a management consultant based in Mechelen on the Brussels–Antwerp motorway, is similar: he often travels from home direct to a client by car to the main Flemish destinations (Brussels, Zaventem airport, Antwerp, Ghent); he also makes a one-day trip to

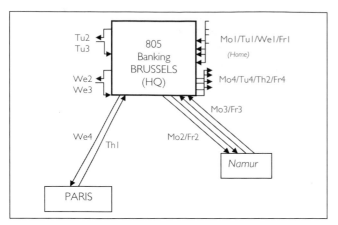

Figure 5.5a Business travel, Central Belgium, case 805

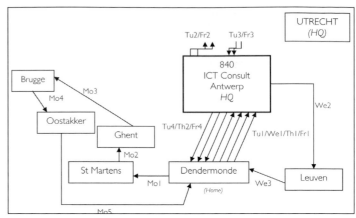

Figure 5.5b Business travel, Central Belgium, case 840

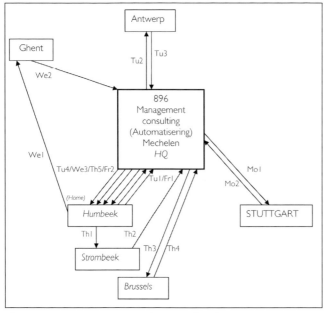

Figure 5.5c Business travel, Central Belgium, case 896

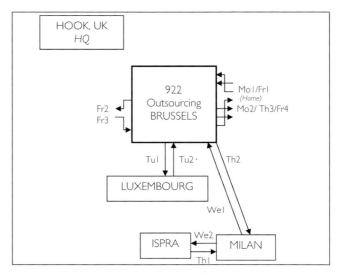

Figure 5.5d Business travel, Central Belgium, case 922

Stuttgart, where this firm has an important office, emphasizing the continuing necessity of face-to-face contact inside the firm. The fourth (922) works in an outsourcing firm headquartered in South East England but with an office in Brussels, the 'international Belgian city'. He makes only one trip in Belgium, to a client in Brussels; otherwise, he travels internationally first by car to

Luxembourg, then by plane to Milan, and on to Ispra – a pattern typical of an internationally-based executive.

RhineRuhr: only two usable results emerged for this region. The first (1169), who works in logistics and is based in Dortmund, travels to meetings outside the MCR, in East Germany and in Austria to visit the firm's headquarters. The second (1198), also working in logistics, has a very different pattern: living in Solingen, commuting daily to work at headquarters in nearby Wuppertal, he makes

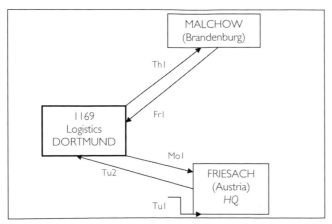

Figure 5.6a Business travel, RhineRuhr, case 1169

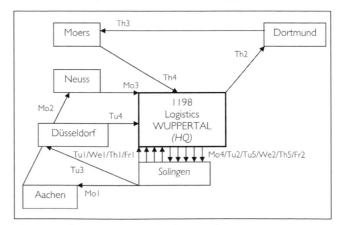

Figure 5.6b Business travel, RhineRuhr, case 1198

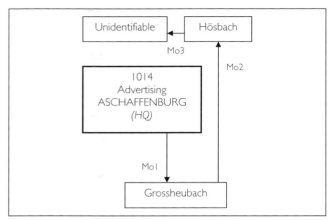

Figure 5.7a Business travel, Rhine-Main, case 1014

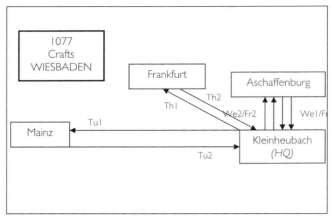

Figure 5.7b Business travel, Rhine-Main, case 1077

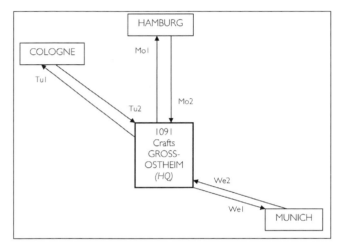

Figure 5.7c Business travel, Rhine-Main, case 1091

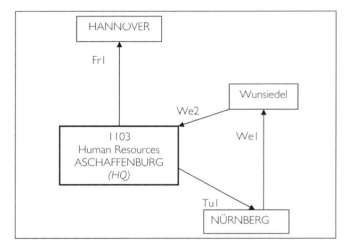

Figure 5.7d Business travel, Rhine-Main, case 1103

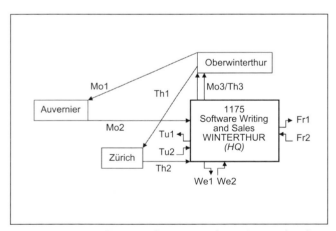

Figure 5.8a Business travel, EMR Northern Switzerland, case 1175

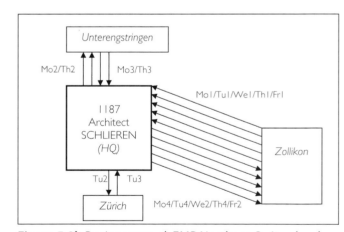

Figure 5.8b Business travel, EMR Northern Switzerland, case 1187

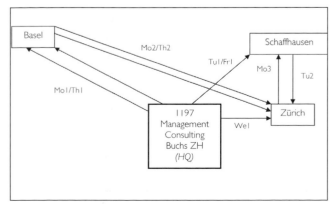

Figure 5.8c Business travel, EMR Northern Switzerland, case 1197

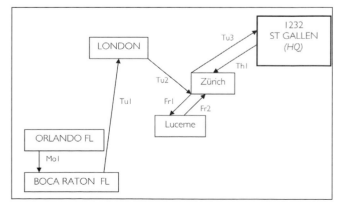

Figure 5.8d Business travel, EMR Northern Switzerland, case 1232

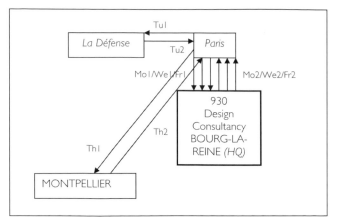

Figure 5.9a Business travel, Paris Region, case 930

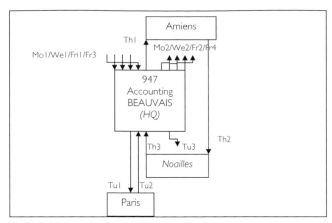

Figure 5.9b Business travel, Paris Region, case 947

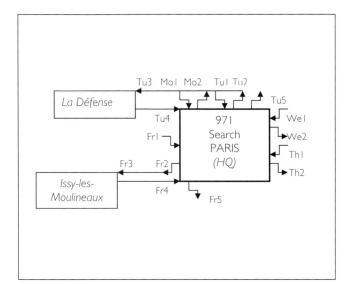

Figure 5.9c Business travel, Paris Region, case 971

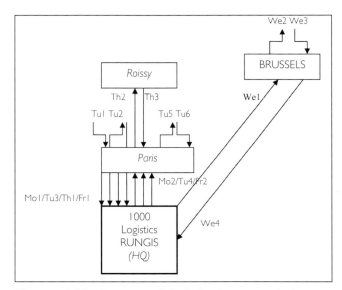

Figure 5.9d Business travel, Paris Region, case 1000

frequent daily trips to other towns in the MCR but never outside it.

Rhine-Main: the first case here is an advertising practitioner (1014) who works out of an office in Aschaffenburg – apparently in a small organization since this is also the headquarters – and makes two very local trips to nearby villages, presumably to contact local businesses. The second (1077) is a slightly odd one: in craft design, he has an office in Wiesbaden but does not appear to visit it, instead working from his home base (described as 'headquarters') in a small village outside Aschaffenburg and visiting different business centres in the MCR on different days. The third (1091) is also interesting: likewise located in a small village, for three days in the week he makes long-distance day trips outside the MCR to major German cities, remaining office-based on the other two days. The fourth (1103) has a complex pattern: a human resources professional based in Aschaffenburg, he makes trips to two major cities, Hannover and Nürnberg, with a

side trip from the latter to a small town near the Czech border. Overall, the picture here is one of small very locally based businesses, albeit with longer-distance travel in some instances.

EMR Northern Switzerland: the cases here are senior managers or in similar positions for APS firms, with local headquarters. They show that journeys within the MCR predominate and that a large part take place within the same functional urban region (FUR), between proximate FURs or between the major FURs (1187, 1197). But there are also journeys to other Swiss FURs (1175 to Auvernier in the FUR of Neuchâtel in the French-speaking part of Switzerland), which is a sign of the relatively balanced spatial economic structure in Switzerland. One example (1232) concerns a journey to Florida, USA. This traveller's firm headquarters office is in St Gallen, but the role of Zürich as a hub is very evident. Zürich connects the centres in EMR Northern Switzerland (or even beyond) to each other, and to other centres in the wider world.

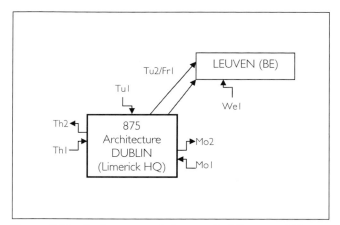

Figure 5.10a Business travel, Greater Dublin, case 875

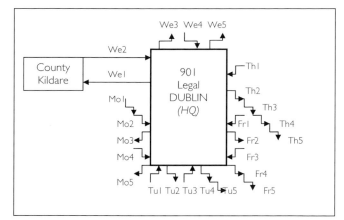

Figure 5.10b Business travel, Greater Dublin, case 901

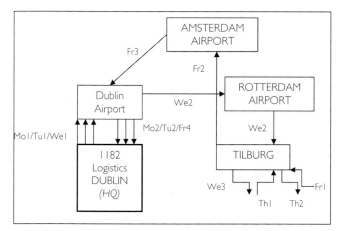

Figure 5.10c Business travel, Greater Dublin, case 1182

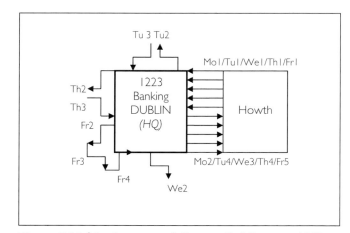

Figure 5.10d Business travel, Greater Dublin, case 1223

Paris Region: the case studies here highlight four features: the importance of spatial proximity; the predominant role of the Paris/Hauts-de-Seine economic core; the role of international relationships for networking professionals; and the one-way relationship between peripheral FURs and Paris, implying that here the MCR hypothesis has only limited validity. Thus the first (930), a design consultant living in Paris and working in the municipality of Bourg-La-Reine in the inner ring of the Paris FUR, makes two trips to clients: one to La Défense, where many headquarters and some design consultancy firms are located, the second to Montpellier, a major French city. The second (947) is an accountancy consultant who lives and works in Beauvais, travelling by car for face-to-face meetings with clients locally and in the immediate region, but also once to Paris: thus, location in a peripheral FUR often means having both a strong local base and a few Parisian clients. The third, in research (971), has business trips only to a few central locations in the Paris FUR; proximity to clients and partners is key to his intensive face-to-face tasks. The fourth (1000) lives in Paris and works in a logistics firm based in Rungis, next to the Orly airport. His business pattern, again, is predominantly restricted to the Paris agglomeration with trips back to his own office, illustrating the importance of efficient

communications within the agglomeration; but he also visits a partner in Brussels, facilitated by easy connections to airports and TGV stations.

Greater Dublin: striking for Dublin, as for Paris, is the high proportion of business trips made within a quite small central business district (CBD), coupled however with some longer-distance international journeys. The first (875) is a senior manager in an architectural practice in central Dublin, with two trips abroad to Leuven, Belgium to meet a client. The second (901), a senior manager in a central Dublin law firm, again has business travel largely in the city centre, split rather evenly between meetings 'in the same firm' and those 'in other firms/organizations', and with only one meeting outside Dublin. The third (1182) is a senior manager of a Dublin-based logistics company based at the airport. Here, contrastingly, there were no business trips in the region, but one three-day trip to the company's Netherlands office. The fourth (1223) is a senior manager in a Dublin-based bank; commuting daily from a residential area into central Dublin, his business travel is essentially confined to central Dublin. Some at least were intra-firm – unsurprisingly, since several Dublin banks are multi-office operations.

Table 5.5 Distribution of phone calls made for all top five office locations

Class	Phones out	Phones in
<3	31.7	31.1
3–5	13.9	10.2
6–10	17.3	19.8
11–20	20.3	22.2
>20	16.9	16.7
Total	**100%**	**100%**
N =	533	293
Average	**10**	**13**

Table 5.6 Distribution of total phone calls per week

| | Phones out | | Phones in | |
Class	same firm	other firm	same firm	other firm
<10	46.3	37.1	40.3	31.3
10–19	10.9	11.4	9.7	12.5
20–34	14.9	14.9	14.8	19.3
35–50	13.1	21.7	18.8	24.4
>50	14.9	14.9	16.5	12.5
Total	**100%**	**100%**	**100%**	**100%**
N =	175	175	176	176
Average	**22**	**26**	**25**	**27**

Table 5.7 Distribution of total phone and video conferences per week for all top five office locations

Class	Phone conferences	Video conferences
<3	11.1	4.3
3–5	1.4	0.0
6–10	10.4	0.0
11–20	13.9	8.7
>20	63.2	87.0
Total	**100%**	**100%**
N =	144	46
Average	**22**	**27**

Table 5.8 Distribution of total phone and video conferences per week

| | Phone conferences | | Video conferences | |
Class	same firm	other firm	same firm	other firm
<10	23.5	26.9	17.6	17.6
10–19	0.0	0.0	0.0	0.0
20–34	15.7	0.0	0.0	0.0
35–50	17.6	11.5	41.2	17.6
>50	43.1	61.5	41.2	64.7
Total	**100%**	**100%**	**100%**	**100%**
N =	51	52	17	17
Average	**17**	**16**	**19**	**22**
Average total sample	**2**	**2**	**1**	**1**

Table 5.9 Distribution of total e-mails sent and received per week for all top five office locations

Class	Sent e-mails	Received e-mails
<3	51.5	48.0
3–5	10.4	13.3
6–10	16.5	15.3
11–20	11.8	15.3
>20	9.9	8.1
Total	**100%**	**100%**
N =	425	248
Average	**8**	**8**

Table 5.10 Distribution of total e-mails sent and received per week

| | Sent e-mails | | Received e-mails | |
Class	same firm	other firm	same firm	other firm
<10	68.5	58.6	69.4	69.4
10–19	7.6	9.6	8.8	8.8
20–34	8.4	10.0	6.1	6.1
35–50	8.4	13.5	6.1	6.1
>50	7.2	8.4	9.5	9.5
Total	**100%**	**100%**	**100%**	**100%**
N =	251	251	147	147
Average	**15**	**18**	**15**	**14**

Telephone traffic

Respondents were asked to enter the top five office locations (outside their own building) for received and made phone calls in as much detail as possible. Table 5.5 gives the class distribution averaged over the five top locations. The class modus is less than three phone calls. On average the phone calls per location can be estimated on five calls out and five calls in.

On a weekly basis the estimated average for phone calls out is 22 within the same firm and 26 to other firms. Received phone calls are on average 25 and 27 (Table 5.6).

As already explained, these returns were centrally mapped. The information (top five origins and destinations) could easily be recorded on a single map for each type of traffic because of the relatively sparse returns on these topics.

Figure 5.11, for telephone exchanges, suggests a considerable degree of polycentricity for most of the eight

Table 5.11 Importance of location factors by country

Importance	BE	DU	SE Eng	RM	RR	FR	RH	NS	Tot
Access to labour supply/skills	4	5	3.5	5	4	4	4	4	4
Access to language skills	4	2	2	3	3	3	3	3	3
Access to venture capital	3	1	2	1	3	3	2	1	2
Opportunities face-to-face contact	4	4	5	4.5	4	4	4	4	4
Opportunities for knowledge transfer	4	3	4	4	4	4	4	4	4
Ability to innovate	4	4	3.5	3.5	3	4	4	4	4
Proximity to customers/clients	4	4.5	4	4.5	4	5	4	5	4
Proximity to other service business providers	3	4	2	3	4	4	3	4	3
Proximity to business competitors	3	4	4	2	3	3	2	3	3
Proximity to government agencies	2	3	2	3	3	3	2	3	3
Proximity to professional and trade organizations	2.5	2	2.5	3	3	2	2	3	3
Credibility of your office address	3	4	4	3.5	4	3	4	3	4
Availability of suitable business premises	4	4	4	4	4	4	4	4	4
Availability of advanced telecom infrastructure	5	4	4	5	4	5	4	5	5
Support from local government	3	2	4	4	3	3	3	3	3
Labour flexibility and employment law	4	4	4	4.5	4	3	4	4	4
Corporate tax structure	4	4	3.5	5	4	4	4	4	4
Personal taxation	4	3.5	4	5	4	3.5	3.5	4	4
Cost of business infrastructure	4	4	4	4	4	4	4	4	4
Cost of labour	4	4	4	5	5	3	4	4	4
Housing costs	3	4	4	4	3	3.5	3	4	4
Proximity to good schools	3	4	3	4	4	4.5	3	4	3
Quality of life	4	4	4	4	4	4	4	4	4
Security (crime/terrorism)	3	4	5	4	4	4	4	4	4
Environmental quality	3.5	4	4	4	4	4	3.5	4	4
Accessibility by plane	4	3.5	4	3	4	4	3	3	3
Accessibility by train	4	3	3.5	3	4	4	4	4	4
Accessibility by car	5	4	4.5	5	4.5	4.5	4	4	4
Accessibility by local public transport	3	4	3	3	4	5	4	4	4

Notes: BE = Central Belgium, DU = Greater Dublin, SE Eng = South East England, RM = Rhine-Main, RR = RhineRuhr, FR = Paris Region, RH = The Randstad, NS = EMR Northern Switzerland, Tot = Total.

study areas, though Rhine-Main, Paris Region and Greater Dublin are obvious exceptions. Notable also is the high proportion of calls made both between the eight areas, and beyond them to other parts of the world – notably the United States and Pacific Asia, and (for the two German regions) other German cities. This last was equally true for polycentric regions such as the Randstad, and for highly-monocentric ones like the Paris Region or Greater Dublin. But the Parisian case (Halbert, 2005a) illustrates a one-way relationship, as for business travel, between more peripheral FURs and Paris: they are linked to Paris, but the Paris economy is not connected to them. Generally, in both these regions there is intensive communication within the central business core and also between this core and distant business centres, but not with the rest of the MCR.

Video and phone conferencing

Phone conferences held with the five top locations number 144. For video conferences the number is far less, 46. For those respondents who hold phone and video conferences the average is rather high (Table 5.7). As can be seen in Table 5.7 only 11 per cent of the respondents hold phone conferences; for video conferences this percentage is far less, only 4 per cent. The averages for all respondents are of course very low (Table 5.8). Figure 5.12, showing the geographical patterns of conference calls (including video), reveals a very similar picture to Figure 5.11, save that the data are very sparse for several regions (e.g. EMR Northern Switzerland) suggesting a degree of monocentricity that may in fact be false.

E-mail

For those who completed questions on e-mail and web-based business communication, the average (modal class)

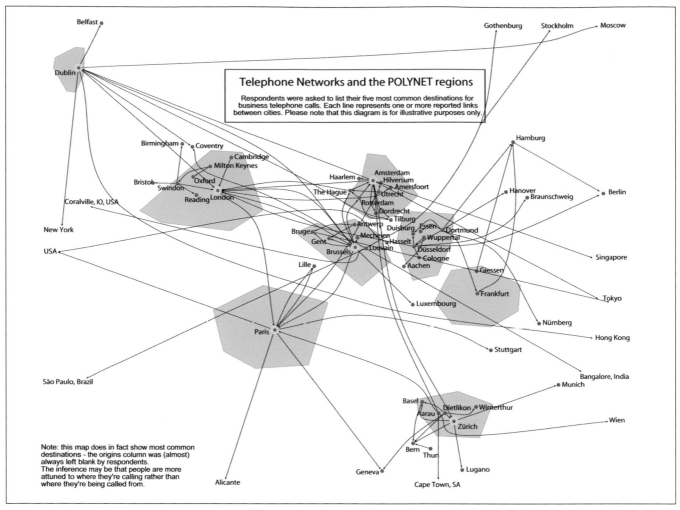

Note: Geissen, Mannheim and Heidelberg are not part of the Rhine-Main MCR.

Figure 5.11 Telephone traffic

of the top five locations for sent and received e-mails is – somewhat surprisingly – less than three per week. On average, each week, as few as eight e-mails are sent and received to these top locations (Table 5.9). The total e-mails sent and received per week in the same firm can be estimated as 15 per week (Table 5.10). Eighteen e-mails are sent to other firms and 14 e-mails are received from other firms in one week: extraordinarily low figures.

Figure 5.13, showing the geographical pattern of e-mail traffic, again demonstrates an almost identical picture to the previous Figures 5.11 and 5.12, save that Rhine-Main now appears as much more polycentric in its system of exchanges, and both Rhine-Main and RhineRuhr have strong contact patterns with other major German cities.

Overall, however, this part of the analysis seems to accord with that for business travel: there are intensive contacts within each MCR but also significant contacts with other MCRs and even more so with other parts of the world. These international contacts however vary greatly from case to case, some respondents being very local and others quite global; and there again appears to be a clear distinction between highly monocentric MCRs, where contacts are either within the central core or international, and more truly polycentric regions where there is also a more intensive pattern of intra-MCR exchanges between individual cities and their regions. Here, it appears that South East England, Central Belgium, RhineRuhr, the Randstad and EMR Northern Switzerland are relatively polycentric, while the Paris Region, Greater Dublin and – perhaps surprisingly – Rhine-Main appear more monocentric in their patterns of virtual exchange.

Location factors

Responses on the relative importance of location factors are set out in Figure 5.14 for both 'First Cities'[2] and for other cities in each region, arrayed in order of importance in the primary city. Interestingly, access to broadband telecommunications is ranked first, closely followed by access to labour and access to face-to-face meeting opportunities, proximity to clients and availability of premises. Public transport access and quality rank higher than car access (though the latter scores significantly higher

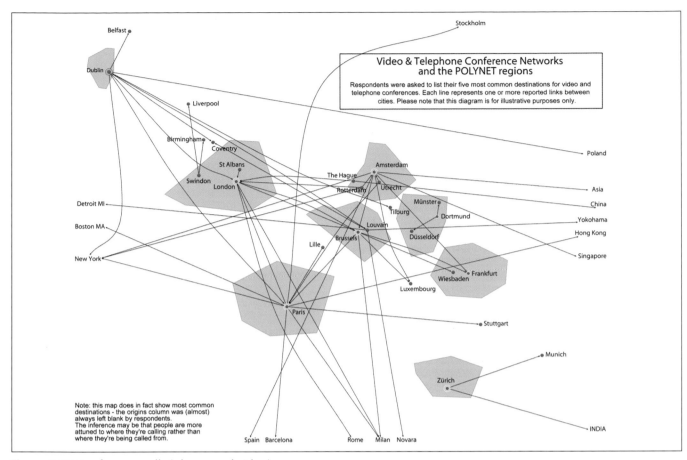

Figure 5.12 Conference calls (phone and video)

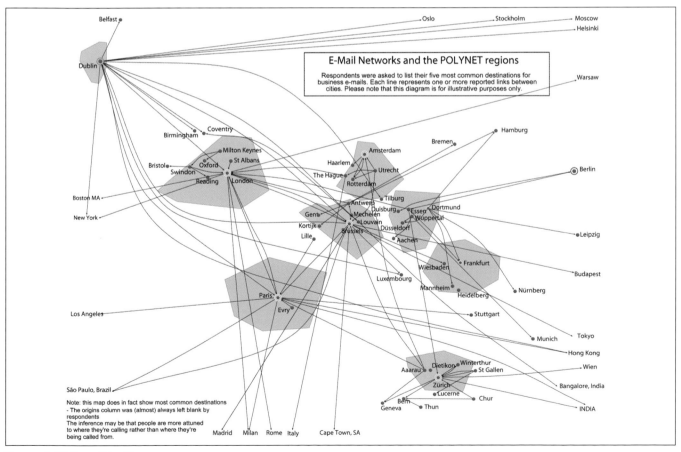

Figure 5.13 E-mail traffic

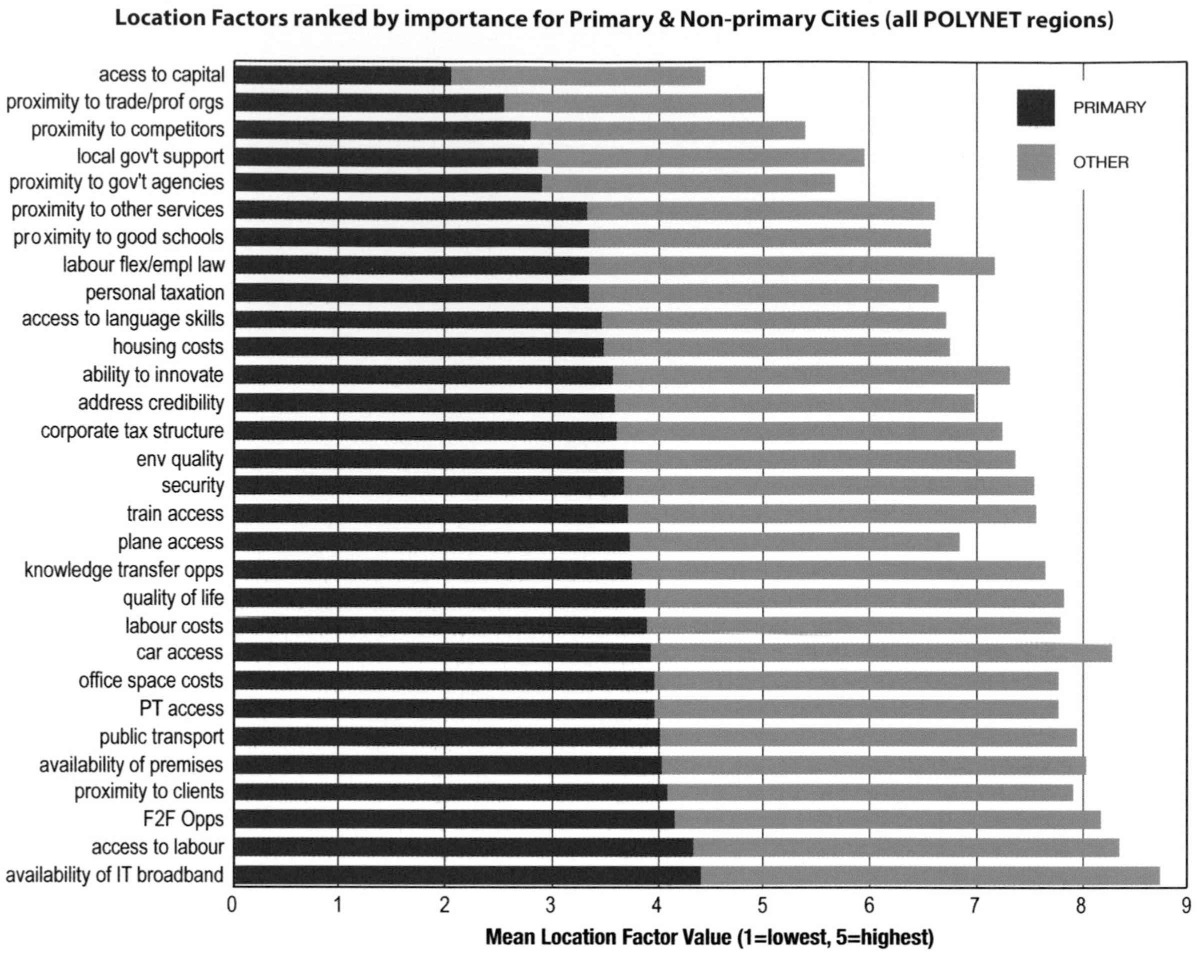

Location Factors ranked by importance for Primary & Non-primary Cities (all POLYNET regions)

Figure 5.14 Location factors: Relative importance

in 'other' cities). Other interesting variations are that airport access and 'ability to innovate' rank higher for primary than for other cities. Generally, tax considerations do not figure very highly, presumably because the most significant tax burdens do not vary much from one location to another in the same country or region; neither do more general factors like quality of local schools or proximity to other services. Access to capital counts as least significant of all, presumably again because it does not vary by area.

Table 5.11 shows the median values[3] for the importance of location factors for the different countries and regions. Obviously the most important factor is 'availability of advanced telecom infrastructure'. The least important factor is 'access to venture capital'.

Conclusion: The elusive measurement of flows

The conclusion must be that the attempt to measure information flows directly, by surveying business people in the course of their everyday work, produced results that fell

far short of the teams' original hopes and expectations. It is natural to ask what, if anything, might have been done to produce significantly higher responses.

From the start, we recognized that this type of intensive diary-based survey research was going to be intrinsically difficult. This has been the invariable recent experience in transportation surveys, and it seems to be becoming progressively worse as time pressures on busy executives increase and as many more requests for research participation descend on their desks. A great deal of preliminary discussion took place both within the London team and at their early workshop meetings with the other teams. From the outset it was accepted that a limited response was likely if not certain, that the results could never claim to be scientifically representative, and that it would in any case be better to have a relatively few in-depth responses than a greater number of low-quality partial returns. For this reason, the original strategy was to concentrate on winning the cooperation of a relatively small sample of senior respondents in the interviews.

The significant change was the decision to use a web-based survey rather than a paper-and-pencil diary. This was based on the experience of the Swiss team in other recent research which had secured an excellent response both in quantity and quality. Since in the event the Swiss response to the survey was one of the best, it may well be that there is a greater surviving sense of civic cooperation and participation in Switzerland than in other countries, while the exceedingly poor response in South East England may suggest that the UK is following the US record of a decline in social capital (Putnam, 2000). It remains doubtful whether any alternative approach would have secured a significantly higher response rate.

The conclusion probably has to be that the only way to achieve better responses would be to involve senior management very actively in the design and the execution of the project. This might be possible if management had a direct interest in the outcome (for instance, because they were engaged in telecommunications or locational consultancy). But this would have defeated the purpose of this particular exercise, which was precisely to investigate the flows of information in a number of different advanced service industries. The final inference therefore is that this kind of research, important as it may be to understanding the functioning of firms and organizations within large and complex metropolitan areas, is almost impossible to achieve satisfactorily. Perhaps somewhere, other researchers will find a way of disproving this rather despairing conclusion.

Nevertheless some important conclusions can be drawn from our research experience, particularly when considered in conjunction with the qualitative interview results which follow in Part 3.

First, as the survey progressed, it became evident that many of the e-mails sent to potential respondents did not reach their intended recipients. This was because the messages, which had a link to the web survey and an attachment containing explanatory literature about the project, were blocked either by anti-spam software or by personal assistants (PAs) who now routinely 'filter' the huge in-boxes of senior managers. The former reason for non-delivery was actually identified in the interviews as a serious problem encountered by advertising, media and design firms needing to send large attachments and links by e-mail. Both reasons demonstrate that an analysis of overall e-mail traffic (rejected at an early stage of the research), even at the level of individual firms, would have told the research teams little about actual high-value informational flows between business cities.

Second, our original intention – to persuade a relatively small sample of the senior managers we interviewed to participate in the survey – was based upon extensive prior interview experience which had demonstrated the importance of establishing strong relationships between researchers and business respondents to gain valuable insights. When we departed from this approach by extending the survey to business actors who had no prior knowledge of the research or the researchers, and who receive many requests to participate in surveys, it was inevitable that their diaries would yield less detailed information. But, although we devoted much time to ensuring that the survey forms should be as simple and quick to complete as possible, they may still have appeared too time-consuming and/or complex to 'cold-call' recipients. Thus the very limitations of the diary survey bring into sharp focus a vital finding from the interviews to be discussed in Part 3: in spite of the widespread and ever-increasing volume of e-mail flows, face-to-face contact proves to be of crucial importance for exchanging high-value information and knowledge, vital to APS.

Finally, though in no way truly representative, the individual cases from the survey analysis appear to yield a reasonably consistent picture. Both the business travel patterns and the patterns of virtual exchange demonstrate that all eight MCRs have an intensive pattern of local exchange coupled with remarkably well-developed links to other major business cities both within Europe and farther afield. These patterns however differ very greatly in individual cases, some businesses being very locally based, others having much more developed and regular external linkages. Finally, there seems to be a quite basic distinction between MCRs that are fundamentally quite monocentric and those that are truly polycentric. The first show patterns of business contact that are highly concentrated either within their First City FUR and even within a small CBD of that city, or between that business core and other distant cities. Here any other centres tend to operate in a one-way relationship with the central core, dependent upon it for some business but without any reciprocal relationship. The second show, in addition, a more balanced pattern of development, with quite extensive relationships between individual FURs that do seem to have a degree of two-way relationship. However, it must be stressed that this may be an outcome of the particular sample, as the interview results – described in Chapters 6–8 – demonstrate a much greater dominance of a single First City, even in apparently polycentric regions. Nonetheless, it appears that the analysis lends support to an observation long made by geographers and planners: that some of Europe's major metropolitan areas are intrinsically more polycentric than others.

Notes

1 Conventional mail and fax traffic were both eliminated for this reason.

2 The leading city in each region; see Chapter 3, p63.

3 The median values are obtained from the individual ratings registered in the web inquiry.

PART 3

Understanding
the Polycentric Metropolis:
Actors, Networks, Regions

6

Firms and Places:
Inside the Mega-City Regions

Kathy Pain and Peter Hall

Evidently, despite their various limitations, the three attempts to quantify the 'space of flows' so far reported – the examination of commuting patterns in Chapter 2, the analysis of advanced producer service (APS) firms' organization in Chapter 3, and the direct attempt to measure information flows in Chapter 5 – all help mutually to reinforce a key conclusion: that the eight mega-city regions (MCRs) demonstrate considerable differences in internal structure. These differences reflect their unique histories, development paths and national contexts. A key challenge in these quantitative studies has been to find a common basis for comparison between the regions, trying first one approach and then another in order to bring out both their common features and their individual points of difference.

The interview studies seek to drill deeper down into the actual processes that underlie these diverse functional geographies. They do so by deliberately eschewing any attempt to quantify: instead, they try discursively to reach qualitative judgements about the operation of these processes and about the relative importance of different factors that influence them.

Face-to-face interviews with firms, business, professional and policy-making institutions aim to shed new light on the ways in which Castells's 'space of flows' and 'space of places' (Castells, 1996) intersect within these regions. As in the previous quantitative analyses reported in Chapters 3 and 5, the research focus here is on the individual actors, their firms and organizations, their connectivities at different geographical scales and the linkages they create between the different urban centres that constitute these MCRs. In order better to understand these multi-layered and cross-cutting relations, we go directly to their source: the evidence of prominent business actors from the eight MCRs, whose daily working practices create the inter-city flows and linkages under examination.

Necessarily, much of the richness and hence the value of this qualitative evidence is specific to each region. However global these actors and the economic world they inhabit, much of their everyday business practice is experienced through their own offices in their own cities. Unlike the quantitative analyses so far reported, we are now centrally concerned with this wealth of local detail: we need to understand its specificity before we try to generalize from it. And this is particularly so, because in probing this experience in the interviews we were concerned to emerge with important conclusions for the next and final stage of the POLYNET analysis: the recommendations for policy. We needed to understand from our respondents what factors they found most important for the efficient operation of the knowledge-based economy, what features in their own regions they found positively contributed or negatively impeded this operation, and what specific recommendations they would make for improvement. By distilling this deep experience, hopefully, we would emerge with a set of tentative proposals which we could put, in the next stage of the analysis, to regional policy-makers.

These specific regional experiences and formulations are described by each of the research teams in eight regional chapters, Chapters 9–16. They use these to make bridges to the discussion of policy, introducing key policy documents for their regions. Later, in Chapter 17, we seek to build an overarching viaduct connecting these eight bridges, comparing the policies and teasing out their common features and differences.

In this and the following two chapters, by way of introducing the regional detail, we seek in advance to draw out some of the key common conclusions that will be supported by the evidence in the regional chapters, shedding light on the way business is conducted within and between the eight MCRs. We consider intra- and inter-regional flows of information, labour and skills and knowledge transfer in relation to globalization of markets, including labour markets and servicing strategies. We seek to identify common themes as well as differences, and to discuss them in the context of the overarching POLYNET research hypotheses and questions, set out in Chapter 1.

The interviews

In its basic methodological approach, the interview survey builds on previous research conducted by the Globalization and World Cities (GaWC) team at Loughborough University. Detailed studies of London-Frankfurt global city relations (Beaverstock et al, 2001) and global business services clustering in the City of London (Taylor et al, 2003) indicated the significance and complexity of the flows within advanced producer services (APS) firms that link North West European cities in a worldwide 'global city network'. POLYNET extends this field of enquiry to cover the eight MCRs of North West Europe. The in-depth, face-to-face interviews with senior business practitioners and organizations in the eight study areas set out to investigate how actual business operations connect the MCRs into the space of flows. Interviews ran in parallel with the quantitative analyses described in Chapters 3 and 5, and continued afterwards.

A sample of firms, selected for the analysis reported in Chapter 3, was selected for interview in each region. Sample sizes were not designed for statistical significance. The target was 60 interviews with senior executives[1] in the eight APS sectors: banking/finance, insurance, law, accountancy, management consulting, advertising, logistics and design consulting. Firms were selected to provide as reasonable as possible coverage of firms operating at the four geographical scales or 'scopes' across these sectors in each region. Teams were encouraged to extend the survey to new locations within or outside the boundaries used for quantitative data collection and analysis as new information on important connectivities became apparent. Selected potential interviewees were contacted initially by letter followed, by telephone call, e-mail or fax. Although researchers were unable to predetermine which organizations would agree to participate, the firms interviewed represent a reasonably accurate overview of non-local firms across the eight sectors. A total of 492 firms and 106 trade, professional and government institutions were interviewed across the eight regions. A further 37 interviews with major London firms from the earlier Corporation of London study were included in the analysis because of their direct relevance. Interviewees were of a very senior level within each organization, the majority being of chair, vice-president, chief executive, managing director or partner, senior or regional manager status or equivalent.

The location of firms interviewed is not statistically representative, but it does reflect the distribution of APS as earlier identified in studying firms' locations. Thus in Greater Dublin, Rhine-Main and the Paris Region, most firms are located in 'First Cities' as defined in Chapter 3 – Dublin, Frankfurt and Paris. In EMR (European Metropolitan Region) Northern Switzerland, the Randstad, Central Belgium and RhineRuhr, there is a wider geographical spread of firms but the largest number of offices and interviews conducted were in First and Second Cities: Zürich/Basel, Amsterdam/Rotterdam, Brussels/Antwerp and Düsseldorf/Cologne, the greater number being in the First City in each case. The South East England case differs: here, most interviews were conducted in urban centres outside London in order to supplement existing interview data from London, but the overall spread reflects the regional position.

Because the interviews were specifically intended to explore subtle and complex processes, the interview survey was intensive. A semi-structured questionnaire (Appendix 2) was designed to allow interviewers to tease out information about the pattern, volume and quality of connectivities and flows associated with their everyday experience of business operations. The interviews were conducted in the language of choice of respondents. Common open-ended questions formed the basis for interviews in all regions, so as to ensure comparability of basic results across the study and to ensure that first responses were a true reflection of the issues that the respondents themselves deemed important. The questions were triggers for deeper discussions in which the interviewer's knowledge increased progressively during each interview, building a comprehensive database on particular circumstances, issues and variables, cause and effect. Suggested prompts were refined by interviewers to probe specific areas of enquiry as new insights and understandings emerged. The interview length was planned to be 30–45 minutes but in many cases discussion extended considerably beyond that. Discussions were tape-recorded and transcribed wherever possible so that non-attributable quotations could be used to illustrate reported results.

Presenting the interview results

The resulting data are qualitative and suggestive, complementing the quantitative analyses reported on in Part 2 of this book. In this and the following two chapters we try to identify similarities and differences and attempt to isolate apparent causal relationships.

We first look at the location of offices in the APS sectors, in particular the evidence of clustering. We relate this to the critical variable of the geographical scopes of these services: global, European, national, regional. We try to trace connectivities within firms and between them, within and between urban areas. More summarily, we consider globalization and its impact on corporate strategies, particularly organizational structures. These are the themes of the remainder of this chapter.

Second, we turn to information and its key role in these services. We seek to understand the processes of knowledge production, transfer and innovation. We look in turn at the roles of virtual communications and of face-to-face contact involving locational proximity. We consider the importance of travel and transport for the latter. Finally, we try to sum up on the relationships between interaction, linkage and flow. These topics are considered in Chapter 7.

Finally, in Chapter 8, we focus on the space of places and the interdependencies between this and the space of flows. We look at the crucial significance of skilled labour and of labour markets. This brings us to the importance of 'place', in particular the role of the POLYNET First Cities in knowledge production. And this leads us on to a fundamental reconsideration of two assumptions on which the study was based: the assumption that MCRs exist and can be defined geographically; and the assumption that polycentricity is a growing reality. Out of this, we conclude by identifying some key issues for sustainable regional management – issues to which we return in Chapter 17.

Office locations and clustering

The interviews confirmed a common relationship between patterns of intra-regional business clustering, sector, market reach and network scope – regional, national, European or global.

Many firms operate from just one regional location to serve the whole MCR or, in some cases, the whole country. The most extreme example is Greater Dublin where very few non-local APS firms are found outside the Dublin metropolitan area. Similarly, in Rhine-Main the small size of the region and good transport infrastructure mean that only one office is generally needed to service both the whole regional and national market from one location, leading to a high concentration of firms in most sectors in Frankfurt. In EMR Northern Switzerland, a 'single business location strategy' reflects not only the small size of the MCR (which like Rhine-Main, has good transport infrastructure) but also the size of the Swiss national market. Firms operating regionally are located in Zürich (most often) or Basel, while firms operating nationally do

so from just one location, either in Zürich (in the MCR) or from Geneva. In general, only firms in accountancy and management consultancy need to support a regional network of offices to be close to their clients whereas advertising, banking and law are more likely to operate from one office location particularly for firms with an international focus.

In other regions a single office location could be in one of several urban centres. In the Randstad, interviewees considered regional transport infrastructure less adequate than those in Rhine-Main and EMR Northern Switzerland, but firms serving the national market generally also operate from just one office in one of the four largest urban centres – Amsterdam, Rotterdam, Utrecht or The Hague (in that order) – from which they can service their clients across the MCR or across The Netherlands. Large management consulting, advertising, insurance and law firms operate in this way whereas accountancy and design firms with regional markets are more locationally dispersed.

A general trend towards spatial concentration of firms is reported in all regions – even in RhineRuhr, which was identified as one of the most polycentric regions in terms of APS office location in Chapter 3, although again the intensity of this process was found to vary between business sectors. In Central Belgium most firms underline the advantages of concentrated locations. While the trend towards concentration into as few office locations as possible is also widely reported in London, a number of major international networks continue to operate significant offices both in London and elsewhere in the MCR. In management consulting, for example, we were told that all South East England based offices must now work internationally and be 'overseas players'. To what extent this is a feature of the depth of APS concentration in the First City, London, will be addressed again in the light of further evidence. The degree of concentration in First Cities, relative to other regional centres, varies considerably across the study regions; there are also differences in the degree of sectoral specialization between urban centres in each region.

Greater Dublin: concentration in just one city is most notable in the case of Greater Dublin which is regarded as 'Dublin-centric' for all business services with the exception of the offices of a small number (relative to other regions) of larger regional and national scope multi-office firms such as design consultancies and accountancy firms. Dublin is regarded as a 'magnet' in the national as well as the regional context. Logistics services are found outside Dublin, especially in Naas-Newbridge, although this is not regarded as constituting a logistics cluster. Apart from these examples, the only other APS presences outside Dublin are the local branches and a few back-offices of banks and financial institutions that are headquartered in Dublin.

Dublin clustering processes show 'a remarkably strong preference for city-central locations' in all sectors except logistics. Within central Dublin, global firms are particularly clustered in central business district (CBD) postcode areas 1, 2 and 4. A number of firms have offices in several locations within the CBD as a result of organic growth, take-over/merger and deliberate locational strategy. In addition to established clustering in area 4, area 1 includes an international financial services cluster developed with the aid of government tax concessions in the former Docklands area.

Rhine-Main: here Frankfurt is the only urban centre in the MCR which currently features notable APS clustering – advertising, corporate law and, particularly, banking and finance. Within the city, banking and law firms are found clustered in close proximity in the western area of the inner city and 'Westend' district. Elsewhere firms are generally located in city fringe industrial parks. Insurance is well represented in Wiesbaden while television and broadcasting are traditionally located in Mainz. An important IT cluster is identified in the southern part of the region with its core in Darmstadt. APS density is higher in the centre of Frankfurt and in the western (Mainz, Wiesbaden) and southern parts of the region (Darmstadt).

Paris Region: Paris and London are highly concentrated APS centres with notable internal sectoral clustering. The Paris team concludes that for their region 'the question is not so much of de-concentration dynamics but rather the explanation and the limits of a concentrated location in the Advanced Producer Service sectors' (Halbert, 2005b, p1). In Paris, major firms form a dense cluster that stretches from the Paris CBD to La Défense and Boulogne-Billancourt. Management consultancy firms are clustered in the heart of the business district in prestigious western *arrondissements* and law companies in the northern 16ᵉ *arrondissement*. Design consultancies are also almost all located in the dense part of the city. While other sectors are less spatially selective, major firms are all located within the CBD. Major accountancy firms are located in an area from Neuilly-sur-Seine to La Défense while small firms are also spread across the Île-de-France and the Paris Region. Finance and insurance headquarters are located in La Défense and central Paris with regional offices in Orléans, Reims and Rouen. Le Mans, an insurance headquarters outside the Paris conurbation, is an exception to the general rule of concentration in Paris and logistics is the least centralized sector, office location being determined by transport infrastructure which may or may not coincide with city locations, a feature in all MCRs.

South East England: London is the largest APS concentration not only in South East England and the UK but in Europe – the only sector that is not well represented there being logistics. A small area of the city contains the dense City of London 'Square Mile' APS cluster and in particular banking and finance, insurance and law firms. Law firms also straddle the area between the Square Mile and the courts at Holborn to the west. Proximity to the judicial system is less important for 'City firms' which specialize in corporate business law and favour locations close to the major international banks which are now located not only in the Square Mile but also in Canary Wharf in the Docklands redevelopment area to the east of the City. A less cohesive cluster including management consultancy firms is located in the West End of central London in proximity to international corporate clients and to Soho which is the creative district for advertising. Major accountancy firms are located more on the fringes and to the west of the Square Mile as well as having a regional network of offices. There is a weaker clustering of design services immediately to the north of the Square Mile and, as in the case of accountancy, a wide regional coverage of small to medium size firms:

The distinction between the situation in Paris and London and that for Dublin is that, in spite of the scale of concentration in London and in Paris, more significant APS activity is found in the MCRs outside these cities, particularly in South East England. Interview evidence in Greater Dublin suggests that 'This "hub"… appears to overshadow the remainder of the regional economy leaving no room for any type of clustering in its hinterland' (Sokol and van Egeraat, 2005b, p7). In the Paris Region, a specialization in insurance services exists in Le Mans – a rather exceptional case – and there is a significant presence of non-local APS firms in Reading, Southampton and Cambridge, in particular, in South East England. Sectoral specializations identified are financial services at Bournemouth and logistics at Milton Keynes. In addition, Reading and Crawley are seen by a number of major accountancy and law firms as emerging clusters for these sectors. Although Cambridge has a large number of design firms, this was not seen as a cohesive, specialist cluster.

EMR Northern Switzerland: Zürich is the largest APS concentration in the region though second city Basel comes closer in size than in the previous cases. Some sectoral specialization between centres is identified in Lucerne and St Gallen (advertising) and Zug (above average presence of accountancy, insurance, law and management consultancy) but the largest international firms in these sectors are concentrated in Zürich. Zürich has the highest concentration of banking services which, together with advertising and legal services, are found in one central location. Elsewhere, close relationships also exist between accountancy, law and financial services. In this case, accountancy and management consultancy firms, which require customer proximity at a very local spatial scale, are represented across the MCR centres.

Central Belgium: here, APS concentration in Brussels is rather more closely followed by that in Second City Antwerp. Accountancy and design are mainly concentrated in Brussels followed by Antwerp and Ghent. The location of the 'big four' accountancy firms (Deloitte Touche, Ernst & Young, PriceWaterhouseCoopers and KPMG) moved from the city centre to the periphery in the 1980s due to their large office space requirements, while smaller firms requiring closer proximity to institutions and law firms remain in the city centre. Brussels is the absolute dominant centre for banking, finance and insurance especially headquarters (HQ) offices which are located in the central area of the city. Advertising is also very highly concentrated in Brussels to be close to large corporate customers and European institutions, with a smaller representation in Antwerp. Brussels is the main location for law firms which are again concentrated in the core of the city. For logistics the biggest concentration is in Antwerp and then Brussels (42 per cent of logistics firms are located in Antwerp due to its harbour and good highway network).

The Randstad: this and RhineRuhr have the widest geographical spread of firms compared with the other MCRs but, within the Randstad, Amsterdam is clearly 'capital city' for APS activity with a concentration of firms in banking and advertising. Amsterdam has four times as many firms as Rotterdam, the second largest concentration (although the number of employees is only 1.5 times as high). Other concentrations are located in Rotterdam (particularly architecture and logistics), The Hague (an even distribution of sectors with many firms servicing the national government institutions) and Utrecht/Amersfoort (management consultancy). Advertising firms are almost entirely clustered in Amsterdam/Amstelveen corresponding to its GaWC global connectivity rankings. It also has a strong financial services sector although, unlike most preceeding cases (Frankfurt being an exception), not all banks within the MCR see a need to be located in Amsterdam. Law, accountancy and insurance firms serving the national market show no patterns of concentration and may have their head offices in any one of the larger urban centres however major, international law firms tend to concentrate in Amsterdam.

RhineRuhr: here, Düsseldorf once again has the largest overall regional concentration of firms but this time other cities – Cologne, Dortmund, Essen, Bonn and Duisburg – also have significant APS concentrations and the MCR has the most significant sectoral specialization between its urban centres. Insurance, logistics and advertising are clustered: Düsseldorf (advertising), Cologne (insurance), Dortmund (logistics), Duisburg (logistics). Management consultancy, advertising, insurance and law operate from one MCR office in one of the four big cities (Düsseldorf, Cologne, Dortmund, Essen). The largest law and accountancy offices are concentrated in Düsseldorf city centre, and advertising is concentrated in central Düsseldorf and in Cologne. Insurance is concentrated not in Düsseldorf, but in two clusters in Cologne, while logistics is concentrated in Cologne, Dortmund and Duisburg-Niederrhein. Management consulting, design and banking/finance have no distinct locational specialization between centres, though management consulting and design are more concentrated in Düsseldorf, Cologne and Bonn.

An important difference between RhineRuhr and the other POLYNET regions is that banking and finance are relatively evenly distributed across the region through a network of branches and are less spatially clustered than in other regions. It seems likely that this reflects the dominant position of Frankfurt as the leading German financial services centre. The existence of a number of nationally important business service centres in Germany has implications for the RhineRuhr and Rhine-Main. This is a matter to which we will return later as we find that differences in national economic context have crucial effects on the internal service geography of the MCRs.

Size of office also shows some correlation with regional concentration and clustering patterns. In general, First Cities contain some of the largest offices in terms of jobs in each region, but an important point for policy is that office sizes vary both within and between the MCRs. Some of the largest offices are found in the First Cities but very small firms are also found alongside the largest offices in densely clustered city centres. Amsterdam provides an extreme example. The mean size of offices is higher in Haarlemmermeer, Amersfoort, Rotterdam, Utrecht and The Hague than in Amsterdam, reflecting the fact that, across the region, firms in insurance, logistics and accountancy are larger while advertising firms (which are clustered in Amsterdam/Amstelveen) can be very small (the mean number of jobs is just three) yet the intensity and quality of their knowledge connectivities is reported as high. Similarly, in the City of London's Square Mile very small offices, for example, in financial services, are located alongside some of the biggest APS offices in the world yet they have disproportionately high global connectivities. Thus the number of staff employed in an office is not necessarily a good indication of the size of an office's network or the importance of the functions conducted there.

Perhaps the most significant finding from the comparative analysis of locational patterns within the MCRs is that just one city stands out in each case as the dominant centre in terms of overall APS concentration, in spite of regional differences in the geographical distribution and clustering of firms. But apart from logistics which has a different locational structure, sectoral specialization between urban centres is more evident as the number of similar size centres increases. Thus sectoral specialization between urban centres is less apparent in MCRs with the most concentrated APS presence in First Cities, for example, London and Paris, and most notable in RhineRuhr and to a lesser extent the Randstad. Intra-city clustering in the central area of First Cities is present to different degrees in each region. Banking and financial services are present in the densest area of the city centres in all cases, but are not clustered in Düsseldorf. Linked to this point, Frankfurt is also an interesting departure from other cases because it is a relatively specialized financial services cluster compared to other primate cities, London and Paris, which have a broader representation of services.

The significance of geographical scope

In this section, we consider the relationship between clustering and network scope. How do firms, operating at different scopes – regional, national, European and global – conduct business from their offices in each MCR? In all the regions, many local business services are provided by small firms with just one office and no other wider service network connections. These firms are not included in the interview survey as they have no connectivity beyond the local level. Also excluded are firms that may belong to wider service networks but which focus on the retail market. As explained in Chapter 3, the focus of our research is on firms that show connectivity at one of the four geographical scopes.

The interviews show that firms operating at any of these network scopes can and do engage with markets from local to global scales from their MCR locations. There are examples of regional and national scope firms in smaller centres that service clients in Europe and other international locations. However, international and global scope firms are quite different in nature because they aim to provide knowledge-based services to clients through a cross-border network of offices. These offices are concentrated in global cities but, depending on office functions, they can also be located in non-clustered regional locations or cover a wide geographical area through a network of offices that services local business

clients. Because they operate through a worldwide global city network, they connect certain cities and places through flows of information and skills by means of virtual communications and business travel. An important area of enquiry in the interview research has been to gain a better understanding of how the MCRs are structured in terms of these different functional network scopes.

Regional scope firms are shown to require a local office presence in two or more small regional centres in order to be very close to important customers for their market. In some cases they also acquire an office in a First or other major city to extend their market reach. This is least common in Dublin and Frankfurt but is a familiar pattern in South East England and to some extent in the Paris Region where firms feel the need to have a 'foothold' in the major global agglomeration. In the cases of RhineRuhr, the Randstad and to a lesser extent Central Belgium and EMR Northern Switzerland, this 'foothold' may not necessarily be in the MCR First City.

National scope firms are shown to be generally located in the larger APS centres to be close to a large number of business clients. *International scope firms* are usually located in the First City or other major centre. Evidence from the interviews across the study shows that, in all cases, First Cities have the highest concentration of firms belonging to global networks. Branch networks and, in some cases, the 'back-offices' of large international firms may also be found in smaller centres, reflecting a functional separation of 'front-' and 'back-office' activities for reduction of office and labour costs. This pattern is noted in the Paris Region and Greater Dublin but seems to be most prevalent in South East England.

In general, the presence of regional to global scope firms, across the urban centres in all MCRs, reflects the same basic relationship between market orientation, network scope and office location resulting in distinctive patterns of clustering in different regional situations. In Greater Dublin and Rhine-Main, Dublin and Frankfurt have a strong representation of national scope firms and a striking dominance of major international and global firms, particularly in their CBDs. The remainder of the Greater Dublin Region has very few firms indeed operating at any of the four network scopes outside the Dublin metropolitan area. In Rhine-Main the majority of non-local firms are located in the Frankfurt functional urban region.

In the Paris Region, similarly, the Paris CBD contains a very high representation of offices of national and international scope firms and has total dominance at the European and global scopes. Offices outside the Île-de-France area are generally smaller and local to regional in scope. There is a general lack of global companies outside Paris – Rouen, Orléans, Reims and Amiens have more firms at the regional and national scales.

In South East England, London has by far the largest concentration of global scope firms and also dominates for European scope firms. But London's scale hides the presence of a significant number of international firms in other MCR urban centres. Reading, Cambridge and Southampton have concentrations of international scope firms, but less-clustered and non-clustered significant global scope firms also exist elsewhere in the region.

In EMR Northern Switzerland and Central Belgium, the offices of international scope firms are most concentrated in Zürich and Brussels, but in these cases, there is also a greater presence of regional and national scope firms. Zürich and Brussels tower above Basel and Antwerp for European and especially global scope firms but these First and Second Cities are more similar in terms of the presence of regional and to some extent national scope firms.

The Randstad, together with RhineRuhr, was identified as one of the most polycentric POLYNET MCRs in Chapter 3, yet even so, in relation to APS, Amsterdam is considered to be 'the most internationally oriented city of The Netherlands'. Most international scope firms, such as global law firms, advertising agencies and corporate and security banks, operate from a head office located in one of the larger cities – mostly in Amsterdam. The four largest cities – Amsterdam, Rotterdam, Utrecht and The Hague – are reasonably balanced in terms of regional and national scope firms but, as for other regions, Amsterdam dominates absolutely at the European and global scales. Rotterdam has some international orientation especially in logistics and architecture but firms in Utrecht and The Hague mainly operate on a national level. Interestingly, the relatively small cities of Amstelveen and Haarlemmermeer have rather high connections at an international level, reflecting their proximity to Schiphol International Airport. Accountancy, and in this case, design (engineering) serve a regional market with firms locating close to their customers.

Relative to other MCRs, RhineRuhr has the strongest presence of regional and national scope firms located in cities other than First City Düsseldorf – Cologne, Dortmund, Essen, Bonn, Duisburg. But in spite of having the most dispersed APS geography of all, headquarters offices for global scope firms are located in Düsseldorf which is the most important location for international law, advertising and accountancy firms. International law firms, for example, have only one office in the region, mostly located in Düsseldorf. Similarly, international advertising firms located in Düsseldorf are also lead agencies for the national advertising market.

Insurance firms in Cologne are increasingly international in scope but operate at a national scale through a network of offices in medium size centres within the region. In common with other MCRs, accountancy firms often have two to three smaller offices in Cologne, Essen and Bonn but international scope firms are located in Düsseldorf city centre. International and national scope logistics firms are concentrated in Cologne, Dortmund and Duisburg-Niederrhein but operate regionally. Management consulting and design consist of mainly middle size firms but the few European and international scope firms have just one location in Düsseldorf to serve the regional and national market. Banking and finance is evenly distributed across the region reflecting an under-representation of international scope firms.

Major banking and financial services are identified as the most importantly connected sector in First Cities, with the exception of Düsseldorf which lacks a strong international banking and financial services concentration and Amsterdam (not all finance is concentrated in Amsterdam, but it is the major financial centre of The Netherlands). The distinction between domestic (national scope) and international (European and global scope) firms in banking, financial services and insurance is an important issue for First Cities: these sectors remain organized on a largely domestic markets basis because of the continued existence of different national regulations and tax structures. Only some financial services are conducted on a truly global basis. In general, domestic banks have large headquarters in their First City and a network of branches serving both business and retail customers. The German case is unusual because, in spite of Frankfurt's position as leading international financial services cluster for Germany, not all domestic banks are headquartered there; other major German cities also have some representation of banking headquarters. In the case of Dublin, Irish banks that have been acquired by foreign entities have been integrated into international networks and could now be regarded as 'national' offices performing back-office functions within larger cross-border firms. These Dublin city-based offices are becoming disconnected from the domestic context losing their national and regional scope. In the case of London, opening up to foreign investment by banks and financial companies in what has popularly become known as the 'Big Bang' of 1986, has made the City of London truly globally constituted in banking and financial services, promoting London's role as an international centre for business services.

In MCRs containing several APS centres of similar size (RhineRuhr, the Randstad, Central Belgium and EMR Northern Switzerland), each centre has a good representation of regional and national scope firms, presumably because they have a choice when deciding their office locations. Sectoral specialization between centres follows from the fact that services cluster together to maximize simple agglomeration economies such as access to clients and skilled labour. In MCRs with one primate APS centre (London and Paris), notable sectoral clustering takes place in First Cities due to the strong representation of firms and sectors located there while sectoral specialization between regional centres is less prominent. It is not clear, from the interview evidence, what part the time-distance between centres plays in the development of sectoral specialization in each region. While some sectors require widespread regional coverage through a network of small local offices, firms operating at national and international scopes are generally concentrated in one city location. But what is clear is that firms with global servicing strategies cluster in the First Cities of each region.

Significantly, there is only one truly globally constituted cluster in each region. These cities are in a different league to other cities in the study: they are the only city in each region with connections not only at a European scale but to the global-city network. Evidence from the region with the least primate urban structure, RhineRuhr, shows that even here Düsseldorf is the major place or node for the international business level and for external flows and relationships. The implications of different locational strategies within the MCRs for connectivity within firms are examined in the following section.

Connectivities within firms

To what extent do distributional and clustering patterns of service firms support regional connectivity between offices within the same service network? In the study of business organization reported in Chapter 3, firms with multiple intra-regional office locations were assumed to have connectivity – but do such firms in fact have frequent and/or important communications and relationships between offices?

It is clear that APS locational strategies are highly determined by service sector and market positioning (the significance of non-economic factors in decision-making is discussed in Chapter 8). Regions having a number of urban centres with similar levels of connectivity could be considered more polycentric than those dominated by one city – but the scope of firms represented in different urban centres is shown to affect intra-firm connectivity with respect to the intensity, quality and direction of flows.

Five situations associated with potential multi-office functional connectivities will first be considered:

1   *Regional scope firms without First City offices.* Here, the interview evidence suggests that multi-office networks choose locations in the largest regional business centres and one or more smaller ones to be close to a large local

client base. Accountancy operates in this way in all the MCRs. Some research teams conclude that the amount of communication between these separate offices is very low indeed as each one is highly focused on its own particular regional market. There are many regional networks of this type in the less primate regions but they are seen as having the least real intra-firm connectivity due to the limited size of their offices and the very localized nature of their markets.

2   *Firms with regional offices and a First City location.* Two-directional flows of strategic value are found in small to medium size regional firms that have opened offices in First Cities Dublin, London and Paris. This situation is likely to be a significant contributor to intra-regional connectivity. Many non-local firms in Orléans, Reims, Rouen and Le Mans and in South East England were found to fit this model. For example, in insurance, a company based in Le Mans also uses its Paris office for strategic exchanges and decisions. In this example, volume of knowledge flows may not be significant but the quality of flows between Le Mans and Paris is high. Importantly, this situation indicates that high-quality intra-firm connectivity can exist in MCRs with a relatively primate First City.

3   *Firms with a First City head office location and regional branches.* Here, connectivities between head office and regional branches have a wide regional spread but follow a 'hub and spoke' or 'centre-periphery' model. In South East England and the Paris Region, these networks are centred on First Cities London and Paris, but in other regions this would not always be the case. In the Paris Region and Greater Dublin, communications between banks and their branches are low in volume; communication is predominantly electronic and with head office. Flows with Paris central offices are only frequent at a certain level of responsibility in senior managerial staff: 'intense interactions with the hub city are not common features of all local/regional staffs who are dealing mainly with issues at this local/regional scale' (Halbert, 2005c, p4). However, South East England does show interesting evidence of higher-quality interactions with head offices in this type of network in cases where regional branches are servicing major international clients located outside London. Again, this indicates the potential for high-quality inter-urban connectivity in a primate MCR.

4   *Firms with a First City head office and regional 'back-offices'.* Such decentralized back-offices are principally reported in South East England and Greater Dublin and may therefore be less common in other regions. In each of the three cases reported, connectivities are directly with the First City and of a strictly support

nature. In Greater Dublin, examples are call centres and customer contact centres. Relations and flows with Dublin are found to be hierarchical and 'The single most important intra-firm flow is with the capital's HO [head office] [in Dublin city]' (Sokol and van Egeraat, 2005b, p6). Communication between regional offices is limited to sporadic phone calls. Back-office activities are located in a number of clustered and non-clustered centres outside London. Three banking and finance offices of large global firms located in the Bournemouth-Poole conurbation undertake routinized and technical support functions. As in the Greater Dublin and Paris Region cases, relations are hierarchical and communications less intense.

5 *Regional offices in logistics services.* Logistics has a different locational basis in all regions, being strongly focused on transport infrastructure. Actual communication flows vary according to specific service activity but in Greater Dublin, in some instances intra-firm communications by intranet, e-mail and phone can be intensive: 'Operational data is generally automatically shared with the head office' (Sokol and van Egeraat, 2005b, p7). In this case, head offices are located in Dublin city but regional networks have a flat hierarchy and some operations outside Dublin are relatively independent. In general, communication tends to be centred on the head office and there is limited contact between branch offices. However, as head offices are not always located in a First City even in more primate MCRs, the logistics sector can contribute positively to intra-regional connectivity. In South East England, for example, two major logistics firms interviewed have located senior functions in Milton Keynes as opposed to London.

However, the most important type of intra-firm connectivity identified in each MCR is found in the densely clustered CBDs of First Cities. The following examples illustrate the consistency of results on this point, regardless of degree of First City primacy.

The Paris Region interviews show 'a different sort of intra-firm connectivities according to the location of firms within the study region' (Halbert, 2005b, p4). The most intense intra-firm flows are within the dense area where most offices of multi-locational firms are located. The triangular-shaped central part of the Paris agglomeration (Paris's western *arrondissements* – La Défense – Boulogne/Issy-les-Moulineaux) is regarded as 'the business campus of most major producer services firms' (Halbert, 2005b, p4). In banking, which is singled out as a sector providing regional intra-firm connectivity, the intensity and quality of flows between Paris and regional offices is of a completely different magnitude to those identified within the central area and between Paris and other global cities. Even small and medium size enterprises (SMEs) located in central Paris have stronger knowledge flows. Intra-firm connectivities between centres outside Paris are limited because the firms are SMEs and because the direction of flows is towards Paris. These types of intra-firm connectivities depict a regional network where central relationships are dominant while there are more secondary interactions between the hub city and other urban centres (Halbert, 2005b, p5).

In EMR Northern Switzerland, firms in Basel have a considerable proportion of relationships at the European and global scopes, but firms with the strongest networks are based in Zürich: 'companies based in the Zürich area generally have stronger business relationship networks … more frequent, some the most frequent, connections of all centres in the metropolitan region' (Glanzmann et al, 2005, p6). Zürich offices are one-fifth more closely networked with other locations than companies of other regions. Even Basel 'trails in this respect' though it had high potential connectivity in the quantitative analysis described in Chapter 3. While the most frequent relationships are at the regional level, intensity drops as geographic distance increases, particularly for SMEs – 1 in 10 at European level and 1 in 20 at global level.

RhineRuhr appeared to have prominent potential intra-regional connectivities in the Chapter 3 analysis, yet Cologne and Düsseldorf are singled out as the two 'most important' APS centres in the region. Cologne is the most important city on the national level but Düsseldorf 'functions as the most important location within the MCR for international advanced producer services' (Knapp et al, 2005, p7) and is the major node for external global flows and relationships.

The Randstad results show that on the international level, major firms generally favour Amsterdam locations, where large multi-national companies (MNCs) can be reached and from which international clients can be serviced overseas. Amsterdam is best connected in intra-firm networks with an international scope, with Rotterdam and Utrecht/The Hague some way behind. Amsterdam is identified as the only global gateway city of The Netherlands with a 'global city milieu'. 'For many global firms Amsterdam is The Netherlands' (Lambregts et al, 2005a, p7).

Rather different conclusions are drawn from the South East England interviews, which suggest that the high-quality and intense flows concentrated in London are associated with significant regional intra-firm connectivity. No less than 72 per cent of all firms interviewed in the centres outside London also have at least one London office. The number is particularly high for Cambridge (95 per cent), Southampton (83 per cent) and Swindon (80 per cent). Forty-six firms interviewed (58 per cent) had another office in the MCR located outside London. In all, just under two-thirds of the companies interviewed outside London were part of European or global scope networks of which banking and finance and accountancy dominated for global connectivity. A mix of scopes and sectors was interviewed to represent closely the APS inventory but a surprising amount of international working was found.

There is considerable evidence of intra-firm connections between regional offices and with London offices, which are clearly critical to the quality and profitability of regional services. Interactions fall into four main categories: support, specialisms, joint working and meetings. These are high-quality interrelations and there are many examples of branch office reliance on transfer of expert knowledge and skills, leverage of London and regional office specialisms, joint working and cooperation, support links and business (including international business) introductions.

'Hard' and 'soft' flows and exchanges of information and tacit knowledge can be found on different geographical scales. For example, knowledge transfer can occur in many different ways – through the visits of directors, senior managers and specialists or via intranet. Strategic information can pass in many directions – from and to London, other regional offices and offices elsewhere in the network. Overwhelmingly London is seen as the location of the most specialized skills and business knowledge and the main source of innovation and key contacts. These connectivities clearly demonstrate crucially important regional functional relations that benefit from London's depth of global concentration.

In conclusion, the evidence on intra-firm connectivities is mixed. The major finding from across the regions is that the most intense, high-quality communications and flows are not taking place in the POLYNET MCRs but in their globally connected First Cities. The volume and strategic value of interactions and exchanges in these cities are of an order that overshadows connectivities elsewhere in the regions – yet the South East England interviews suggest that depth of global concentration can be associated with regional economic growth. The implications of these results for inter-urban linkages are considered next.

Inter-urban linkages

Given the complexity of relations between the scopes, sizes, service sectors and functions of networks and the diversity of specific regional situations, summarizing and comparing results on inter-urban linkages is far from straightforward. But some points can be tentatively established.

In the analysis of firm structures reported in Chapter 3, it was assumed that less primate MCRs would have more centres with strong regional connectivity on the basis of the multi-office networks represented there. But the interviews suggest that everywhere, in both primate and polycentric regions, actual communications between offices serving the regional market are often low in both volume and quality of communication flow. The most intense and high-quality flows are concentrated in just one or two cities in each MCR; global connectivities are found only in the First Cities of each MCR.

Considering first two primate MCRs, the Paris Region and Greater Dublin, the Paris Region interviews 'show no particular evidence of a polycentric pattern in the producer services linkages. This confirms the clustering of service operations in the central part of the Paris agglomeration' (Halbert, 2005b, p5). In Greater Dublin, low intra-firm connectivity across the region translates to a low level of linkage between urban centres and it is important to note that while Dublin's international financial services are global in network scope, they are regarded as: 'largely disconnected from the Irish context' (Sokol and van Egeraat, 2005b, p8).

More surprisingly, in the Randstad, which is considered one of the most polycentric regions, very limited evidence of functional linkages within the MCR is found and those that are identified are within First City, Amsterdam: 'Looking at the regional concentrations of APS sectors, one might expect functional linkages. Apart from advertising, these linkages are generally very limited' (Lambregts et al, 2005a, p9).

However, there is also evidence to suggest that depth of global concentration in London is leading to geographically wider, high-quality, intra-firm communication flows in South East England. These are high-value interactions linking London to key business clusters in a wide surrounding area. The clusters are not generally based on sectoral lines but are 'regional service clusters' that are interlinked through the networks of offices located in them – knowledge flows through regional business circuits as well as between the individual clusters and London. The nature and value of these linkages seems to be not so much about volume of communication flows but leverage of skills and knowledge that allows higher-value business services and advice to be offered outside London. This may involve servicing contracts for international firms 'with a local presence' and, in some cases, working internationally.

Here, the interviews emphasize the significance of particular regional clusters. The Cambridge sub-region is described as 'a vital driver for national economic growth' and Southampton is regarded as the key commercial market for the 'South Coast Metropole'. Crawley-

Gatwick is seen as a place that you need to be in: 'Where do we get our work from – where are the regional corporate banking centres? Where are the lawyers?... Many of them are in Crawley-Gatwick' (Accountancy, South East England). Reading is seen as a 'professional services centre' that you need to be near: 'where the people who give out work and make recommendations to clients are based' (Law, South East England). While South East England offices outside London do not seem especially highly integrated into the international economy, there are considerable intra-firm connections that create functional links between a number of service clusters. These linkages prove crucial in promoting a functional regional knowledge economy.

So far, the interview results have been discussed exclusively in relation to intra-firm relations. But, across the study, with the exception of the Randstad, the interviews show that other relationships are vitally important. In Central Belgium, proximity of actors, subcontractors and clients and concentrated customers is sought by firms. In RhineRuhr, communication and relationships with other firms in the same sector and different APS sectors, suppliers and service providers, regional bodies and institutions are important for all sectors. And in EMR Northern Switzerland, the financial services sector is identified as having a central role in inter-sector networks: '...financial service providers play a central role in these inter-sector relationships. They have the most frequent and most significant relationships of all APS sectors investigated'. This is due to their function as 'company financiers and advisers' and 'as intermediaries between the various sectors, maintaining the relevant networks of relationships and communications' (Glanzmann et al, 2005, p5).

Sectors, markets and corporate strategy: The regions in a global context

Very evidently, geographical scope proves crucial for location. Firms and offices that serve wider-than-local markets show a strong tendency to cluster in First Cities, in primate and polycentric MCRs alike. One crucial consideration is how this is affected by the tendencies towards globalization that are now everywhere evident.

The interviews show that globalization of markets and service provision, generating intense market competition, is an ongoing driver for change in all APS sectors across North West Europe. Consolidation, restructuring and integration into international networks are the common stories in all sectors and all MCRs. There is agreement that firms must be responsive to changing market conditions at a variety of scales to survive.

Firms and organizations see globalization as inevitable: a 'one-way journey'. Larger national scope firms are now expected by clients to provide a cross-border 'seamless service' and intense domestic competition is a spur to extend market reach and scope. Local markets are everywhere increasingly crowded, intensifying competition for regional scope firms. Firms of all sizes report the need to achieve increasingly wider and deeper market reach to remain competitive. Small and medium size firms are joining networks or specializing in market niches at all geographical scales.

The need for increasing cross-border capacity combined with local market depth creates frequent conflicting priorities for larger firms, requiring constant adjustment. As already seen, consolidation is taking place in all sectors but integration into cross-border networks is not an end-game – as illustrated in one of the most globalized sectors, advertising. Vertical break-up and re-consolidation are constant as agencies compete for business. There are not many full-service providers in any sector and, to compete, a firm must be at least as good as a specialist in any market segment. Firms at the regional to global scopes must be flexible. Cross-sector alliances are common: the big four accountancy firms continue to overlap with consultancy and law to provide integrated services to clients. Advertising overlaps with marketing and communications; management consulting with information technology (IT) and logistics, banking with insurance, and so forth.

Firms must keep even closer to their customers while reaching out beyond regional and national markets to extend their client base. In several MCRs, firms describe how traditional client relationships are breaking down. Where firms lack capacity to generate knowledge and information solutions in-house, they are bought in from outside. Diversification to differentiate services in the market is also a key trend.

These pressures – local versus global, specialization versus diversification – also necessitate changes in management structures and internal organization. The biggest international APS networks require functional specialization between service centres on a global scale. Organizational structures service the three global regions – the USA, Europe/North Africa and Asia – with high-value, high-complexity functions concentrated in the three global hub cities. Matrix management allows management functions to decentralize geographically across a network of APS centres and there is evidence from interviews that this model is becoming increasingly popular with medium and large size firms in the MCRs. Key international clients are looked after by one partner or senior manager who focuses on this relationship and there is evidence of some senior management roles decentralizing from London to Europe and from First Cities to other regional centres.

Specialization and diversification of services is creating cross-disciplinary ways of working, causing the breakdown of traditional boundaries. This applies particularly to the banking and insurance, law, accountancy and management consulting sectors with the formation of multi-disciplinary practices and 'formal' splintering and restructuring in response to industry regulation in the latter two sectors. National regulation is identified as a key issue for business.

In addition to these common changes, there are specific sectoral and regional differences. As already discussed, in banking, finance and insurance relatively few firms operate globally. There are continuing barriers (regulation, lack of obvious cost savings/revenue enhancement and, in some cases, national pride) but consolidation is proceeding on a cross-industry basis through mergers and acquisitions within and between banking/financial services and insurance, and most banks perceive the need to extend their market reach. Consolidation, concentration and specialization are ongoing in all MCRs to minimize cost and centralize skills while maintaining a local presence 'on the ground'. A key difference is that continental European banks require a London office as well as a domestic HQ to be international players.

Law is the least globalized of the six major APS sectors (banking and finance, insurance, accountancy, law, management consultancy, advertising) in the study area: the key global centres remain London and New York and only a few firms are seen as operating at a truly global scope. But over the last five years demand for cross-border legal services has led to a spate of take-overs, mergers and strategic alliances led by London firms.

In contrast, accountancy/management consultancy is the most globalized. The big global firms, led by the big four accountancy firms based in London and New York, see the European Union (EU) as a huge and expanding market. In all MCRs, there is a presence of a few big accountancy firms and many middle and small size firms. This is the sector with the widest networks of regional offices. These firms also nearly dominate the management consultancy sector now, although post-Enron, consultancy and accountancy services have broken up in terms of fee income.

Advertising was the first sector to operate on a global basis due to early demand from MNCs. The large conglomerates demonstrate constant global restructuring, consolidation and disaggregation due to intense competition and rivalry among firms. The two main European creative clusters are London and Paris but advertising services have the greatest requirement of all sectors for local interpretation – hence networks, based in major cities, extend across North West Europe.

The design sector seems to be the least globalized of all eight POLYNET sectors. Architecture and planning services are dominated by small and medium size practices, local in scope while often servicing clients nationally as well as regionally. But in the UK there are also some very large multi-disciplinary practices incorporating civil engineering, planning, architecture, surveying and property consultancy.

In all MCRs, logistics operates on an entirely different locational basis. Logistics services have to be available literally everywhere. Advanced coordination functions are located on the basis of physical infrastructure nodes while communication through networks is virtual. Respondents have described this as the most 'global-local' sector and the most virtualized. The sector has been adapting continuously through consolidation to create a seamless, pan-European or global service.

Consolidation and restructuring are likely to be ongoing processes, but what will be the likely effects for the different urban structures of the MCRs?

On the world scale, major APS concentrations have occurred in only a few selected 'global cities'. Within Europe, London is regarded as the international business services platform, particularly for wholesale activity, while other POLYNET First Cities play the role of 'regional centres' for global service networks, allowing firms to access the expanding EU market and 'articulating' the MCRs into the global city network.

Nor does this seem likely to change. Matrix management and virtual communications make it technically possible for firms to disperse geographically, yet all the evidence from POLYNET suggests that a process of concentration is continuing within global networks across North West Europe.

There is evidence of the dispersal of some 'back-office' functions in some MCRs to reduce costs, either locally within a region or to more distant locations like Eastern Europe or Asia. But interviews showed that such outsourcing could operate in tandem with functional re-concentration. Cost savings may be outweighed by loss of quality and management control and political risk. Paradoxically, alongside the evidence on dispersion, continuing concentration of front-office high-value, high-complexity and strategic decision-making functions is seen as crucial in London. Indeed, evidence from across all the MCRs confirms the continuing need for concentration of global firms in spite of developments in information and communication technology (ICT) and management methods.

The explanation is the vital need for innovation, creativity and the production of new ideas. Ideas and skills are 'transferred through the network'. Specialization leads to a concentration of skills in a few centres but also to the dispersal of knowledge products for use globally. Close proximity of universities and technical colleges is seen as important for knowledge production, though increasingly, skills cannot be learned in traditional educational establishments.

First Cities have a key role as information nodes and are consistently described as 'information gateways', 'global articulators' and in similar terms. London's global concentration gives it a special role as a European information hub. First Cities have distinct forms of 'knowledge milieu'. But this varies: Frankfurt for instance is not generally regarded as having the right 'ingredients' for creative production.

In international networks, innovation and knowledge production come from intense interaction within the network and, importantly, from interaction with competitors and clients. Interviews in all the regions highlight the advantages of concentrated locations allowing close proximity to many actors. In London and Paris, inter-firm competition and cooperation go hand in hand. Larger firms, servicing a wide range of corporate and institutional clients, at times work together in multi-disciplinary teams and provide services and advice to each other. These interrelationships are important for information and knowledge exchange, but the flows taking place are not easily identified or quantifiable.

Consolidation and restructuring allow more specialisms to be brought into networks. Equally, disaggregation through de-merger and the creation of new alliances creates new specializations. Both trends allow the transfer of skills and knowledge and promote innovation – but, again, actual flows are difficult to measure.

Inter-office relationships are also increasingly complex. A French bank undertakes back-office functions for an overseas operation in London at night to achieve optimal cost-effectiveness. Two German banks operate virtual offices between Frankfurt and London, sharing information and knowledge.

So there is a paradox. Technology facilitates new modes of organization which achieve greater operational efficiency. In some important respects, these could make geography appear irrelevant. Yet firms still emphasize the importance of concentration, because their key raw material is fresh knowledge – and in its generation and transmission, traditional face-to-face communication still plays a vital role. In Chapter 7, we turn to look more closely at the role of communication technology in the 'space of flows' and its locational significance.

Note

1 The most senior managers were interviewed where possible as they are most likely to have an overview of changes and leading edge developments within their firm and business sector.

7

Flows and Relationships: Internal and External Linkages

Kathy Pain and Peter Hall

Advanced producer services (APS) companies have been profoundly affected in their daily worldwide operations by the rapidly increasing scale and scope of operation and competition, in particular by processes resulting from globalization. That is clear from the interviews with key industry players, reported in Chapter 6. But these impacts have been mediated and, to no small degree, triggered by equally rapid and revolutionary advances in the technology of information generation and exchange. The POLYNET interviews have thrown new light on these changing patterns, in particular their significance for the location of APS companies within the mega-city regions (MCRs).

The big change in the last decade, noted in all regions, is the massive rise in electronic and virtual communications. E-mail and intranet are major communication modes but are used more for internal communications, within APS networks, than external communications. But, as will be seen later in this chapter, traditional face-to-face contacts still retain a critical importance and have profound locational consequences.

Virtual communications: Internal

The interview results on business communications are largely consistent across the POLYNET study, albeit with different behaviour patterns reflecting the variations in regional APS processes and structures, discussed in the previous chapter. The modal split between different kinds of communication varies according to whether communications are internal or external, size of firm, type of service and nature of market. Here the main conclusions are summarized, starting with internal communication within the company.

E-mail

E-mail is the key mode in terms of volume and is replacing fax. The estimated modal split of a chief executive officer (CEO) in a Rhine-Main design consultancy is representative of the whole MCR cross-sectoral interview sample: '60 per cent e-mail, 30 per cent telephone and 10 per cent for written communication of all sorts' (Design, Rhine-Main). While telephone remains very important, and is used intensively in some cases, e-mail is 'a big one these days'; 'Increasingly people carry very little stuff on paper any more. If it's not in the [computer] system, you probably haven't got it' (Management consulting, Greater Dublin).

The important benefits of e-mail include the ability to communicate and send information and data quickly and asynchronously across time zones anywhere in the world, together with ease of large-scale data storage. But a major disadvantage is managing the increasing volume of communications, many of which are unwanted, including spam. Many senior managers now use a personal assistant (PA) to manage their in-box as flagged in the discussion of e-mail in Chapter 5. A senior decision-maker in insurance in the Paris Region, for example, receives over 100 e-mails a day and does not access these until his PA has sorted them. London interviews revealed this to be a common practice among top global business decision-makers in the City of London. Simple volumes of e-mail flows are therefore a poor indicator of the value of interactions between recipient in-boxes.

Intranet

Intranet is used by small as well as large companies which have wide area networks (WANs) to communicate on an international scale. The majority of firms interviewed in South East England had some form of intranet activity.

Knowledge management systems, such as shared electronic databases and internal diaries, are in widespread use. Network size is a key factor in firms' ability to invest in and benefit from advanced information and communication technology (ICT) applications. Larger APS networks are able to make a greater investment in hardware, software and technical support, with competitive advantages in terms of access to information and knowledge exchange. Dedicated lines, with shared back-up practices, are used to achieve security of data transfer in the law, banking and accountancy sectors. Potential benefits are illustrated by an example in the Randstad:

We have a knowledge system in which all firms and employees are connected. With simple search operations we can worldwide find people specialized in cases concerning energy companies for example, which makes team formation easy and quickly possible (Design, The Randstad).

A design firm in South East England illustrates the way in which resources, skills and knowledge can be pooled and accessed across a global office network:

They're not running a library out in Australia because we're running it here. So they've got access to all our documentation, all our resources, reference material, archives and everything else … our picture libraries … are all held here because our server is much, much more powerful than theirs (Design, South East England).

The benefits, in terms of volume and quality of information flows, are greater in larger firms that include more specialisms and skills across their office networks, but even small firms gain advantages. In Central Belgium, for example, the internet and data processing standardization effectively reduces the physical distance between regional insurance brokers and headquarters offices. In RhineRuhr, collaborative tools such as whiteboards, chats or instant messaging are widely used. Clearly it would be extremely difficult to quantify the volume or value of information and knowledge exchanges associated with this mode across space.

Telephone

Telephone remains a key mode: it is considered quicker and more personal than e-mail. A company chairman in the Paris Region exchanges around 30 to 40 phone calls a day, while the regional director of a bank can 'spend his working days talking on the phone' (Banking, Paris Region).

Video-conferencing

Video-conferencing is generally seen as a way of reducing travel costs for large firms but installation costs are expensive for small firms. Respondents show that this mode is mostly used across the regions, and some firms use it extensively for long-distance communications at management level.

Examples of low use are EMR (European Metropolitan Region) Northern Switzerland, because of the high cost, especially for small companies, and Rhine-Main, where video-conferencing is little used even when expensive equipment has been installed. For some interviewees 'there is no added benefit of the technique compared to traditional telephone calls or telephone conferences'; face-to-face communications are preferred. In South East England, out of the total sample of firms interviewed in centres outside London who had used video-conferencing, most saw it negatively. Complaints mainly centred on limitations of the technology.

South East England evidence shows that video-conferencing is largely used by firms operating at the European and global scopes. Examples of high users interviewed in the region are in the accountancy, banking/finance and law sectors. A US investment banker based in London is convinced that the technology is advancing fast and will reduce long-distance travel for meetings further. Two firms interviewed in South East England use inexpensive web cams for one-to-one video-conferencing, one of which uses this for communications with their offices in New Zealand as well as within the UK.

In Central Belgium, video-conferencing is commonly used in the law, management consultancy and informatics sector (in the last case this includes its use in communications with clients). Greater Dublin also reports common use of this mode among firms interviewed. Video-conferencing is almost exclusively used for internal international communications/management functions and it is possible that this could be linked to the relatively large presence of foreign banks in Dublin but a similar link is not found in Rhine-Main.

Examples of firms using video-conferencing in the Paris Region include an insurance company which uses video-conferencing in its national office network and a leading design consultancy at La Défense that has an entire floor equipped for international video-conferencing. Similarly in London, a bank headquartered in Edinburgh and a Rhine-Main headquartered bank, both of which have key offices in the City of London, use video-conferencing for regular weekly communications between a large number of staff without the need of expensive and time-consuming travel between offices.

Conference calls

Telephone conference calls are fairly widely used for internal communications between offices when two or more people need to communicate at the same time. One major insurance company in South East England uses international conferencing with Europe on a daily basis. Video-conferencing and telephone conference calls facilitate long-distance communications within a network which would often not otherwise take place, thereby increasing the volume of distance communications. But although both modes create a 'virtual office space' and facilitate remote working, neither is regarded as a substitute for personal face-to-face contact.

Virtual communications: External

While e-mail facilitates interaction, face-to-face meetings, supported by a great volume of telephone contact, are regarded as vital for external communications. In banking, e-commerce is a key platform for cross-border market reach for the volume of customers but valued contacts require face-to-face interaction. Nevertheless, other electronic modes promote distance interaction.

Extranet

Extranet is not generally discussed by interviewees, and interview evidence shows that it is not widely used in South East England. When it is used, this is generally for contact with high-value business customers as a supplement to face-to-face contact and for customer convenience. One interesting example of knowledge exchange between a firm and its clients through extranet is that of a logistics firm in which: 'A lot of our sites are actually customer systems – so some customers have our systems in their business and vice versa' (Logistics, South East England). But, as the Swiss team comment: 'When it comes to gaining new contacts and keeping them, face-to-face contact has not been replaced by telecommunications' (Glanzmann et al, 2005, p12).

Electronic documents and fax

Interviews in London suggest that fax is still used to transmit documents speedily, if these are not available in e-format, for example, in legal services work. And in Rhine-Main, printed materials, for example, in the communications sector, are still physically transported when a firm wants a message to get the focused attention of a recipient. However, only three interviewees in the South East England interviews mentioned fax as a communication mode and this was to say that their use had greatly declined with their increasing use of e-mail.

In general, electronic documents are replacing paper except in the case of the law, accountancy and insurance sectors, but even in these sectors the situation may be changing:

As to the clients, there is still a lot of paper involved in decisions and in tax returns ... of course more and more correspondence happens via e-mail. That is increasing. We have a client letter, that we have expanded by an e-mail newsletter – that is slowly increasing (*Accountancy, Rhine-Main*).

Yet in London, one of the big four accountancy firms is working towards being an entirely 'paperless office'.[1]

Mobile technologies

Ongoing development of mobile technologies – mobile phones, laptop computers and mobile internet such as 'Blackberries' – allow communication flows to continue even while business people are travelling, facilitating mobility: 'Internet has ended the inconvenience of distance' (Accountancy, Paris Region). Other Paris Region comments, from three different advertising agencies, highlight the diminishing importance of geographical distance in APS:

My objective is to always be available in less than 20 minutes to a client, wherever I am... Time proximity is much more important than actual geographic proximity (*Advertising, Paris Region*).

A client has got to be able to contact me within 24 hours. What matters is not physical proximity but psychological proximity (*Advertising, Paris Region*).

What keeps together all the many offices of [the firm] is not workers' mobility, nor common business projects but ICTs as all our virtual tools are shared, from intranet websites to all the databases (*Advertising, Paris Region*).

Electronic communication has in some ways made geographical distance irrelevant – and this, in theory, should encourage the dispersal of functions from the central zones of North West European APS hubs. Yet there is no evidence for the dispersal of key decision-making functions.

Irish financial services interviews provide a good example. A decentralized customer services centre in the Dublin hinterland handles the bulk of customer relations nationwide, yet customer phone calls and letters still pass through Dublin before being processed at the dispersed location. Electronic communications allow the Dublin 'hub' or 'node' to connect into the international space of financial services flows, but the intensity of its linkages within the region are limited. On the other hand, one example was found of a European scope APS firm located outside Dublin which has virtual communication flows that bypass the First City. Another example is that of a regional scope firm in the MCR that outsources certain technological support work to India:

We get that done in India and we have never seen … in fact one of the firms we deal with, we've never spoken to them. All I have ever done is to communicate with them by e-mail (Design, Greater Dublin).

In South East England, there are many examples of offices outside London that are highly connected to global networks through e-mail, phone, intranet and other modes. Yet, on a pan-North West European scale, command-and-control functions for international services remain concentrated in London, facilitated by the co-presence of electronic connectivity and physical concentration. The use of virtual modes has not caused functions that require proximity to move away from clustered central London locations.

What is not clear is how it would be possible to quantify and compare both the volume and value of flows, associated with service networks, across space. Chapter 5 already showed the difficulties of obtaining any raw quantitative data on flows, quite apart from the difficulty of evaluating the value of the communications. Of the virtual modes discussed, telephone, video and telephone conferencing and fax may offer most potential for reasonably accurate measurement; but less easily measurable e-mail and intranet modes are likely to be the most important modes for intense information and knowledge exchange.

However, it is important to remember that the firms interviewed across the study see virtual communications as complementary to face-to-face contact: face-to-face contact is the most highly-valued mode of interaction of all. Electronic communications are seen as complementing but not substituting for face-to-face contact. Conversely, enhanced electronic communication is regarded as having increased the need for face-to-face contact. Hence, the need for concentration is in some ways diminished by web and intranet communication. For example, there is less need for insurance brokers to be located near to headquarters. But the overwhelming view emerging from the interview reports replicates the conclusion in the Central Belgium report: 'information highways will never replace physical highways'.

The next section considers why face-to-face contact and meetings remain so important.

Face-to-face contact and locational proximity

The critical importance of close proximity for face-to-face contact in APS services hinges on the absolute need to establish personal relationships and mutual trust between different actors – between staff and clients, within front-office teams and with other firms. There are some variations in the results between regions as to the degree of proximity to other actors required by different sectors, which seem to reflect the location, size and scope of firms interviewed in the different cases. It is not possible to cover all specific combinations, but some common principles apply across the study and are described here.

The focus on relationships is a top priority for all firms in all regions, but the need for physical closeness between different actors varies within a given MCR, according to the type of business activity and the market level at which firms are operating. In RhineRuhr, for example, the frequency and intensity of external communication is reported to vary from regular to rare.

At the regional scale of operations, purely regional players need to be very close to the client at a local level. Membership of local institutions and clubs and personal relationships are prioritized. Regional offices are connected through their networks but face-to-face contact between these offices is infrequent: it is the client relationship that matters. The frequency of face-to-face contact seems to be related to spatial proximity. A manager of a regional practice in Greater Dublin claims that: 'Part of the reason we would be employed [locally] is because we are able to instigate that face-to-face contact' (Design, Greater Dublin).

Relationships for firms operating at the international level, and located in the 'First' or other major centres, are regarded as more formally and less personally based; here, close proximity to other service providers becomes as important as proximity to clients. First City central business districts (CBDs) are described as 'a big village' for the business community, both in Dublin and in London. This is the 'village' some regional firms join when they take offices in these larger cities:

When you live in the village you meet people in the village and it's good for business and you keep your face and your name and the contact going and we need to be kind of where the action is (Management consulting, Greater Dublin).

In Dublin, senior managers in design consulting and advertising perceived the CBD as displaying 'a cluster effect'. When asked about the current advantages of their location, most managers prioritized two key factors – proximity to and accessibility by their clients and accessibility for staff including, importantly, their senior managers.

A slightly different grouping is the regional offices of global scope firms. Back-offices have little need for local relationships, other than for labour recruitment purposes, but 'branch' offices require close relationships in the regional business community (where they compete for clients with pure regional scope firms), as well as having important contact with other branches, head office and 'the network'.

Co-location

Spatial compactness is highly valued by firms located in the most concentrated First City global APS clusters. There are powerful reasons for co-location: the presence of a large number of clients, institutions, information technology (IT) infrastructure, skills and depth of labour market. But agglomeration economies in these highly centralized clusters include accessibility to other service providers and what seems to be a form of 'city capital' – an intensity of personal exchanges derived from interrelationships between firms. London interviews show that presence in centralized clusters, and proximity to them, reflect the importance of this form of social capital for particular services and markets.

In some sectors a 'network of personal contacts' and 'tight relationship' with other firms is reported to be critical – as in the case of two accountancy firms in Greater Dublin. In London, the most senior decision-makers in international networks emphasize the importance of very close proximity to related business services which are sometimes both service providers to, and clients of, each other. These relationships, founded on a mutuality of interests, are particularly noted in banking, financial and legal services and in other services that are located in the City (the Square Mile). For example, accountancy firms located within – or on the edge of – the Square Mile willingly pay the high price for their locations because proximity to the most dense APS infrastructure is critical for their business. Equally, legal services firms located between the Square Mile and the law courts and 'West End' strike a balance between requirements for proximity to concentrations of different actors.

Clustered locations centralize the most high-skilled, high-value and strategic decision-making and management control functions and are said to be absolutely necessary for the operation of multi-disciplinary, multi-firm client teams in London. In legal services in RhineRuhr, the same point is made:

The individual, professional and geographical proximity is important for us. If a case affects several law segments or sectors we compose teams from different praxis groups and, by request, we include other consultants within our teams (Law, RhineRuhr).

Close working between firms takes place in the financial services sector in Zürich and in London and is described as playing a crucial role in inter-sector relationships. In Zürich, financial services have the most frequent and significant business relationships of all the sectors investigated, due to their role as company financiers and financial advisers. In London, banks (particularly US investment banks) are reported to have a central 'anchor' role in the City APS cluster. Continental European banks interviewed in the Square Mile see their presence in the cluster as an essential 'training camp' for innovation and transfer of skills and knowledge through their domestic or international networks.

In management consulting and design, the importance of closeness to major clients seems to take rather more precedence over closeness to other service providers – and in advertising, closeness to suppliers in the media sector is reported as very important. Logistics is different from all other APS sectors: very little proximity to clients and other services is reported, helping to explain the unclustered locational strategy noted in this sector in all regions as reported in the previous chapter.

Face-to-face contact

Regular face-to-face contact facilitates both formal and informal relationship-building and is regarded as: 'impossible to replace' (Accountancy, Greater Dublin) in all regions. Face-to-face contact is prioritized at certain stages of the client relationship and project development, including initial and key project stages, and also during multi-firm team work on client projects. The importance of 'seeing the colour of their eyes' is often repeated in interviews. A financial services manager in the Paris Region describes the extra-economic nature of business relations: 'Finance is a story of men. You have to see each other'. Small firms in particular, aim to develop long-term client relationships in what is commonly described by management consultancies as 'people business' and cultural and social factors seem to be important in this process.

Similarly, being close to other service providers has much greater significance than ease of physical access by foot. Geographical situation has value for interrelationships: 'It's the eye to eye contact, the continuous contact, the chemistry' (Banking, London).

It is to do with building trust and whether someone can deal with me or not. The other side is that we want to meet the client, as we can't analyse him completely, if we haven't spoken to him, haven't seen him in his own surroundings (Management consulting, Rhine-Main).

Trust is an essential factor for cooperation in the most high-value exchanges which are: 'knowledge intensive, individual and incapable of standardisation, which applies to all advanced producer services' (Glanzmann et al, 2005, p12).

Because of this, local proximity is highly valued for regular and spontaneous face-to-face contact in situations and gatherings appropriate to the culture in each MCR. In Paris, for example, business lunches are reported to be one of the ways to achieve a long-term relationship with a customer. In the logistics sector in RhineRuhr, *Stammtische* (round tables) have become popular events for informal relationships between intersectoral actors:

It is no longer necessary to play golf, if you want to make and cultivate contacts, you can just go to a Logistics Stammtisch, where you sit in a snuggish pub, meet nice people and can also talk about business *(Logistics, RhineRuhr)*.

High-value, high-complexity functions also require regular face-to-face contact between skilled staff and specialist teams in which close working is seen as highly important for innovation. This makes home-working an occasional activity for most staff working in highly clustered locations, although hot-desking takes place because of the requirements for very frequent travel for some staff. Physical presence in central offices varies, as shown by a Rhine-Main example:

The range is wide. We have investment bankers who are on the road five days a week and we have investment bankers who are on the road seven days a week and worldwide. And at the same time we have customer service workers in, for example, Aschaffenburg who are never away from the office *(Banking/finance, Rhine-Main)*.

International scope banks in London describe operating a 'virtual office' in which their front-office 'people' can be located anywhere in the network at a given time as in the case of a senior manager in a German bank interviewed in London: 'I'm basically someone who works in both centres'.

Home-working
Although some staff travel extensively, face-to-face contact within one office is in most cases regarded as essential. Some home-working takes place but is not reported as important except in the case of the management consultancy sector and in the Randstad. In the Randstad, mobile internet devices such as the 'Blackberry' are now used by many employees in law firms:

We're very confident about Blackberries. Many employees working part-time at home because of young children can stay in close contact with the office *(Law, the Randstad)*.

Home-working is noted in Central Belgium in the management consultancy sector where employees need to be close to clients. The same pattern was identified in the Rhine-Main where:

Everyone in our company has the possibility to work at home. There is a remote access to the whole system… Our employees are doing much of their work weekends or in the evening. As our locations are all continents our employees are working round the clock, day and night for the firm *(Management consulting, Rhine-Main)*.

In contrast, in advertising and accountancy there is very little home-working. In the case of advertising this is because 'It's a team job with a lot of brainstorming and close contact with colleagues' (Advertising, Rhine-Main). But in accountancy, the Belgian team noted, the reason is the confidential nature of the work.

Business meetings and travel
The need for frequent face-to-face contact leads to increasing travel wherever offices are not in close proximity or walking distance. At the regional level, travel for meetings is essential and frequent, and takes place mainly by car in all MCRs. For international scope firms, regular management meetings are required on different spatial scales and may take place at regional and national head offices in a variety of network locations. Meetings involving a variety of actors from different global locations also often now take place near to airports as well as at central city headquarters (HQ). Project based meetings are dependent on the stage of transactions and on the stage of client relationship development. In London, frequent meetings are reported to be especially important when setting up and closing deals and at other strategic project stages when working in big multi-firm teams. Logistics again differs in this respect, apparently requiring less face-to-face contact with clients, though in South East England, strategic client meetings are held in London.

This need for close face-to-face contact alongside e-communications, described as 'hi-tech, hi-touch' in London management consultancy, is a key reason for continuing central city clustering making efficient long-distance travel essential to develop and maintain relationships at the international scale. Interviews in the Paris Region make this point:

Direct contact remains indispensable. ICT technologies are practical but can only be complementary *(Design, Paris Region)*.

Some things cannot be sensed through a phone call. You have to see your interlocutor *(Insurance, Paris Region)*.

Nowadays anything can be done at a distance. Yet we have a golden rule: nothing is discussed via the internet. Information can be transferred thanks to e-mails but discussion deserves face-to-face *(Advertising, Paris Region)*.

While high-volume basic information exchange now takes place through e-contact, high-value knowledge exchange takes place through face-to-face contact. In the next section, the consequences for transport networks and infrastructure – road, rail, metro, air and transport hubs – in the MCRs are considered.

Travel and transport

In all regions and in most APS sectors there is clear evidence of the vital importance of mobility for front-office, client-facing staff, both within the regions and at an international scale. Across the study there are examples of high levels of mobility for face-to-face meetings and work which must cut across commuting patterns; in fact, for some staff, it appears that the nature of their work may make a regular daily commuting pattern impossible. This relates to people working chiefly within one MCR, or on a national basis, who have to make frequent journeys to clients in a variety of locations, and to staff in international firms who make regular trips abroad.

One major banking and finance firm in South East England revealed that within the firm such staff are referred to as 'gypsies'. A London example is a banker who travelled to New York, Zürich, Paris, Tokyo, Hong Kong, Buenos Aries, São Paulo and Miami in just three working weeks. Another increasing phenomenon is staff who are based in two or more offices and maintain a regular presence in each, for example, a senior executive interviewed working in London, runs a worldwide company based in New York and commutes to London from his home in Frankfurt on a weekly basis. The following interview extracts illustrate the prevalence of a variety of business travel patterns:

Computers have eliminated many problems but not all; there need to be as many meetings as before (Insurance, Paris Region).

I spend a day a week in the office. Typical week, take this week as an example … yesterday I was up in Birmingham, today I'm in the office, tomorrow I'm in Doncaster, Friday I'm in Swindon (Logistics, South East England).

Sixty per cent of our staff will be out for more than 80 per cent of their time (Accountancy, South East England).

In a situation of an important closing, it could be possible we are moving a team for a month to New York or London (Law, the Randstad).

People move around inside those client teams. So if something big has to be rolled out across the world, well probably lots of Brits will move around with it (Management consultancy, London).

All of the big networks now can service any client pretty much in any location anywhere – certainly in Europe (Advertising, London).

I work on the train you know, you just move into a mindset of Virgin from Edinburgh to Liverpool is my office today (Management consulting, South East England).

Our skills are brought from all over Europe to London. We see London as the hub of our European network so the skills fly in and fly out and go to where the clients are (Banking, London).

[One client] works in London, lives in York and picks up information about his file from his extranet on his laptop on the way between York and London (Law, South East England).

Implications for transport infrastructure

The long-term importance of good transport infrastructure is emphasized across all the MCRs, but the level of satisfaction with existing infrastructure varies significantly from region to region. An interview in the Randstad demonstrates that 'time-distance', as opposed to geographical distance, is the major accessibility issue:

As I am living in a small city near Utrecht, travelling by car to Brussels is much faster. When going to Paris everybody in the office makes use of aeroplanes from Schiphol airport. In time this can never be beaten by train (Finance, the Randstad).

Across the study, particularly important modes include: for secondary centres, regional infrastructure, motorways and fast rail; and for First and other major cities, intra-urban and international accessibility. Specific reported deficiencies are presented in the regional reports, but brief summaries for each MCR are listed below. What is clear is that failure to continue to invest in transport infrastructure could prove the big stumbling block for future APS regional growth, as inefficiencies are a barrier to the most important form of regional knowledge flow: highly-skilled staff travelling into, out of and within the regions for face-to-face contact.

South East England: transport infrastructure is seen as a key issue in South East England. In London the urgent problems are the need for improvement to the Underground, commuter rail services, central London traffic congestion and investment in the east–west Crossrail line to connect the City to Heathrow international airport. In the rest of the region, improvements to road and rail infrastructure and parking facilities are needed, with specific issues quoted in each of the eight urban centres studied.

The Randstad: public transport is generally regarded as impractical, especially when travelling to several locations within one day; saving time is the key determinant of mode. Business destinations are frequently not within easy reach of the main train stations that provide inter-city services, and travel by train, bus, tram and underground, is not regarded as a pleasure. Travel within The Netherlands is most often by car and, for international journeys, Schiphol is the most popular airport. In the south and east of the MCR, Rotterdam and Düsseldorf airports respectively, are also used.

Central Belgium: existing transport infrastructure requires improvement. Commuting into and out of cities and city traffic congestion are both seen as a drawback for business. TGV (Train à Grande Vitesse) lines to The Netherlands and Germany are needed but there is a perceived lack of state investment in infrastructure.

RhineRuhr: internal accessibility is relatively good by road and rail but public transport systems need better integration. Rail travel involves delays due to the large number of centres requiring station stops and there are traffic bottlenecks on motorways. Long journeys are quicker by car. Relatively poor international accessibility by air is a disadvantage for the region and particularly for Düsseldorf and Cologne.

Rhine-Main: transport infrastructure within the MCR is seen as good for air, rail and road but car is the most common mode for business travel because of its flexibility and because it saves time. That it provides privacy for making telephone calls en route is also seen as an advantage. Train is used to some extent for regional travel and to other major German cities outside the region and it has been suggested that development of high-speed rail links could expand the boundary of the functional MCR.

EMR Northern Switzerland: the rail and road transport system is seen as very good but improved transport infrastructure, linking the region's city centres to one another, is seen as a way of enhancing Zürich's gateway city role. Road and rail infrastructure in Zürich is seen as approaching the limits of its capacity. Airport development is required to maintain international capacity but there are noise pollution implications.

Paris Region: few professional trips occur between secondary urban centres; the concerns are accessibility to Paris and national and international travel. For many international firms based in Paris, trips to other European First Cities are weekly, with London, Brussels and Amsterdam being mentioned often in the interviews.

Greater Dublin: inadequate transport infrastructure is identified as one of the biggest challenges for the MCR, particularly public transport infrastructure. APS related flows between Dublin and Belfast appear limited; both cities have stronger transport links with the outside world, including London, than with each other.

Conclusion: The continuing importance of physical accessibility

The evidence from all the MCRs indicates that business efficiency and quality of life are both damaged by poor accessibility. In general First Cities have the best connectivity to transport infrastructures for all modes – car, train and air – nationally and internationally. The implications of the evidence on virtual communications and physical movement for linkages and flows in the regions are now summarized.

The evidence on e-communication, presented above, demonstrates the challenges of accurate measurement of virtual information flows and knowledge transfer.

E-mail is identified as the most regularly used and highest-volume APS communication mode, but the total number of e-mails sent and received clearly bears little relation to the actual number of flows that finally reach, and have value for, intended recipients. Telephone calls are a second important mode in terms of volume and, interview evidence suggests that the 'information value' of calls is likely to be generally high, as this mode is regarded as a substitute for face-to-face contact. However, even here, as in the case of e-mail, calls are directed through and screened by PAs. Calls within office networks are typically internal as is the use of intranet and other data sharing systems, making these exchanges 'invisible' to external observers. Hence in all cases, the cooperation of individual communicants is needed to quantify the volume of actual and usable flows received via these different modes.

The POLYNET web survey attempted to gain the cooperation of senior decision-makers in such a study but – as explained in Chapter 5 – this was largely unsuccessful and a very low number of useful responses to the survey was achieved. Although the interview evidence, described in this report, does not allow us to quantify the volume of flows between APS centres in the study, it does provide valuable insights into the geography of information and knowledge flows that pass between and through APS networks in the MCRs.

The interview evidence on the importance of face-to-face contact in these 'knowledge services' suggests that highly-clustered CBDs of globally connected First Cities, and travel between them, are the most important means by which highly specialized knowledge is transferred within and between cross-border APS networks. The position of the First Cities of each MCR in functional international APS networks therefore powerfully links them together in terms of information and knowledge transfer.

The costs of labour, property and servicing are high in these centres, yet the largest international firms continue to concentrate strategic decision-making functions and expertise there. Evidence indicates that functions that are dispersed either to the edge of larger cities or to other less clustered regional locations do not require close proximity and agglomeration advantages to remain competitive, but others do. The need for continuing concentration of services in Central Belgium to address existing inefficiencies associated with too much geographic dispersal is made strongly in interviews.

Evidence on phone calls made by firms in the Paris Region shows the intensity of information exchanges in the dense central part of the city and a concentration of interactions that mirrors physical concentration there. The web survey evidence for Greater Dublin illustrates the strong linkages found in the interviews in central Dublin and strong international links with the UK, especially London, the rest of Europe and, to a lesser extent, Hong Kong in East Asia. Links between the Greater Dublin MCR and the rest of Ireland appear relatively unimportant.

Similarly, evidence from the Randstad and EMR Northern Switzerland shows how, for multi-national oriented service firms, the importance of international links and good accessibility prove critical. Yet SMEs (small and medium size enterprises) have extensive national networks and are shown to have a great deal of interaction in EMR Northern Switzerland at the local/regional level

suggesting the potential for development of a 'regional added-value system'. South East England seems to have the most notable evidence of the existence of just such a regional system.

Accessibility is clearly a key issue for the development of inter-city linkages at the international and intra-regional levels. Evidence on the complementary nature of virtual and face-to-face communications in the RhineRuhr suggests that accessibility needs to go beyond the concept of 'time-space' to include 'organizational proximity'. In terms of physical travel, 'time-distance' takes precedence over geographical distance for interviewees, while transport infrastructure itself increasingly becomes a locus for virtual information and knowledge exchange.

Finally, the RhineRuhr evidence shows how 'to a large degree, the evolving infrastructure of the internet is reinforcing old patterns of agglomeration' (Knapp et al, 2005, p14). 'Connectivity agglomeration' has become an asset of APS networked cities which are literally 'e-gateways' for the MCRs.

Thus physical and virtual spaces are clearly intertwined in the pattern of connectivity both within and between regions. And this relationship is complex: despite revolutionary changes in remote communication, it appears that physical proximity and accessibility continue to retain all their old importance for information transfer, or even to enhance it. In Chapter 8, interdependencies between the 'space of flows' and the 'space of places' in the MCRs will be further examined.

Note

1   See Chapter 6, p95.

8

People and Places: Interrelating the 'Space of Flows' and the 'Space of Places'

Kathy Pain and Peter Hall

The various elements discussed in the last two chapters – spatial scale, corporate organization and the technology of communication – interact in complex ways to shape the location of knowledge-based advanced producer services (APS) and thus the urban spatial organization of the mega-city regions (MCRs). In seeking to understand these interactions more precisely, we need now to look more closely at the factors that firms find most important for competitive success. Our interviews give a wealth of information on this subject; in this chapter we present the most important conclusions.

Skills and space

The most important conclusion is the critical role of people. APS businesses handle knowledge: knowledge is both their raw material and their finished product, and is thus the only source of their competitive success. And this knowledge, however exchanged, is embedded in the heads of the people they employ. How they recruit their workers, what attracts these people to one city rather than another, what are seen as the key factors underlying their rapid and instant access to new knowledge, are all crucial to such firms' performance and ultimately their survival.

So access to skilled and specialized labour emerges from the interviews as a key determinant of where firms locate within the MCRs. (This finding is supported by the web survey results from Chapter 5, which showed access to skilled labour to be one of the two main office location factors, the other being access to clients.) So important are they, that in the Paris Region skilled employees are referred to as 'collaborators' or 'partners'. One Paris interviewee

goes so far as to refer to his staff as his 'gold nuggets'. In London interviews, employees are generally referred to as 'our people'. Elsewhere firms stress the key importance of highly skilled labour which 'creates more value-added'. Flexible and creative working are regarded as 'among the most sought-after attributes'.

Where young skilled people and senior business decision-makers want to live, and to work, thus becomes a crucial determinant of the geography of the regional knowledge economy. Highly skilled professionals in international firms are attracted to particular major cities, especially to the First Cities of each POLYNET region. The locational preferences of APS workers and the location of firms are clearly 'two sides of one coin' and are mutually reinforcing processes. In Paris and Dublin, labour supply and demand interdependencies are described as a 'lock-in' through which labour and firms are tied to the First Cities.

Recruitment and labour markets

Firms in all the regions see it as important to be close to universities and colleges which form the sources of their labour supply but they recruit regionally and nationally for skilled jobs from the top institutions. In the Paris Region, this means that domestic recruitment is in practice dominated by the region itself, because prestigious universities and schools are geographically concentrated there.

But in addition, there is evidence that the specialist skills required by advanced business services cannot simply be acquired through formal education; they have to be acquired on the job. An EMR (European Metropolitan Region) Northern Switzerland interviewee explains that 'Tailor-made employees … are rarely found on the labour market'. The ability 'to adapt quickly to new methods and gain new practical knowledge' is more important than specific education and training:

Universities can only generate basic knowledge. But in our business (re-insurance) implicit or passive knowledge is absolutely necessary. It's only the firms themselves, that can teach those kinds of skills *(Insurance, EMR Northern Switzerland)*.

In London one City law firm explains how they 'cherry-pick' top graduates from leading UK universities and train staff 'on the job' to their own specific business requirements.

The scale of recruitment also depends on the specific skills required. Specialized skills and top management positions are recruited on a global scale: 'For really highly qualified people in many areas, you have to look worldwide' (Management consulting, Rhine-Main). Whereas SMEs (small and medium size enterprises) generally recruit locally without difficulty in all the regions, larger firms operating in international and global scope networks compete for highly skilled labour, compelling them to recruit in an 'elite international labour market' to attain the skills they need. Even at the level of the international labour market, a major management consultancy interviewed in London reports a serious global shortage of skills.

Innovation and labour diversity

However, the internationalization of labour is not simply an outcome of a shortage of supply; for firms in some sectors, cultural mixing is considered an important business asset and a form of 'knowledge capital'. Paris Region interviews suggest that multi-cultural teams bring 'freshness' into a firm, promote knowledge transfers from other countries and allow the development of more global approaches. A diversified labour market is said to 'facilitate encounters, it reinforces potential connections and it maximizes knowledge production'; 'the social capital that represents the sum of all the workers' networks is a source of agglomeration economies for producer services firms' (Halbert, 2005b, p12). In one firm interviewed in Paris, of 12 staff working in capital fund management, only two are French. Similarly, in London, a US investment bank has 'focused on [diversity] in the trading rooms since 10 years ago and they finally did it corporately'. A main reason was 'to do business in Europe' (Potts and Pain, 2005, p24). In some sectors, Amsterdam is also seen as benefiting from worldwide interactions through the internationalization of labour.

Across the study, First Cities are reported as having the highest, or sometimes the only, concentration of highly-skilled international labour in each region. Secondary centres, critically, lack this advantage of depth of 'skills

with diversity'. For example, in the Randstad, architecture, which is concentrated in both Rotterdam and Amsterdam, is reported to be highly dependent on international creative labour: 'We have many international projects. Dutch employees in proportion to foreign employees are about 20:80' (Design, the Randstad). But here, Amsterdam is the only city 'with a considerable international workforce', which in this case also includes advertising and finance, both of which are concentrated in Amsterdam.

Reasons for concentration

The reason that firms in First Cities report an extreme reluctance to change office location is to a large extent explained by the need to retain their workforce. One Dublin respondent says that moving would be 'suicide in this business'. In Paris and London the precise location of firms in each city is in fact closely related to where high-skilled labour and senior managers wish to work and can conveniently commute. For example, most highly qualified professionals live in the city of Paris and in the neighbouring western part of the Paris Region; many respondents admit that their location in the central metropolitan triangle is to facilitate their employees' access. Similarly, many London-based managers live either in the prestigious, highly priced areas of West London or further out in the countryside, while a majority of (lower paid) support staff commute from the city suburbs and urban fringe. Established (socio-economically related) housing location preferences, and travel patterns to specific transport nodes, are a major constraint on even a small shift of office location within central London.

Skilled and senior staff are also reported to be highly reluctant to move from the centralized 'city labour market'. As already described in Chapter 7, the 'virtual office' phenomenon has not brought about a significant change in locational working patterns in the MCRs. It complements, not replaces, face-to-face contact, by making documents instantly available at meetings: 'the time of heavy and crammed briefcases is over' (Accountancy, RhineRuhr).

Regional firms, branch and back-offices

Labour skills are similarly important to firms in deciding where to locate back-office activities. One senior institutional respondent in London explained that some activities outsourced to India are returning to South East England. One reason is that skills requirements for back-office functions are rising, particularly in the customer contact area, and these are available close to London. Skilled support staff are recruited locally in all regions without much evident difficulty, but there is a perception that education and training need to be honed to meet increasingly sophisticated APS customer requirements.

In relation to regional firms and branch networks, one interviewee in Greater Dublin claimed: 'We tend to get more out of them than a Dublin practice would have of their staff' (Design, Greater Dublin). Relocating outside the city is to escape from the 'overheated labour market' to places where staff are 'cheaper, more loyal and more flexible'. But the prime reason for most new office openings, take-overs and in situ growth outside London is reported to have been to get closer to developing markets. Access to cheaper labour was not quoted as a reason and business expansion in the MCR outside London, in any case, usually involves some relocation of London-based staff.

This is supported by evidence from London firms: that to achieve significant labour cost savings it is necessary to move functions out of the UK altogether, as has been the case with off-shoring of back-office activity over a number of years. Furthermore, interviews with firms outside London suggest that in-commuting to secondary centres is now extensive and that in some cases this involves staff living on the outskirts of London who reverse commute. An accountancy firm explained that this facilitates business: 'because quite a few of our clients are in London as well, it does mean that people could be working in London for six months of the year anyway' (Accountancy, South East England). If anything the interview evidence suggests that patterns of working in the MCR are bringing London and its secondary centres closer together.

The significance of 'place'

Both international labour and international firms value some cities more than others as places to live and work. The interviews show that firms' locational decisions are not based solely on rational economic criteria: the personal preferences of senior decision-makers can be highly influential. Intangible cultural and social factors play a part. Interviewees in London point to the fact that senior American managers, for example, in investment banking, feel comfortable with living in London for cultural as well as linguistic reasons. Similarly Düsseldorf's large Japanese community has historic cultural links to that city. Some regional reports emphasize that 'environmental quality' and 'quality of life' are highly regarded throughout the region – yet only a few cities in the study attract international highly-skilled labour and jobs, which goes to highlight their distinctive qualities. Paradoxically, though, the cities attracting the largest firms, with many highly-paid employees, are invariably those most compromised environmentally by traffic congestion and pollution.

City symbolism

The symbolic status attached to a First City office location

is critically important for international firms. In EMR Northern Switzerland, Zürich and Basel have more cultural facilities and are the only cities that have an international image for firms operating at an international or even national level. These cities 'have an important place in the consciousness of APS firms'. Yet Zürich has a special role within the region, as the location for 'top-rank financial firms with international presence'. 'We could do our job just as well in another town than Zürich. But our customers wouldn't understand why we are in say, Winterthur and not in Zürich. It would affect our reputation' (Management consulting, EMR Northern Switzerland). A prestigious address in Zürich is reported to be justified: 'by more narrow economic necessity in only a few cases' (Glanzmann at al, 2005, p14). This 'prestige' function 'like the gateway function, is not something it is possible to extend to other centres of the metropolitan region'. For many firms the desire for a 'good address … is instrumental' (Glanzmann at al, 2005, p11).

Similarly, in Paris, management consultancy firms cluster in the central area of the central business district (CBD) with the most prestigious addresses. In Greater Dublin, the highly clustered CBD is most popular with senior managers. Dublin 2 is described by one interviewee as a 'professional quarter of the town'. Address is also important to firms in the Randstad, and most firms located in nearby Amstelveen use 'Amsterdam' in their external communications. Having a London address with the right postcode is likewise considered critical to the image of 'international players' in London. Interestingly, some firms refer to their location as 'London' on websites when they are actually located elsewhere in the MCR, implying a perception from outside the UK or Europe that South East England constitutes a 'London city region' for APS business.

City milieu

In addition, different city milieux are identified as significant for the location of APS employees and firms. In all regions, a distinction seems to exist between business and creative milieux. For example, in RhineRuhr, Cologne has a cosmopolitan image but Düsseldorf is the favoured location for the young and highly skilled. Overall in Germany, Hamburg, Berlin and Cologne are considered better locations for advertising than Frankfurt. While Frankfurt has more 'international flair', it is reported as failing to attract 'creative minds' (Fischer at al, 2005c, p17). Similarly, Antwerp is considered 'trendy' for creative workers in Central Belgium who don't like to work in Brussels (Aujean et al, 2005b, p19).

Cities with clusters of firms in several sectors seem to benefit from the presence of different milieux. For example, Amsterdam's international workforce is shown to work in a broader spectrum of services than Rotterdam because it is both a creative and a financial centre. Being located in Amsterdam is regarded as 'a big advantage in attracting labour'. It is the 'one and only city with a considerable amount of international workforce' and the major city in the MCR with 'global attitude'. Creative workers are well represented there: 'They love Amsterdam. People are happier here' (Advertising, the Randstad).

In London and Paris, too, specific milieux are identified. Being located in the appropriate central city milieu is regarded as more important than close proximity to clients for advertising and design firms in London. 'Urban assets' such as architecture and streetscape, art galleries, theatres, clubs, restaurants, bars and shops are important, but it is the people present in particular areas of the city who seem to constitute the creative environment. Although Canary Wharf in London has an international mix of firms and employees, the development is identified as a 'banking environment' for 'suits' whereas the Soho area is identified as the milieu for 'creatives'.

A Dublin architectural practice said that a move from the city would be a matter of 'losing soul'. 'How could you operate in Drogheda? Half your management team would leave; all the sales people would look for a new job in Dublin' (Insurance, Greater Dublin). 'If we were up in Dundalk, we wouldn't be able to recruit the people ... if we move down to Cork or even 50 miles out of Dublin, we would have no staff' (Advertising, Greater Dublin). In South East England interviews the south coast town of Brighton (which was not included in the interview survey) is identified by a prominent London institutional representative, and by a number of firms outside London, as increasingly attractive to APS employees, some of whom commute to London as well as to other centres in the MCR. A Crawley-Gatwick interviewee reports that: 'A lot of people live in Brighton and work in Crawley-Gatwick because Crawley-Gatwick is the financial centre and Brighton holds the life-style' (Accountancy, South East England).

The evidence on the precise qualities that attract people and skills to particular places suggests that interrelationships between the 'space of places' and the 'space of flows' in the MCRs reflect 'soft' social, cultural and economic processes. In general, location seems to have more to do with these global city processes than with physical infrastructure. The significance of the relationship between flows and places for knowledge production in First Cities is considered next.

The role of POLYNET 'First Cities' in knowledge production

The flows of knowledge between the MCRs can only be properly understood in a much wider context: that of the entire global city network. South East England interviews re-confirm the role of London within the three global APS regions – USA, Europe/North Africa and Asia – as the European hub for international business services. Its concentration of firms, skills and specialisms gives it unique depth of business infrastructure within the European region. Firms with Continental European headquarters (HQ), interviewed in London, regard the City's role as 'the production' or 'kitchen' for their international business. The co-presence of so many foreign and global firms, clustered in London, leads to a great intensity of interactions and exchanges between its APS networks. London therefore plays the role of an international 'meeting point', where many of the most valuable knowledge exchanges take place: those involving face-to-face contact. As one foreign banker in London put it: 'People are coming to London and you meet people here, you don't have to go to other places' (Banking, South East England). In Dublin, conversely, some interviewees describe the city as 'to some degree a satellite of London'; 'a financial suburb of London'; 'tiny'; 'almost irrelevant'; '[London is] the hub in information flow and also the money. The money flows through London as well' (Management consultancy, Greater Dublin).

The First Cities in the POLYNET study vary considerably in size, and this is reflected in their relative global network connectivities already shown in Table 1.2, p10. But collectively, the interview findings demonstrate the critical importance and inter-connectedness of all the First Cities as 'knowledge gateways'. Evidence, both on virtual and face-to-face communications, reveals the great volume of interactions between these First Cities and the wider global city network. The multiple drivers for concentration of firms and labour, analysed in Chapters 6 and 7, generate a distinctive MCR 'hub function' for information and knowledge in all eight cities, which sets them apart from all the other places in their respective regions.

Knowledge and innovation are described by our interviewees as not only generated in networks, but also dispersed through them. Knowledge production can occur centrally at First City HQ and also spontaneously at the network periphery. Rhine-Main examples illustrate this process of knowledge development and transfer. In insurance and accountancy, knowledge products are developed at HQ or research and development (R&D) locations in the MCRs and by working in multi-disciplinary specialized teams in close cooperation with clients 'on-site'. Knowledge and innovation is produced, centralized and managed to minimize duplication and reduce costs by being made usable for the whole network. In another example, an information technology (IT) consultancy developed new products in a small branch office in the United States. These were centralized at HQ in Rhine-Main, sent to India to be software-crafted and finally sold and distributed. An interviewee explains that:

The best thing here is 'best practice-sharing'. You take the ideas from colleagues at different locations in different countries depending on their ability to deliver the best solutions at a given time. That is our way to achieve high performance at every location in our network *(IT consulting, Rhine-Main)*.

APS clusters are also being developed in Rhine-Main (particularly in R&D), so that different firms, not necessarily in close proximity, can benefit from the comparative advantages of network structures and a skilled labour pool.

Importantly, as already discussed, knowledge is also exchanged between firms and cities. This happens through collaboration in client teams, cross-servicing relationships and working 'on-site', consolidation and restructuring. In addition, the so-called 'labour churn' produces ongoing 'cross-fertilization' of ideas and knowledge between firms. Unlike many other products, key knowledge products – a firm's employees – are not a fixed asset. Competition for, and 'poaching' of, skilled people is a further 'invisible' way in which knowledge flows between, as well as within, cross-border networks.

The complexity of cross-cutting interactions, within and between firms, creates complementary relations between the POLYNET First Cities as information and knowledge are produced, exchanged and circulated through different modes. London's role as a global hub gives it a concentration of decision-making and 'command and control' functions, but matrix management adds a further layer of complexity. Senior management positions can now be decentralized across a network of centres. Underlying a functional specialization between London and other First Cities, the globalization of knowledge production can produce a structure whereby cities perform complementary roles.

The interrelationships between the 'space of flows' and the 'space of places' may raise important issues for the sustainable management of the regional knowledge economy, which will be treated in the final section of this chapter. However, we next return to the POLYNET research questions, specifically to consider the hypothesis that: *APS knowledge flows extend beyond the global city network creating linkages between other towns and cities in North West Europe at a city region scale leading to a spatial phenomenon – the global MCR.*

The regional knowledge economy: Polycentricity and the mega-city region

There is a major overarching question that has run through the study: *how should the area of the global MCR be defined?* In returning to this question in the light of the interview evidence, the entire relevance and value of the MCR concept also require fundamental re-evaluation.

The interviews show that, in general, the POLYNET MCR definitions have little relevance for the firms operating within them. In all regions, the reference points for firms are markets, and their market areas usually bear little relation to these definitions.

Taking into account their markets, the advanced producer service firms are not very much interested in the Rhine-Main region's delimitation … it is difficult to evaluate the dynamics of change in the regional knowledge economy. However, our understanding is that the dynamics rather affect the national and maybe European or global connectivity of the advanced producer service firms located in the Rhine-Main region and only to a much lesser extent their intra-regional connectivity *(Fischer et al, 2005c, p19)*.

Firms very rarely organise their operations on the basis of the MCR as defined. Only the major accountancy firms and a couple of financial services firms discuss their 'region' in a way that roughly corresponds to the POLYNET MCR and, for the former, London represents a separate region for international functions. Many regional firms interviewed actually operate on a sub-regional basis; some have offices just outside the MCR, in Bristol, Cardiff and Midlands towns. The evidence on cross-cutting functional linkages suggests that MCR boundaries have 'soft' edges and need to be defined in loose and flexible ways *(Potts and Pain, 2005, p30)*.

Business flows, linkages and interactions are fluid and hard to quantify in the spatial context … it could be said that Dublin dominates not only the city-regional economy, but also the entire Irish economic space … the matter is further complicated if the position of the Greater Dublin region within the international space of flows is taken into consideration … this all leaves the definition of Dublin's mega-city region rather open and inconclusive *(Sokol and van Egeraat, 2005b, p15)*.

Many of the firms we interviewed are part of national, European or global networks and operate from one office in a First City or other major city to service a market stretching beyond MCR boundaries. This, we have seen, results from the business drivers that lead to the concentration of activity into as few centres as possible. For these firms, it is relationships within the centres in which they are located, and between the major business cities to which they travel, that appear to predominate – in other words, a spatial scale of inter-city relations:

For secondary urban centres, the mega-city region exists, as Paris hub city region is the business horizon for most of them. On the contrary, for Paris firms, there is no such thing as a mega-city region *(Halbert, 2005b, p13)*.

All in all we may conclude that the Randstad is definitely an advanced producer services concentration, perhaps even a cluster, both from a national and an international perspective. The region (through its firms) would seem to play a more important role in global business service networks than could have been expected on the basis of its relative size. As such the region would seem to incorporate certain qualities of a 'mega-city region'… Does the Randstad represent a regional space of flows? Yes and no. Of course there is, as the result of the density of firms and business, a dense network of knowledge flows. But at the same time it is not something that seems to be attached to the Randstad very strictly. An important part of the knowledge flows are as much global as they are regionally embedded, both within firms' networks and externally. Knowledge would seem to be a quality of the firms and their (international) networks rather than a regional quality *(Lambregts et al, 2005a, p24)*.

The other group of firms we interviewed belongs to regional networks which have two or more offices within the study area. But the MCRs, as defined in this study, have little meaning for many of these firms either. Their focus is on specific local market areas and is very much related to particular business centres with a concentration of existing and potential clients. In this case, the focus is the local scale of the specific business centres in which firms operate. Wider regional relationships have been found to exist for firms that have offices both in a First or major city and in other secondary centres in the area around them. These are regional firms with an office in a First City and national and international firms with regional branch or back-offices. However, once again, MCR boundaries are of little relevance to the foci of these firms. Regional offices and branches again focus at the local scale of specific business centres, while back-offices do not service a market but provide functional support for a network HQ:

We have learned more about the fact that there is a poorly developed perception of the region as a complementary urban configuration … nevertheless there is an organisational network of business services within the region and its offices are also linked into networks on the national and international scale *(Knapp et al, 2005, p17)*.

The Belgium MCR is made up of autonomous FURs under the leadership of Brussels:

On the international scale, the Belgium MCR is dominated by Brussels. Brussels is the only city in Belgium where multi-national firms are located *(Aujean et al, 2005b, p19)*.

From the point of view of firms and markets, the conclusion drawn across the study regions is therefore that MCR boundaries, and indeed any regional scale boundaries, appear arbitrary. However, a number of highly important issues for APS firms do emerge from the studies. They relate to a variety of policy spheres: regulation, spatial concentration, transport, housing, education and inter-urban relations. Some have specific relevance at the MCR scale but also at national and European scales. These are discussed further below. Hence, while the geographical delimitation of the MCR is not something to which a majority of firms relate, they nonetheless find social, economic and policy processes within these city-region areas critical for their operation. The conclusion from the studies is that there is a crucial policy agenda at an MCR scale, but that specific boundaries are not relevant to functional relations in APS. These functional relations replicate the overlapping structure of markets and therefore cannot be strictly delimited:

Zürich has shown itself to be of central importance to the whole metropolitan region… The central functions of Zürich, and to a lesser extent also Basel, radiate out into the metropolitan region, and the benefits of this can be felt even in more distant centres… An essential prerequisite for making the most of this potential [of Basel] is a better functioning cooperation and coordination across political borders *(Glanzmann at al, 2005, p15)*.

Reconsidering polycentricity

The second key research question to be addressed concerns the issue of 'polycentricity': *to what extent flows associated with concentration of services in primary business services centres in each region are associated with polycentric development at the regional scale?*

All the evidence points to the essential advantages of the concentration of APS, operating as part of national and international networks, within the MCRs. The agglomeration economies associated with APS clustering have critical importance for the knowledge economy at regional, national, European and global scales. As discussed above, concentration and clustering promote depth of knowledge production that is associated with the skills and diversity represented in knowledge milieux. And, as demonstrated, this process of concentration is driven by the globalization of markets and services, facilitated by developments in information and communication technology (ICT), long-distance travel and regulation. The breaking down of barriers to cross-border business creates operational requirements from which firms, business and professional bodies agree there is no going back. Globalization has increased competition everywhere at the local market level, requiring firms to develop sufficient size and operational scale to engage with cross-border markets. Concentration is not only essential for cost reduction but for knowledge production:

Few firms are working or plan to work in a polycentric way. Most firms underline the advantages of concentrated locations: proximity of other key actors, subcontractors and clients *(Aujean et al, 2005b, p19)*.

The evidence appears at first sight to lead to the conclusion that these trends run quite counter to the entire concept of the polycentric urban region. But the reality of MCR relationships is more complex than it appears. On the one hand, the advantages of concentration for knowledge production appear to be diluted by being spread across a number of centres at a regional, and sometimes a national, scale. But there are substantial differences between First Cities – London, Paris, Frankfurt and Dublin – which have appeared more primate than other First Cities within their regions. These differences seem clearly to relate to the national contexts of these First Cities.

For example, Frankfurt's position in Rhine-Main seems to be influenced by the functionally polycentric German national urban structure, in which a number of major cities are also important (and specialized) APS centres. Frankfurt has less all-round concentration of services than London or Paris – and this may limit its functional connectivities within the MCR and, potentially, on other geographical scales. While Frankfurt remains the key regional international hub for the MCR and the key hub within Germany for financial services, regional centres outside Frankfurt have more independent linkages at a national scale though not with each other:

The Rhine-Main is shaped by a very distinct pattern of polycentricity. Each FUR (functional urban region) has strong individual linkages on the national level that show some degree of sectoral and in the case of Darmstadt FUR and Hanau FUR also geographical specialization. Only relatively few linkages could be detected on the regional level. In conclusion, Rhine-Main appears as a polycentric region in the sense that the FURs complement each other on the national level. However, in the case of the big transnational companies with European and international scope, Rhine-Main shows a less polycentric structure due to a very dominant position of the Frankfurt FUR *(Fischer at al, 2005c, p20)*.

Dublin's dominant position at regional and national geographical scales is also likely to be influenced by its national context in which linkages with Belfast, in the north, are weak. In all cases, differences in regional situations can be seen to reflect national differences that have evolved historically over long periods of time:

It could be argued the process of simultaneous spatial decentralization and centralization is indeed at work in and around Dublin city... However, it seems that much of the spatial decentralization is being accommodated within the Dublin metropolitan area... It is therefore the Dublin metropolis that, perhaps increasingly, resembles a 'multifunctional and multinuclear structure' *(Sokol and van Egeraat, 2005b, p16)*.

Polycentricity has also been found to be scale-specific: polycentricity at a national scale does not automatically translate to polycentricity at the regional scale. For example, while the Paris region appears primate at regional and national scales, it is part of a polycentric urban structure at a European and international scale:

As flows are mainly converging towards the dense part of the hub city or circulating within it, leaving only a very restricted proportion of linkages between non-Parisian urban centres, if it is to be said that there is any sort of polycentric pattern it is one of hierarchical polycentricity. In this regard, the hub city is the gateway and articulator for the entire case study region *(Halbert, 2005b, p14)*.

There are further complexities. The interview evidence demonstrates that functional configurations cannot be directly mapped on to MCR spatial configurations. For example, the Randstad appears from its spatial configuration of similar urban centres to be polycentric, yet the results of this research reveal a quite different picture functionally. In practice, weak intra-regional functional linkages have been found between the Randstad MCR cities:

The region's morphological polycentric structure is not something that receives a lot of thought among APS providers. It is not generally associated with certain advantages. It is easier to think of particular disadvantages... But to what extent does the Randstad function as a polycentric Mega-City-Region?... [For SMEs and MNCs (multi-national companies)] the Randstad offers a rich pallet of business opportunities and an attractive pool of potential employees. At the same time however, the Randstad as a spatial entity does not coincide with the spatial scope of the operations of either category. For the vast majority of SME-oriented firms the Randstad is simply too big ... for MNC-oriented providers, business does not stop at the edges of the Randstad *(Lambregts et al, 2005a, p24)*.

On the other hand, South East England, which has a spatially primate regional structure of urban centres, seems to benefit from massive global APS concentration in London. Strong functional linkages have been identified between centres within the MCR, many of which cross-cut a 'hub-and-spoke' spatial configuration. These linkages are facilitated by developments in ICT but are not caused by them:

Intra- and extra-firm connectivities take many forms and many of the most important interactions are not readily apparent. While e-mail flows are high volume, face-to-face contact remains high value and essential to knowledge production and transfer. As new (non local) offices open to access regional markets, functional linkages are woven in… Virtual communications facilitate the development of functional polycentricity, but an overriding conclusion is that they do not drive it *(Potts and Pain, 2005, p30).*

The overwhelming conclusion is that, collectively and individually, the POLYNET First Cities have a special role in their regions – a role that in many ways links them more closely to each other, in terms of an intensity of interactions in knowledge production, than with other cities and towns in their regions. These First Cities have key connections beyond their regional and national economies through their strategic positions in the world-wide global city network. They act as knowledge gateways at the intersection between the 'space of flows' and regional markets. This seems to be true for spatially polycentric and monocentric MCRs.

As in the case of the first research question, specific regional boundaries are found to obscure the overarching urban processes that structure MCR functional and spatial relations. Geographical scale has important relevance for policy but specific regional boundaries confuse the issues relating to the nature of (polycentric) inter-urban relationships.

A question mark remains as to whether – as seems likely – intra-regional functional linkages, identified in (spatially monocentric) South East England, are actually *caused by* the very intensity of global interactions in London. If this is the case, then the highly paradoxical conclusion must be that APS concentration has positive benefits for functional polycentricity at an intra-regional sub-nodal level. This finding is in keeping with the conclusion of individual MCR reports concerning the importance of all the POLYNET First Cities within their regional setting:

With the help of the qualitative interviews it has become more obvious that Düsseldorf is by far the most important place as a location for advanced producer firms, and as well the most important node within the MCR RhineRuhr through which international flows of communication is conducted… The interviews and the web survey have given no evidence that high quality knowledge flows strengthen flows to lower order regional centres

within the MCR RhineRuhr but hypothetically it can be taken for granted … there are some hints that such processes are taking place especially within the management consulting and advertising sector in Düsseldorf and Cologne and to some extent within the logistics centres Cologne, East Ruhr Region and Duisburg–Nordrhein *(Knapp et al, 2005, p17).*

If we simply consider the fact that Zürich continues to have important central functions, which it is not possible for other centres to take over, then the metropolitan region cannot be described as specifically polycentric … it is practically impossible to 'polycentralize' these [soft] factors, or at least this can only be achieved on a very long-term basis … but the smaller FURs of [the MCR] are increasingly being perceived as valid alternative locations, above all by APS companies… *(Glanzmann et al, 2005, p16).*

Conclusion: Ten key issues for sustainable regional management

Finally, we seek to summarize conclusions from this part of the study, with particular reference to interrelationships between the 'space of flows' and the 'space of places' in sustainable regional management. We can do this in the form of ten propositions.

1 None of the MCRs sees a future without urban concentration of APS. The First Cities in each region are identified as having a key role as global knowledge 'gateways' that benefit from depth of concentration and clustering of labour, firms and clients.

2 Close proximity for face-to-face contact in First Cities is shown to be the most important mode for strategic knowledge transfer. All regions see the enhancement of First City concentration as vital to the regional knowledge economy. Six important features of successful global APS clusters are identified in the interviews:
   • high-skilled international labour supply;
   • concentration of global firms;
   • representation of multiple APS sectors;
   • inclusion of international banking/financial services;
   • international 'city image';
   • presence of 'financial' and 'creative' milieux.
   These are characteristics of successful clusters and not 'location factors' identified by firms. They identify key processes associated with APS knowledge production as opposed to physical infrastructures.

3 There is a distinction between 'environmental quality' or 'quality of life' which are generally regarded as good at the level of the MCRs, and what attracts international high-skilled labour and senior APS decision-makers to particular cities. These 'soft' features

are hard to create, if absent, but should be protected by policy-makers where they exist.

4 The concept of regional spatial polycentricity is found not to be compatible with functional linkages between cities. It is vital that policy focuses on inter-urban functional relations that cross-cut regional administrative boundaries for sustainable development of the regional knowledge economy.

5 Inter-urban functional relationships are complementary not competitive, and should not be confused with 'competitiveness' in markets. Cities should not see themselves as competitors.

6 Policy intervention to create or disperse clustered 'global city' APS could not succeed as they rely on concentration for knowledge production. Policy at national, regional and local First City levels needs to ensure that historic, market-led city centre clustering is not disrupted.

7 Functional regional interlinkages should be facilitated by addressing specific issues that cannot be resolved through market processes, such as investment in large-scale infrastructure. Transport is highlighted as a crucial area for management as well as investment.

8 European Union (EU) and state policy and regulation are of critical concern for firms. Regulation of markets and services shapes business opportunities and strategies and has a crucial effect on concentration in specific countries and cities.

9 At a regional government scale, policy should focus on the economic profiles and issues of individual urban centres. At a national government scale, in some cases a 'champion' for business services may be needed. Firms should be encouraged to participate more actively in relevant political processes.

10 There is a need for long-term vision and joined-up thinking that crosses policy and geographical boundaries. Coordination between policy levels vertically and horizontally is needed, including integrated economic and spatial planning.

These ten propositions have important implications for policy formulation in each region – implications to which we return in Chapter 17. Before however we do this, we need to look in more detail at the specific position of each region. To what extent are they special and different from each other, and, if so, how has that impacted on the development of policy responses? This is the burden of Chapters 9–16.

PART 4

Visiting the Polycentric Metropolis:

Regional Identities, Regional Policies

9

South East England: Global Constellation

Kathy Pain, Peter Hall, Gareth Potts and David Walker

South East England is unique among the eight mega-city regions (MCRs). It is by far the largest POLYNET region, extending even beyond the area mapped in Chapter 2: west into the South West and north into the southern parts of the East and West Midlands regions. Most significantly, the quantitative analyses of commuting (Chapter 2) and advanced producer service (APS) networks (Chapter 3) have revealed important functionally polycentric relationships covering a wide arc in the west of the region, paradoxically stemming from the strength of London's global linkages.[1]

This has deep roots. South East England has historically been the main focus of economic activity and wealth production in the UK. From about 1730 to 1930, this pattern was temporarily modified by the Industrial Revolution which generated new industrial and urban concentrations in the Midlands, North of England, Wales and Scotland. But since then London and the South East have reasserted their primacy, first through new manufacturing industries and latterly through APS for global markets, making this the UK's most productive and prosperous region in terms of gross domestic product (GDP) per head. Even as defined in Chapter 2, the MCR extends up to 110 miles (180km) from central London and has an area of 11,268 miles^2 (29,184km^2). At the 2001 Census it had a population of 18,984,298 and a total employment of 9,040,000.

The analysis of commuting flows (in Chapter 2) shows that, viewed more closely, it consists of no less than 51 functional urban regions (FURs) dominated by London, which – extending for an average of 30 miles (50km) from the centre – has a total population of 9,025,960 people, just over half the total MCR population, and overlaps six of the other 50, sometimes completely surrounding them. The next largest FURs, Southampton and Portsmouth,

have just over 600,000 people, one-twentieth the size. There are seven FURs with between 300,000 and 500,000 people, another seven in the 200,000–300,000 bracket, no less than 26 falling between 100,000 and 200,000, and eight with less than 100,000, a distribution that confirms the picture of the MCR as dominated by small to medium size towns and their spheres of influence.

London's dominance is just as complete in terms of employment. Of a total 2001 employment in the MCR of 9,040,000, the London FUR accounted for 4,336,000, or 48 per cent. Otherwise, as with population, employment was distributed quite evenly among the other, medium size, FURs. The largest single employment centres were Oxford with 307,000 jobs and Southampton with 286,000; and almost half of all employment centres had between 50,000 and 100,000 jobs. Thus, while London remains the dominant centre in the region, with by far the greatest concentration of business service firms, these other centres have grown and attracted a range of business service industries which form a substantial part of their economic activity.

South East England: A web of global connectivity

The GaWC (Globalization and World Cities) analysis of APS world city network connectivity, mentioned in Chapter 1, has demonstrated London's extraordinarily high connectivity to other global cities worldwide and to the other POLYNET First Cities. While these connectivity rankings might imply a world (and European) hierarchy of service centres, in reality the analysis shows quite the opposite: it demonstrates the connectedness of cities, especially London, within the space of information flows.

The primary location of London's intense global connectivity is the small densely clustered area of the City of London 'Square Mile' with Canary Wharf just to its east, but a spider's web of informational exchanges stretches invisibly across the MCR. The evidence from over 100 interviews with senior decision-makers in firms, trade, professional and government institutions reveals a crucial difference between London's MCR and the others: high-value knowledge-based interactions mirror the potential intra-regional linkages mapped in Chapter 3.

The maps shown in Figure 3.2, p61 are based on data collected in each region showing the potential connectivity of MCR offices within business networks operating at regional, national, European and global scales (here called 'scopes'). The polycentricity – and its opposite, primacy – of each region is compared using a number of different measures. As explained in Chapter 3, across these assessments, South East England appears to sit between the most primate regions (Greater Dublin followed by Rhine-Main, then Paris Region) and the most polycentric (RhineRuhr followed by the Randstad). One way in which polycentricity is assessed is by looking for an even distribution of *intra-regional linkages* between major service centres. On this criterion, whereas the Randstad and (particularly) RhineRuhr have many relatively equal linkages between centres – RhineRuhr has nine major links involving five MCR centres that bypass First City Düsseldorf – South East England has just one (Reading–Southampton), suggesting London's relative primacy (Figure 3.2a, b and d). Another way is by examining differences in the *connectivities* of the MCR First Cities and their secondary centres at different network scopes. Based on this assessment, at the regional scope, South East England again appears primate, while at the opposite extreme RhineRuhr appears hardly primate at all; Cologne has 99 per cent of Düsseldorf's regional scope connectivity, while Reading has only 52 per cent of London's (Table 3.5, p59).

However, there is an anomaly between these quantitative results and the interview evidence, which has found strong intra-regional linkages only in South East England. This almost certainly reflects differences in the connectivity of the POLYNET First Cities that are not apparent or taken into account in the potential assessment of polycentricity or monocentricity. South East England interviews, from firms headquartered outside the UK, in North West Europe and beyond, suggest that London's global super-connectedness results in unique regional-scale advanced service linkages; furthermore, despite London's evident morphological monocentricity, these have a cross-cutting geography that suggests greater functional polycentricity in South East England than in other MCRs. Even though the analyses in Chapter 3 do not permit

comparisons of overall regional connectivity between the MCRs, it appears significant that South East England is less primate in its global scope connectivity than in its regional scope: it is firms outside London, forming part of global networks, that make South East England more functionally polycentric relative to other MCRs.

Some important points emerge from evaluation of the qualitative and quantitative evidence. Although morphologically polycentric RhineRuhr has a more even distribution of regional scope connectivities across its centres than other MCRs, the interviews reveal that in practice regional scope networks contribute least to MCR functional linkages, because of the limited size of their offices and the localized nature of their markets. Hence, in RhineRuhr, the intra-regional linkages bypassing First City Düsseldorf are paradoxically associated with weaker functional polycentricity. In contrast, South East England's linkages are supported by London's greater global connectivity and specialisms. These inter-urban linkages help achieve leverage of global skills and knowledge *through* London, thus offering high-value business services and advice to global multi-national companies (MNCs) *outside* it, building a true network of globally connected offices in the MCR.

This leads to a further interesting distinction between the MCRs. Sectoral specialization between regional centres was shown in Chapter 6 to be prominent in the cities of RhineRuhr, followed by the Randstad, Central Belgium and EMR (European Metropolitan Region) Northern Switzerland. In contrast, sectoral specialization was limited in the Paris Region and hard to detect at all among the service centres of South East England. South East England has relatively well-balanced sub-regional clusters of APS activity, well connected to London and to each other. And the co-presence and close proximity between creative and financial 'knowledge milieux', found in London and Paris, seems to add significantly to their agglomeration economies. A key question for further research is to what extent sectoral specialization between APS service centres reflects the need to enhance agglomeration economies when service activities are spread relatively thinly across a number of centres which lack concentration at a regional and inter-regional scale, as seems to be the case for the morphologically polycentric system of German cities.

If morphological polycentricity fails to produce an even regional distribution of functions, what can be said of the distributional effects of functional polycentricity? A key finding from South East England is that linkages between its most highly-connected service clusters mirror the uneven west–east commuting pattern identified in Chapter 2. While business services are found throughout the South East, advanced service networks are located in the most developed western area of the expanding region.

Service providers on the eastern side of the MCR are more commonly smaller local firms operating from just one location and/or are largely servicing the retail consumer market. The western side of the MCR has the strongest network linkages to and through London to other UK, European and global cities, reflecting established socio-economic development patterns and transport infrastructure. Functional polycentricity has not led to a balanced spatial distribution of functions here, and this raises further unresolved questions concerning the historical and national contexts that shape territorial development patterns – the role of communications infrastructure, centres of excellence and the presence of demand for global services. Thus the consideration of polycentricity in South East England brings us back to a finding of previous global city research: the crucial importance of the past in constructing present and future interdependencies between the space of flows and the space of places (Pain, 2005). The main conclusions from the South East England analysis are summarized next, before turning to consider how the evidence from POLYNET can inform policy.

The interview evidence

From the interviews, seven key conclusions emerge with specific relevance to South East England.

The need for concentration

Concentration of global functions in London should not be seen as inhibiting activity in other cities, either regionally or nationally: these highly clustered and specialized functions require concentration and they actually support different functions in other centres. South East England's network connectivities extend across the UK and internationally.

Supporting market-led clustering

Sustainable APS clusters cannot be created by policy; existing clusters should not be disrupted because their agglomeration economies cannot be replicated elsewhere by design. Policy should focus on alleviating blockages to market flows through long-term planning and managed investment.

Infrastructure investment is essential

Functional polycentricity has major implications for physical infrastructure and environmental sustainability. Economic globalization and e-technology are not leading to greater self-containment of settlements; e-communication actually stimulates business travel. The strong message from London and the South East is that increased investment in transport infrastructure is critical just to support existing business flows – and this requires coordination and adequate resources.

Multiple policy scales are involved

Inter-urban functional relations cross-cut administrative and departmental boundaries, leading to a need for long-term vision and coordinated inter-authority approaches to economic and spatial policy, primarily: European Union (EU) and national regulation, transport management and urban housing development. London and regional economic and planning agencies, central government – the Treasury, Department for Trade and Industry, Office of the Deputy Prime Minister (ODPM), Department for Transport – and the private sector should all be involved.

Complementarity of functions

POLYNET reveals the complementary nature of inter-urban functional relationships. Service network flows produce inter-office and inter-firm cooperation, hence the notion of market competitiveness should not be conferred to inter-city relations. Cooperation between cities and regions is needed – competition is counterproductive in urban networks.

A network approach is needed

The research findings suggest that a key challenge for policy will be to engage with the MCR as a networked space comprising all geographical scales from the local to the global. Complex interactions between flows and space make strategic, integrated economic and spatial planning vitally important to sustain existing flows into London and the South East and to address issues of uneven development between two regions – a functionally polycentric West and an under-linked East. The key functional role of London at regional, national and European scales, together with multi-scalar implications for polycentricity, movement and infrastructure, mean that cross-border and transnational cooperation through linked policy networks will be essential to sustainable management of the South East England MCR.

Building the structure

Though this huge highly-interlinked MCR is a crucial ingredient in the success of the UK national economy, policy-makers have not yet recognized its importance, nor have they yet developed policies to promote it. A key starting point will be studies that further identify the key triggers for polycentric development. Two in particular demand attention. First, the role played by increasingly sophisticated patterns of demand that link APS (banking, accountancy, law; media, design services); second, patterns of accessibility, both electronically (high-speed broadband)

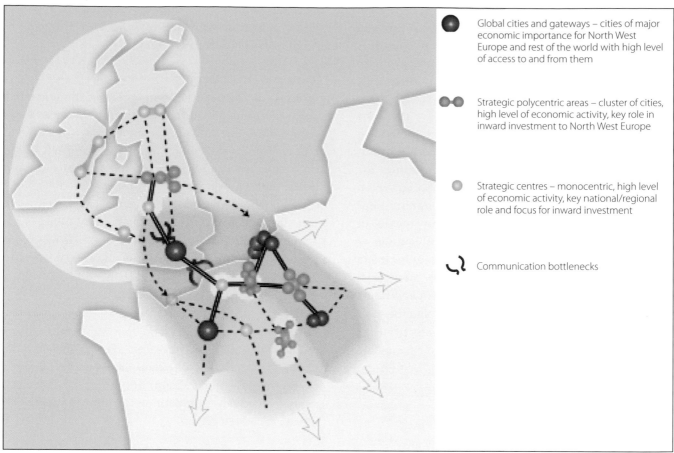

Global cities and gateways – cities of major economic importance for North West Europe and rest of the world with high level of access to and from them

Strategic polycentric areas – cluster of cities, high level of economic activity, key role in inward investment to North West Europe

Strategic centres – monocentric, high level of economic activity, key national/regional role and focus for inward investment

Communication bottlenecks

Source: NWMA Spatial Vision Group, 2000, Figure 3.1, p30

Figure 9.1 NWMA Spatial Vision 2000

and face-to-face (better physical linkages by both road and rail, both radially out from London, and – even more crucially – orbitally between the other centres). Both these factors will prove critical for further enhancing the flows of information between South East England's dynamic urban service clusters and the wider regional, UK and EU economies.

Policy responses

UK spatial planning policy has recently demonstrated a remarkable degree of consistency and coherence, both between different spatial scales and also in engaging with the Europe-wide scale. Indeed, in some respects it can be interpreted as delivering key objectives of the European Spatial Development Perspective (ESDP), most notably the aim of developing a more polycentric urban system. This can be seen by tracing the common themes down through the spatial scales: European (the ESDP itself), North West Europe (the North West Metropolitan Area (NWMA) Spatial Vision); national (the UK Urban White Paper, Sustainable Communities); regional: (ODPM Growth Corridors/Areas), regional divisions (Regional

Spatial Strategies (RSSs): South East, East of England, South Midlands, South West), and finally sub-regional–cross-regional (Milton Keynes– South Midlands).

The European scale[2]

The ESDP makes a distinction between the core 'Pentagon' and the rest of Europe (see Figure 1.1, p5). The central principle is to promote polycentricity by diverting growth from the Euro-Core to Euro-Periphery, especially through Structural Funds, to encourage growth in less-developed regions, cities (European Commission, 1999). Such a process has been hugely successful in cities like Madrid, Lisbon and Dublin in the 1990s; it promises to be equally successful in Eastern European capitals like Budapest, Prague and Warsaw in this decade. But the paradox is that if so, it may have the effect of promoting national monocentricity in these countries, as indeed it has earlier done in Spain, Portugal and Ireland. However, for the purpose of the present chapter it is important to notice that the South East England MCR (strictly, London) is located on the extreme north-west edge of the Pentagon; part is inside it, but the larger part is outside.

The NWMA Spatial Vision of 2000 (NWMA Spatial Vision Group, 2000) transforms the ESDP into operational objectives (see Figure 9.1). The core is one of the world's foremost world command centres; super-connected internally and externally. But this paradoxically is producing an unbalanced pattern of development with congested links between South East England and the European mainland, threatening economic performance and environmental sustainability. The key therefore, the Vision document argues, is to develop 'counterweight global gateways and economic centres' in the Midlands and Northern England, and to strengthen alternative corridors, bypassing the core cities, such as Hull–Immingham–Rotterdam, or Southampton–Le Havre.

The UK national scale

UK national policy, developed in the report of the Urban Task Force (Urban Task Force, 1999) and the Urban White Paper (Department, Environment and the Regions, 2000), sets a national objective that 60 per cent of all new residential development should be on brownfield (previously developed land) and that a 'sequential test' should be used to ensure that existing urban areas are developed first, followed by urban extensions and only then by new communities; there is a built-in bias towards urban compaction. This in effect is a uniform national requirement, which somewhat ignores the fact that circumstances vary between the UK regions.

The ODPM Sustainable Communities strategy was published in 2003 (ODPM, 2003). It tries to address a geographical imbalance: in the North of England there is housing oversupply, in the South a housing shortage. The UK government's answer for the North is nine 'pathfinders' to develop a combination of regeneration and selective demolition; in the South, it is to concentrate additional housing in four growth areas forming corridors running out from London along high-speed rail lines: Thames Gateway, Milton Keynes–South Midlands, Ashford and London–Stansted–Cambridge. Together, these would provide for another 200,000 homes above previously planned levels. The government will provide £446 million for essential infrastructure in Thames Gateway and £164 million for the other three areas.

For South East England, the 2003 strategy deliberately develops a series of key spatial objectives. It consciously aims to stress certain key growth directions at the expense of others (Figure 9.2). Thus the entire western and south-western sectors of the region, which have demonstrated the greatest dynamism over the last 50 years, are simply ignored: the strategy states that growth will be diverted eastwards into the two major northern growth corridors, the first through Luton, Milton Keynes and Bedford (with an outlier in Aylesbury), Northampton and the three Northamptonshire towns of Wellingborough, Kettering

Table 9.1 Proposed new homes and jobs in southern England to 2031

	Homes	Jobs
Milton Keynes–South Midlands	+370,000	+300,000
London–Stansted–Cambridge	+130,000[a]	132,000[a]
Thames Gateway	+120,000[a]	+300,000
Ashford	+31,000	+28,000

Note: a To 2021.

and Corby, the second via Stansted airport and Cambridge to Peterborough. This is associated with development of a so-called 'science arc' between Oxford and Cambridge, and exploitation of three 125 miles per hour (200km/h) high-speed rail lines serving these corridors, one of which (the West Coast Main Line through Milton Keynes) has been recently upgraded. Likewise, south of London growth is effectively diverted into Thames Gateway and the expansion of Ashford, which in some ways can be regarded as a Thames Gateway outlier since in both growth is aligned along the new 190 miles per hour (300km/h) high-speed Channel Tunnel Rail Link (CTRL) from London through Kent, due for completion in 2007.

This pattern, commonly called beads-on-a-string, has been consistent from the launch of the strategy early in 2003 through all subsequent reiterations and refinements, and has been carried down into regional spatial strategies.

The proposal in the 2003 report, and subsequently, is driven by a perceived need to ensure the competitiveness of London and the South East, by accommodating the growth associated with their economic success in areas where new and expanded communities are needed. Specifically, as shown in Table 9.1, major development is to be provided for in the four growth areas to the year 2031.

Though not the largest of the growth corridors in a geographical sense, Thames Gateway has received special attention because its development became a strategic priority earlier, in 1991, and consequently proposals have been developed to a high degree of detail. It builds in turn on the London Docklands regeneration project of the 1980s and 1990s; both aim to turn London's growth away from the more favoured and dynamic west to the less favoured east, but Thames Gateway does so on a far larger geographical scale, for some 40 miles (70km) to the east of London.

The key piece of transport infrastructure is the CTRL, as mentioned above to be completed in 2007, with four station stops: London St Pancras (terminal), Stratford, Ebbsfleet and Ashford International, each integrated with local transport, and with major regeneration including commercial development around each. The basic strategy,

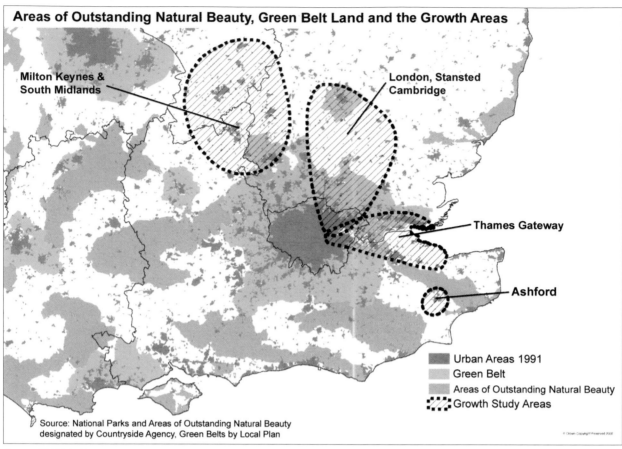

Areas of Outstanding Natural Beauty, Green Belt Land and the Growth Areas

Milton Keynes &
South Midlands

London, Stansted
Cambridge

Thames Gateway

Ashford

Urban Areas 1991
Green Belt
Areas of Outstanding Natural Beauty
Growth Study Areas

Source: National Parks and Areas of Outstanding Natural Beauty
designated by Countryside Agency, Green Belts by Local Plan

Source: ODPM, 2003a, p47

Figure 9.2 Sustainable Communities Strategy 2003

published in 1995, has shown detailed subsequent fine-tuning (particularly in terms of housing targets) but little fundamental alteration. It stresses major commercial regeneration at Stratford and Ebbsfleet but also a heavy emphasis on new homes around these nodes and also between them, as at Barking Riverside on the north side of the Thames. Here in particular, a complication is that available funds for transport infrastructure have not always been available in sufficient amounts or at the right time. Barking Riverside is not served by the CTRL, which passes at high speed on its northern edge, and lack of funds for an extension of the Docklands Light Rail system have in effect put the development on hold until after 2010.

In consequence, development in and around the nodes looks likely to take precedence. A major commercial development at Stratford, begun in 2005 and likely to be substantially complete by 2012, incorporates a very large regional shopping centre, commercial office developments intercepting the commuter flows that will pass through the station, and high-density residential development, some of which forms the Olympic Village component of the successful London bid for the 2012 Olympic Games (in which the stadium is to be built close to the new international station).

Given the magnetic effect of the new station, and the difficulty of developing the intermediate sites, one evident effect must be to stimulate pressures for higher-density residential development in nearby areas, especially sites in the Royal Docks that have been left undeveloped since the financial crisis of 1989–1994. These have the merit of available transport infrastructure (the Jubilee Line underground extension of 1999; the Docklands Light Railway extension scheduled to open in 2009), feeding into the Stratford station, thus in effect supporting development of a high-intensity mixed-use area.

Very much the same pattern seems to be emerging around the second intermediate station at Ebbsfleet, just over the London border in the county of Kent. Here, a very large chalk quarry, which was still being worked in 2005, is shortly to be developed as a high-density residential area, exploiting the dramatic improvement in accessibility to central London after the opening of CTRL domestic services in 2009. This area will be bisected by a line of the new reserved busway system for the area, the first parts of which were already under development in 2005, which will connect the huge retail park at Bluewater, Europe's largest, with the commercial

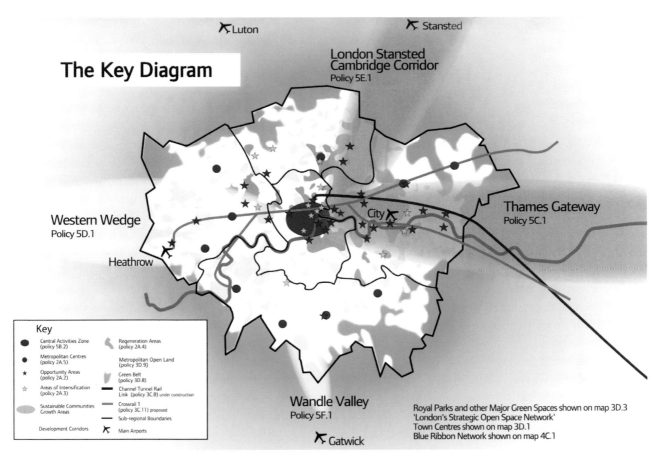

Source: Mayor of London, 2004, p50

Figure 9.3 Mayor's London Plan 2004 key diagram

development around the CTRL station. In effect, this area is developing as a very large new town in all but name.

The third intermediate station, at Ashford in Kent, is separated from Ebbsfleet by some 40 miles (60km) of very attractive countryside, much of it highly protected from development. The town, close to the English portal of the tunnel, is planned for massive expansion which will effectively double its size by 2025.

The regional scale

The national strategy, and specifically its southern England component, is being translated into new-style statutory plans being drafted in consequence of a major change in the English planning system. The Planning and Compulsory Purchase Act 2004 introduces a simpler, more flexible plan-making system at both regional and local levels. The Act abolishes the County Structure Plans, which have provided the strategic level of planning since the late 1960s, replacing them by statutory RSSs produced by new Regional Planning Bodies (RPBs), which also replace the former Regional Planning Guidance. These, inter alia, specify housing targets for each district/borough. There is a much greater emphasis throughout on strategic allocation of housing and other land uses at regional and (where appropriate) sub-regional level.

The Mayor's London Plan, 2004

The first of these new strategies to appear, the Mayor of London's London Plan, was published in draft in 2002 and then, after Examination in Public, in final form in 2004 (Mayor of London, 2004). It occupies a special place since it was produced under separate legislation of 1999 which established a directly-elected Mayor for Greater London in 2000.

The plan follows national – and regional – priorities in seeking to correct the historic east–west imbalance in London and its wider region (Figure 9.3). The Docklands project began to reverse it; Thames Gateway builds on the momentum. To the east, concentrations of multiple deprivation coincide with large-scale opportunities for physical regeneration. Therefore, the plan shows a strong easterly bias in employment and housing. No less than 14,000 new homes, 60 per cent of the London total, are to be built in Central and East London; 32,500 out of 42,400 new jobs are to be created here, 77 per cent of the total. It might well be argued that these figures have the nature of a planner's fantasy, since there is no set of policy instruments that could deliver them. But the Mayor could argue that the trends are strongly in this direction and that the conventional public wisdom, as so often in the past, will be proved wrong.

But this needs substantial sums of money for new transport links and land preparation. Transport in particular will require major investment. The biggest scheme, Crossrail, could cost over £16 billion in total, and there is a £7–8 billion funding gap between the cost and the total of public and private commitment. Even important smaller schemes, like the Docklands Light Railway extension to Barking, are so far unfunded. The risk therefore is that developments may not happen, or may not happen in time to support key elements of the development. In addition, transport and housing proposals are not always well integrated. It is surprising that the plan's biggest single residential development, Barking Riverside, is not underpinned by the plan's biggest single transport investment, Crossrail.

It is evident that in developing the plan in detail, especially its sub-regional components, adjustments are being made. This is particularly evident in the east, where much of the activity is concentrated. The lack of investment for transport almost inevitably means that in important areas – Barking Riverside, for instance – implementation of the plan will need to be postponed. In addition, planning orthodoxies may increasingly do battle with the private sector and its clients – as was evident for instance at the plan's Examination in Public in Spring 2005.

Outer London might be regarded as one of the plan's big missed opportunities. The plan does not seriously consider the possibility of creating a 'polycentric London'. It suggests raising housing densities around town centres with good access to public transport, but it is unclear how this will be achieved, since many of these areas have conservation area status. There is a need for better transport – especially orbitally. The proposed Orbirail is not yet funded, and plans for orbital bus routes are weakly developed; road plans are generally non-existent, except for a new Thames Gateway bridge.

The Regional Spatial Strategies, 2004–2005

Outside London, the indirect influence of the ESDP is clearly seen in a new generation of RSSs produced by new RPBs for each of the English standard regions, with separate strategies from the devolved bodies for Wales and Scotland, in anticipation of a major change in the UK planning law.

There are two important general points about the new RSSs. First, with the conspicuous exception of London, they are produced by bodies that are not democratically directed; the intention of the UK government was that progressively, through referenda in each region, the RPBs should be directly elected, but in October 2004 this option was rejected in North East England and will not be pursued.

Second, and very importantly in South East England, their boundaries – which are those of the so-called Standard Regions used for statistical purposes – do not correspond at all well to the realities of economic and social geography. The Greater South East contains all or part of no less than five of the eight English Standard Regions: London, South East, East of England, East Midlands and South West. London is divided from the rest of the region since it has a directly elected Mayor responsible for the development of its RSS (the 'London Plan'); this has a definite geographical logic, as it corresponds approximately to the built-up area of Greater London which since the 1940s has been constrained by the Metropolitan Green Belt, and the inner boundary of which is approximately marked by the 125 mile (200km) London Orbital Motorway, the M25. But other regional boundaries bisect two of the major growth corridors in the Sustainable Communities strategy: Thames Gateway is divided between the South East and East of England RPBs (and also London), though this has a certain logic in physical geography since it corresponds to the wide Thames Estuary between the counties of Kent and Essex; while the Milton Keynes–South Midlands strategic corridor is divided between the South East, East of England and East Midlands RPBs.

At the end of 2005, the five RPB strategies are at different states of production. London's, which was produced under separate legislation in advance of the others, is complete. Those for the South East, East of England and East Midlands were produced in consultation and then draft stages from late 2004 through 2005 and were yet to go to public examination at the time of the study; the South West has not yet produced a draft so its strategy (affecting the western fringes of South East England, in the Bournemouth–Poole and Swindon areas) could not be considered in this study.

The South East Strategy (2005) was published in draft in July 2005 after extensive consultation. It presented three alternative levels of growth: 25,500, 28,000 and 32,000 dwellings per annum. Public consultation found sharply divided views: a face-to-face survey showed 38 per cent supported growth at 25,500 per annum, 35 per cent 28,000 per annum and 22 per cent 32,000 per annum, while a questionnaire showed 68 per cent favoured 25,500 per annum, 20 per cent 28,000 per annum and 9 per cent 32,000 per annum. The Assembly concluded that 28,900 per annum would be appropriate while supporting early progress in eliminating or reducing a backlog of provision (SEERA, 2005, pp31–33).

The plan calls for future development to be focused in and around urban areas, in order to conserve land and support sustainable development patterns, maximizing the viability of existing infrastructure, especially public

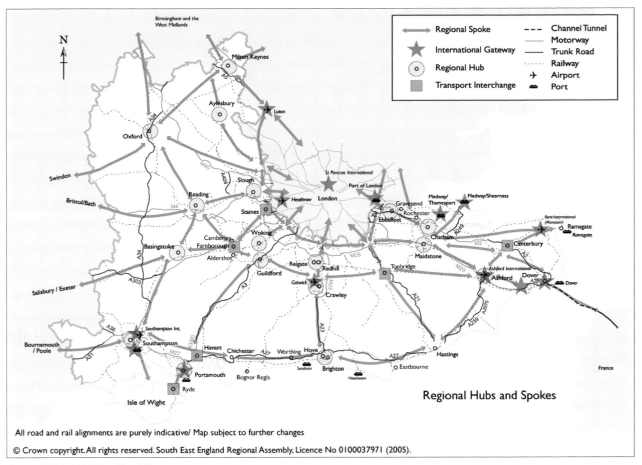

Source: SEERA, 2005, Map T2, p103

Figure 9.4 South East Spatial Strategy 2005 hubs and spokes

transport, and service provision – both community services such as education, health, social and cultural facilities, and also water and energy supply. Development should therefore be concentrated within urban areas and at least 60 per cent of all new development should be on previously developed land and through conversions of existing buildings (SEERA, 2005, p52). On transport, the plan proposes developing the role of regional hubs that increase the level of accessibility by public transport, walking and cycling, including high-quality interchange facilities between different modes of transport; these will become foci of economic activity, with higher-density land uses and/or mixed land uses that require a high level of accessibility so as to create 'living centres' (SEERA, 2005, pp93–94). They will be supported by a network of regional spokes: corridors of movement that will support a complementary and integrated network of rail and express bus/coach services (Figure 9.4).

The East of England Regional Spatial Strategy (2004) also plans for an enhanced rate of growth, concentrated in key locations in the government's Sustainable Communities growth corridors. In Thames Gateway these include Basildon, Southend-on-Sea and Thurrock; in the Stansted–Cambridge corridor, Cambridge, Harlow and

Peterborough; and in the Milton Keynes–South Midlands corridor, Bedford and Luton–Dunstable; the strategy accepts the earlier Milton Keynes–South Midlands sub-regional strategy as a basis for strategy in that zone (EERA, 2004, pp18–19).

The East Midlands Regional Spatial Strategy (2005) is based on a sequential approach based as far as possible on five existing Principal Urban Areas (PUAs), one of which, Northampton, is in South East England – plus significant new development in Corby, Kettering and Wellingborough (identified as growth towns in the Milton Keynes–South Midlands sub-regional strategy), plus smaller-scale development in sub-regional centres including Daventry (GOEM, 2005, pp15–17). Here again, the approach is completely consistent with the government's Sustainable Communities strategy and thus with ESDP strategic objectives.

This consistency arises in part because of the prior existence of the Milton Keynes–South Midlands sub-regional strategy, spanning three regions – East of England, East Midlands, and South East – and produced through a separate coordinated process. Produced in draft in July 2003 and publicly examined in Spring 2004 (EERA, 2004, p98), it has then simply been incorporated into the RSS. It

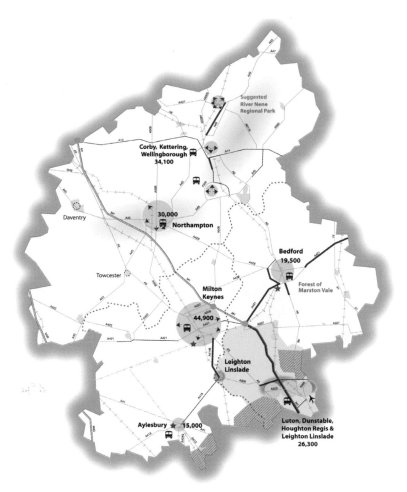

Source: ODPM/GOSE/GOEM/GOEE, 2005, Figure 1, pp10–11

Figure 9.5 Milton Keynes–South Midlands sub-regional strategy 2003

concentrates major development into six growth areas: Aylesbury, Bedford–Kempston–Northern Marston Vale, Corby, Kettering and Wellingborough, Luton–Dunstable–Houghton Regis, Milton Keynes and Northampton (GOSE/GOEM/GOEE, 2005, p13). In all these there will be an integrated approach to accessibility, aiming at reducing dependence on private car use through an improvement in public transport provision (GOSE/GOEM/GOEE, 2005, pp59–60). The resulting planned growth will be substantial: 169,800 new homes over the period 2002–2021 (Figure 9.5).

The local context: Powers and money

South East England thus demonstrates a remarkable consistency of approach in translating broad pan-European strategic spatial objectives, through a sub-European level and into national and regional planning strategies, despite the obvious anomalies of a democratic deficit and anomalous regional boundaries. There are however two major questions for the future, concerning implementation at the local scale.

First, the government has proposed and local authorities have accepted a great variety of Special Purpose

Vehicles (SPVs) for local delivery: Urban Development Corporations (West Northamptonshire, Thurrock and East London); Urban Regeneration Companies (Corby, Peterborough); Local Strategic Partnerships (Kent Thamesside, Milton Keynes); an unspecified 'Local Delivery Vehicle' (North Northamptonshire); a commercial consortium (Stratford City); and other arrangements (including a special mechanism for delivery of London's 2012 Olympics bid in the Lower Lea Valley of East London). These have varying powers and resources, and some are highly dependent on goodwill and support from the local authorities, which may not be so readily forthcoming after changes in political control which occurred in the May 2005 elections – notably, from Labour to Conservative control in Northamptonshire and from no overall control to Conservative in Oxfordshire.

Second, though the government has allocated £330 million for spending on specific infrastructure and housing projects to support the strategy in Thames Gateway, with another £136 million across the other three growth areas (Ashford, Milton Keynes–South Midlands and London–Stansted–Cambridge) with the intention of leveraging private sector investment of over £2 billion, both the South East and East of England RPBs have refused to support higher levels of housebuilding unless considerably more is on offer. Their stance has been reinforced by an independent consultancy study, suggesting a funding gap of £1900 million in the South East and £6012 million in the East of England region (Roger Tym & Partners, 2005). This remains a major point of contention between the central government and the regional bodies, and a major source of doubt about whether the strategy can be implemented on the scale and at the speed envisaged.

Key questions for policy

Continuity of planning policy, cascading down from the European scale through national policy for sustainable communities, to the RSSs for the constituent regions of South East England, undoubtedly reflects a determination on the part of the UK government to adhere to the policies in the ESDP and Lisbon Agenda (European Council, 2000) – at least in principle, and with a domestically oriented slant. However, the strongly centralized nature of government in the UK allows central government to set policy agendas for the regions, assisted by a 'democratic deficit' in English regional government. However, this remains an approach strongly based on land use planning; though the intention may be to implement a more far-reaching *aménagement du territoire* on the French model, the necessary structures and instruments for implementation appear to be lacking.[3] This is most evident in an apparent lack of integration between land use planning and transport planning. The need for improved transport infrastructure and internal accessibility has been shown to be critical to sustain flows (essential commuting and business travel) across an MCR that is far larger than existing South East England administrative boundaries. This requires joined-up strategic planning between districts and other government departments including the Highways Agency, Network Rail, Civil Aviation Authority and Department for Transport.

The London strategy will inevitably prove expensive and will require central government support, particularly for transport investment and land preparation. It raises the question of whether the housing targets, in particular, are realistic. The Rowntree Foundation has shown that in recent years, actual housing completions have been barely one-third of the need as calculated by the Mayor's own housing commission. The major regeneration sites depend heavily on transport investments to make them commercially viable: not only the very ambitious and expensive east–west Crossrail, but also more modest schemes like the Docklands Light Railway extension to Barking Riverside which is not currently funded. And the major development proposals are not always coherently limited to transport investments: Crossrail does not serve a major development like Barking Riverside at all.

There is therefore a central question about the London Plan. Although its basic strategy is generally supported, even by its critics, it is vulnerable to changes – especially, economic. It will require big resources in order to achieve the ambitious targets – not all of which can be raised by London itself, at least without some major new source such as a development land tax, which would require national legislation. And, in places, there appears to be a certain lack of integration between transport and proposed development. The question remains: can it be achieved on the scale foreseen? If not, part of the resulting pressure – particularly on housing – may fall on neighbouring regions.

Here, too, doubts remain. Effectively, while the RSSs try to develop from the old emphasis on land use planning towards wider spatial strategies on the French model, they remain limited in terms of powers of implementation. Even within a few months of their publication as a basis for consultation, the responsible Regional Assemblies for the South East and East of England regions have begun to scale down the planned level of development, on the basis that the necessary investment in infrastructure is not forthcoming. This represents the most serious obstacle to their implementation, and it is reported that the Treasury is seeking to devise new ways of involving private developers in advance preparation of infrastructure. Here the obvious problem revealed by POLYNET is that the areas where large-scale investment is needed, to the east of London, are also the least well connected to the knowledge economy; hence, leverage of private finance is likely to be most difficult in just the areas where investment is needed most. Essentially, the UK is still very far from the system of concerted national and regional planning that has been practised in France since the 1950s, and which provides the conceptual basis for the ESDP.

The concept of spatial planning, as currently embodied in South East England policy frameworks, has yet to reconcile fully functional interrelationships between 'economic flows' and 'places' – both fine-grained and strategic vision is required. RSSs across the MCR show a strong alignment but effective powers, vital to finance development needs resulting from global drivers, lie outside the remit of regional authorities. Most UK taxes are determined, collected and redistributed locally according to nationally determined priorities. Increased re-investment of taxes levied in London and the South East will be needed to support its unique role in knowledge and wealth creation. And there is a lack of governance at the MCR scale. Decision-making on transport, housing (numbers, type, location) and skills ultimately takes place at central – across many departmental groups and quangos – and local levels. Future strategic decision-making on these issues must involve regional agencies and the private sector. Inter-regional competition for inward investment and differing local interests on accommodating growth pose a threat to key UK and EU economic development priorities. Policy coordination is required both horizontally and vertically to promote sustainable management of MCR assets and flows and grow the Pentagon.

Finally, Europe's 'competitiveness' in the global economy, coupled with internal cooperation between cities and regions, is strongly encouraged both in the ESDP and the Lisbon Agenda. Yet, as seen in policy documents, a competitive instinct remains at a political level. London business is seen as 'under constant and strong pressure from competitors in other countries' and 'other top global economies in North America, Asia and Europe' are discussed as being 'our real competitors'. The functional complementarity of business relationships between city regions in North West Europe should inform territorial cooperation.

The policy documents reveal some obvious contradictions. Functional polycentricity, associated with South East England's buoyant service economy, covers a wide area, resulting in pressures for development (housing and employment) that conflict with objectives for self-containment (minimization of movement). In spite of developments in information and communication technology (ICT), more balanced intra-regional development is leading to increasing cross-commuting and business travel which cannot be effectively supported by public transport. There are challenges for regional planning: the scale of the MCR, which comprises parts of four regional administrative areas in addition to South East England, and the range of market processes and public-private influences that shape its future development. In particular a wide range of central government interventions are not integrated with objectives for the regional economy.

So there are two pointers to future policy: first, to bring the North of England and Midland core cities, and their surrounding city regions, closer to London; second, in parallel, to 'grow South East England' into the Midlands by promoting better connections along sustainable community growth corridors. Critical preconditions for sustainable management of the functionally extended MCR will be integrated planning that takes account of potential complementarities that interlink the space of places in the global space of flows. These challenges represent an agenda that goes beyond POLYNET.

Notes

1 In contrast, conventional 'morphological polycentricity', as found in the RhineRuhr and the Randstad, need not be associated at all with 'functional polycentricity'; there, indeed, it is associated with weak intra-regional functional linkages.

2 This section is equally applicable to all eight regional chapters. It is placed here to provide a general context for all of them, though – as shown below – it is especially relevant to the South East England case.

3 We return to this important point in Chapter 17.

10

Randstad Holland: Multiple Faces of a Polycentric Role Model

Bart Lambregts, Robert Kloosterman, Merijn van der Werff,
Robert Röling and Loek Kapoen

The Randstad Holland is commonly portrayed as one of Europe's most pronounced polycentric mega-city regions (MCRs). It combines a political capital, a financial capital, a cultural capital, first-class international gateway functions (the port of Rotterdam and Schiphol Airport) and a highly-skilled, cosmopolitan labour force. But these assets are not located in just one city as in London or Paris; they are distributed over a number of historically distinct cities in the western part of The Netherlands. Relationships between these cities date back centuries or more. Already in the 16th century, for example, excellent water-borne transport connections fostered the development of a marked division of labour between them, the remnants of which can still be traced today ('t Hart, 1994; Kloosterman and Lambregts, 2001). Since then, however, complexity has increased enormously. Successive rounds of (global) economic restructuring have radically reshaped the area and still continue to redefine the roles and perspectives of both individual cities and the Randstad region as a whole. At the same time, the advance of motorized transportation has been a boon to (individualized) mobility, increasing the freedom of location for households and firms alike. Patterns of linkages and interdependencies between and among the cities, towns and villages of the Randstad area have correspondingly become more complex. As a result the Randstad has become a complex, multi-layered mosaic of places, markets and flows, rife with implicit and explicit intra-regional interdependencies and hierarchies and connected to the rest of the world in intricate ways. It can be argued that currently business services industries play the key role in the ongoing reconfiguration of the region's

spatial appearance, its economic functioning and its incorporation in the global economy. After all, many service activities have recently been (and still are) among the fastest growing industries and are, moreover, subject to strong processes of globalization (UNCTAD, 2004). In this chapter we will explore the question: what does the functioning of the business services sector tell us about polycentricity in the Randstad and how do current policy frameworks relate to this?

The Randstad as a polycentric business services complex

The Randstad: Key characteristics

The Randstad is the horseshoe-shaped urban configuration in the western part of The Netherlands. It roughly runs from Dordrecht and Rotterdam in the south, via The Hague and Leiden in the west to Amsterdam in the north and Utrecht and Amersfoort in the east. These cities surround a predominantly rural area called the 'Green Heart'. The outer borders of the Randstad are not precisely defined (see Figure 10.1).

The Randstad measures about 43.5 miles by 46.5 miles (70km by 75km) (16 per cent of the Dutch land area) and houses about 6.6 million people (40 per cent of the Dutch population). They live in a large number of mainly medium size cities and an even larger number of smaller towns and villages. At the end of 2004, the region included 12 cities with more than 100,000 inhabitants and another 12 in the range 70,000–100,000. The most populous cities are Amsterdam (739,000), Rotterdam

Figure 10.1 Overview of the Randstad

(596,000), The Hague (469,000) and Utrecht (275,000). In The Netherlands, these cities together are often referred to as the 'Big 4'. The co-presence of so many individual smaller and larger cities in a relatively small area gives the Randstad its typical polycentric appearance.

The Randstad is also the country's economic powerhouse. It is home to some 3.2 million jobs (45 per cent of Dutch employment), most of them in various kinds of services. In terms of spatial distribution, employment generally closely follows population (see Figure 10.2). The main population centres and their surroundings are also the main employment centres, with the possible exception of Schiphol airport, which has developed into a massive logistics and services centre of its own.

The Randstad's global connections are effectively facilitated through the port of Rotterdam (Europe's largest), Schiphol Airport (Europe's fourth largest), and the Amsterdam Internet Exchange (the largest in Europe after London). A dense network of road and railway corridors connects the cities of the Randstad with each other and with other parts of the country and North West Europe at large. A high-speed train connection with Brussels and Paris is to open in 2007.

At first glance, therefore, locational differences within the polycentric MCR of the Randstad seem to be eroded to the point of insignificance. Population and employment centres are almost evenly spread across the region; nearly every centre has access to the same infrastructure (both transport and communications) and is, moreover, located within one-hour travel time of Schiphol Airport. Beneath this picture, however, there also exists a more fine-grained pattern of functional divisions and interdependencies. They can be illustrated, for instance, by taking a closer look at the Randstad's business services complex.

Changing the focus to business services

The Randstad stands out as The Netherlands's most services-oriented region. At the end of 2002, 752,000 or 54 per cent of the country's jobs in business services were located in the Randstad. Business services accounted for 24 per cent of total employment in this region compared to 16.5 per cent in the rest of The Netherlands (Central Bureau of Statistics (CBS) employment statistics). Within the Randstad, the Amsterdam and Utrecht regions are particularly important business services strongholds. Here,

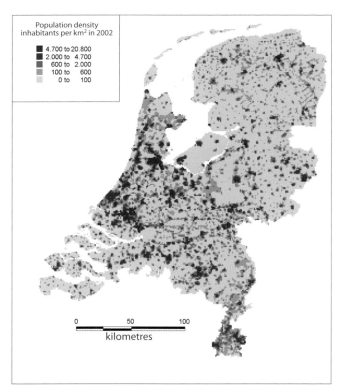
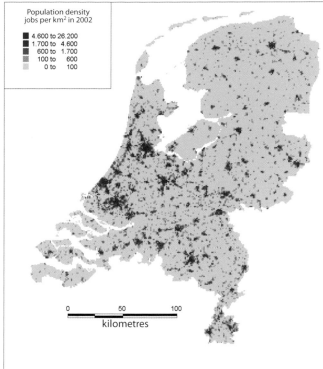

Figure 10.2 Distribution of population and employment, based upon CBS data

the business services' share of local employment is almost 30 per cent.

The Randstad's lead in business services over the rest of The Netherlands is not of recent date. As the country's most urbanized region, the Randstad was the first region to undergo the transition from a predominantly industrial to a predominantly post-industrial or service economy. Its head start has since then diminished somewhat, but the latest figures show that the strongest job growth in business services again occurs notably in the Amsterdam and Utrecht regions and in the area in between. Growth here is stronger than the national average and much stronger than in the southern half of the Randstad.

Within the Randstad, considerable differences exist as regards the services profiles of the different major cities (see Figure 10.3). Amsterdam, as the country's long-standing trade and financial centre, stands out as the region's prime services centre. It has by far the largest concentration of financial services in the country and also leads in law and advertising firms. The city's large numbers of (Dutch) multi-nationals provide ample demand for advanced producer services (APS) of many kinds. On top of that, the city is also favourite with foreign services firms entering the Dutch market, a picture that was confirmed by a small research study carried out in 2004 (Lambregts and van der Werff, 2004). From a sample of 78 global business services firms with one or more offices in The Netherlands (taken from Taylor, 2004a) almost three-quarters of the headquarters (HQ) were located in Amsterdam or one of

its surrounding municipalities (Amstelveen notably), with only a handful of offices left for Rotterdam, Utrecht and some smaller places in between (see Figure 10.4). This marked concentration of global business services HQ in the Amsterdam area led the researchers to contend that, within the Randstad, the global city milieu to which global business services tend to be attracted (cf. Sassen, 2001) is very much monopolized by Amsterdam and its immediate surroundings.

The city of Utrecht and the eastern part of the Randstad are characterized by a strong presence of design (engineering) and management consultancy firms. Many of the large Dutch firms in these sectors have their HQ in this area.

The economy of the southern part of the Randstad differs significantly from that of the northern and eastern parts. The Hague is first of all the seat of the national government and a wide range of related public and semi-public institutions. As such, it does attract its fair share of business services, but the sector at large is not as well developed as in the Amsterdam region. Accountants, design consultants (especially engineering) and law firms are quite well represented but for financial services, advanced logistics, advertising and management consultancy the reverse is true.

Rotterdam, in turn, still heavily depends on its port as far as the economy is concerned. After Haarlemmermeer (the municipality that hosts the national airport Schiphol) the city is home to the largest concentration of (advanced)

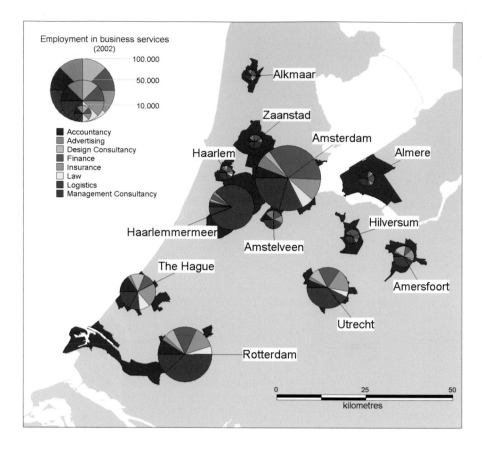

Source: LISA, 2002

Figure 10.3 Business services jobs in selected Randstad centres

logistics services in the Randstad. Accountancy is another well-represented sector in the city; several of the country's largest accountancy firms have their HQ in Rotterdam. The city is also renowned for its concentration of highly successful architecture firms (Kloosterman, 2004). Finance, advertising and management consultancy are among the sectors that are quite underrepresented in the Rotterdam area.

In what sense is the Randstad a polycentric business services complex?

So while in terms of population and total employment distribution the Randstad appears as a rather undifferentiated polycentric conurbation – in effect a single urban field – the above analysis, however schematic and partial, shows that beneath this 'unmistakable' poly-centric picture of the Randstad there exists a far more complex and multi-layered reality that is shaped by subtle divisions of labour and highly localized agglomerative forces. For every indicator demonstrating the 'polycentric' nature of the area there is another showing that the area also has more 'monocentric' characteristics. A comprehensive under-standing of the area needs to take into account both its monocentric and its polycentric features, and be open to the ways in which they interrelate. In the next section we will explore the latter issue in some more detail.

Complicating the picture: Connectivity and intra-firm linkages

Multi-level connectivity through office networks

Detailed quantitative study of the office networks and inter-office linkages of some 175 Randstad-based business services firms (Lambregts et al, 2005c) (see also Chapter 3 for details of the methodology) reinforces the multi-layered picture described above. In terms of connectivity it appears that overall regional interconnectivity in the Randstad is strong. This means that multiple cities (rather than just one or two) are relatively well connected, both with each other and with a range of other cities through the office networks of business services firms. The latter is especially true for Amsterdam and Rotterdam. Amsterdam is the city that is best connected at the regional level (i.e. within the Randstad) while Rotterdam, quite surprisingly, is the city that is best connected at the national level (Figure 10.5a, b). Utrecht and The Hague are reasonably well connected with other regional and national centres as well. The 'connectivity gap' between the four largest cities and the smaller centres of the Randstad at first sight seems major, but it is actually quite minor when viewed from a comparative perspective (see Chapter 3). Interestingly, of all the minor Randstad centres the most peripherally

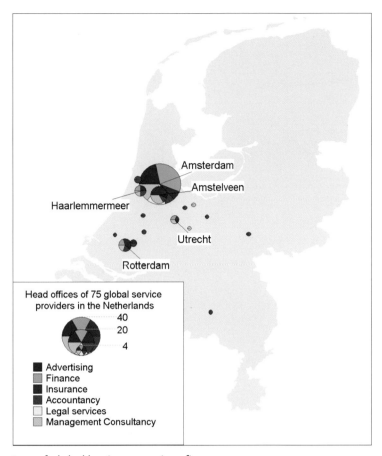

Figure 10.4 Dutch headquarters of global business services firms

situated cities of Alkmaar and Amersfoort achieve the highest regional and national connectivity scores.

Thus while at the regional and national scales Amsterdam and Rotterdam compete closely for the status of 'most connected' city, the story is quite different at the European and global scales. Here, Amsterdam emerges as the country's internationally best-connected city, with Rotterdam following at some distance (Figure 10.5c, d). Utrecht and The Hague are number three and four, again at some distance. Noteworthy is also that minor centres located in the vicinity of Schiphol Airport (i.e. Amstelveen and Haarlemmermeer) gain some places in the European and global connectivity rankings compared to the regional and national rankings. Amsterdam's clear lead in European and global connectedness without doubt has to do with its popularity as a place of settlement among global services providers (see above).

Intra-regional linkages – again through office networks

The same quantitative analysis of office networks also produced an overview of the potential intra-regional linkages between the Randstad's 12 major business services centres (Figure 10.6). The strongest linkages are between Amsterdam and Rotterdam (meaning that these are the pair of cities for which most firms find it necessary to have

a simultaneous presence). Next are the connections between this pair of cities and The Hague and Utrecht. Alkmaar and Amersfoort maintain relatively strong connections with each of the four largest cities in the Randstad. The other minor centres are not particularly well linked to each other and/or the larger centres in the region. An exception is Haarlem, which maintains reasonably strong connections with Amsterdam. The 'strength' of all other linkages is less than 60 per cent of that of the strongest linkage: Amsterdam–Rotterdam.

Connected cities or divided markets?

The above findings give rise to different – in parts even paradoxical – interpretations. First, and less problematically, the connectivity scores presented suggest that whereas dominance in terms of connectivity at the regional and national levels is shared among four cities, a single city (i.e. Amsterdam) demonstrates outstanding quality if European and global levels are considered. This finding suggests that the Randstad is more polycentric as a regional system in its national context than as an MCR in the European and global contexts: a statement that supports the findings in the previous section.

More caution is needed, however, in interpreting the meaning of the intra-regional networks analysis and this requires a complementary qualitative interview

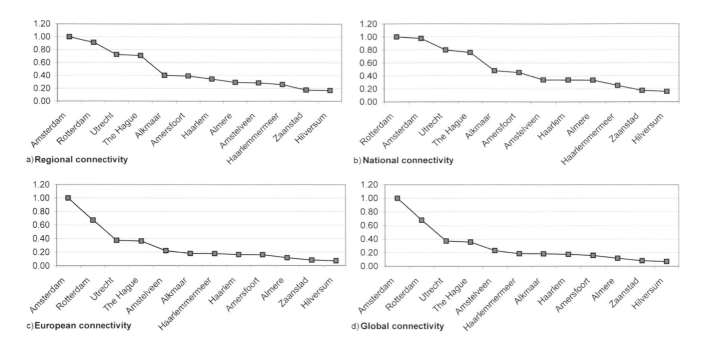

Figures 10.5a, b, c, d GaWC connectivity indices: Office networks

methodology, to be discussed in detail in the next section. The outcomes of the quantitative analysis suggest that a dense and well-spread network of business services flows exists between the main business services centres of the Randstad. The layout of the network also differs significantly from the commuting networks analysed in the project (see Chapter 2). This analysis showed that the strongest commuting linkages are predominantly defined at the level of individual city regions (for example, those of Amsterdam, Rotterdam and The Hague) and that 'pan-Randstad' commuting is (still) a rather modest phenomenon. Figure 10.6, on the other hand, suggests that the opposite is true for business services flows. Here, the strongest linkages typically occur between the four largest cities and not so much between the largest cities and their surrounding subcentres. But caution is definitely necessary here. Interview evidence indicates that the dense network of intra-regional linkages found is above all the result of many business services firms apparently finding it necessary to have offices simultaneously in Amsterdam and Rotterdam and often in a number of other cities as well. It is tempting to focus on the (supposedly) frequent and meaningful forms of interaction between the offices and hence to conceive the region as a 'polycentric system of business services centres', the cities of which are more or less closely tied to one another through (intra-firm) business services flows. This is, however, but one possible interpretation of the patterns found here. A second one is that many firms do not find it feasible to serve the entire Randstad region from a single office. Their clients are spread across the Randstad but cannot be 'serviced' from a single, strategically chosen location. As such, the region may be polycentric in the sense that markets are dispersed and that several economic centres of gravity co-exist, but it does not function simultaneously as a polycentric system (or region) in the sense that, for example, one centre can easily be served from another. In this interpretation, the Randstad is made up of several (at least four) largely separate business markets. It is also this interpretation that helps us to make sense of the relatively strong 'links' that were found between the comparatively peripheral cities of Alkmaar and Amersfoort on the one hand and the four largest cities on the other. While seemingly many firms consider it feasible to serve smaller centres such as Zaanstad, Almere, Amstelveen and Haarlemmermeer from their offices in Amsterdam, the cities of Alkmaar and Amersfoort are located so far away from the main centres as to justify the opening of additional offices. Presumably, these cities, like the four largest ones, constitute 'business markets' of their own.

So altogether, the outcomes of the connectivity analysis on the one hand confirm the idea of the Randstad being 'polycentric' in more than one way, while on the other they add complexity to the picture by suggesting that the Randstad may not be as coherent an entity as presumed, and rather should be understood as a loose collection of smaller regions instead. In the next section, this suggestion will be explored in more detail.

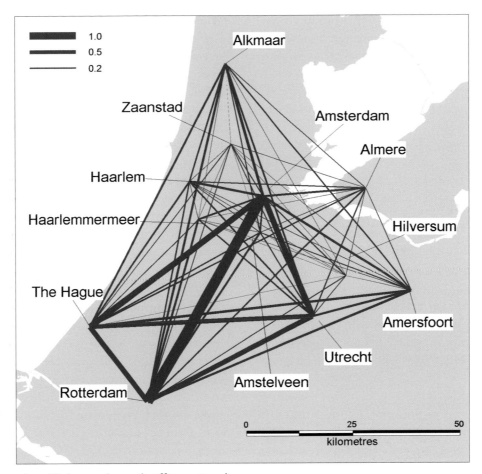

Figure 10.6 Intra-regional linkages through office networks

Business services markets in the Randstad

Within The Netherlands, the Randstad is without doubt the region where most of the business and corporate decision-making takes place, including the bulk of internationally oriented business. While it is not an absolute requirement to be actually based in the area in order to serve this rich and diversified business market (as is proved by companies that successfully acquire business in the Randstad from places such as Arnhem and Tilburg), most of the larger and growth-seeking Dutch APS firms feel the need to have a presence here. Next to an abundance of business opportunities, the Randstad also constitutes an extensive pool of highly qualified labour. By strategically choosing its location, a firm can give itself direct access to more than a million potential employees with a university or college degree. The Randstad's northern and eastern parts may be slightly better endowed in this respect than the southern part (Marlet and van Woerkens, 2003). For only a few business services industries are labour markets more locally defined. Examples include advertising agencies and specific financial services, which basically rely on the Amsterdam region for labour (that is, if they want to attract the most talented of people).

The fact that a large percentage of global business services find it necessary or attractive to have a presence in Amsterdam and/or the wider Randstad area (see above) also confirms the idea that from a global perspective the Randstad represents an attractive market for business services firms. Interviews with high-ranking managers of 64 Randstad-based business services firms (for a full report see Lambregts et al, 2005a) generally confirmed and even reinforced this picture. Many Dutch-based branches of internationally networked firms were reported to do relatively well compared to branches of the same firms in other countries. Quite often they are either significantly larger than could be expected on the basis of the small size of the Dutch economy, or they play an active role in the management of the networks of which they are a part. Reasons for this (as mentioned by interviewees) include: the traditional outward/international orientation of the Dutch economy and its entrepreneurs; the fact that The Netherlands are for many other countries an acceptable (i.e. because of its small size, not very threatening) entity to which to allot executive tasks; and – last but not least – the fact that the Randstad or Dutch services market is well developed, not least because it is the HQ of a relatively large number of multi-national companies (MNCs) that give rise to a comparatively large and (because of their often complex and globalized operations) sophisticated demand for business services.

The same interviews, however, also produced the insight that the Randstad is not considered to be a 'single' market by each and every firm. There appears to be a crucial dividing line between services firms with a client orientation towards small and medium size enterprises (SMEs) on the one hand and firms predominantly servicing large and MNCs on the other. For both categories, the Randstad offers a rich pallet of business opportunities and an attractive pool of potential employees, but for neither does the region necessarily coincide with the spatial scope of their operations. For the vast majority of SME-oriented service providers the Randstad is simply too large. The spatial scope of their markets is usually more limited, in part because they depend so strongly on presence and visibility in local networks for the acquisition of business. To take full advantage of the Randstad's business potential, such firms therefore need offices in various cities across the region as it is, for example, virtually impossible to operate successfully on the Amsterdam SME market from Rotterdam and vice versa.

Alternatively, for MNC-oriented services providers, business does not stop at the edges of the Randstad. They consider the whole of The Netherlands as their 'hunting ground'. Quite a number of them are capable of serving the whole country from a single, often Randstad-based office that only occasionally is complemented by a subsidiary office, for example, in Eindhoven. While face-to-face contacts do form a crucial part of their day-to-day operations (just as for SME-oriented firms), their ability to acquire new business usually does not depend strongly on 'local visibility'. Most of the MNC-serving business firms rank among the 'big names' in their fields and will be invited to pitch for a job based upon their reputations and previous experiences rather than on local visibility. Firms that service both SMEs and MNCs often maintain an extended network of regional offices for their SME-oriented operations while attending to their MNC clients from a single (HQ) office in the Randstad.

So from a business services perspective, the 'nature' of the Randstad is again diffuse rather than unanimous. For some the Randstad consists of several separate or partly overlapping geographical markets while for others the area just constitutes the 'centre court' of a larger entity: the entire Dutch market for business services. Because of its distinct concentration of business opportunities (and qualified labour supply) the Randstad gets (international) recognition as 'a market', but in practice its boundaries are as fluid as can be.

Governance and policy

The multi-form picture emerging from the above directly resembles the region's institutional and policy context. From an administrative and institutional perspective, just as from a functional perspective, the region is every inch as much a multi-layered patchwork; and spatial policies for the Randstad also continue to waver between taking the region as a functionally integrated system or a loose collection of subsystems. The country's fifth official planning memorandum, issued in 2004, changes little in that (Ministerie van Volkshuisvesting, Ruimtelijke Ordening en Milieu (VROM), 2004).

The Dutch administrative structure basically consists of three different tiers: the national, the provincial and the municipal. As regards spatial planning, national government provides the overall policy framework (long-term goals, general strategies) while executive planning powers tend to be in the hands of the municipalities. A key responsibility of the provinces (12 in total) is to ensure a minimum level of coordination between local development initiatives and to check whether they are consistent with ongoing national policy directives. This structure has been in place for more than 150 years, with tasks and responsibilities (in the field of spatial planning) occasionally shifting back and forth between tiers. The latest trend is predominantly one towards (further) decentralization of powers.

The Randstad, which is presently divided between about 175 municipalities and four provinces, is one of the regional constructs that fits uneasily in the three-tier structure (others include the functional urban regions (FURs) around the major cities). Calls for the establishment of a fully fledged metropolitan authority for the Randstad have been made on several occasions. However, such a large-scale reconstruction of the 'House of Thorbecke'[1] as it is called in The Netherlands, has over the years proved a mission impossible and probably will continue to be so for a while. Nevertheless, in order to address the emerging reality of a 'regional world', refuge has been taken in alternative (some would say second-best) solutions such as the scaling up of the local level (e.g. by way of merging municipalities) and the promotion of inter-municipal and, albeit to a lesser extent, inter-provincial cooperation.

In effect, fragmentation is therefore still the key word in any description of the administrative landscape of the Randstad, although admittedly, local and regional actors increasingly seem to open up to different forms of cooperation in order to get things done – or at least discussed. The most prominent example is the by now formal cooperative platform called *Regio Randstad*. In this administrative platform the four Randstad provinces (i.e. North Holland, South Holland, Utrecht and Flevoland), the four largest cities and their respective city regions undertake joint activities that are in the interest of the (international) competitive position and quality of life of the Randstad. It is also the discussion partner of the national government as far as issues relating to the Randstad at large are concerned. Its mission is largely compatible with that of the *Vereniging Deltametropool* (or Deltametropolis Association), a rather diverse and active Randstad-based think tank and interest group that strongly promotes a metropolitan development perspective for the Randstad area. Next to these, the region is home to many smaller and often more informal platforms for cooperation. Examples include the 'Administrative Platform for the South-wing', the 'North-wing Conference' and the 'Administrative Platform for the Green Heart'. Not all platforms and arrangements work equally smoothly or achieve continuous success, but many are proving to be quite resilient and they are excellent vehicles for building trust and developing a common understanding of regions' spatial development problems and challenges.

This development comes at a time when Dutch spatial policy-making is imbued with a widespread sense of urgency to get the faltering economy up and running again. Pressure is even high enough to have spurred the four ministries that produce spatially relevant policies to coordinate their activities and strategies, which is not a foregone conclusion in Dutch policy-making. The extent to which this joint approach will make itself felt when the broad policy strategies outlined in the various White Papers are further refined and implemented remains to be seen. Experience shows that the walls between policy departments tend to crumble only very slowly, but one never knows.

In terms of content, current spatial, economic and transport policies at different levels generally seem to be based on a sound understanding of the conditions and dynamics on the ground. Of course, interpretations and interests between and among departments and administrative tiers do differ to some degree, and also the solutions and strategies that are proposed in consequence are not always fully compatible, but on the whole there have been less unanimous times in Dutch spatial planning. Perhaps the most interesting difference in point of view is that between the national government and the united Randstad authorities. While both share the opinion that it is notably the Randstad – as the motor of the Dutch economy – that should be enabled to strengthen its international competitive position and hence to get the Dutch economy moving again, they advocate different spatial development strategies for the region. Whereas the national government assumes that the Randstad is best helped by strengthening its constituent parts (i.e. the North-wing, the South-wing and the Utrecht region) the Randstad authorities would rather ensure that the constituent parts come to function as one so as to make better use of the metropolitan potential that they consider to be inherent in the region.

POLYNET research findings for the Randstad tend to provide support for both views. Analysis of travel-to-work patterns pointed out that the lion's share of commuting indeed remains confined to the level of individual city regions and the Randstad wings. And from the interviews with business services firms it has become clear that for a substantial share of the firms – that is above all the category of business services firms catering to SMEs – the same city regions and 'wings' function as their main areas of operations as well. However, the analyses also indicate that for another category of issues the Randstad may indeed form a more meaningful level for analysis and policy-making. For business services firms that service MNCs, the entire Randstad constitutes a market. Even though many such firms for a variety of reasons prefer to be located in the Amsterdam region, it is the business potential offered by the Randstad as a whole that attracts them to the area (if they come from abroad) and that enables them to prosper and eventually become European or global players of their own (if they originate from the area itself). It is findings like these that support the call for promoting market integration through travel time reduction, as made by the *Regio Randstad*, and the claim made by the *Vereniging Deltametropool* that an integrated, metropolitan approach is vital to secure the survival and further strengthening of the Randstad's high-level international functions.

Note

1 Johan Rudolf Thorbecke (1798–1872) was a celebrated 19th Century Dutch politician who, in 1848, almost single-handedly drafted a revision of the Dutch constitution based on a 'three-level' system of power (state, province, municipality) which has survived and is known as the 'House of Thorbecke'.

11

Central Belgium: Polycentrism in a Federal Context

Christian Vandermotten, Marcel Roelandts, Laurent Aujean and Etienne Castiau

Polycentrism is promoted as an answer to diseconomies of scale resulting from congestion affecting large urban areas, and as a strategic tool for development and improved spatial equity. What is the impact of polycentrism in Belgium, a country characterized by a very small, quite densely urbanized territory divided into three autonomous regions within a federal context of government?

The legacies of the urban system

A map of population densities in Belgium shows a sharp contrast between a northern densely populated part, approximately corresponding to the territory of the Flemish region, and a southern, less densely populated, part: the Walloon region, especially south of the Sambre and Meuse valleys. The Brussels-Capital region, with 1 million inhabitants, is completely enclosed within the Flemish region, though its southern part is close to the Walloon region's boundaries. Its peri-urban extension, and to an even larger extent its labour pool, stretches largely over Flanders and Wallonia.

The Belgian urban system is dominated by Brussels. Although in the early 19th century Brussels had a population quite similar to that of the Flemish cities of Antwerp and Ghent, the capital progressively asserted itself after independence. Today, the Brussels morphological area has almost twice as many inhabitants as Antwerp and six times more than Ghent.

In Flanders, the medieval urban system was essentially a Christallerian network related to the early development of trade activities and the simultaneous agricultural intensification, except in the north-east (Saey, 1981; Vandermotten and Vandewattyne, 1985). This ancient urban framework developed and reinforced itself with the revival of Flemish economic dynamism, already visible in the inter-war period, and has asserted itself particularly since World War II. This has led to peri-urbanization and general urbanization in the north of the country, structured by a dense network of medium and small size cities. Such 'rurbanization' was brought about by the early intensity of workers' commuting by rail, developed from the 19th century onwards in order to avoid excessive working-class concentrations in cities, considered a social threat by the governments of those days.

The Walloon urbanization for its part is concentrated in the former industrial and coal area, developed in the 19th century along the Haine, Sambre, Meuse and Vesdre valleys. In Wallonia, pre-industrial urbanization was much more limited than in Flanders, so that the urban developments linked to industrialization have led to the emergence of a poorly structured linear conurbation.

Table 11.1 Population and surface area of the Belgian regions

	Total population (1 January 2005)	Surface area (km²)	Density (inhabitants per km²)
Flemish region	6,058,368	13,522	448
Walloon region	3,402,216	16,844	202
Brussels-Capital region	1,012,258	161	6287
Kingdom of Belgium	10,472,842	30,528	343

Source: SPF Economie – DG Statistique et information économique (2005)

Table 11.2 Principal Belgian urban areas in 2003

	Morphological area[a]	Remaining functional urban area[b]	Total
Brussels (Brussel)	1,524,019	1,286,126	2,810,145
Antwerp (Anvers) (FL)	816,041	599,443	1,415,484
Liège (WAL)	428,935	279,551	708,486
Ghent (Gand) (FL)	250,629	370,902	621,531
Charleroi (WAL)	325,563	200,301	525,864
Mons–La Louvière (WAL)	301,958	137,340	439,298
Hasselt/Genk (FL)	132,128	520,544	652,672
Leuven (Louvain) (FL)	102,602	79,462	182,064
Brugge (Bruges) (FL)	134,708	158,022	292,730
Kortrijk (Courtrai) (FL)	223,584	13,292	236,876
Namur (WAL)	105,705	153,209	258,914
Mechelen (Malines) (FL)	99,172	26,198	125,370

Notes: a Defined on the basis of all adjoining communes of more than 650 inhabitants/km^2.
b Defined on the basis of all communes having more than 10 per cent of their active population occupied in the economical area.

Belgium's institutional context in the field of territorial planning

Language differences, and even more divergent and conflicting economic and social histories, have led to a progressive process of federalization of Belgium, beginning in the 1960s and 1970s, culminating in an explicitly federal structure in 1993.

Wallonia is currently faced with the legacy of its industrial past: a lack of state-of-the-art advanced producer services, a high unemployment rate, redevelopment problems and large areas of industrial wasteland. In contrast, Flanders has benefited from sound development during the 'Golden Sixties', notably due to numerous multi-national investments but also its dense network of small and medium size enterprises (SMEs). As for the Brussels-Capital region, it is cut off from its natural hinterland by its regional boundaries, so that considerable peri-urbanization of population – mainly involving medium- and high-income level groups – and peripheral establishments of new firms tend to benefit the two surrounding regions.

The Belgian State, traditionally not very interventionist, has only been concerned with territorial planning since the 1960s, and then within a context of prosperity, once seen as unlimited, and functionalist views which have supported rather space-hungry Fordist developments. The coverage of the whole national territory by land use plans has not favoured a parsimonious management of space. Intense peri-urbanization has increased daily commuting movements and caused growing problems linked to a lack of cross-subsidization of resources between urban centres and their peripheries. This question is particularly crucial in Brussels, where it is compounded by the presence of regional boundaries.

Following the country's federalization, each of the regions has become fully responsible for territorial planning. Federalism in Belgium, contrary to other federal states like Germany, is characterized by the absence of a national structure for consultation, regulation, or cross-regional cooperation. In a context of harsh competition, the regions position themselves as competitors rather than as parts of a complementary system.

A polycentric system?

The labour market

Critical questioning of the polycentrism concept is often obscured by a lack of definition of the concept itself and of the spatial scale on which it is being analysed.

In terms of the workforce, even though commuting is well developed right across Belgium, the labour pools of the regional cities remain quite individually distinct (Figure 11.1). Brussels's labour pool, which provides nearly 80 per cent of the labour force in its economic core, covers the totality of the central part of the country, almost the whole of the former province of Brabant (currently the Walloon and Flemish Brabant provinces), huge parts of the north Hainaut and Namur provinces, the eastern part of East Flanders, several communes to the south of the Antwerp province and the west of Liège province. In addition, Brussels draws on a considerable mass of employment in the large cities outside its own functional urban region (FUR). In Belgium, the image of the job market is certainly not one of a polycentric system. Labour flows are particularly weak on both sides of the linguistic border, except those towards Brussels. Moreover, the labour pool of the city of Luxembourg is aggressively extending into the far south-east corner of Wallonia.

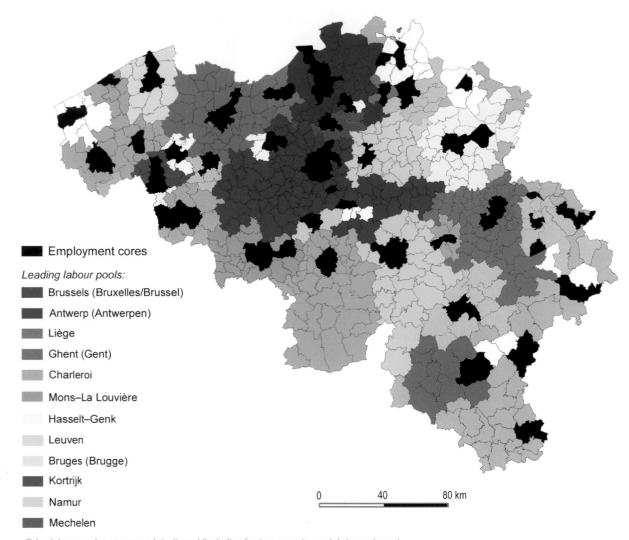

Employment cores

Leading labour pools:

Brussels (Bruxelles/Brussel)

Antwerp (Antwerpen)

Liège

Ghent (Gent)

Charleroi

Mons–La Louvière

Hasselt–Genk

Leuven

Bruges (Brugge)

Kortrijk

Namur

Mechelen

Other labour pools not separately indicated (including foreign countries, mainly Luxembourg)

Figure 11.1 Central Belgium: Labour pools

Brussels: An almost exclusive international position

Whatever the criteria considered – location of international institutions or of head offices, organization of conferences, etc. – Brussels, with its central position in the home market, appears as the only Belgian city with significant international weight, dominated by the presence of European institutions. According to Globalization and World Cities (GaWC) studies, Brussels is defined as a 'world incomplete city' (Beaverstock et al, 1999a). In addition to the presence of 'classic' subsidiaries of numerous multi-national companies (MNCs), the city is sometimes chosen by the latter for their European headquarters (HQ), while Belgian firms of international scope – though there are not many of these – mostly choose Brussels as their decision-making centre. Many MNCs setting up in Belgium opt for a location in Brussels or its periphery, without trying to establish subsidiaries in other Belgian cities. This is especially true of sectors such as advertising or law offering very specialized services to

international organizations whose clients are concentrated in the Brussels metropolitan area, albeit not always located in the European district. This also applies to international companies specializing in airport logistics based around Brussels airport at Zaventem. Due to the small size of the country, these firms have no difficulty in serving the whole of the national market from their Brussels base.

As far as advanced producer services (APS) are concerned, Brussels' primacy is especially evident, if we include the nearby Flemish periphery around the capital's airport (Zaventem).

If we consider the international connections of APS firms located in Belgium (Figure 11.2), once again the dominant international position of Brussels is largely confirmed.

Apart from Brussels, Antwerp is the only city benefiting from international connections of relative importance, but those connections are specialized in functions linked to harbour logistics activities and engineering services associated with the industrial weight of the city (Derudder and Taylor, 2003).

Table 11.3 Total employment and salaried employment in APS in the nine main cities of Belgium

Main cities	Total employment	Number of salaried jobs in APS	Proportion of salaried employment in APS (%)
Total of Brussels	690,172	114,817	17
Brussels-Capital region	*599,193*	*98,739*	*17*
Zaventem	*90,979*	*16,078*	*18*
Antwerp	272,063	37,498	14
Ghent	134,344	9965	7
Liège	94,470	6424	7
Hasselt-Genk	84,220	4757	6
Charleroi	79,007	3836	5
Leuven	59,591	7936	13
Brugge	57,388	3178	6
Malines	35,733	3322	9

Source: Office National de la Sécurité Sociale (ONSS) (2001)

The spatial functioning of the national economy

The leading role of Brussels in the national economy has already been stressed: Brussels-Capital provides 19.2 per cent of total national added value and, if we add the peripheral Hal-Vilvorde *arrondissement*, which includes most of the new activities located in the suburbs, that percentage rises to 25.5 per cent. By comparison, the Antwerp, Ghent and Liège *arrondissements* respectively account for 11.8 per cent, 5.4 per cent and 4.4 per cent. Brussels's supremacy is even more obvious with respect to management activities: in the financial sector, percentages reach 57.2 per cent for Brussels and its periphery, 10.8 per cent for Antwerp, 3.7 per cent for Ghent and 3.3 per cent for Liège. The weakness of the last percentage clearly reflects the weakness in the advanced tertiary sector of the old industrial cities of Walloon region.

Compared with observations at an international level, Belgian cities however appear to form part of a more polycentric structure, at least on the Flemish side, if one considers intra-firm networks at national level (Figure 11.3). But here too, the great weakness of the Walloon cities in the field of APS, and the absence of structural connections between Liège and Charleroi, are striking.

It should however be pointed out that the GaWC methodology tends to overestimate horizontal relationships between subsidiaries. This overestimation is probably stronger at the level of local subsidiaries than at an international level. Interviews with firms' managers reveal the strong dominance of vertical hierarchical relationships. In only three of the nine investigated sectors (law, engineering and design consultancy, accountancy) is an operational mode closer to that of a cooperative polycentric structure noticed. Meanwhile, this operational mode is seen as an unavoidable fact rather than an efficient

aspect of spatial organization: although proximity to clients and local markets is an imperative for those sectors, their managers admit they nonetheless aim for a maximum of scale economies and thus concentration. Thus, in all APS sectors managers declare that scale economies always increase productivity, both inside the firm (grouping of all activities and abilities in a single place) and outside it (proximity of suppliers, subcontractors, customers, labour force, know-how, decision centres, etc.). Only two factors are seen in some respects as detracting from increased productivity: mobility (due to congestion costs in the most central areas) and quality of life.

Consequently, none of the interviewees considers polycentric spatial organization an alternative or a credible perspective in managing his or her enterprise. Within a knowledge economy, the human factor, confidence, face-to-face meeting, concentration of competences, and informal debates are considered extremely important and cannot be replaced by cold computer contacts or other communication techniques. Of course this does not mean that all sectors are identically concentrated or that location strategies are all similar. Depending on specific imperatives – differentiated strategies of competition or cooperation, pursuit of corporate image by means of a prestigious central area address, the search for a green peripheral working environment, etc. – location choices may vary considerably from sector to sector. But, in APS sectors in particular, the dominant trend remains geographical concentration, even in the periphery of a large urban area (Brussels in the present case) and, if possible, concentration at the metropolitan level rather than intra-metropolitan level, in order to avoid the high property prices in city centres.

In conclusion, the functioning of the Belgian economy does not appear much affected by polycentrism, despite the density of the urban system. At the very most, the recent trend, at least for some tertiary subsectors, is

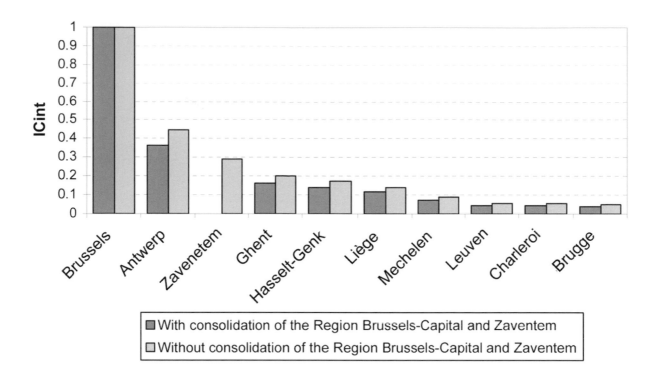

Figure 11.2 Central Belgium: International connections of APS firms

oriented towards a peripheral deconcentration around Brussels, however this does not affect decision centres at the highest level.

The notion of polycentrism in territorial planning patterns

It should again be emphasized that the guidelines in territorial planning are now defined in Belgium exclusively at a regional level. We have already seen that regional cooperation in this field – as in many others – is extremely limited. Meanwhile, each of the general plans in each of the regions is in line with European Spatial Development Perspective (ESDP) views.

The ESDP has been much debated, both at European and Benelux levels. The first discussions took place as early as the 1970s. The ESDP is strongly marked by the original objectives of the European Community, which aimed at improving integration, if possible also at territorial level, thanks to a balanced urban and regional development. The ESDP is a product of strong interventionist policies within a neo-Keynesian perspective. Yet aims have evolved over time, and recent changes have been added in a neo-liberal direction, with the notion of 'urban and territorial competitiveness'. As it now stands, the ESDP attempts to combine cross-urban cooperation with territorial competition and competitiveness through the regulating concept of polycentrism.

In the light of these objectives, we will now examine how the concept of sustainable polycentric development is reflected in regional development patterns, not merely as a spatial planning concept but also as an operational tool.

The Schéma de Développement de l'Espace Régional Wallon

The preliminary Schéma de Développement de l'Espace Régional Wallon (SDER) drafts in the 1980s still reflected a self-centred view, considerably influenced by the sudden emergence, from the early 1960s, of a regionalist claim resulting directly from the dramatic effects of the industrial crisis in the old coalfield areas and from a strong mistrust of Brussels. Indeed, the capital, which was home to the head offices of the companies that had dominated Belgian industry for more than a century, was considered a bourgeois city, responsible for Wallonia's misfortunes. This opinion was expressed in a project aimed at basing Wallonia's redevelopment on a 'poly-city', a long east–west conurbation throughout Wallonia, badly structured for historical reasons, offering few services and whose two major poles, Liège and Charleroi, rather than complementing each other in times of difficulty, appeared as competing with one another. In that project, Wallonia was seen as isolated and cut off from Brussels.

Fortunately, these views were abandoned in the 1998 version of the SDER. The new pattern places Wallonia back in its Western European context and takes into account the qualitative weakness of its urban system. The

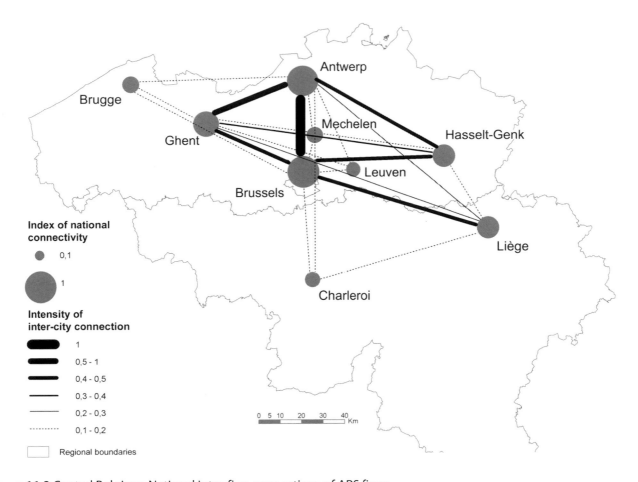

Figure 11.3 Central Belgium: National intra-firm connections of APS firms

Walloon territory is organized around two Eurocorridors, and the pattern aims at improving the cities' structuration by placing them into cross-regional cooperation networks, around or with external poles: Brussels, Lille, Luxembourg, and the polycentric Hasselt–Maastricht–Aachen area including the city of Liège.

This project is still encountering considerable resistance from some Walloon policy-makers, who have deep memories of the Region's industrial and social past. Also, practical institutionalization of projected trans-regional cooperation is evidently encountering many difficulties. Nevertheless, the Walloon polycentric project principally appears as a quite serious attempt to address the weakness of the Walloon pattern of urbanization and the expensive and sterile internal competition between Walloon poles, especially Liège and Charleroi.

Brussels-Capital region Plan Régional de Développement

The notion of polycentrism is obviously meaningless for an urban pattern that only involves the central part of a metropolitan area, the more so as we have underlined the lack of true operational cooperation between Brussels and the other regions, among them the surrounding Flemish

region. The basic concerns of the Plan Régional de Développement (PRD) authors are two: preventing Brussels-Capital region from losing middle-class wealthy inhabitants, and controlling, as much as possible, deconcentration of economic activities to the benefit of the periphery, especially those in high added-value service sectors. It is only recently that a degree of dialogue has been initiated between the Brussels-Capital region, the other two regions, and the federal authorities, accompanied by a cooperation agreement on the financing of a rapid-transit rail system (RER) around Brussels, whose impact on the evolution of Brussels' peri-urbanization remains however uncertain. In addition, some reluctance seems perceptible in the actual implementation of cross-border cooperation agreements with other European metropolises, especially Lille.

The Ruimtelijke Structuurplan Vlaanderen

In contrast to Wallonia, Flanders has from the start included Brussels in its territorial planning patterns. Indeed, Flanders considers Brussels as its capital: a historically Flemish city, even if outside the region's boundaries and with a majority of French-speaking inhabitants.

The concept of a polycentric urban network is quite notable in the Ruimtelijke Structuurplan Vlaanderen (RSV). For example, through the idea of 'concentrated deconcentration', which means a redistribution of population and some activities to existing cores so that the urban system will be reinforced and densified in order to counter peri-urbanization. In particular, the 'Flemish Diamond', which includes Brussels in a rhomboid-shaped area whose three other vertices are Ghent, Antwerp and Leuven, is designed as a European-level integrated urban network. This Flemish Diamond, structuring the central space of the Belgian economy, should provide Flanders with a competitive position in relation to other large mega-city regions (MCRs) of North Western Europe, such as the Randstad, RhineRuhr, the UK's South East England and the Paris Region.

However, the polycentric view as developed in the RSV has to be interpreted at two different levels.

In terms of spatial planning, the concern is to structure the occupation of space between large, medium and small Flemish cities, quite close to each other, so as to preserve maximum of open spaces between them.

In terms of international positioning, the notion of polycentrism, and especially that of the Flemish Diamond, is a powerful marketing tool. The purpose is to sell potential investors the image of a strongly urbanized Flemish region, including the large Brussels metropolitan area with its multiplicity of services, transport network and international image, offering them potential competitive advantage. On more micro-geographical scales, the RSV also stresses cross-border cooperation between Courtrai and Lille, Cologne–Liège–Hasselt–Genk, as well as the network of coastal urban centres and the Hasselt–Genk dipole.

Conclusions

In the Belgian context, the notion of polycentrism does not appear to correspond to an effective functional reality, though the map of the urban system shows an overall high degree of urbanization and a dense network of diversely sized cities which tightly structure a large part of the national territory.

Polycentric organization seen functionally, as the functioning of networks, also appears quite far from both concrete spatial strategies and from managers' reflections.

Moreover, it remains uncertain whether the development of a networked polycentric structure would effectively lead to increased efficiency. In a dense spatial structure such as the Belgian one, where most networks are organized in a star pattern around Brussels, more polycentrism could mean increased environmental burdens, the potential for reduced public transport use, and increased invasion of open spaces by housing and activities. In any case, it would be necessary to propose a well-considered mix between the current structure and a more polycentric one, but only after accurately examined the advantages and disadvantages in all relevant fields. It would also be necessary to combine polycentrism with a strict control of land uses, particularly as regards concentrated clusters of economic establishments, if not of housing, in the neighbourhood of railway stations for instance.

It is far from obvious that polycentrism would lower commuting volumes by bringing jobs closer to the commuters' places of residence, for the following reasons: (a) if the labour pool of an urban enterprise is spread widely across the periphery, it is not easy to determine an optimal location at one point of this periphery, unless the workforce is compelled to move to the new workplace; (b) living and working patterns of households are more and more multiple and unstable; (c) and finally, it has been noted that the development of a diversified supply of employment is only possible in urban centres. Indeed, if relocation of firms from Brussels to the periphery is a reality, the contrary is also true, notably some firms had previously opted for the periphery but decided to return to the city, mainly for reasons of access to labour, especially the skilled labour force. It seems that, most of the time, a significant part of the workforce does not follow a firm that moves to the periphery.

In addition, in the Belgian context, more polycentrism could mean increasing budget problems in the Brussels-Capital region, and consequently social problems, without necessarily solving those of the central communes of other large cities that are in difficulty, given that decentralization would benefit their peripheries and therefore attract still more peri-urban populations.

It only remains to consider the normative aspect: polycentrism seen as an objective. Indeed, competition would involve cooperation, and would finally result in a better territorial balance brought about directly by economic evolution rather than being organized by policy measures in a Keynesian fashion. Doubtless, in certain cases such cooperation and specialization solutions may appear attractive and profitable, especially to prevent some cities from launching development strategies in all directions, because this would mean those cities failing to achieve sufficient results in any given area and so stimulate their economies. This is particularly true of the large Walloon cities, which are weaker than their Flemish counterparts. Meanwhile, it is also true that some inter-city cooperation is constrained and leads to unequal relationships between strong metropolises and weak neighbouring cities. In other cases, reality is very different from the cooperation originally promised. For instance, Hasselt–Genk is supposed to make up a dipole in which each city's assets should develop in a complementary way. But in practice, competition and division of all forms of infrastructure prove to be the rule. In the same way, complementarity between Aix–Liège (with its *Train à Grande Vitesse* (TGV) station) and Maastricht (with its airport), though provided for in the plans, is far from being a reality: if Aachen and Maastricht have indeed reached an agreement on the airport question, Liège has nevertheless developed its own Bierset airport. After a phase of appeasement following Bierset's specializing in freight, conflicts are now resuming with Liège's strategies to develop passengers charter traffic.

Thus – rather paradoxically – polycentrism, which aims at granting more economic and decisional weight to lower levels of the urban hierarchy, in practice requires a relatively strong central power to supervise the sharing of competences and to impose complementarity between the different urban centres. In the absence of such strong regulatory power, polycentrism will remain wishful thinking: the principle of every man for himself will produce ever more uniform cities, taking up the same benchmarking recipes. And a relatively weak central power will turn the idea of polycentrism into a kind of icing on the cake, aimed at satisfying everyone. The problem is precisely that Belgium represents an extreme case of weakness of the central power and of jealously preserved autonomies at both regional and local levels.

12

RhineRuhr: 'Polycentricity at its Best'?

Wolfgang Knapp, Daniela Scherhag and Peter Schmitt

When considering the urban system in Germany, especially its network of large metropolitan regions, and RhineRuhr as one important node of this network, one needs first to emphasize that we are dealing with a somewhat specific – perhaps unique – case in North West Europe and even beyond. Some of its special characteristics are shared with Rhine-Main, as discussed in Chapter 13; others make it truly unique.

RhineRuhr: A unique case?

First, contrary to most other countries in Europe, the German national urban system is characterized by a dense network of vital small and medium size cities along with only a dozen bigger ones with populations of more than half a million inhabitants. Numerous trade relations in the Middle Ages, scattered regionalism and, particularly, the decentralized German federal system of government have led to a distinctly polycentric urban system with no single city holding a clear dominant position. The only exception, to some degree, is the chequered history of Berlin, which was among the premier league of European metropolises until World War II. As a consequence of this, a distinct division of labour has developed, sharing out national level and metropolitan functions among a handful of urban regions such as Hamburg, Munich, Berlin, Frankfurt and to some extent even Düsseldorf and Cologne, as well as Stuttgart and Hannover. Munich, for example, specializes in the research and high-tech industry sectors; financial services and the chemical industry are especially concentrated in Frankfurt; knowledge-based producer services and the media sector have developed an above-average presence in Hamburg, Frankfurt, Düsseldorf, Cologne and Berlin; Stuttgart and parts of the

RhineRuhr region have specialized in classical technologically oriented industries, such as automotive and mechanical engineering. The same scattered geography is evident with regard to international control, organizing or gateway functions, which are carried out by various institutions or infrastructures located in several larger urban agglomerations. Because of this spatial 'division of labour', the network of metropolitan regions is able to compete with international metropolitan areas, even if Germany lacks a global city region like London or Paris.

Secondly, comparing mega-city regions (MCRs) as selected by POLYNET, another crucial aspect becomes obvious. This concerns not only their size but, even more evidently, their different urban configurations. In this respect, RhineRuhr seems to be a unique case not only in Germany, but also – together with the Dutch Randstad – in Europe. In contrast to polynucleated regions such as London and South East England or the Paris Region with one dominant core city, RhineRuhr consists of a number of historically distinct cities and lacks a clear leading city which dominates in political, economic, cultural and other aspects. Instead, several larger cities, which do not differ much in terms of size or overall economic importance, together with a greater number of smaller cities, all constituting independent political entities, are located in relatively close (daily commuting) proximity to each other (Knapp and Schmitt, 2002). However, this relatively balanced size of the larger cities masks a functional hierarchy: the complex system of RhineRuhr can be seen both as a hierarchy and as a case of sectoral specialization. At the level of the cities (see below) the picture of a relatively low degree of hierarchical relationships has long shaped the image of the region in the minds of regional actors and does justice to the strong feeling of competition that exists in the bigger cities, because every city is alert to the threat of negative discrimination. Hence, such an inter-urban polycentric configuration is in many respects qualitatively different from those with a dominant core, and the creation of functional, strategic and regional/cultural identities appears very challenging in this particular case.

The mega-city region RhineRuhr

RhineRuhr, named after the region's two most important rivers, is by far the most urbanized area in the Federal State of North Rhine-Westphalia, with about 12 million inhabitants and more than 5 million jobs located between Bonn in the south, Mönchengladbach in the west and Dortmund in the north east. Besides Düsseldorf (with 572,441 inhabitants and 333,561 employees[1] in 2004), the capital city of North Rhine-Westphalia, the metropolitan core cities of this large city cluster include Cologne (966,021/439,882), Bonn (311,002/143,119), Essen (598,189/206,494), Dortmund (589,734/191,801), and finally Duisburg (506,478/154,292), complemented by a dozen medium size cities and a vast number of smaller towns. Marked by the morphological polycentricity already described, an ongoing process of spatio-economic scale enlargement makes the functional urban region (FUR) a logical basis to capture urban economies as well as the everyday worlds of inhabitants, and also appears as a realistic (co)operation area for city-regional activities (see Figure 12.1).

There are some promising signs that RhineRuhr is increasingly interconnected through a number of relational ties, even though empirical verification – with the exception of travel to work patterns – is still lacking. Commuter flows have intensified during recent decades, especially between neighbouring economic core cities, but also involving cross-flows between secondary centres. Düsseldorf is by far the most important core for in-commuting from Duisburg, Essen, Mönchen-gladbach, Cologne, Krefeld, and Wuppertal. Cologne and Bonn as well as Essen, Bochum, Dortmund in the Ruhrgebiet also emerge as strongly interrelated cities. A look at the self-containment of overall urban labour markets (i.e. the share of resident employed workers employed in a city) confirms this picture of a remarkable functional polycentricity with respect to both commuting patterns and self-containment, at least in most parts of RhineRuhr. The rates of self-containment of labour markets have decreased in all 11 high-order centres of RhineRuhr, whereas the total rates of in-commuting have increased in the last decade.

Evolving patterns of service network flows

In comparison to other European Metropolitan Regions, RhineRuhr still has a relatively strong industrial base, which has contributed to various high-tech industrial profiles in different fields. Nevertheless, the secondary sector is more strongly represented outside RhineRuhr than inside, and the service sector in general, and the

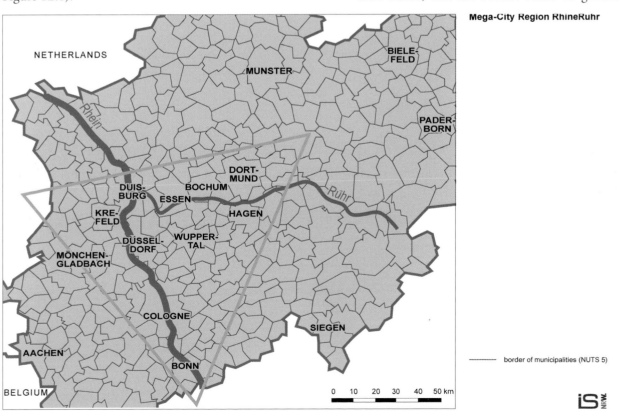

Mega-City Region RhineRuhr

border of municipalities (NUTS 5)

0 10 20 30 40 50 km

Figure 12.1 The MCR RhineRuhr

advanced producer services (APS) sectors in particular, have a higher share within the region than in the rest of North Rhine-Westphalia. The share of APS sectors together varies from 24.7 per cent (Düsseldorf), 22.2 per cent (Cologne), about 16.0 per cent (Bonn, Essen, Dortmund) down to only 8.7 per cent (Duisburg) in 2001. A closer look at the business services structure of the metropolitan cores might give a first hint of a degree of division of labour and maybe even functional polycentricity within RhineRuhr. Whereas Cologne is traditionally the main location for insurance, design and media services, Düsseldorf – followed by Cologne – constitutes the leading centre for advertising within RhineRuhr and, together with Essen, also the most important centre for management consulting, as well as law and accountancy. Logistics firms are well distributed within the region, namely in Cologne in the south as well as close to the eastern (Dortmund) and the western (Duisburg) entrance of RhineRuhr (Table 12.1 and Figure 12.2).

Apart from logistics, APS cluster in central (micro) locations within single cities. Most of the headquarters (HQ) of insurance firms in Cologne, for instance, are located within the city centre or nearby in the southern part of the city. Advertising agencies, design, law and accountancy and management consulting companies in Düsseldorf are also clustered within the central business district (CBD) and adjacent areas (e.g. the restructuring of the city port into a location for media (Media Harbour)),

the new trade centre in the eastern part of the city). Most of the logistics firms, however, are located near to nodes of the transport system like airports (Cologne, Düsseldorf) or ports (Duisburg) and all of them are naturally close to the numerous motorway junctions.

Not only does this geography of APS concentration indicate some polycentric division of labour between the metropolitan cores of RhineRuhr, but also the geographical scope of firms and the connectivities of urban centres identified in the quantitative analysis of business networks (described in Chapter 3), suggests a potentially high degree of polycentricity. The big FURs or high-order centres have extremely high levels of connectivity at the regional scale, all over 0.4; Düsseldorf, Cologne, Dortmund, and Essen score over 0.8 (Figure 3.2d, p61, and Table 12.1). The more balanced the relative importance of a set of cities, the higher is the degree of polycentricity at the regional scale in this respect, and RhineRuhr can thus be considered as relatively polycentric in comparison to other MCRs in Europe in terms of the geography of its regional scope business network functions. A closer look at the intra-regional linkages of the main cities shows especially strong linkages between Düsseldorf–Cologne, Düsseldorf–Dortmund and Essen–Cologne (Figure 3.2d). To what extent lower-order regional centres are involved in this network is an open question, but there are some suggestions that such processes are taking place, especially within the management consulting, advertising and

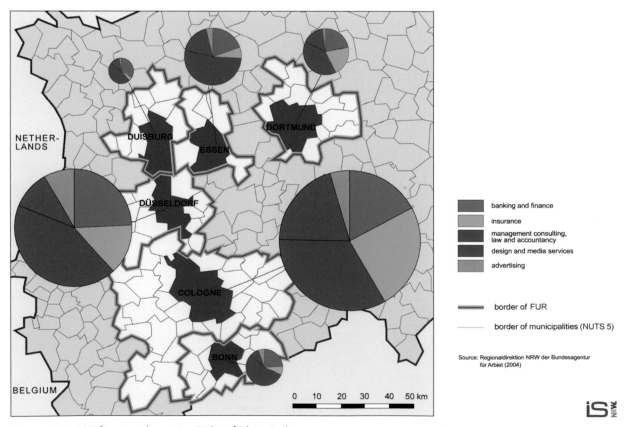

Figure 12.2 APS firms in the main FURs of RhineRuhr

Table 12.1 GaWC connectivity indices of FURs in the RhineRuhr region[a]

FUR	Regional	National	European	Global
Düsseldorf	1.00	0.97	1.00	1.00
Cologne	0.99	1.00	0.61	0.58
Dortmund	0.90	0.77	0.37	0.34
Essen	0.89	0.75	0.42	0.39
Bonn	0.79	0.65	0.29	0.26
Duisburg	0.77	0.60	0.24	0.22

Note: a Connectivities are reported as proportions of the highest score = 1.00.

Source: Own survey, compiled by GaWC

logistics sectors. Furthermore it is important to recognize that the inter-urban connectivities suggested by this quantitative analysis are only suggestive of interactions between the MCR cities. These can only be confirmed by evidence from interviews with the actors working there, to be considered shortly.

Beyond the regional scale, the analysis of office networks of APS firms shows less balanced connectivities (Table 12.1). Whereas at the regional and national levels both Düsseldorf and Cologne are level, the relative importance of the FUR Düsseldorf within RhineRuhr increases with higher geographical scales. At the European/global level, the FURs Cologne and Essen achieve only between 61/58 per cent and 42/39 per cent of Düsseldorf's value. While both Düsseldorf and Cologne are important national scale APS centres, crucially, Düsseldorf is the main international gateway that connects the region to wider international flows.

The complementary configuration of locations: A framework for business planning?

Polycentric urban networks are often associated with the notion of synergy: the assumption is that the individual cities in these clusters of closely located cities relate to each other in a synergistic way, making the polycentric urban regions more than the sum of their parts by means of cooperative and complementary relationships and externalities arising from them (Camagni and Salone, 1993; Capello, 2000; Meijers, 2005). Synergy in polycentric urban regions is generated through regional organizing capacity and related cooperative behaviour (horizontal synergy) and complementarity, i.e. differentiation in the economic roles or profiles of cities, in urban facilities or business milieux coupled with regional demand (leading to vertical synergy) (Meijers, 2005, p770). Cooperation, between city administrations and on a sub-regional basis – for instance in the Ruhr area – seems

to be increasing, but what is needed is regional organizing capacity. The ability to coordinate development regionally through an institutionalized framework of cooperation, debate and decision-making in pursuit of regional interests in which public and private stakeholders participate is so far lacking in RhineRuhr (see below). The second synergistic mechanism, functional complementarity, seems to be present in so far as the main cities in RhineRuhr have developed different economic profiles leading to a sectoral division of labour at the regional scale however this does not of itself construct functional linkages between RhineRuhr cities. Moreover, a feature of the RhineRuhr cities is their functional specialization in that HQ and APS functions cluster in larger cities, while only few cities have developed international functions.

To what extent a polycentric urban network is seen as a specific locational advantage and how far RhineRuhr as such plays a vital role in strategic business planning today remain open questions. As a result of our interviews within the APS business sector as well as business organizations (Chambers of Commerce, Local Development Agencies), one can confidently state that these stakeholders have a poorly-developed perception of a 'RhineRuhr' region as a complementary urban configuration. The urban network and emerging division of labour among historically distinct core cities and new centralities beyond their boundaries – as well as the polynuclear urban region as a home to a wider variety of actors giving rise to a more diverse collection of potentials, ideas and driving forces, profiles and creative environments – do not seem to be perceived as a locational advantage for these regional agents. Neither did the interviewees consider the region to be a single operational unit, mainly because of the fragmented political/administrative landscape and the lack of regional identity and regional consciousness of inhabitants and stakeholders. Moreover, the region is considered as a more or less non-specific large conurbation with good access to markets, clients or qualified staff rather than as a polynuclear frame of reference for business strategies.

When discussing competitive advantages and disadvantages, the interviewees were more prepared to consider RhineRuhr as a whole, even though they had also stressed the uneven economic performance of its different sub-regions. In particular, the Ruhrgebiet was only regarded as a candidate for the national league. Only together with Düsseldorf, Cologne and Bonn would the region acquire the assets to enter the premier league of European city regions.

The interviews also gave further evidence that Düsseldorf is by far the most important place as a location for APS, as well as the most important node within RhineRuhr through which international flows of communication are conducted. Cologne and other urban centres even more show a considerable gap in comparison with Düsseldorf in terms of international relationships. Together with Cologne, Düsseldorf is also seen as the most important location on the national scale. Both cities benefit from their 'supportive socio-cultural milieu', which places them above all other centres within RhineRuhr as the most attractive for living and working.

Discussing some of the factors companies may consider when deciding where to locate their business, 'access to markets, customers or clients' and 'availability of qualified staff' are seen as most important by about two-thirds of our respondents. However, communication issues like 'transport links with other cities and internationally' and the 'quality of telecommunications' are also essential factors.

In general, labour markets, skills and education in RhineRuhr were valued positively. Specialist training for specific skills is provided in different places within the region, for instance: insurance – Cologne; information technology (IT) and media – Cologne and Dortmund; advertising and design – Düsseldorf; logistics – Duisburg; and these opportunities for study are often important factors companies consider when deciding where to locate their business. On the other hand, disadvantages relating to higher education, research and development, and technology transfer – especially for smaller firms – are also emphasized.

When comparing RhineRuhr with other European regions, its relatively good regional transport infrastructure and accessibility at different scales come to the fore in spite of some minor weaknesses. Besides a number of voices emphasizing the role of face-to-face contacts – and calling, therefore, for upgrading of the relatively well-developed regional public transport system – above all, intercontinental flight connectivity is criticized. Concerning availability of high bandwidth capacity, Düsseldorf and Cologne are of particular importance, both for the internet providers who are keen to promote a highly interconnected and widespread European network architecture and also for diffusing high bandwidth internet accessibility throughout the European territory and, naturally, beyond. The availability of IT-broadband is, therefore, a positively valued location factor in RhineRuhr.

While the perception of RhineRuhr as a functionally connected polycentric city region is poorly developed, interviewees recognized that the regionalization of business activities, of everyday life and more complex commuting, together with the 'old' disadvantages of large conurbations with their environmental problems and/or social tensions, present real challenges for future policies, both at federal state level and for new regional governance structures. Thus, the question arises whether policy-makers have an understanding of the growing potential for the functional connectivity of the MCR economy and of the reality of RhineRuhr as a complex and differentiated, but also as a complementary, configuration of different locations. Does the polycentric region represent an objective, or even a framework, for strategic planning and regional development policies?

Problems in policy-making: Institutions, substance, trajectories, perceptions, concepts

Since the establishment of its legal base in 1965, strategic spatial planning in Germany has focused chiefly on securing a more balanced geography of economic development, rather than on supporting further concentration within agglomerations, in order to ensure comparable conditions throughout the country. Here the central-place concept, based on Christaller's neo-classical theory (1966 (1933)), has been developed into a directive instrument for spatial planning at state and regional levels, implementing social welfare policies throughout the country (at least in times of prosperity), by securing the widespread provision of amenities to the population and their access to social infrastructure. As a direct consequence, the economic role of cities was restricted to their regional-level functions. For a very long time there has been no political will or even a motivation to think about the possible strategically superior role of a selected number of cities or metropolitan regions in a national or even international context: such policies, it was felt, might aggravate regional disparities and spatial injustices. Hence, spatial policies to boost metropolitan regions and their functions have not been on the political agenda. Even today, this 'substantial pillar' of spatial planning and policies is still apparent from a careful reading of strategic documents and plans. But, all that said, since the beginning of the 1990s one can detect a gradual, but crucial, adjustment of norms, objectives, methods and instruments. They are rooted, as in many other European countries, in a somewhat neo-liberal rhetoric: they refer to the competitive performance that selected urban agglomerations might achieve. Moreover, the specific situation in Germany has been profoundly affected by reunion in 1990 and by strong de-industrialization processes, contributing to the transformation of the national economy from outstanding prosperity to stagnation and the general diversification of the geo-economic map. Evidently, since then a shift of stress regarding spatial planning has become imperative – as strategic documents and new spatial development concepts suggest.

In relation to this, most notable is that since 1995 almost a dozen German urban agglomerations, among them RhineRuhr as well as Berlin, Hamburg, Munich, Stuttgart and Rhine-Main, have been conceptualized no longer as being congested areas which should be protected from further growth, but as constituting a critical mass for economic competitiveness in a national as well as an international context. Hence, they are characterized as 'driving forces' or 'motors of spatial development' and are designed officially as 'European Metropolitan Regions' by the Standing Conference of Ministries Responsible for Spatial Planning (*Ministerkonferenz für Raumordnung*, MKRO). One effect is that this new strategic spatial category functions as a new 'discursive frame' for such urban agglomerations at a larger scale, allowing them to negotiate spatial policies that boost their competitive assets and improve their innovative and symbolic functions as well as enhancing their external and internal accessibility in the 'space of flows' (Blotevogel and Schmitt, 2005).

In RhineRuhr, this new strategic option stimulated by the MKRO has been incorporated promptly as a formal objective in the 1995 *Landesentwicklungsplan* (State Development Plan) for North Rhine-Westphalia. But, though the European Metropolitan Region (EMR) RhineRuhr portrayed there almost corresponds to the MCR we have defined for POLYNET, the plan neglects any reference to its function as a polycentric urban region. This can be traced back to the general perception by state, regional and urban planners in North Rhine-Westphalia and RhineRuhr alike: that functional polycentricity is not conceptualized or even conceived as a regional challenge (Schmitt and Knapp, 2001), even though RhineRuhr might represent a textbook case. Moreover, the State Development Plan – the only existing strategic document relating to the MCR RhineRuhr – fails to contain any comprehensive description of what the spatial construct should represent. The description of the overall goal seems more rhetorical in nature than a precursor to an advanced framework of proposed measures:

The greater significance of the European Metropolitan Region RhineRuhr for spatial development in North Rhine-Westphalia, in Germany and in Europe has to be taken into consideration when development of the spatial and settlement structure is at stake *(translated from MURL, 1995, p16).*

Besides this modest strategic guideline, the political and planning discourse about RhineRuhr as a critical mass (in terms of overall population or economic output of a wide territory), able to exploit the competitive advantage of similarly sized metropolitan regions, has so far been conducted in a very diffident way. The reasons are multi-faceted (Knapp et al, 2004). One of the most interesting is a displacement of the power geography: it is feared by the state government that this MCR might become a political project at the expense of other areas and, maybe even more conflictual, would result in a powerful 'RhineRuhr state' within the 'state of North Rhine-Westphalia' (Knapp and Schmitt, 2003). It is patently evident that the state government reassures itself by stating that North Rhine-Westphalia does indeed possess a region of European importance in terms of population, infrastructure endowment and facilities. Secondly, one needs to point out that most (not only political) stakeholders have not become sufficiently aware of the existence and the economic importance of this, by far the biggest urban agglomeration in Germany: what we have termed the MCR RhineRuhr. Apart from some ineffective marketing campaigns, there have been no efforts to develop new positive images of this officially new-born spatial construct called the EMR RhineRuhr, which could serve as a 'framework' for communication as well as for an advanced discourse that goes beyond the circle of primarily academic debates. Even though the term 'metropolitan region' has become very popular and has been incorporated in discursive practices in the professional arenas in Germany, the 'spatial image' of a 'united RhineRuhr-region' has in no way become a 'hegemonic project'.

This is, however, rooted in another dilemma that inhibits strategic discourse on this spatial category in general and its functional polycentricity in particular: the institutional patchwork and policy response at the sub-regional level. First it needs mentioning that at the sub-state level, regional planning is carried out by the *Regierungspräsidenten* (district commissioners) in cooperation with the *Regionalräte* (regional councils) formed by political representatives of the cities and counties of a *Regierungsbezirk* (district administration of the state government). This regional tier of physical planning ('regional planning' in the German context) forms the link between state and local planning (i.e. urban land use planning) in North Rhine-Westphalia. In relation to the MCR RhineRuhr, the difficult issue is that the region falls under no less than four different *Regierungsbezirke*. Because those authorities first and foremost take responsibility only for their own territory, the polycentric MCR RhineRuhr has not become a mutual shared challenge for regional planning stakeholders in North Rhine-Westphalia (Schmitt et al, 2003).

In the medium or long run, a rather promising institutional platform to tackle spatial development issues for the MCR RhineRuhr might be the *Regionalverband Ruhr* (RVR, Regional Association Ruhr). After almost 30 years of insignificance, the RVR has regained some of the historic strength it had in the years when, after establishment in 1920 (and then named *Siedlungsverband Ruhrkohlenbezirk*, SVR), it was the forerunner for regional governance in Europe. Known between 1979 and 2004 as the *Kommunalverband Ruhrgebiet* (KVR, Ruhr District Association of Communities) this regional association comprising the municipalities of the Ruhrgebiet had until recently served mainly as a regional marketing institution with a few additional functional and information dissemination tasks. Since October 2004 the new association has had to deal with development of trans-municipal informal master plans (e.g. for transport, leisure, regional landscape management, etc.). However, the RVR neither holds a formal regional planning competence, nor does it work as a regional development agency incorporating development and marketing of business sites at the regional level with any decision-making power. Another dilemma is its legitimacy, as its representatives are not directly elected by the inhabitants of the Ruhrgebiet. Thus, only the future will show whether the RVR is able to improve cooperation among the local authorities of this part of RhineRuhr or perhaps even open the door for other municipalities along the Rhine, like Düsseldorf or Cologne. For the moment, the participation of the 'metropolitan region Ruhr' in the international trade fair for the property market, *Marché International des Professionnels d'Immobilier* (MIPIM), in Cannes or the common application of the Ruhrgebiet for the European Cultural Capital 2010 are seen as positive first steps in demonstrating a more cooperative spirit, at least within the Ruhrgebiet. In terms of the evolution of the MCR RhineRuhr, it is notable that there is a faint stirring of opinion in favour of a RVR-type organization for the cities along the Rhine. Significantly, the newly elected North Rhine-Westphalia state government favours restructuring the five Regierungsbezirke into three 'regional associations' – one being the RVR for the *Ruhrgebiet*, receiving back its formal planning powers, and another an RVR for the Rhineland (covering Düsseldorf, Cologne and Bonn and their hinterlands). This simplification might aid coordination within the MCR RhineRuhr.

However, one should not forget the existence of the many autonomous county-free cities (in particular 11 higher-order centres with more than 200,000 inhabitants) and 10 counties and their constituent local government authorities, which presently together shape the MCR RhineRuhr. They usually follow the principle of self-interest – even though nowadays, a higher level of (sub)regional cooperation plays an important role in the political rhetoric. The state government's desire for greater regional cooperation thus evokes an apprehension on the part of local government authorities: that they might be forced to give up their self-governing status, which is deeply rooted in the German basic law. Although none of the relevant local stakeholders attempts to tackle planning and/or political issues above and beyond local interests at the scale of RhineRuhr, some regionalization initiatives have opened the road for a new quality of supra-local cooperation (inter-municipal commercial spaces, regional retail concepts, common applications for contests or model projects). Optimistically, such steps can be seen as further potential platforms for the consolidation of cooperation at the scale of the MCR RhineRuhr.

Besides these difficulties in shaping something like metropolitan governance appropriate to the geographical scale and functional polycentricity of the MCR RhineRuhr, another substantial deficiency may prove even more crucial. The polycentric urban pattern in RhineRuhr can be traced back to the distinct industrial development history of the Ruhr coalfield: its long history as the industrial heartland of Germany, and partly even of Western Europe, has left its mark not only on its physical appearance and polycentric structure, but also on specific perceptions and, crucially, conceptions of spatial development policies. In the Ruhrgebiet a strong coalition of the huge steel and coal industry firms, the trade unions and the Social Democratic Party has established itself over some decades. Industry in general, and in particular specific branches (mechanical engineering, chemical industries, environmental protection industries, high-technology steel), have played a key role in North Rhine-Westphalian politics. Moreover, because of the division of labour among German metropolitan regions, it has been difficult to find a niche to establish advanced APS-profiles as in Frankfurt, Hamburg or Munich. Because of this, APS-oriented policies have never existed in North Rhine-Westphalia in an advanced form. It often seems that the only branches and value chains that might contribute to new jobs and social welfare are in relation to manufacturing industry. In other words, APS-oriented policies are hardly recognizable at state level, only at the level of a few cities such as Düsseldorf, Cologne or Dortmund. The first two cities are strengthening their position as media or design cities, while Dortmund has gained a national reputation as a centre of IT, micro-systems technology (MST) and, together with Duisburg, of logistics. Economic policies in North Rhine-Westphalia in general, and RhineRuhr in particular, are still very much technology and industry driven: infrastructural endowment, supply of business sites for industrial manufacturing facilities, (higher) education and internationalization strategies. This becomes most obvious in the state government's efforts to promote 12 so-called but rather vaguely defined 'fields of competence' in the Ruhrgebiet to strengthen their diversification activities and stimulate economic activities in associated branches (e.g. logistics). These 'fields of competence' simply build on existing profiles and value chains dominated by established industries.

Before its defeat in the May 2005 state election, another much more distinct concept was introduced by the Social Democratic–Green Party state government: a distinct concentration of economic, labour market and technology policies to shape so-called 'fields of technological excellence' in North Rhine-Westphalia. The idea was to lead enterprises, scientific organizations, universities and employees towards internationally outstanding performance in six selected 'fields of excellence': IT-based systems integration and micro-systems; logistics and transport systems; life sciences; new materials and technologies and solutions for their application (like mechanical engineering, the steel or chemicals industry); energy and environmental tech-nologies; and finally, literally translated, 'knowledge-based producer services'. This last might give a first indication of a rethinking of those policies with a major impact on spatial development. It remains to be seen if the new state government (a Conservative–Liberal coalition) will take this further, giving APS and their development potential a higher standing in the policy-making in North Rhine-Westphalia generally and in RhineRuhr in particular.

RhineRuhr: 'Polycentricity at its best', but a challenge for strategic spatial planning and policy

In this chapter we have tried to provide a structure and an interpretative framework for our research findings concerning the MCR RhineRuhr and its functional polycentricity, mainly as constituted by APS. Further, we have shown how they relate to the current institutional and political make-up.

Today, RhineRuhr can be seen as an emergent functionally-connected polycentric urban network with a potential for increased regional competitive advantage, through economies of scale and scope generated by the MCR as a whole. But, because of the rather disappointing

regional understanding of the sectoral and growing functional specialization between the cities of RhineRuhr, the lack of any strategic identity, and the related vague or fragmented and inconsistent image of the region, both inside and outside it, RhineRuhr can be seen as a 'hidden metropolis' that fails to draw on its potential resources.

RhineRuhr demonstrates a remarkable degree of functional polycentricity in most areas, in its intensive and relatively complex commuting patterns, and in the geography of its 'APS clusters', which show some polycentric divisions of labour between the metropolitan cores, and in the geographical scopes of firms and potential functional connectivity of urban centres. However, both economic stakeholders and policy-makers show poorly developed perceptions of a 'RhineRuhr' region as a complementary polycentric urban configuration. The region is considered as a more or less non-specific large conurbation with good access to markets, clients and qualified staff, rather than as a polynuclear space of opportunities for business strategies. The polycentric region, and in particular the growing functional complexity and connectivity of its economy and settlement structure, neither form an object nor a framework for strategic planning and regional development policies.

Within North Rhine-Westphalia, the MCR RhineRuhr can thus be seen as a 'sleeping giant', unable to play its potential role due to its inadequate institutional structures and its related failure to develop a common vision of future development. Most critical is that so far the state government has failed to take the initiative to frame a 'substantial policy discourse' on the future of its biggest urban agglomeration. RhineRuhr is still not perceived as a heuristic or even as a strategic spatial image; at best it is seen only as an analytical spatial frame. Even though regional stakeholders display a distinct awareness of the different and highly specialized sectors of the regional economy and its diversified profiles and areas of competence, they still demonstrate a rather disappointing understanding of the potentials for increasing functional connectivity and the 'hidden division of labour' within the regional economy. The MCR RhineRuhr is neither perceived as a complex and differentiated region, nor as a complementary location. There is no frame of reference for marketing and business activities; due to the incoherent and diffuse image of the region as perceived by outsiders, interest for attracting inward investment mainly focuses on Düsseldorf. Although 'polycentricity' in the sense of a variety of options (urban profiles, landscapes, availability of space) is seen as an advantage, more often the multitude of different stakeholders and conflicting interests spread across the MCR are seen as an obstacle to cooperative action.

To sum up, only some elements of a functional identity, but little strategic and no regional cultural identity, are recognizable. An imaginative spatial *Leitbild* (guiding vision) and its implementation through strategic projects is not evident, because neither a functional nor a cultural or strategic identity has so far developed. This is surprising, since the POLYNET findings imply a different style of governance encompassing the entire MCR as a framework capable of meeting different challenges. Additionally, there is a growing political interest in questions relating to metropolitan regions and their functions, which is more than a passing fancy. Although the EMR concept can be regarded as somewhat hazy, suiting political rhetoric and useful as a 'discursive frame' to support claims for federal or European Union (EU) subsidy, there is increasing discourse in Germany suggesting that metropolitan regions should be strengthened because of their underlying growth potential. Yet surprisingly this is not so in North Rhine-Westphalia, where political efforts are concentrated merely on upgrading a 'Ruhr metropolis', leaving cities along the Rhine to strengthen their roles as distinct growth poles on their own.

The growing reality of an emerging functionally connected polycentric MCR RhineRuhr suggests a different strategy. Instead of continuing a 'wait and see' policy, the central and fundamental task for the future is a complex and difficult one: enhance a broad (not only economic) regional discourse, combine this with the formative power of organizing capacity and regional governance, and begin to formulate the strategic issues concerning the development of a new and distinctive economic cluster. Therefore, we think that there should be much more room not only for a quite abstract academic discussion on the pros and cons of a 'EMR RhineRuhr', as is presently occurring, but also for considering the potential to enhance the region's outstanding multi-level polycentric networking connectivity in the space of flows and places.

Note

1   Social security contributors only.

13

Rhine-Main: Making Polycentricity Work?

Tim Freytag, Michael Hoyler, Christoph Mager and Christian Fischer

With a worldwide reputation as leading European financial centre and international transportation hub, the city of Frankfurt frequently comes to stand for the larger heavily urbanized region in which it is embedded. Frankfurt's concentration of banking prowess, symbolized visually in its skyscraper skyline and perpetuated linguistically in the city's nicknames 'Mainhattan' and 'Bankfurt', has dominated the international perception of the Rhine-Main metropolitan region. Rhine-Main, however, is far more than just an appendix to the 'global city' Frankfurt. As Germany's second largest urban agglomeration after RhineRuhr, the region is home to 4.2 million inhabitants, about 5 per cent of the country's population, of which roughly one-third lives in one of its five major urban centres: Frankfurt, Wiesbaden, Mainz, Darmstadt and Offenbach. Historically, these have developed independently as cities in a territorially fragmented region, a legacy which continues to be reflected in their distinctive economic profiles, competitive localism, and lack of regional identity among the population of Rhine-Main. Nevertheless, functional relations between the municipalities in the mega-city region (MCR) Rhine-Main (see Figure 13.1) have intensified ever since the onset of industrialization in the 19th century. Today, Rhine-Main is one of the most dynamic German metropolitan regions, competing with and complementing ten other 'European Metropolitan Regions', designated by the state's coordinating body for spatial planning.[1]

Rhine-Main: Polycentric region in a polycentric urban system

This multitude of highly networked German city regions, characterized by economic specialization and a spatial division of urban functions, is to some extent an outcome of German historical territorial fragmentation and the contemporary federal organization of political power and administration (Blotevogel, 2002). Within the polycentric national urban system, Rhine-Main is characterized by a concentration of internationally operating advanced producer services (APS) firms in the cities that constitute the polycentric region. This chapter outlines the development of Rhine-Main as Germany's leading cluster of global business services and investigates the multi-scalar organizational geographies of professional service firms, which connect the region to wider economic flows. We proceed in three steps. First, we briefly trace the evolution of Rhine-Main as a major urban region and as Germany's premier location for APS. We then focus on the role of business service firms in creating a functionally connected polycentric region, drawing on quantitative measures of connectivity and interviews with selected firms and institutions. Finally, we consider the tensions between the identified relational geographies of interconnectedness and the multi-layered territorially based structures of governance and spatial planning.

The evolution of Rhine-Main as a metropolitan region

Within the Rhine-Main area, the cities of Frankfurt, Mainz, Wiesbaden and Darmstadt have long been major competing centres of political and economic power (Bördlein and Schickhoff, 1998). Frankfurt, venue for the coronation of German kings in the Middle Ages and a free city of the Holy Roman Empire with financial sovereignty and freedom for its courts and administration since the end of the 14th century, developed into an important centre for trans-regional trade, fairs, banking and book printing. The city had only limited functional connections to its direct hinterland since Mainz, and, after 1806, Darmstadt and Wiesbaden possessed their own territories and acted as seats of clerical or secular rulers. After different stages of re-territorialization and the annexation of wide parts of the region by Prussia in 1866/1867, the area of the present Rhine-Main MCR stretched across three different territories until it was reorganized again during the Third Reich (Freund, 2002). The present day delimitation of the *Länder* (federal states) borders of Hessen, Rhineland-Palatinate and Bavaria, which cut across the Rhine-Main region, is an outcome of the post-war federal reconfiguration of Germany.

Industrialization in Rhine-Main took off in the middle of the 19th century. The first major industries were established along the river Main outside Frankfurt's city boundaries. In some cases, notably Offenbach, these were planned to counterbalance the dominant economic and political position of neighbouring Frankfurt. The development of early radial railway links in the 1840s and 1850s, reaching out from Frankfurt, connected the new industrial cores with a rural hinterland. Growing commuter flows from the towns provided the economic cores with industrial workforce and fuelled early territorial integration. After the establishment of dye works in Höchst and the foundation of Opel, then a sewing machine and bicycle manufacturer, in Rüsselsheim, these two small settlements grew rapidly into industrialized cities by the end of the 19th century, thus contributing to a growing morphological polycentricity of the region. By the late 1800s further industrial locations had evolved in Darmstadt, in Hanau, which benefited from its pre-industrial tradition in metal processing, and in Aschaffenburg, an early centre of paper manufacturing and textile industries (Bördlein and Schickhoff, 1998). In the first half of the 20th century, chemical industries and automotive engineering emerged as the key industrial sectors in Rhine-Main, supplemented by electrical and mechanical engineering. However, industrialization in Rhine-Main was a geographically uneven process. Wiesbaden, for example, a spa with international flair and a casino, successfully prevented the establishment of early industries within its city limits.

After World War II, central urban functions that had concentrated in Berlin, the nation's capital since the foundation of the German Empire in 1871, were redistributed in a then divided Germany. Frankfurt successfully maintained its traditional role as a major fair and exhibition centre, and was able to regain its position as leading financial centre from Berlin. Major banks, several insurance companies and important wholesale and industrial firms relocated to the region that was part of the American occupation zone. Some key institutions were founded in Frankfurt (such as the *Bank deutscher Länder*, a predecessor of the Deutsche Bundesbank, and the *Kreditanstalt für Wiederaufbau*, which was set up in 1948 to finance reconstruction projects after the war); these proved to be crucial for its future development as a major financial centre (Holtfrerich, 1999). At the same time, the enlargement of Frankfurt airport (a response to the Berlin blockade in 1948–1949) laid the foundation for its future development into a European air traffic hub.

Mainz and Wiesbaden regained their historical positions as political centres of power as newly declared federal state capitals of Rhineland-Palatinate (1950) and Hessen (1946). In addition, Wiesbaden gained central federal institutions such as the Federal Statistical Office and the Federal Criminal Police Office, and profited from the relocation of several insurance headquarters (HQ) from Berlin. Later, design consultancies and architecture firms were established in the city. Mainz developed a strong presence of media companies in close proximity to the *Zweites Deutsches Fernsehen* (ZDF), one of the main public national broadcasting companies. In Darmstadt – the self-proclaimed 'City of Science' – urban economic policies after 1945 called for the creation of workplaces for the highly skilled in publishing and natural and technical sciences. The Technical University, founded as one of the first of its kind in Germany in 1877, developed a reputation in electrical engineering, architecture and information science that attracted several public research organizations (e.g. the control centre of the European Space Agency), high-tech telecommunication companies, software consultancies and information technology (IT) firms.

During the last 30 years, the metropolitan region has been reshaped by fundamental changes in the distribution of population and firm location (Keil and Ronneberger, 1994). Tendencies to relocate residential population from the urban cores to the rings have been reported for Rhine-Main since the 1970s (Institut für Kulturgeographie, Stadt- und Regionalforschung, 2000). Processes of suburbanization of population continued in the 1980s and intensified in the 1990s after German reunification, with a stagnation of population numbers in the urban cores and a strong, centrifugal increase in small and medium size towns in the rings (Table 13.1). In 2001, more than 1.7 million people were employed in Rhine-Main. Whereas the number of workplaces in the MCR increased about 15 per cent between 1981 and 1991, especially in mid-size towns of the inner rings adjacent to the urban cores, the small increase of about 1.7 per cent in the following decade was geographically much more disperse.

The suburbanization of both workplaces and living places in different areas of Rhine-Main have created a landscape of urban sprawl and regional deconcentration.

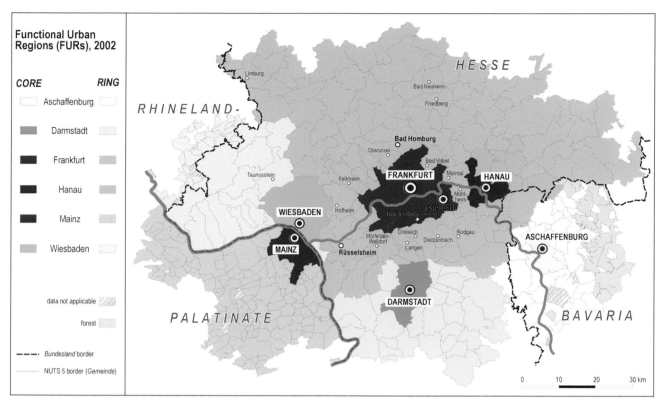

Figure 13.1 The MCR Rhine-Main

Morphologically highly amorphous, this phenomenon has been described as *Zwischenstadt* – a city in between – where borders between urban cores and rural periphery have become blurred (Sieverts, 1999). Patterns of functional linkages have strengthened as commuting flows intensified within and across the different parts of the region. For example, in municipalities like Eschborn, Schwalbach am Taunus or Sulzbach am Taunus to the north and north west of Frankfurt, more than 90 per cent of all employees commute in whereas more than 75 per cent of the residential workforce commute out. The 270,000 daily in-commuting employees underline the dominant economic position of Frankfurt's core within the region (Fischer et al, 2005a).

The process of de-industrialization and tertiarization of economic activities since the 1950s has led to considerable growth of the APS sector and a geographical redistribution of economic functions in Rhine-Main. In the major urban centres, the number of service sector employees began to increase in the 1960s while the hinterland continued to be dominated by manufacturing until the end of the 1970s. A marked decrease of workplaces in manufacturing in the following two decades could only be partially absorbed by the rising service sector and particularly affected the old industrial centres in

Rhine-Main. In 2001 73.5 per cent of the employees worked in the service sector, a plus of 12.5 per cent in only ten years. Although jobs in the tertiary sector are still concentrated in the major urban cores, an increasing number of these workplaces are now found in the suburban surroundings of the cities (Fischer et al, 2005a).

The changes in Rhine-Main's economic structure are embedded in a growing internationalization of economic relations. European integration and the transformations in Eastern Europe have added further to the complexity of regional economic change. For example, foreign direct investment (FDI) in Hessen underwent rapid growth during the second half of the 1990s. At the same time, outgoing direct investment of German financial companies increased even faster than financial sector FDI (Schamp, 2002), fostering a process of internationalization that has anchored the region ever firmer within European and global flows of capital. The accelerated integration of Rhine-Main in new national and international networks, made possible by the dynamic development in information and communication technologies (ICT), has created new organizational and functional geographies that follow a different spatial logic from territorially bounded administrative responsibilities or commuting patterns that connect parts of the larger region.

Table 13.1 Basic socio-economic figures and trends of FURs in the Rhine-Main region

		Population, 2001	Population change		Employees, 2001 (social security contributors only)	Employment change		Degree of tertiarization, 2001 (%)	Change in tertiarization, 1991–2001 (%)
			1981–1991 (%)	1991–2001 (%)		1981–1991 (%)	1991–2001 (%)		
AB	Core	67,028	8.2	4.6	39,288	16.8	−6.1	65.2	11.0
	Ring	205,368	8.7	9.2	50,959	11.4	2.8	46.2	17.2
	FUR	272.396	8.5	8.0	90,247	13.8	−0.2	55.4	15.2
DA	Core	137,776	0.5	−0.8	87,632	11.3	−8.2	71.2	10.6
	Ring	328,472	5.9	9.5	69,985	20.5	10.4	62.7	14.6
	FUR	466,248	4.2	6.2	157,617	14.8	−0.8	67.7	11.8
FR	Core	815,044	2.5	0.1	583,547	10.1	1.8	83.8	13.0
	Ring	1,600,823	4.9	7.7	471,803	22.6	4.9	66.8	13.2
	FUR	2,415,867	4.1	5.1	1,055,350	15.2	3.1	76.6	13.1
HU	Core	87,809	0.6	1.0	47,088	4.9	−16.9	60.9	15.3
	Ring	89,346	4.9	8.6	13,455	23.1	8.2	59.3	8.3
	FUR	177,155	2.7	4.7	60,543	7.7	−12.3	60.5	140
MZ	Core	183,134	−4.2	2.0	101,186	18.1	1.4	78.9	n.a.
	Ring	287,248	8.7	13.7	62,033	10.5	15.0	61.8	n.a.
	FUR	470,382	2.9	8.8	163,219	15.3	6.2	72.4	10.8
WI	Core	268,716	−5.2	3.2	122,885	11.5	0.2	71.7	n.a.
	Ring	177,016	2.9	7.0	41,030	15.9	8.6	66.1	n.a.
	FUR	445,732	−2.2	4.7	163,915	12.5	−2.3	76.3	10.7
Rhine-	Cores	1,559,507	0.3	1.0	980,652	11.1	−0.8	79.8	n.a.
Main	Rings	2,688,273	5.6	8.7	707,708	19.9	5.4	64.8	n.a.
	Total	4,247,780	3.5	5.7	1,688,360	14.5	1.7	73.5	12.5

Note: AB = Aschaffenburg, DA = Darmstadt, FR = Frankfurt, HU = Hanau, MZ = Mainz, WI = Wiesbaden.
Sources: Statistische Landesämter Bayern, Hessen und Rheinland-Pfalz

Connecting Rhine-Main: Organizational geographies of advanced producer service firms

Business service locations in Rhine-Main

In Rhine-Main, the percentage of employment in services increased across all functional urban regions (FURs) between 1991 and 2001 (Table 13.1). However, the FUR Frankfurt clearly is the preferred location for APS firms (see Figure 13.2). While the inner city of Frankfurt houses a major cluster of globally operating knowledge-intensive business services – the HQ of major banks and other financial services, internationally operating law and accountancy firms and advertising agencies – back-office activities, firms with less need of face-to-face contact, and smaller APS firms can be found on the city fringe and in surrounding municipalities. A mix of service firms is present in all FURs, but insurance firms are especially well represented in Wiesbaden, IT consultancies in Darmstadt, and logistics firms in Frankfurt (particularly around the airport), Aschaffenburg and Hanau.

Networking the region: Intra-firm linkages in and beyond Rhine-Main

The analysis of office networks of APS firms (Fischer et al, 2005b; following Taylor, 2004a) underlines Frankfurt's dominant position as the major APS cluster in Rhine-Main: at all scales, the Frankfurt FUR shows the highest degree of connectivity (Table 13.2).

The relative importance of Frankfurt as an APS centre increases with geographical scale. At the regional level, the FURs of Wiesbaden, Mainz and Darmstadt achieve between 61 per cent and 44 per cent of Frankfurt's value. Aschaffenburg and Hanau are less well connected and score about a quarter of Frankfurt FUR's regional connectivity. This rank order remains consistent across all scales with the exception of the national scale, where Mainz ranks a little higher than Wiesbaden and Hanau overtakes Aschaffenburg. In terms of European and global linkages, all FURs fall clearly behind Frankfurt, which reflects the city's position as an international financial centre and gateway to the German market. More detailed analyses of connectivity patterns between each FUR in Rhine-Main and other German cities reveal distinctive

Table 13.2 Connectivities of FURs in the Rhine-Main region

FUR	Regional	National	European	Global
Frankfurt	1.00	1.00	1.00	1.00
Wiesbaden	0.61	0.22	0.13	0.11
Mainz	0.57	0.24	0.09	0.06
Darmstadt	0.44	0.17	0.08	0.06
Aschaffenburg	0.27	0.07	0.04	0.03
Hanau	0.25	0.08	0.03	0.02

Note: The Frankfurt FUR shows the strongest linkages (connectivity = 1) at all scales; connectivities for other FURs are reported as proportions of the highest score.

geographical network profiles for individual FURs (Fischer et al, 2005d). Frankfurt, for example, is particularly well connected with the other major cities Berlin, Munich, Hamburg, Düsseldorf, Stuttgart and Cologne, reflecting a locational strategy of leading service firms present in key nodes of the German economy. Hanau's linkages, in contrast, are focused on cities in the Ruhr area, a result of the specialization of its APS firms in logistics and industrial consultancy. The spatially distinctive network connections of FURs in Rhine-Main point to the complementary nature of business service locations in the polycentric metropolitan region.

Within the region, aggregated intra-firm office linkages show a clear primary radial pattern connecting each FUR to the Frankfurt FUR (Figure 13.3). A secondary triangle of interconnections exists between the FURs of Wiesbaden, Mainz and Darmstadt. Connectivities are highest between Frankfurt and the FURs of the two *Länder* capitals Wiesbaden and Mainz, followed by Darmstadt. The strength of these linkages and the relatively low connectivities with Hanau and Aschaffenburg reflect the longstanding west–east disparities in tertiary employment in the region and the closer association of firms in Wiesbaden, Mainz and Darmstadt with the financial sector that dominates in Frankfurt.

This mapping of aggregate intra-firm connections across Rhine-Main suggests that firms with more than one

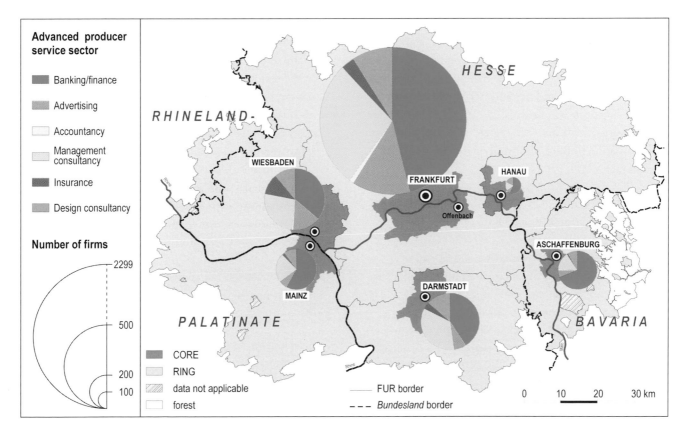

Source: Hoppenstedt firm database 2003

Figure 13.2 APS firms in the FURs of Rhine-Main (selected sectors)

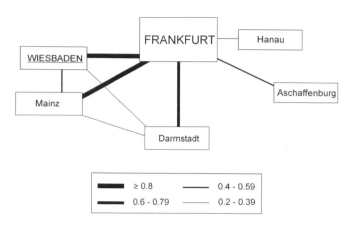

≥ 0.8   0.4 - 0.59

0.6 - 0.79   0.2 - 0.39

Note: Values are calculated as proportions of the prime link (Wiesbaden–Frankfurt).

Figure 13.3 Network connectivities between FURs in Rhine-Main

office in the region tend to locate one of their offices in the FUR Frankfurt. Frankfurt serves as both integrator for regional flows and as global gateway that connects the region to wider international flows.

Places and flows: A qualitative analysis of service business connections

The quantitative modelling of communication and information flows in the region and beyond was supplemented by a qualitative analysis of 61 interviews conducted with representatives of APS firms and selected institutions in all six FURs that constitute the MCR (Fischer et al, 2005c). Where a firm is located in the region and how it is linked to other places is highly dependent on the history, size, sector and network scope of the business conducted. From the responses of interviewees four major modes of organizational strategies and networks of information and communication flows can be deduced in Rhine-Main:

1 Most of the global business service firms articulated the need to be present in Rhine-Main in close proximity to other multi-national companies (MNCs) especially in the banking and finance sector. Due to the region's limited size, these firms often operate only one office to cover the entire region and sometimes even the whole German market. In general, cross-regional intra-firm flows do not appear to be very intense. By far the most important location for globally-oriented APS firms in Rhine-Main is the Frankfurt FUR as the major economic core. Proximity to clients, competitors and other highly specialized business services are key locational factors. Foreign firms with global reach in the banking and finance, management consulting and corporate law sectors are especially willing to pay high

rents for a specific address, for example, in Frankfurt's Westend, to be able to participate in face-to-face contacts in Frankfurt's premier APS cluster.

2 For firms with a distinctive national service strategy, Rhine-Main is also a 'must' location, providing immediate access to Germany's leading APS cluster and Frankfurt's international gateway function. These businesses are not necessarily located in the Frankfurt FUR but cluster according to the functional specializations of different APS locations in Rhine-Main. This business strategy is supported by a reliable transport infrastructure that ensures fast and easy access to other locations within the region and beyond. This is especially true for Frankfurt International Airport, one of the key locational assets of Rhine-Main.

3 Some insurance firms and banks, traditionally more hierarchically organized, follow a clearly defined strategy of servicing the region. Consequently, they operate more than one office in Rhine-Main to ensure an area-wide presence for acquiring new business and catering for sub-regional markets. However, firm-specific regionalizations rarely correspond to administrative or political delimitations of Rhine-Main. For example, firms in the Darmstadt FUR in southern Rhine-Main have developed strong ties with cities in the neighbouring Rhine-Neckar region like Mannheim, Karlsruhe and Heidelberg. A similar pattern exists in the Mainz FUR, which shows strong intra-firms connections with the cities of Kaiserslautern and Saarbrücken to the west of Rhine-Main.

4 Many of the business service firms that were established in the region and evolved 'bottom-up' to service a national or international market, remain located outside Frankfurt's inner-city APS cluster. The excellently rated transport and telecommunications infrastructure allows easy connections both physically and virtually from anywhere in the region. Moreover, local business taxation and office rents tend to be much lower than in the inner city of Frankfurt. The most important reason not to move over larger distances however was the fear of losing personnel.

In general, over the last ten years or so, locational patterns of APS have proved to be highly persistent on the level of FURs, although relocations on a micro level have occurred. The interviews provide no evidence that functions located in the Frankfurt FUR are now being undertaken in other regional centres within Rhine-Main. Neither is there strong evidence for increasing relocation of APS functions from the five smaller functional urban regions to the Frankfurt FUR. It is, however, difficult to evaluate the dynamics of change in the regional knowledge economy, which is often initiated from outside the region in the national, European and global networks of individual firms.

Only a few APS firms reported a strategic division of their regional business functions. In the banking and finance sector, back-office functions of major companies were relocated to office spaces outside the FUR cores, mainly in the 1990s. Other firms create products at their headquarters, for example, in Mainz and Aschaffenburg, and maintain a small Frankfurt office in close proximity to transnationally operating clients. Knowledge and innovation are produced by and in the firms' networks, sometimes in multi-disciplinary project teams that may include specialists from diverse locations, firms and service sectors. The centralization of these ideas and their economical utilization in the service business network pose major challenges for the firms independent of their geographical location.

There are several features that senior executives identify as specific assets of Rhine-Main. These locational advantages go beyond single locations and clusters in close proximity and point to potentials of the regional economy as a whole. For example, while highly skilled professionals are recruited nationally and internationally – with the notable exception of Darmstadt where a local labour market for IT consultants has emerged – the regional labour market for support staff is regarded as one of the best in Germany. Furthermore, the excellent intra- and inter-regional accessibility of Rhine-Main and the integrated regional and national transport infrastructure are highly appreciated. The region is perceived as being well equipped with institutions of (higher) education (e.g. universities in Mainz, Frankfurt and Darmstadt) as well as with private and public research and development (R&D) facilities. Especially for IT and design consultancies, these institutions serve as potential nuclei for cluster formation, as is the case for the IT sector in Darmstadt. Additionally, attractive landscapes, good environmental quality, adequate housing supply for professionals, and the mixture of different international influences in the main urban centres add to the interviewees' picture of the Rhine-Main region as a place to work, travel and live.

The region's external image, however, is often reduced to Frankfurt's skyline and the reputation of its leading city as financial centre. A predominant association with banking and finance fails to do justice to the polycentricity of the region and its diversity and was occasionally seen as detrimental for attracting highly skilled personnel. Advertising and corporate law respondents in particular perceived Frankfurt as a place with limited appeal for young professionals, keen to experience modern urbanity and inspiring cultural milieux. This is in part due to the relatively small size of Frankfurt (c. 650,000 inhabitants) in comparison to the major global cities in Europe, and the competing attractions of other leading German cities, especially Munich, Berlin and Hamburg.

Fragmentation and cooperation in Rhine-Main

It is this perceived inter-metropolitan competition in both a national and international context, fuelled by an all-pervading globalization discourse, which has refocused the attention of both economic and political actors in Rhine-Main on possible ways to overcome the mismatch between the potentials to promote MCR functional interrelationships and the political and administrative fragmentation in Rhine-Main. Current debates build on a long and well-documented history (e.g. Scheller, 1998; Bördlein, 1999) of attempts to reform metropolitan governance for Frankfurt and its surrounding municipalities. Despite phases of intensive discussion in the late 1960s/early 1970s, and again in the late 1990s, the intersection of federal structures (i.e. three states share part of the region) with strong local government (i.e. relatively autonomous municipalities) has so far prevented the development of effective regional governance structures and institutions and fostered informal and voluntary forms of cooperation.

Both state and private initiatives have been proposed in recent years to develop a coordinated strategy of regional economic development that creates a more unified and marketable image of Rhine-Main, built on the premise that a common metropolitan voice would help to boost the prospects of economic agents and municipalities within the region. However, large-scale (trans-*Länder*) administrative reorganization currently seems unlikely.

An important step to overcome the lack of joined-up thinking came with the establishment of the *Planungsverband Ballungsraum Frankfurt/Rhein-Main* (Frankfurt/Rhine-Main Conurbation Planning Association) in 2001, following legislation by the state of Hessen to strengthen communal cooperation in Rhine-Main. Its main objective is the integration of regional planning and local land use plans for 75 municipalities at the centre of the Hessian part of the region. However, the work and authority of this association is geographically limited (only part of the region centred around Frankfurt is incorporated), and its restricted range of responsibilities leaves much of the cooperation between Frankfurt and its neighbouring municipalities to voluntary arrangements. It is supplemented by a new *Rat der Region* (Council of the Region), a body with representatives of each municipality with over 50,000 inhabitants that is responsible for the coordination of municipal cooperation in the conurbation. A specific longstanding problem is the financial imbalance between Frankfurt and the region: while Frankfurt as central city provides much of the social and cultural infrastructure used by the population of the surrounding municipalities, the financial burden is carried by the city alone, which has seen declining tax revenues compared to many of the wealthier communities in the region.

Private initiatives have played a major role in the recent articulation of the wider functional Rhine-Main region. These include the *Wirtschaftsinitiative Metropolitana FrankfurtRheinMain e.V.* (a promotional initiative of major firms in the region) and the IHK-Forum *Rhein-Main* (Forum of the Chambers of Commerce), which extend their activities beyond federal state boundaries. Both private and public actors come together in a new organization, *FrankfurtRheinMain GmbH International Marketing of the Region*, which started work in August 2005 to market Rhine-Main (across federal state boundaries) internationally. In contrast to this economically driven perspective, a sense of regional identity is much less developed in the population of the polycentric region. With the aim of explicitly addressing this deficit, the *Wirtschaftsinitiative* initiated the first *Regionalwerkstatt* in 2004, a regional workshop that gathered different political and economic actors and the public to develop collectively ideas about the future of Rhine-Main. The workshop found strong resonance in the region, with over 600 voluntary participants. The resulting collection of ideas can be interpreted as one of the first attempts at a regionalization 'from below', although it still awaits a conclusive outcome (Langhagen-Rohrbach and Fischer, 2005).

While the initial ideas of the *Regionalwerkstatt* continue to be developed into concrete projects, a key policy document, the 'Strategic Vision for the Regional Land Use Plan and for the Regionalplan Südhessen', has been developed jointly for the area of the *Planungsverband Ballungsraum Frankfurt/Rhein-Main* and the wider spatial planning region Südhessen (Planungsverband Ballungsraum Frankfurt/Rhein-Main and Regierungspräsidium Darmstadt, 2005). Although this is limited to the Hessian part of Rhine-Main, it covers a major area of the functional MCR centred around Frankfurt. The Strategic Vision outlines aims for the development of Frankfurt/Rhein-Main in the next 15 years. Throughout the document, polycentricity is stressed as a regional asset that needs to be maintained and further developed.

The Strategic Vision acknowledges the functional complementarity of the various urban centres in the region and explicitly encourages municipalities to develop and strengthen their own economic profile in order to engage in 'productive competition'. The balance between competition and cooperation is seen as potentially beneficial to the region. Furthermore, the document highlights potential synergies through densely networked cities on different scales – both within the region and within wider European transnational networks. It remains to be seen how these development goals will be translated into more concrete measures in the final version of the regional land use plan of the conurbation, and how coordination with other parts of Rhine-Main outside the remit of this plan will be achieved.

Conclusion

This chapter has presented a brief introduction to the multi-layered polycentricity that constitutes Rhine-Main. Several dimensions of polycentricity can be distinguished: while the region can be construed as a morphologically polycentric region, albeit dominated by the largest metropolitan core, Frankfurt, MCR functional polycentricity is a more complex and highly scale-dependent phenomenon. Frankfurt serves as European and global hub for knowledge-intensive business services in the region and is the preferred gateway for foreign producer service firms who seek access to the German market. As a node in the world economy, Rhine-Main displays monocentric characteristics focused on the core of Frankfurt's FUR. It is at the national scale that connectivity patterns of other FURs in Rhine-Main reveal the complementary nature of APS provision across space: while all FURs are primarily connected to Frankfurt within the region, each shows a distinctive profile of connectivity with other German cities. It is this inter-regional *complementarity* of functions which gives the MCR its overall economic vitality: Frankfurt's ability to attract globally operating service firms depends not least on the region's capacity to provide a wide range of supportive services that are themselves well embedded within Germany. From this functional service perspective, polycentricity works well for Rhine-Main – but its relational character defies confinement to a territorially bounded space, however fuzzy the delimitations.

In contrast, institutional polycentricity in the region is firmly anchored in a territorial logic and has long been a contested issue. The intersection of three federal states, several planning regions and a few hundred municipalities in the MCR Rhine-Main, have stood in the way of efficient regional coordination and cooperation. Strong autonomous municipalities and weak regional institutions that cover only part of Rhine-Main in ever-shifting constellations have prevented the development of integrated policies across the MCR. This fragmentation of political and planning responsibilities has made it difficult to establish a coherent vision of Rhine-Main, not least because a sense of regional identity has yet to emerge fully in the population of the wider region. The ongoing debates about regional reform and the active involvement of both economic and political actors in the development of major initiatives to institutionalize and market the region, however, reveal a high degree of awareness of the need to strengthen regional coordination and cooperation. Addressing the tensions between territorially-based political power and the new economic geographies of interconnectedness calls for a continuing engagement in 'creative governance' (Kunzmann, 2004) to make polycentricity work effectively in Rhine-Main.

Note

1 *Ministerkonferenz für Raumordnung* (MKRO) (Standing Conference of Federal and State Ministers Responsible for Spatial Planning). The designated regions are Berlin/Brandenburg, Hamburg, Rhine-Ruhr, Rhine-Main, Stuttgart, Munich, Halle/Leipzig-*Sachsendreieck* (potential metropolitan region) (1997), and Nürnberg, Hannover-Brunswick-Göttingen, Rhine-Neckar and Bremen/Oldenburg (2005).

European Metropolitan Region Northern Switzerland: Driving Agents for Spatial Development and Governance Responses

Lars Glanzmann, Simone Gabi, Christian Kruse, Alain Thierstein and Nathalie Grillon

Switzerland, a country that is conceived and structured in small political and geographical units, is currently experiencing a phenomenon described in a recent publication as 'Urbanscape Switzerland' (Eisinger and Schneider, 2003). Its authors put forward the key question: 'How do areas change?' Urbanized landscapes, they argue, assume a key role in economic and societal development. The systemic structures of these areas are becoming increasingly complex and more difficult to understand. Morphological descriptions of settlement structures that change over time no longer suffice. Vertical and horizontal networks link together actor and action systems and thus form the predominant characteristic of urbanized landscapes, as found in metropolitan regions such as Northern Switzerland. Most of these functional network effects occur almost unnoticed by the public. Even Swiss spatial planning guidelines still struggle to acknowledge the existence of a functional spatial level such as the European Metropolitan Region (EMR) of Northern Switzerland – with the backbone of the agglomerations of Zürich and Basel its most potent node.

'Urbanscape Switzerland' and the knowledge economy

The knowledge-based economy gains increasing importance for economic and social development in Switzerland, still a small and open economy. For lack of indigenous natural resources – apart from the tourism export sector – the Swiss economy grew predominantly on the basis of technological innovations and specialized producer services such as financial services. In 2001 about 22 per cent of all jobs in Switzerland were defined as knowledge based (Dümmler et al, 2004). Furthermore, due to its small size, the high share of exported goods and services is a distinct feature of the Swiss economy.

Firms in the knowledge-based sector – whether they are high-tech manufacturers or offering advanced producer services (APS) – are dependent on locations that serve as nodes to the global network of flows of knowledge, excellence, capital and talent. Thus, there is an increasingly internationalized competition between places for these scarce resources. Although size does not play a crucial role per se, at least a certain threshold of scale-related quantities and qualities of location factors comes into play in order to be able to compete in this big picture. In fact Switzerland has a series of recognized economic landmarks such as the financial place of Zürich, the international organizations such as the United Nations Organization, the World Health Organization and the World Trade Organization and the *Conseil Européen pour la Recherche Nucléaire* (CERN) research centre in Geneva or the watch and micro-technology manufacturing cluster in the Arc Jurassien. But looking from outside in, it makes no sense to try to distinguish the two locations of Basel and Zürich. Metropolitan city regions have become a functional spatial scale where at least implicitly centres of excellence,

Table 14.1 Basic data for the EMR Northern Switzerland

	Population 2002	Area km²	Population per km²
Zürich city	358,500	87.8	4083
Zürich FUR	1,080,700	1085.8	995
Basel city	169,300	37.0	4576
Basel FUR (Swiss part)	479,400	481.1	996
EMR Northern Switzerland (Swiss part)	3,959,900	11,794.9	336
Switzerland	7,347,800	41,284.5	178

innovative firms, efficient public infrastructure and proactive stakeholders form a coalition for change. But we must make no mistake: in order to deploy the full force of such a coalition, the first necessity is a heightened awareness of the broader public of the need to recognize themselves as an important proactive element.

Switzerland faces a growing concentration of population in functional urban areas (FURs). Three in four people live in areas that are officially defined as urban. However, this does not necessarily coincide with dense spatial concentration. Urban areas extend and grow into semi-rural areas where 'green' intermediate urbanized spaces leave people with an ambiguous notion of 'neither-nor'. This state of mind has spread all along the Central Plateau from Lake Geneva in the west to Lake Constance in the east of Switzerland.

This description sheds light on the fact that spatial trends in today's emerging knowledge economy are hard to detect, complex and controversial. Despite the excellent Swiss public transport and communication systems, there is ongoing concentration of APS in the main cities, most of all in Zürich. But even Zürich, Switzerland's largest city with about 365,000 inhabitants, is much too small for a full-scale urban system. Knowledge networks extend beyond the borders of cities and single conurbations, to encompass nearby towns and urban regions. Certain networks like the Swiss cluster in medical technology even embrace the whole of Switzerland with its neighbouring regions as the dominant spatial scale of interlinkages for innovation (Dümmler, 2006).

Thus, Northern Switzerland is one of the smaller but relevant players in Europe's system of metropolitan regions. EMR Northern Switzerland extends over an area that can be reached within an hour from Zürich airport. With conurbations like Basel, Lucerne and St Gallen it includes about one-half of the Swiss population, on only a quarter of the Swiss surface area. It is not only the main focal area of the Swiss population, but also the central area of the Swiss economy. In 2001, gross domestic product (GDP) per capita was about 19 per cent higher in EMR Northern Switzerland than in the rest of Switzerland, with more dynamic growth (Bundesamt für Statistik, 2004).

The canton of Zürich (with about 17 per cent of the Swiss population) alone produces about 22 per cent of the total Swiss value added (Stiftung Greater Zürich Area Standortmarketing, 2003).

However, EMR Northern Switzerland encompasses numerous cantons and municipalities whose borders have hardly changed since the establishment of contemporary Switzerland in 1848. Because of the history of decentralized federalism with a positive overall performance of that institutional regime, the cantons and municipalities insist very much upon keeping their sovereignty. Thus, this 'Swiss system' is so much engraved in the administrative everyday life of Swiss policy-makers and the constituency, that the emergence of functional metropolitan systems is hard to detect, let alone to promote. Although there is a long way to go in managing metropolitan regions in policy terms, the functional interlinkages already exist today.

Advanced producer services and spatial development in European Metropolitan Region Northern Switzerland

EMR Northern Switzerland is a morphologically polycentric region, with two large centres (Zürich and Basel), three medium size centres (Lucerne, St Gallen and Winterthur) and about 20 smaller centres. Thus, there is a relatively well-balanced distribution of population in the metropolitan region (Table 14.1 and see Figure 14.1).

In contrast, the distribution of APS jobs is more uneven (Table 14.2). The top location for APS is Zürich, followed by Basel. St Gallen, Zug and Lucerne are secondary APS locations, and Winterthur is a weak APS location despite its relatively large size. Smaller centres, with the exception of Zug, are more or less weak APS locations, with Baden-Brugg and Aarau the strongest among them. About 30 per cent of all APS firms in Switzerland are located in the FURs of Zürich, Basel, Zug, St Gallen, Lucerne, Baden-Brugg, Aarau or Winterthur.

It is vital that these FURs should act as locations for APS firms which offer secure and well-paid jobs for highly

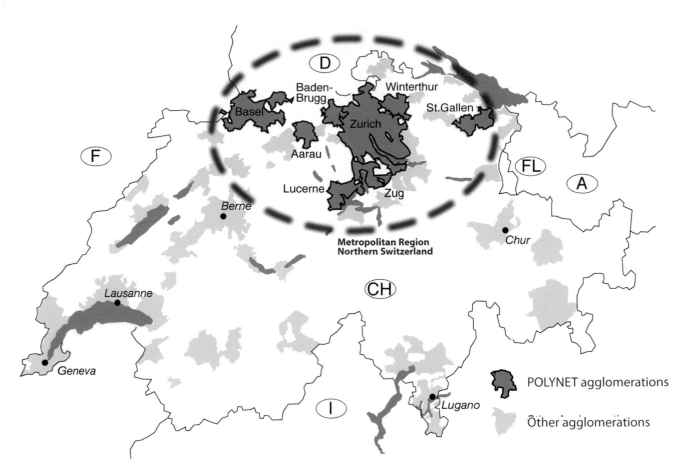

Figure 14.1 The EMR Northern Switzerland

educated people, helping public authorities to lower social costs and raise tax returns. But not all FURs offer the same attractive conditions for APS firms. One very important precondition is the facility to communicate with plants or other firms in locations anywhere in the world. Furthermore cross-border APS firms themselves serve as agents that connect smaller locations to larger economic cores and enable knowledge to flow between them. Thus, locations with well-connected cross-border APS firms are in a better position to keep or attract advanced jobs. It is thus interesting to look at the portfolio of APS firms in the centres of Northern Switzerland, and the spatial patterns of their connectivities.

An analysis of these patterns reveals a hierarchical and strongly interlinked metropolitan system of business networks (see Figure 14.2). It clearly confirms the thesis that Zürich, and to a lesser extent Basel, are global gateways for the whole of Switzerland. Zürich is an indispensable location for many global APS firms, and is thus well connected to the most important economic centres on all continents. On the other hand, Zürich and Basel are also well connected in terms of their organizational linkages, with regional centres in Switzerland. Figure 14.2 shows that all FURs in Northern Switzerland are more connected with Zürich than with any other centre. This leads to the conclusion that Zürich, in

Table 14.2 APS employment in EMR Northern Switzerland FURs

FUR	APS employees	Total employees	APS employees (%)
Zürich	139,404	676,040	20.6
Zug	12,209	65,233	18.7
St Gallen	15,431	91,203	16.8
Basel	35,084	287,560	12.2
Lucerne	11,566	107,577	10.8
Baden-Brugg	6095	58,876	10.4
Winterhur	5803	59,511	9.8
Aarau	4018	47,077	8.5

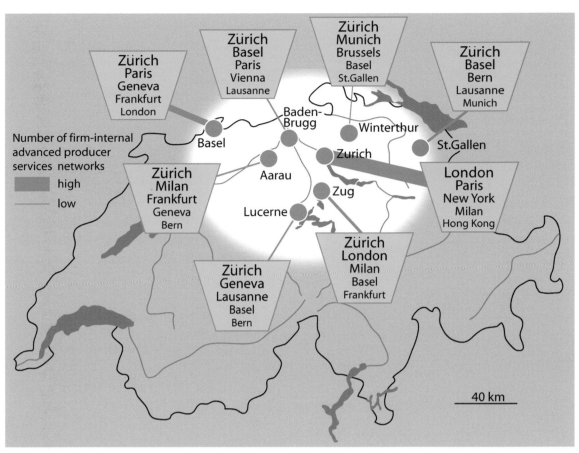

Figure 14.2 FURs in EMR Northern Switzerland and their integration in firm-internal APS branch location networks: The top five locations in each FURs network

cooperation with Basel, serves as a vital 'hinge' or 'hub' of knowledge flows between the Swiss regions and the world.

Global connectivity figures for smaller centres are, as expected, smaller than the figures of the two large centres, Zürich and Basel. For APS firms not located in Zürich or Basel, it is more difficult to establish cooperation with firms abroad. A good assumption is that, the smaller a centre is, the smaller its global connectivity is, but interestingly there are cases that diverge from the expected. One case is Zug, a small agglomeration of about 90,000 inhabitants, which is globally much more connected than expected on the basis of its size. Zug is a very specialized low-tax location, which attracts many global trade firms, and is half an hour by train form Zürich.

On the other hand, the medium size FURs of Lucerne and Winterthur are relatively weakly connected by APS firm networks. In the case of Winterthur, one explanation is the still surviving industrial past, combined with its proximity to Zürich, which almost turns Winterthur into a suburb. Lucerne is also relatively dependent on manufacturing industries and also on tourism.

Figure 14.3 shows cooperation links between APS firms located in different sub-regions of EMR Northern Switzerland. It confirms the suggestion that Zürich is the central, but not the only, hub of knowledge and information flows in the metropolitan region. Zürich is involved in almost all the regional or national APS networks, where knowledge flows between locations. Crucially, cooperation networks between APS firms in different subcentres, leaving Zürich out, are rare.

Most APS firms operating on a global scale are located in Zürich. Basel also plays the role of a business network hub, albeit a smaller one. As both Basel and Zürich are generally too small to carry entire APS networks alone, their APS networks intermix. The result is an economic 'backbone' Zürich–Basel, with great importance for the entire Swiss economy. It is therefore possible to understand these morphologically separated nodes as a 'functional gateway' that imports APS business-relevant knowledge from the globe to Switzerland, or exports it, vice versa.

There are similar potentials for cooperation networks and knowledge flows at the national and regional level. Zürich is the most central location in national APS business networks. One reason lies in the fact that Zürich is generally chosen as a location by those companies which occupy a central role in economic networks. An important example here is the financial sector. Through their central position in a business network, these companies have corresponding radial connectivities with APS firms in the other centres of the metropolitan region as described in

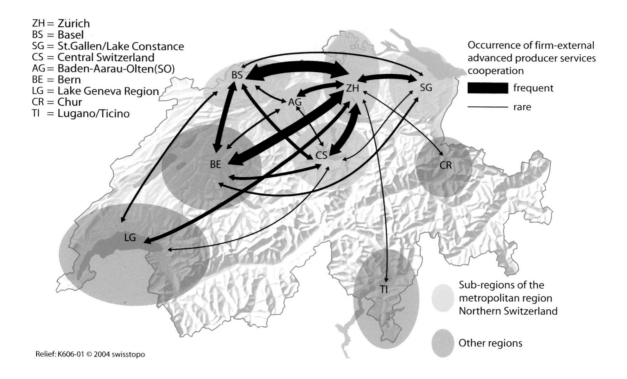

ZH = Zürich
BS = Basel
SG = St.Gallen/Lake Constance
CS = Central Switzerland
AG = Baden-Aarau-Olten(SO)
BE = Bern
LG = Lake Geneva Region
CR = Chur
TI = Lugano/Ticino

Occurrence of firm-external
advanced producer services
cooperation

▬▬▬ frequent

──── rare

Sub-regions of the
metropolitan region
Northern Switzerland

Other regions

Relief: K606-01 © 2004 swisstopo

Figure 14.3 Firm-external cooperation between APS firms in different sub-regions

Chapter 3. The geographical location of companies, and the spatial pattern of their relationships, therefore depends on the centrality of their position in a functional economic network. This means that a better appreciation of the spatial pattern of functional complementarities in APS networks becomes possible when there is greater knowledge about relations and value chains within and between APS branches.

A second important link exists between Zürich and Bern, the Swiss capital, which is outside the EMR Northern Switzerland area. This strong tie is surprising as Bern shows only limited economic dynamism. But Bern as the capital of Switzerland is still an important location for formerly federal companies (e.g. telecommunications) that are integrated in cooperation networks of APS firms. Other functions that Bern has as a capital can also be surmised to be relevant here.

APS links from the German speaking EMR Northern Switzerland to the French and Italian speaking parts of Switzerland are quite rare. Language barriers play a great role here, most of all because they separate different markets. For most APS firms in EMR Northern Switzerland, markets in the Lake Geneva region or the Ticino are less important than markets in Germany or Austria.

What do these patterns tell us about polycentricity in the EMR Northern Switzerland? First of all it is clear that the region cannot easily be defined either as polycentric or as monocentric. While the morphological pattern is indeed polycentric, the functional spatial patterns show a much higher complexity. While the large centres of Zürich and Basel have direct links to global economic centres, medium size and small centres miss the advantages of those direct links. To different degrees, they depend on functional links with one of the large centres, in most cases with Zürich, to be connected to global flows of business-relevant knowledge for their local economy.

But there is a potential for more APS activities in medium size and small centres. There is an evident trend: that APS firms recognize advantages of locations in subcentres outside Zürich, such as better availability of affordable land or better accessibility by car. However, a very close location to high-quality infrastructure (e.g. an airport and universities) is the main argument for many APS firms to locate or remain in Zürich. For highly specialized firms this will not change, but for some APS firms agglomeration costs in Zürich (e.g. growing traffic congestion) are becoming too high. Subcentres of EMR Northern Switzerland, due to the excellent transport system, the relatively high quality of life and other factors, are more and more considered as possible alternative locations. This is leading to a more polycentric distribution of APS activities in the region, though not to a functional equality of all centres, as some APS activities remain dependent on highly central locations.

As this system of functionally interlinked urban sub-centres overlaps administrative borders of sovereign regional authorities, uncoordinated local strategies for spatial and economic development represent an obstacle for the management of the metropolitan region as a whole. The lack of correspondence between political spatial planning institutions and the reality of spatial development is addressed in the next section.

Spatial development policies in Switzerland: Where to go from here?

In the previous section we discussed the empirical findings on functional networks that link actors and action systems that have influenced and formed the urbanized landscape of EMR Northern Switzerland.

The spatial development tendencies identified there point to two central, highly related issues that are critical for future spatial development policy responses in Switzerland:

First, there is a need for institutional and strategic answers to the reality of spatial development at the functional-spatial level of the region. These answers have to move beyond the decentralized federal system of cantons and municipalities where necessary, requiring a widened awareness and problem scope.

Second, there is a need to deal with the mismatch between the functional logic of the actual driving forces for spatial development on the one hand and the terri-torial, normative logic, which is still the foundation and mindset behind spatial planning policies.

Spheres of operation and approaches to metropolitan governance

Referring to the first issue, future effort has to focus on the transformation of territorial governance, not as a reinvention, but based on ongoing debate, approaches and experience.

For many observers from the European Union (EU), the Swiss federal system is a role model for the solution of their own development dilemmas. Nevertheless, the current Swiss situation shows the fragmentation of jurisdictions and deficiencies in governance capacity for solving inter-community, inter-canton and international problems (OECD, 2002; Thierstein et al, 2003; Blöchliger, 2005). It is important to bear in mind that the existing Swiss administrative system consists of three tiers, the confederation, 26 cantons and about 2900 municipalities, each having its own spatial planning responsibilities. The emphasis for planning is at the level of the cantons, whose task is to integrate spatial claims by means of structure plans. The communes are generally responsible for land use planning. Lastly, under the constitution, the confederation is responsible for the legislative framework, for formulating planning principles,

for coordinating formal spatial policies both internally and with the cantons.

Beyond the existing system, the discourse on territorial organization ranges from fusion of cantons and municipalities on the one hand to voluntary cooperation for specific operational tasks on the other. In the field of spatial planning, large cantons often delegate supra-municipal spatial planning tasks to so-called public law regional planning associations, in which municipalities cooperate for planning purposes. Over the last decades, an increasing number of single- or multi-purpose district bodies (special districts) have been founded on a regional level. For instance, each Zürich municipality belongs to an average of six dedicated organizations. The consequence is the jeopardizing of controllability, manageability and integral regional performance as well as the ability to find solutions to problems.

In 2001 a Tripartite Agglomerationskonferenz (TAK) (Tripartite Agglomeration Conference) consisting of the three levels – federal, cantonal and municipal – was founded to promote vertical cooperation in policy fields relevant for the metropolitan regions. A study of the TAK has proposed agglomeration conferences as institutional bodies for the, up to now, merely statistical perimeters of the agglomerations (Tripartite Agglomerations-konferenz, 2004).

A recent outcome of a political decision-making process points the way to the preparation for a reform of federalism: the reorganization of the inter-governmental financial equalization scheme and of the respective functions of the Federation and the cantons (*Neuer Finanzausgleich* – NFA) provides an opportunity to test the fundamental understanding of governance. At the core of the Federal Council's new financial equalization is the idea of shifting decision-making capacity from the federal to the canton levels for tasks of the core cities that extend over canton borders. Thus, in order to deal with specific inter-cantonal issues, the cantons are required to cooperate in order to earn and distribute federal funding. This is the case for universities, specified medical clinics, and large-scale cultural infrastructure and transportation projects in agglomerations. The Federation maintains the competencies to allocate funding if cooperation among the cantons does not take place. The second instrument of the new financial scheme, which is of consequence for urban regions, addresses the balancing of socio-demographic burdens. It shifts financial means to the core cities because the core cities of agglomerations have a greater share of socially weaker members of society, causing higher expenses and less tax revenues. The scrutinizing of respective functions of the Federation and the cantons provides an opportunity to test the fundamental understanding of governance within a federal system.

This debate represents a 'down to earth' approach, in which the institutional framework of the three-tier federal system of Switzerland remains basically unchallenged. On a more visionary basis, authors from different professional backgrounds have recently proposed approaches to metropolitan governance, the definition of new spheres of operation or visualizations of possible urban futures in Switzerland (Blöchliger, 2005; Diener et al, 2005; Eisinger and Schneider, 2003; Rellstab, 2004).

These visions and new approaches are necessary, since the existence of functional interrelations in EMR Northern Switzerland is not yet sufficiently rooted in the awareness of most policy-makers or the constituency. Despite the development trends at metropolitan levels, the areas of focus and action for institutional bodies responsible for spatial development are largely determined by awareness of problems on a local, smaller regional or, at most, canton level.

The functional and territorial logics of Swiss spatial development policies

The second issue that emerges from the reality of spatial development trends is the mismatch between functional and territorial logics.

As a normative setting for spatial development, Switzerland has adopted the strategy of polycentricity outlined in the European Spatial Development Perspective (ESDP) (European Commission, 1999). In the 1996 Swiss planning policy guidelines (*Grundzüge der Raumordnung Schweiz*), the Federal Office for Spatial Planning proposed the cooperation within a network of a connected system of cities (*vernetztes Städtesystem Schweiz*) as the response of the Swiss federal system to the challenges of competition between European city regions (Federal Office for Spatial Planning, 1996). Also, the 1996 Swiss planning policy guidelines helped to identify the significance of agglomerations in the social and economic development of Switzerland. As late as 1997, with the revision of the federal constitution, the Federation started taking more account of the concerns of the agglomerations.

The Federal Council's 2001 agglomeration policy reinforced these steps in order to emphasize the need to support cantons and agglomerations in solving their problems of settlement and transportation infrastructure development, life quality and horizontal and vertical cooperation. Its aim is to support the cantons and communities in their activities and to improve horizontal cooperation within agglomerations (Federal Council, 2001).

Another attempt was the Federal Council's approval for the Strategy for Sustainable Development in 2002, an action package elaborated by the inter-departmental commission for sustainability, as a result of the 1992 United Nations Conference on Environment and Development in Rio de Janeiro. The strategy includes 22 measures for the sectors of economy and competitiveness, financial policy, research, spatial development, mobility, to name just a few. A specific goal for regional policies and spatial planning is the stabilization of the overall use of land (footprint) at 400m^2 per person (Federal Council, 2002).

As the most recent document that complies with the normative direction of the previous documents, the Federal Office for Spatial Development has presented the *Report on Spatial Development* in March 2005 (Federal Office for Spatial Development, 2005) as a follow-up to the 1996 Swiss planning policy guidelines. Based on its analysis of development trends and scenarios, the 2005 Report on Spatial Development outlines a spatial development concept with the following major integrative strategies:

- maintaining and improving physical and virtual international connections (by air traffic, roads, high-speed trains);
- creating two connected networks: the first network comprises new, statistically defined (morphologically) polycentric metropolitan regions (Zürich, Geneva–Lausanne, Basel, Bern, Ticino); the second network is made up of the remaining cities and agglomerations;
- creating strategic urban networks in areas outside the metropolitan regions.

Despite the planning policies of the past decade, the Federal Office for Spatial Development has had to acknowledge that development has not moved towards the objectives of a sustainable spatial development, but has encountered extended urban sprawl, growing mobility and accessibility along with the decline of structuring open spaces (Federal Office for Spatial Development, 2005, p7).

Obviously, there is a missing link or a mismatch between the principle and strategy of sustainable polycentric development as outlined in the ESDP and adopted by Swiss planning policies on the one hand and actual spatial development tendencies on the other.

The mismatch between reaching the normative objectives of spatial planning and the driving forces of actual spatial development tendencies, that follow a functional logic, is best represented by federal policies outside the narrow scope of spatial planning policies, specifically the political debate about the new regional policy. For the past decades, regional policy has been designed to support infrastructure investment in mountain areas and enterprises in economically disfavoured areas through targeted individual support (OECD, 2002, p12).

Recently, approval of the new regional policy has been on the political agenda, with a great deal of sceptical response from rural stakeholders and other status quo beneficiaries. At the beginning of the debate, the authors of the new regional policy set out to take the territorial complementarities between rural areas and agglomerations into account. The goal was to direct the emphasis of the new regional policy towards the inclusion of agglomerations, accepting that the national economy is highly dependent on the functioning of larger cities and agglomerations. In other words the proposed legislation adopted a functional view of the Swiss territory as an interlinked value-added production system (Corpataux et al, 2002).

However, this focus on the whole country rather than rural areas would have required a difficult balancing act. From the overall regional policy budget of 70 million Swiss francs (CHF), 30 million would be allocated to wide area projects that support cooperation between rural areas and agglomerations and 40 million would be allocated to support local and regional projects in rural areas (Federal Department of Economic Affairs, 2004). Thus, in the political process, policy-makers have declined officially to link the two policy fields. They refused to connect the low level while promising agglomeration policies 'best practice models' with the new regional policies (Anon, 2005, p13). The difficulty in connecting agglomeration policy and traditional regional policy shows that there is insufficient political will to create inter-sectoral cooperation between spatial planning and economically oriented policies or between rural and urban policies. For the time being, this makes it difficult to coordinate efforts for more efficient, sustainable management of spatial planning.

It is obvious, that, in comparison with the discussion on the new regional policy, the isolated efforts of the spatial planning sector have a comparably small impact on economic development or on managing the spatial impacts of economic decisions.

Moreover, even the budget for the regional and spatial planning policies, that make up the spatial development policies, is comparatively limited. The Federal Office of Spatial Development and State Secretariat for Economic Affairs do not administer laws related to spatial development, which have substantial budgets allocations. For instance, over the period 1997–2003, federal expenditures for regional policy averaged around CHF 69 million (Federal Department of Economic Affairs, 2004, p57). The means for other sectoral policies, which have an impact on spatial development in the widest possible variety of areas (agriculture, transportation, communication, education, energy, security policy and public buildings), yet do not follow the territorial logic of spatial development

policies, are much higher in comparison.

Conclusions and recommendations

The objective behind the ESDP's concept of polycentricity is to achieve territorial cohesion between economically strong areas and the weaker, less dynamic rural areas or smaller cities. Territorial cooperation between medium and smaller size cities or agglomerations that are within certain proximity is supposed to make them stronger, more economically potent in the competition with other larger cities or regions within the EU. However, in reality cooperation does not occur on a normative basis. The prerequisite for functional networks is problem pressure and/or economic interdependencies between spatial units. These lead the autonomous institutional units to consider advantages of cooperation.

However, the reality of economic structures shows that the centres in EMR Northern Switzerland are indeed strongly linked by APS organizational networks. Smaller centres depend for their economic development on strong central cities, where APS relevant knowledge is either produced or imported for the entire region. These links shape a large metropolitan region. But as these interrelations do not correspond with visible morphological structures or administrative entities, they are mainly hidden. This means that a problem is making itself evident, but is difficult to notice or grasp.

Thus, a first priority for action is to make hidden economic links and dependencies visible and accessible to relevant policy-makers, planners, and last but not least to the public at large. Disseminating factual information to a wide public is important in Switzerland, as its direct democratic instruments like the referendum often leave the final decision to the people. There is a need for more scientific work on metropolitan regions, more research and consulting institutions to inform policy-makers and planners, and more exposure in the popular media to inform the public of the issues.

However, recognized pressing problems must not lead to uncoordinated individual measures at local or regional levels, as this would maintain the complex tangle of isolated policy institutions and cooperation concepts. It takes a coordinating authority to ensure that new governance instruments are implemented in the contexts of functional regions like EMR Northern Switzerland, and in the functional structure of the whole of Switzerland. There are strong indications that this arbitrator's job can only be done on the basis of a top-down principle. The question whether, consequently, the Swiss Federation has to assume this role, has to be answered in the near future.

15

The Paris Region: Polycentric Spatial Planning in a Monocentric Metropolitan Region

Ludovic Halbert

Paris is the only French global city (Hall, 1966; Sassen, 1994). This unique position results from a concentration of political, cultural and economic functions, first under the monarchy and later under successive republics.[1] The French capital benefited not only from the location of numerous political bodies but also from changes in the productive system such as the 19th century Industrial Revolution and more recent economic globalization. Nowadays, the Paris metropolitan area is a textbook case study of a First City in a 'macrocephalic' national urban system. With over 11 million inhabitants, the Paris urban area is eight times the size of its nearest contender, Lyon. In terms of employment, the Île-de-France – the administrative region of Paris – concentrates 21 per cent of the national workforce (against 18 per cent of the total French population) and as much as 40 per cent of the highly qualified workers. Most national and international headquarters (HQ) and related services are located in the Paris region which offers them an office capacity of over 360 million ft^2 (40 million m^2): the second in Europe, closely following that of London. Multi-national enterprises find the most productive workforce in the Paris area: gross domestic product (GDP) per inhabitant and per employee are respectively one-third and one-half higher than in the rest of the national territory. This high productivity benefits the national economy both directly, and more indirectly via massive tax transfers (Davezies, 1999).

The Paris urban area has been the engine of recent economic changes, anticipating what is now happening in dynamic French cities like Lyon, Toulouse or Grenoble. As always, major economic innovations and changes first benefit the most important cities before diffusion trends occur. The development of business services has been led by the Paris urban area (Halbert, 2004), which explains its remarkable economic specialization: it reports a share of workers in these sectors one-third greater than in the remaining main metropolitan areas.

However, this national level concentration of employment in the first metropolis goes hand in hand with a deconcentration of activities from the historic City of Paris to the rest of the urban area – first to the immediately surrounding Paris agglomeration, but second also to the rest of the Île-de-France and to its surrounding regions. Since 1962 at least, censuses show the growth of peripheral locations in terms of both inhabitants and jobs. Many secondary cities have steadily developed, feeding increasing commuting flows. This results in the development of an enlarged urban area – a mega-city region (MCR) in POLYNET terminology – around the Paris metropolis, as

Table 15.1 The different statistical perimeters of the Paris Region

	Inhabitants	Jobs	Area (km^2)
Île-de-France region[a]	11,131,000	5,342,000	12,070
Paris FUR[b]	10,077,000	5,403,000	12,000
Paris MCR (strict contiguity)[b]	12,185,000	6,062,000	20,390
Bassin Parisien FURs (soft contiguity)[b]	15,692,000	7,661,000	43,110

Sources: a INSEE (2004); b INSEE (1999) (POLYNET perimeters)

Table 15.2 Employment in the City of Paris and the surrounding rings (based on département perimeters)

Location	All sectors	Business services	Share of business services in total employment (in %)
Paris City	1,600,820	666,440	41.6
First ring[a]	1,771,920	729,730	41.2
Second ring[a]	1,669,260	520,520	31.2
Third ring[a]	2,962,700	638,200	21.5
Total	8,004,700	2,554,870	31.9

Note: a Three rings of *départements* surrounding Paris City. The first two are part of the Île-de-France administrative region, whereas the third ring consists of around ten *départements* belonging to five different regions.
Source: National Census, INSEE (1999)

attested in the recent literature (Gilli, 2005). If commuter flows are mainly centripetal, linking secondary cities to the Paris agglomeration (which still concentrates a majority of MCR jobs), some sub-regional interactions exist, especially in the northern Oise Valley (Beauvais, Compiègne, Creil), in the eastern half (Reims, Châlons-en-Champagne, Vitry-le-François) or in the further Loire Valley (from Tours to Orléans). The geography of commuting in the MCR shows only a slightly polycentric system.

Employment deconcentration is a complex trend that needs further study. Are all activities affected equally? More precisely, are the major sectors of the knowledge economy following the same pattern, whereby historically most of the corporate complex (HQ and related producer services) were located in the western districts of the City of Paris? Obviously, the business district of La Défense is more a prolongation of the Parisian *arrondissements* than an example of deconcentration at a metropolitan scale. Yet one must remember that the PAT (*Politique d'aménagement du territoire*), at least since the 1960s and down to the 1990s, has sought to limit the strength of Paris and to divert its economic growth to other national secondary cities. This policy worked to some extent, even though most industrial deconcentration has been to the closest cities around the Île-de-France region, potentially favouring the enlargement of the Paris MCR rather than reducing spatial imbalances at the national scale as the initial goal intended. To what extent have advanced producer services (APS) been following this trend? Has a more polycentric metropolitan knowledge economy developed, inducing intense flows linking the different constituting functional urban regions (FURs)?

These questions are strongly linked to the specific geography of Paris. However, there are at least three relevant scales. Polycentricity *within* the Paris metropolitan area – that is to say ignoring the national, European and global scales – can be seen either at the *agglomeration* level (Paris and the secondary economic poles such as the *Villes Nouvelles* or the airport platforms), at the strict *metropolitan region* level (Île-de-France region and the

contiguous surrounding FURs of Chartres, Beauvais, Compiègne, etc.) and at a larger *metropolitan level* according to a softer contiguity criterion[2] thus including most of the Paris Region cities, among which medium size urban centres (Rouen, Orléans, Reims, Amiens, Le Havre, etc.) dominate. Deconcentration and polycentricity may vary utterly from one level to the next.

Concentration/deconcentration: Advanced producer services in a monocentric MCR

Business service deconcentration: Static photograph and moving picture

Business services still have a very central location. According to the latest census data (1999, see Table 15.2), Paris City and the first ring of *départements*, covering more or less the inner suburbs, have over 40 per cent of their employment in this sector, which represents no less than 10 per cent over the Paris Region average. Yet Table 15.3, showing employment and business services growth in the rings surrounding Paris (based again on the French administrative *départements*) attests the absolute decline of Paris City. Strong growth is registered, noticeably in business services, in all surrounding rings. The first and second rings are both located in the Île-de-France, which means that according to POLYNET perimeters they are part of the Paris FUR. In other words, if a strong deconcentration trend exists, it seems still to benefit the Paris urban area more than the furthest secondary cities of the MCR. Among the latter, the Paris Region's western FURs are seen to grow faster than those located in the eastern half.

To some extent, if one were to look only at broad sectoral employment figures, the 'still photograph' of the Paris metropolitan region would be one of a strong concentration in the central area of the agglomeration (Paris City and the inner suburbs, the first ring in Tables 15.2 and 15.3) while the 'motion picture' of the last 30

Table 15.3 Employment change in the City of Paris and the surrounding rings (based on département perimeters) 1982–1999

Location	Absolute variation 1982–1999		Yearly variation 1982–1999 (%/year)	
	All sectors	**Business services**	**All sectors**	**Business services**
Paris City	−207,137	−39,679	−0.7	−0.3
First ring	143,005	298,564	0.5	4.1
Second ring	401,383	347,426	1.9	5.3
Third ring	85,096	175,773	0.2	2.2
Total	422,347	682,084	0.3	2.1

Sources: National Census, INSEE (1982, 1999)

years would be one of intense deconcentration, first to all suburban locations within the Île-de-France region (the Paris FUR) and some secondary urban centres.

Yet this geography of business services employment does not indicate how the Paris metropolitan system really works. In a knowledge economy that increasingly relies on flows of information (Castells, 1989), it is necessary to understand the *relations* between the different urban centres to evaluate the extent to which a polycentric system exists. In other words, is deconcentration resulting in a functional polycentric system? And what is the role of the Paris central area: a city that is slowing down as if unable to compete with new secondary centres on the edges of its agglomeration or even of its FUR? Or is it rather the engine fuelling a deconcentration process through an increasing competition for central spaces?

Theoretical intra-firm flows: A radial geography

The theoretical space of flows of APS in the Paris MCR described in Globalization and World Cities (GaWC) methodology (Chapter 3, page 00) is much more centre-periphery than plainly polycentric. There are no major links between non-central FURs except for one between Reims and Rouen (see Figure 3.2g, p61). All other interactions are therefore binomial, associating Paris and the other FURs in an impressively radial pattern. This hierarchical organization is not too surprising, considering not only the French history of economic concentration but also the fairly limited size of secondary cities in the surrounding areas. However, the GaWC analysis shows a differentiation between the closely located cities on the outskirts of the agglomeration and other, farther distant, cities both on the fringes of the Paris FUR itself and in the Paris MCR. When weighting intra-firm FURs' connectivity by the number of inhabitants or jobs, APS connectivities are much stronger between Paris and its immediately surrounding cities such as the airport platform of Roissy or the *Villes Nouvelles* (Cergy-Pontoise,

Marne-la-Vallée, Saint-Quentin-en-Yvelines and Evry-Sénart in our case) than between Paris and more remote FURs. Similarly, these closely located cities of the agglomeration are more globally linked than other secondary FURs, probably benefiting in this regard from the central core area which shows the strongest global scope. Despite the increasing use of information and communication technologies (ICTs) – which have sometimes been argued to diminish the importance of geographical distance (Cairncross, 1997), proximity still has a role to play in the regional economy.

Here the GaWC quantitative analysis must be augmented by qualitative methods, since the intra-firm connectivities that are measured remain theoretical in nature. Some connectivities between FURs may reflect firms' locational strategies rather than the effective geography of flows. Interviews with APS senior executives demonstrate that despite firms' ability to network, their workers do not communicate freely in an unstructured virtual space of flows; dominant patterns and hierarchical structures still exist.

Flows in the MCR: A qualitative analysis

The 60 interviews conducted in the Paris MCR, both in the Paris central core and in other secondary cities, provide qualitative insights into the underlying logics of effective business flows. Because there is no evidence that people involved in the knowledge economy network freely in the Paris metropolitan region, intense cross-regional flows do not appear to be the most important aspect of everyday life in the APS world. Nonetheless, some interactions are occurring – whether occasionally or frequently – between the constituent FURs. As many APS firms interviewed have an office in the Paris core area – i.e. the firm's HQ – and one or more branch offices in secondary FUR cities, some strong connectivities are observed between the First City and the others. The most obvious correspond to top-down interactions resulting from the concentration of command, innovative and wholesale functions in the Paris core area, while other offices may be less knowledge intensive and/or have more retail-oriented functions servicing sub-regional markets. This co-exists with bottom-up interactions. Obviously this is the case when a firm has its HQ in a secondary FUR and issues commands to other cities including Paris. However, this simple pattern sometimes becomes more complex as temporary functional shifts occur, such as when important events – for example, stakeholders' assemblies or strategic meetings with partners – are held in an office located in Paris. In some cases high value-added tasks that will be used by other offices in the firm's network can be produced in secondary cities when a particular skill is available. Finally, some limited interactions between secondary FURs cross-cut the Paris core area. However, this is often the result of a local firm trying to enlarge its market at a sub-regional level rather than a truly polycentric metropolitan strategy.

The horizon of APS differs according to the scope and the location of the firms in the MCR. If a firm located outside the Paris FUR works at a sub-regional or a regional/metropolitan scope, it often sees the Paris agglomeration as a complementary place in which to do business, thus inducing centripetal flows that can combine with criss-cross interactions with other secondary FURs. However, if on the contrary an MCR firm enlarges its scope to the global market, no matter whether it is a small and medium size enterprise (SME) or a multi-national company (MNC), it sees the Paris core area as the *only global gateway* that will make it possible to gain access to the international market. In this regard, strategic interactions are mostly with the Paris agglomeration because it is the MCR's only global gateway. In return, and not unexpectedly, Paris agglomeration APS firms do not regard surrounding secondary cities as important for their development. For them, their scope is both the Parisian market and the major national and international cities. Therefore, the functional geography of the Paris MCR is not best characterized as a fully polycentric network but as a still very hierarchical geography of flows.

The Paris core area: The global gateway and the regional integrator

Why is the Paris core area still such a strong pole for the metropolitan economy despite the obvious tendency of employment to deconcentrate?

First, economic globalization stresses the importance of global gateway cities as a necessary asset for APS firms. They are the places where regional firms can find the opportunities to access global markets and where global firms can find local insiders to fine-tune their services to the special characteristics of regional/national markets.

Moreover, concentration in the Paris core allows close proximity and easy access to both partners and the large and skilled workforce required. Seemingly, proximity to partners – which in other projects may in fact be competitors – is necessary as soon as essential competences are not available within the firm. Consequently, the concentration of APS and skilled workers in the Paris agglomeration leads to a territorial lock-in situation. The resulting hypothesis is that the more knowledge oriented the economy becomes, the more clustered the central core of the Paris MCR may be. This can be explained by a mix of scale and transaction economies as well as milieu effects. In this last regard, as in most other global cities, because the knowledge economy is information intensive, the strong development of ICTs has not diminished the importance of face-to-face contact in the Paris region. Accessibility therefore remains a key issue for the future of the metropolis, especially within the central area where APS place an absolute value on the benefits of density.

In conclusion, the POLYNET study shows not so much a deconcentrated concentration leading to a functionally polycentric system in the Paris case but rather the strength of the central area (the Paris core and to some extent the Paris agglomeration). Deconcentration trends are most likely the indirect consequences of the strong demand for central spaces. Less central activities or basic business services functions are relocated on the periphery of the Paris agglomeration or in secondary FURs; advanced services remain in the Paris global gateway, thus leading to a hierarchical pattern of interactions between the main centre and secondary poles.

The predictable dynamics should be a continued deconcentration so long as the productive system's specialization in business services increases. The functional division of labour may be reinforced. It is impossible to see exactly how a more polycentric system might be strengthened unless some secondary FURs were to gain momentum and, in consequence, start to attract more up-scale functions (a size effect, see Boiteux-Orain and Huriot, 2002 for a theoretical approach). However, most likely APS will keep concentrating in the Paris First City as it is increasingly the gateway and articulator of flows, both within the metropolitan region and with other international MCRs. Will this benefit the regional and the national economy? Or in other words, should it be regarded as a negative result that a more polycentric structure fails to develop in the first French metropolitan region? The review of national and regional policy documents gives some clues on the policy-makers' preferred answer, and on the ways in which they take the development of the regional knowledge economy into account.

The limits of polycentric planning

It is impossible to discuss the numerous policy documents in detail in this chapter. Instead we address them by asking some cross-cutting questions:

- Are APS of any importance in spatial planning policies?
- Is the metropolitan scale adequately taken into account?
- How is the concept of polycentricity implemented in the Paris case?

The regional knowledge economy: From theory to implementation

Many French spatial planning documents take the new rhetoric of globalization into account, at least since the 1990s. Influenced by evidence from scientific literature, key concepts and debates are discussed in the introductory and contextual chapters of many planning documents: globalization dynamics, the knowledge economy and the connectivity of metropolitan regions. Important determinants for firms like the increasing need for accessibility, development of ICTs and reinforcement of labour force skills are often mentioned. Even though its influence is hard to evaluate, the Lisbon Agenda may have fuelled the growing interest in knowledge-related activities, regardless of the fact that the accent is currently placed more on industrial innovation, research and higher education than on APS (see the *Schémas de Services Collectifs* or the most recent *Pôle de Compétitivité* policy at the national level but also various regional level documents such as *Projets d'Action Stratégique de l'Etat* (PASERs), *Contrats de Plan Etat-Région* (CPERs) and *Schémas Régional d'Aménagement et de Développement du Territoire* (SRADT)).

Yet, there are still some differences between the introductory chapters of the spatial planning documents that state their overall strategies and their more operationally-oriented parts. Many policy documents prove to be too unspecific and fail to deliver focused proposals in terms of economic development issues. For instance, despite the interest shown in the concept of the knowledge economy, the ability to address economic and spatial issues specific to the main functions and sectors of the new economy fails to appear clearly. For example, APS and high-tech industries are often treated as one single category despite their potentially very different spatial logics. Moreover, analysis of policy documents shows that the linkages between the knowledge economy and the rest of the regional economy are not discussed, almost as if two unrelated economies co-exist. This may result, for instance, in an inability to address the urgent issue of social polarization, described in the global city-related literature.

Lack of metropolitan scale in policy-making

A second issue is the importance of metropolitan governance. There is a strong momentum – now largely widespread in the Île-de-France after some initial reluctance – for cross-municipal and sub-regional political cooperation. This mostly results from the new competences given to local authorities by the successive 'decentralization' laws, which favour both institutional cooperation between local institutions and joint spatial planning documents (such as the *Schémas de Cohérence Territoriale*).

However, despite this growing cooperation, a deficiency in terms of governance is still noticeable at the metropolitan level. The mismatch between administrative boundaries and the soft functional perimeters of the MCR, combined with the impossibility of creating new institutions at the relevant scale,[3] makes it very difficult in the Paris case to achieve a metropolitan network bringing together all competent institutions. The short life of the *Charte du Bassin Parisien* in the 1990s (only five years) is a striking example of this as the national government, the Île-de-France and the seven other regions never managed to overcome their differences. Since then, metropolitan issues are no longer addressed in a common strategy in the Paris MCR. If the metropolitan scale or at least cross-regional interactions are taken into account in most recent planning documents (see the two regional schemes – SRADT – published recently in Champagnes-Ardennes and Picardie regions for instance), global cooperation will probably remain the unsuccessful attempt of the 1990s rather than a project for the near future. The absence of the Paris MCR in DATAR's (*Délégation à l'Aménagement du Territoire et l'Action Régionale*) call for metropolitan projects in 2005 is highly illustrative. In this regard, what can be called political polycentricity proves not to work efficiently at the metropolitan scale.

Polycentrism: The spatial planning paradigm in a monocentric MCR

Polycentrism cannot be explained by a lack of interest in the notion of polycentricity itself. On the contrary, it has probably been one of the planning principles most used by policy-makers – both at the national level with the PAT and in the Île-de-France region's *Schémas Directeurs*. The success of the concept is not unrelated to the fact that since Jean-François Gravier's famous book of 1947 (*Paris et le Désert français*), most observers depict a situation of intense concentration and monocentricity at both levels, national and regional. A first hypothesis therefore is that polycentricity in spatial planning policies offers an alternative scenario for less imbalanced spaces in the future. This relates in practice to a second explanation for the widespread use of polycentricity as a normative spatial planning tool. Whether as an inheritance of the 18th Century *les Lumières* philosophers' taste for rational order or the result of the long unquestioned assumption that lack of concentration improves social cohesion, it is often believed that all kinds of geographical disequilibrium are unacceptable and unsustainable. A third explanation for the preference for polycentric planning in most documents is not explicitly expressed but rather induced: the notion has the ability to ease territorial political competition; unlike more monocentric models which give the advantage to one dominant location, it offers each territory the opportunity to be taken into account. Unfortunately, one must admit that despite the existence of a shared project, the major risk with political polycentricity is of falling into a strategy of dispersion in order to satisfy all partners – which in many cases is in fact a lack of strategy.

Two examples of polycentricity-oriented documents in the Paris region: One concept but conflicting results

The *Contrat de Plan Interrégional du Bassin Parisien* (CPIBP) (1994–1999) was the only successful attempt to build a trans-regional planning scheme associating the national government and the eight administrative régions of the Paris Region. It proposed two development scenarios depicted in the 1992 White Papers which refer to two normative approaches of polycentricity. The 'multi-polar and centralized scenario' insisted on the so-called 'natural' dynamics observed at this time with the reinforcement of the Île-de-France region and of a very hierarchical polycentric pattern limiting the development of more peripheral cities.[4] The second scenario, referred to as 'the metropolitan network scenario', could refer in POLYNET terminology to the polycentric MCR. Paris Region cities were to reach a greater autonomy vis-à-vis the capital region and access the rank of European metropolis, thanks to increasing cross-regional flows. This latter scenario, which was privileged by both the state and the eight régions, favoured a redistributive logic aiming at reducing spatial inequities through the promotion of a more polycentric geography in the entire Paris Region.

The *Schéma Directeur de la Région Île-de-France* (SDRIF) was written during the same period (1994) and makes extensive references to the agreement reached at the Paris Region level. This regional document relies on a long history of polycentricity: 'The principle of polycentricity already present in the 1965 and 1976 Schémas is the basis for the urban organization to be developed' (Préfecture de la région d'Île-de-France, 1994, p33). However, even though the polycentric planning concept is at the very core of the document, its implementation (as shown by its central map) is not so much at the Paris Region scale but

within the Île-de-France region. Using the same term and inscribing it in the same general framework, the SDRIF therefore gives an utterly contrasting content to that in the trans-regional document (CPIBP). Polycentrism is understood here as an attempt to limit the growth of Paris City in favour of the rest of the region. In practice, the importance given to the *Villes Nouvelles* and other poles on the fringes of the agglomeration tends to strengthen the Parisian core area rather than divert its economic growth to the Paris Region cities. Indeed, even though they were inspired by the British New Towns, the French *Villes Nouvelles* are much closer to the capital city than in London's case (15.5–22 miles/25–35km at most from Notre Dame Cathedral). Predictable urban deconcentration dynamics have progressively integrated them into the agglomeration perimeter, resulting in a limited deconcentration which differs from the CPIBP's objectives.

The limits of polycentricity in terms of spatial planning are not to be underestimated. First, the use of the same concept at different scales – as shown above – can give utterly conflicting results. Second, even though it has often been depicted as favouring environmental preservation, increasing morphological polycentricity might in fact have the reverse effect. It may encourage space consumption via development of new urban settlements (unlike urban regeneration and higher-density policies) and may induce increasing commuter flows. As non-central interactions grow faster in more morphologically polycentric systems, the share of car journeys is unlikely to be reduced even though public transportation is known to be more environmentally sustainable. Third, it is now demonstrated that deconcentration trends weaken poorer people's economic security. As they move further from the central labour markets to find a home, low-paid and low-skilled workers face increasing transport costs (money and time) and see their job opportunities diminished because of lower accessibility (Wenglenski, 2004). Fourth, polycentric deconcentration may harm economic development, as most knowledge-intensive firms argue that clustering and global connectivity are the major drivers for their development.

More awareness of metropolitan issues?

If the 1990s were a period of 'redistributive polycentrism' aiming at reducing the weight of Paris to assist the development of other cities, the start of the 21st century seems to be associated with growing concerns for economic cooperation. In the last ten years, many studies (both academic and political) have acknowledged the Paris central area's role as a key asset in global competition and have stressed potential complementarities with the surrounding cities of the Paris Region. The latest CPERs (2000–2006) which link the national government with each separate region all express the same necessity to improve cross-regional cooperation. The two recent SRADTs (in Picardie and in Champagne-Ardennes) stress potential interactions with the Île-de-France cities and with other surrounding regions as key issues for their economic development.

The striking failure of the 1994 CPIBP will probably limit any attempt towards a general spatial planning document at the MCR level for some time. However, growing interactions and complementarities may eventually lead to an increasing awareness of metropolitan governance-related issues. It is difficult so far to predict how long it will take before it is shifted up to a priority level in the political agenda. At the time of writing, the debates regarding the revision of the SDRIF do not prove as cross-regional as one could have expected.

Conclusion

The POLYNET results for the Paris MCR stress first the need for a better assessment of business services, APS and more generally all knowledge-intensive activities (including some industrial sectors) in planning documents. Their underlying spatial logics and numerous triggers should be taken on board more effectively. Moreover, potential interactions between the regional knowledge economy and the rest of the economic structure are still insufficiently understood. In order to be sustainable, high value-added activities need to be used as levers for a more widespread economic development that would prevent increasing social dualization.

Second, a radical extension in the concepts and instruments often present in the policy documents is needed. Spatial planning becomes less relevant whereas strategic approaches prove more efficient. Territorial homogeneity is less important than spatially differentiated policies: focused investments on key territories and key issues are more efficient than dispersed policies even though this may initially arouse strong political discontent.

Polycentricity must be questioned too. Is it such a good thing? And at which scales is it most relevant: within the Paris agglomeration, within its MCR, at the national, European/global scales?

Third, metropolitan governance is also at stake. There are numerous metropolitan issues to be resolved, both in the Paris central area and at cross-regional MCR levels. To achieve this, a multi-scalar and global approach allowing horizontal and vertical cooperation has still to be invented. Indeed, to tackle the different metropolitan issues (economic growth, social cohesion, environmental sustainability and territorial integration), it is important to develop a trans-sectoral strategy able to deal with the various scales (from local to global) and to bring all public and private bodies into a shared strategy.

Fourth, the POLYNET study stresses the need to prevent any attempt to go back to the policies that tried to reduce the weight of Paris within the MCR. The central core area proves to be the engine of economic growth; it is the powerhouse not only of the MCR but also of the national and – together with other cities – the European territory.

Notes

1 For an introduction to the history of Paris, see Marchand (1989).

2 This criteria of softer contiguity used in the Paris MCR case study is explained by the fact that the rural municipalities separating most FURs of the Paris Region are of very small size in terms of population and consequently that commuting data are not accurate enough to exclude them from a FUR. Therefore, FURs separated by a small number of non-polarized rural municipalities can be considered as part of the same MCR.

3 Both for practical reasons, as the metropolitan geography is an almost ever-changing one, and because of political reluctance.

4 Ten years later, and at a distance, this scenario seems in fact to correspond to the development of the Paris urban area into a larger-scale metropolitan one.

16

Greater Dublin in the Celtic Tiger Economy: Towards a Polycentric Mega-City Region?

Chris van Egeraat, Martin Sokol and Peter Stafford

In the decade leading to the millennium, the Republic of Ireland underwent spectacular transformation from a peripheral, backward economy to one of the best performers within the European Union (EU). Much of the growth occurred in the Greater Dublin region, making it into one of the most prosperous areas of the North West European 'Europolis'. The region could be seen as the powerhouse of the Irish 'economic miracle', or an engine of the 'Celtic Tiger'. Importantly, much of the economic activity and jobs created were generated within the 'new economy' in general, and the advanced producer services (APS) in particular. The growing international importance of Dublin in this respect has been recognized by the Globalization and World Cities (GaWC) Study Group and Network, labelling Dublin as an 'emerging global city' (Taylor et al, 2002c, p100).

What is not clear, however, is whether the emergence of Dublin as a 'global city' will be accompanied by its transformation into a '*polycentric* mega-city region (MCR)'. The emergence of such a 'city region' is confidently expected amid growing specialization of economic activities and continuous improvements in transport and information and communication technologies (ICTs). As Peter Hall (2001, p74) argues, under such conditions many business functions (back-offices, logistical management, new style headquarters (HQ), media centres, etc.) relocate over time to decentralized locations giving birth to an extremely complex and sophisticated internal geography of global city regions. He contends that this geography is 'quintessentially polycentric' (Hall, 2001, p73), dominated by vital *internal* linkages and information exchanges (Hall, 2001, p72). Elsewhere Hall describes this process of

business decentralization as an 'outward diffusion from [big cities] to smaller cities within their urban fields or spheres of influence' (Hall, 2004, p1). The process of 'outward diffusion' therefore could be seen as key for the formation of a 'polycentric city region' or 'multi-core metropolis' (Hall, 1999, p19). The emphasis of the present chapter is thus on 'outward diffusion' of businesses with a particular focus on APS.

Further conceptual work is obviously needed to grasp the meaning and the definition of 'polycentricity' and of the 'polycentric city region' or 'polycentric urban region' (Parr, 2004; Davoudi 2003; Kloosterman and Lambregts, 2001; Turok and Bailey, 2004; inter alia see also Sokol and van Egeraat, 2005a). However, as Chapter 2 has demonstrated, the Irish capital city and its hinterland evidently deviate from a polycentric ideal, however defined (cf. Yarwood et al, 2004). There is therefore a clear need to examine and understand processes underpinning the functional and spatial structure of the Greater Dublin region.

This chapter aims to contribute to this endeavour by addressing two key questions. The first question is whether a tendency towards a more polycentric pattern of APS sectors is occurring within the Greater Dublin region. This question will be addressed in the next section, arguing that there is only a limited tendency in this direction. The second question is whether the existing strategic planning policy framework supports a tendency towards a polycentric city region. This issue will be discussed in the following section, suggesting that while strategies to support polycentricity do exist, their implementation may prove problematic. Based on these findings, the concluding section will argue that to assume the

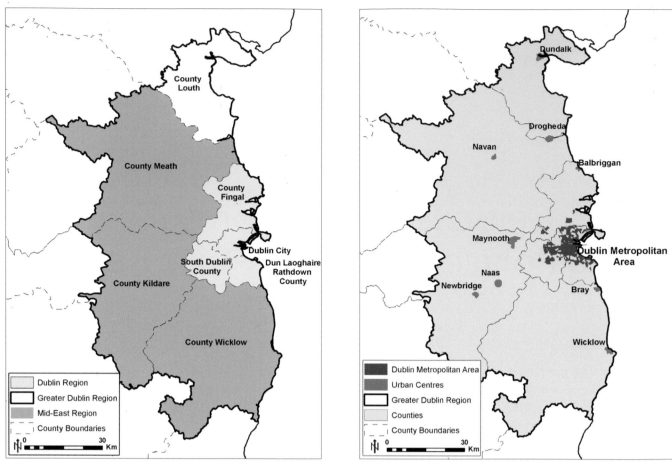

Figure 16.1 The Greater Dublin Region, regional/local authorities and urban centres

emergence of a polycentric MCR in the case of Dublin may be premature.

The information presented in this chapter was collected from various sources. First, interviews were conducted with senior staff of multi-location APS firms[1] located in the Greater Dublin region. An outline of the methodology is included in Chapter 6 (for further details, see Sokol and van Egeraat, 2005b). In total, 88 firm interviews were conducted in 8 APS sectors. The sectoral breakdown was as follows: 25 interviews in banking/finance, 19 in insurance, 10 in logistics, 8 in law, 7 in accounting, 8 in design consulting, 6 in advertising and 5 in management consulting. As for the geographical coverage, out of 88 interviews, 62 were conducted in Dublin and 26 in the urban centres outside Dublin.

Additional information was collected during 21 interviews with institutional actors. More quantitative data were collected through a web survey among managers of APS firms in the study region (for details see Chapter 5). A total of 19 firms in the study region returned usable questionnaires. The policy section is based on an analysis of relevant spatial policy documents (for an overview see Stafford et al, 2005) and information obtained during two focus group meetings involving 20 key actors representing institutions from the Greater Dublin region.

The study region, here called the Greater Dublin region, has been defined as encompassing the official Dublin Region (containing the local authorities of Dublin City, Fingal, South Dublin and Dun Laoghaire-Rathdown), the official Mid-East Region (containing counties Meath, Kildare and Wicklow) and County Louth (see Figure 16.1). It therefore corresponds to what the Regional Planning Guidelines refer to as the 'Greater Dublin Area' (see below), extended to include County Louth. Within this study region, a total of nine urban centres was identified as possible constituent urban centres of a potential polycentric city region: Dublin, Dundalk, Drogheda, Navan, Maynooth, Naas-Newbridge, Bray, Wicklow and Balbriggan. Dublin, here also referred to as the 'Dublin Metropolitan Area', is defined as the official Dublin Region excluding Balbriggan. This town is treated as an urban centre in Dublin's 'hinterland'.

Tendencies towards polycentric development in the Greater Dublin region

Does the Greater Dublin region display a polycentric development pattern? To answer this, Table 16.1 first presents the locations of offices of multi-location APS

Table 16.1 Multi-location APS firms in the Greater Dublin Region[a]

	Accountancy	Advertising	Banking and finance[b]	Design	Insurance	Law	Logistics	Management consultancy	Total
Dublin	22	23	303	73	89	53	50	32	645
Balbriggan			4			1			5
Bray	1		5		1	1			8
Drogheda	1		5	1	5	1			13
Dundalk	2		7	2	2	6	2		21
Navan			5	1	2				8
Maynooth			3			1			4
Naas	1		8	1	3	4	2		19
Wicklow			4		1				5
Total	27	23	344	78	103	67	54	32	728

Notes: a Different companies of one group counted as one firm.

b Funds are not counted as firms. Fund managers and trustees are counted as firms.

Source: van Egeraat et al (2005)

firms in the Greater Dublin region. The situation is graphically presented in Figure 16.2. These first data paint a picture of the opposite of polycentricity – a very monocentric region, dominated by Dublin. If we treat all offices of a firm in Dublin as one single office, then the Greater Dublin region counts 728 offices. About 90 per cent of these are located in Dublin, often in city-central locations (see Sokol and van Egeraat 2005b). Some of the urban centres outside Dublin, notably Maynooth, Balbriggan and Wicklow, have only a handful of multi-location APS firms.

As regards the sectoral distribution, one of the clearest observations is that banking and finance is the strongest sector in all the urban centres outside Dublin. The advertising and management consultancy sectors are not represented outside Dublin. As regards Dublin, banking and finance is by far the largest sector with 47 per cent of the multi-location APS firms. Other well-represented sectors include insurance (14 per cent), design (11 per cent) and logistics (8 per cent). Although all multi-location advertising and management consultancy firms in the region are located in Dublin, the two sectors account for a relatively small proportion of non-local APS firms in the capital.

The interviews provided further evidence of significant differences in terms of size and functionality between the offices in Dublin and in the urban centres outside Dublin. Operations in Dublin were typically national head offices, representing the biggest office of the network and the largest pool of expertise, and possessing the key managerial and command functions. In fact, in several cases (most frequently in advertising, law and management consultancy sectors) Dublin is the firm's sole office location, not only within the Greater Dublin region

but also in Ireland. The size of the interviewed offices in Dublin varied widely both between and within sectors, ranging from 14 people in a design consultancy office to several hundred in a large bank HQ (Sokol and van Egeraat, 2005a, b).

In contrast, the APS sector in the urban centres outside Dublin is extremely underdeveloped. Apart from banking and insurance firms, very few significant APS firms have offices in these urban centres. Exceptions can be found in design consultancy and accountancy where a small number of firms have a regional or national scope of service provision. Furthermore, the banking and insurance firms are generally represented by small local branches of firms headquartered in the capital. Apart from this there are only two sizeable financial operations, both back-office administration centres.

The interviews and web survey were also used to explore another important aspect of city region polycentricity – the extent and pattern of the actual intra-firm flows of information and people. There are important sectoral particularities in the way business is conducted over different operational scopes and in the related intra-firm information flows (Sokol and van Egeraat, 2005b). However, there are only a few model situations where any significant amount of intra-firm information flow would occur between urban centres in the Greater Dublin region.

The first involves the office networks of 'domestic' banks[2] and insurance companies. Large domestic banks typically have a large head office operation in Dublin and a network of branches across the country. However, while there is frequent communication (on a daily and weekly basis, mostly via electronic channels) between branches and head office, the communication *between branches* is very limited. Typically, a branch would have only sporadic

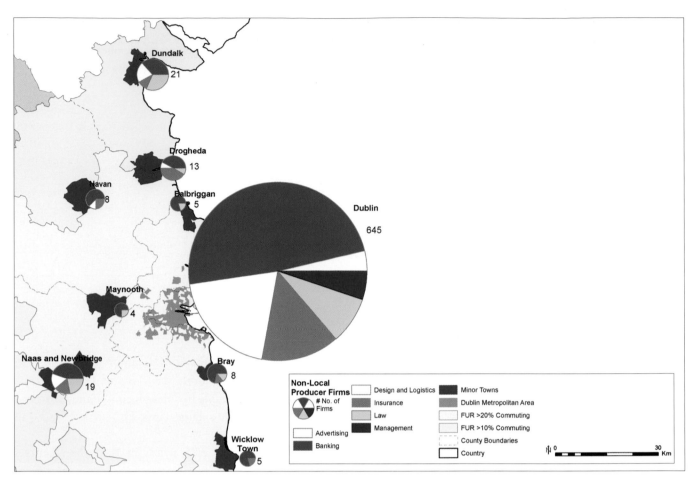

Figure 16.2 Distribution of multi-location APS firms in the Greater Dublin Region, 2004

(telephone) contact with other branches in the network. Decentralized offices of banks in the form of call centres or customer contact centres in Dublin's hinterland are a variation on the same theme. Again, the single most important intra-firm information flow is with the head office, rather than any other part of the bank's network. It is questionable whether the presence of such branches should be interpreted as part of a polycentric development since the function of the branches is clearly subordinated to higher-level decision-making, invariably located in Dublin.

A second type of intra-firm regional connectivity is found in the office networks of regional players from smaller urban centres around the capital that attempt to 'invade' Dublin's market by establishing an office presence there. Such a strategy, although rare, was noted in the accountancy and design consultancy sectors. Here, the prevailing direction of relational flows could be said to work in the opposite direction as in the case of the banking and insurance sector. Finally, regional office networks of logistics firms tend to be characterized by intensive operational contact. Most operational data are generally automatically shared with head office and the level of face-to-face contact is limited. Again, communication tends to

be head office (Dublin) centred with little communication between individual branch offices.

Whereas the level of intra-regional information flow is clearly limited, the interviewed offices of APS firms located in Dublin are often highly connected internationally. Many Dublin offices, notably of 'international' banking and insurance firms, form an integral part of wider international networks, either as 'front-offices', serving the Irish market, or as 'back-offices', responsible for a particular function in the international intra-firm network. In both cases, these offices have no regional or even national intra-firm linkages. Within the international network the Dublin offices generally have limited command and coordination functions. These usually reside in higher order 'hubs', notably London.

The situation can be captured using Castells's (1996) conceptual framework of the 'space of flows'. At the regional level of analysis Dublin clearly functions as a 'hub' in the regional space of flows. It is, however, the only hub. The urban centres outside the metropolitan area function as 'nodes' in the space of flows although one could argue that some of the smaller regional centres should not even be considered as 'nodes' given their extremely limited number of linkages. At the international level of analysis, given the limited presence of international-level command functions, Dublin is 'just' a 'node' in the space of flows (Sokol and Egeraat, 2005a, b).

The evidence clearly does not support the idea of a polycentric city region. Rather, the location patterns and information flows of APS firms point to a monocentric region dominated by Dublin. There are numerous reasons for the concentration of APS firms in (central) Dublin. One of the primary factors mentioned during firm interviews and in the web survey concerns the labour market. For many businesses, Dublin is by far the most important pool of required skills in the region. In addition, the city centre is seen as the best-connected location where firms can attract staff commuting from all around the metropolitan area and beyond. Dublin also represents the most important market for many of the interviewed firms. Face-to-face contact remains very important in many business transactions, and for many firms an office in Dublin, particularly in central Dublin, provides proximity to the majority of their clients.

In addition, several respondents pointed to the advantage of proximity of suppliers of professional services in Dublin. Several managers also highlighted the connectivity to transport infrastructure both nationally and internationally. Notably, many respondents mentioned the proximity of Dublin Airport as a crucial factor, providing access to both affiliated offices and international clients abroad. Other factors included the attractiveness of the urban environment, the need for a prestigious location, advanced telecom infrastructure and the availability of suitable office space.

To a great extent the concentration of APS firms in Dublin can be interpreted as a process of cumulative causation (Myrdal, 1957), started by historical factors, notably Dublin's position as the centre of public administration and the legal system. However, government policies since the 1980s have further contributed to the concentration. A case in point is the concentration of banking and insurance firms in the International Financial Services Centre (IFSC) located in central Dublin. This government scheme offered a reduced corporation tax rate of 10 per cent for companies involved in internationally traded services, conditional on a location in the IFSC (Williams and MacLaran, 1996).

There are also several disadvantages associated with a location in Dublin, particularly with a city centre location. Negative factors mentioned during the interviews include traffic congestion, cost of office accommodation and lack of parking spaces for staff and clients. However, the pull of Dublin, and particularly central Dublin, remains strong. The interviews with firms in Dublin specifically aimed to unveil the potential for the relocation of Dublin-based firms to smaller urban centres outside Dublin. Most firms expressed a strong reluctance to do so, indicating that they would risk losing both staff and clients. The perception is that the pool of suitably skilled labour in these urban centres is too small, particularly for larger operations. In addition, the firms' current staff is often very reluctant to move. A manager in the insurance sector contemplated a hypothetical move from Dublin to Drogheda in the following way: 'How could you operate in Drogheda? Half your management team would leave; all the sales people would look for a new job in Dublin' (quoted in Sokol and van Egeraat, 2005b, p14).

A number of firms are considering relocating their offices out of central Dublin and there is some evidence of incipient decentralization of firms or business functions (see also MacLaran and Killen, 2002). However, most of this decentralization has benefited other more peripheral Dublin locations, notably along the M50 orbital motorway. In addition, a small number of firms, particularly in the banking sector, have relocated some more routine, back-office operations to the urban centres outside Dublin or further afield. However, it would be too soon to see these as elements of a new emerging functional structure of the polycentric city region. Indeed, there is no guarantee that any future relocation will automatically favour urban centres within the Greater Dublin region. Some operations may simply be outsourced or decentralized to more remote parts of Ireland or even internationally.

Planning policy and implementation

We will now consider whether the existing planning policy framework supports a tendency towards a polycentric city region in the future. We will first outline the existing planning policy framework, after which we will deal with the issue of implementation.

In Ireland planning policy is created at three different levels of public administration. At the national level the Department of Environment, Heritage and Local Government (DELG) is responsible for the central coordination of spatial policy. It issued the *National Spatial Strategy for Ireland, 2002–2020: People, Places and Potential* (DELG, 2002), the key guiding document for spatial planning in Ireland. At the regional level responsibility for spatial planning rests with the Regional Authorities that are required to prepare Regional Planning Guidelines. The Greater Dublin Region is administered by three regional authorities but two of these (the Dublin Regional Authority (DRA) and the Mid-East Regional Authority (MERA)) have developed a single set of planning guidelines covering both regions – *Regional Planning Guidelines: Greater Dublin Area* (DRA and MERA, 2004). Finally, spatial planning responsibility at the local level rests with the county councils and city councils. These local authorities are required to prepare development plans. Regional authorities, in the preparation of their guidelines, and local planning authorities, in the preparation of their local development plans, are required to have due regard for the development strategy advocated by the National Spatial Strategy (NSS).

These recently issued key strategic planning and development policy documents do embrace the concept of polycentric city regions. The NSS specifically promotes the idea of polycentric development approaches. It believes in developing each Irish region independently, responding to its own specific needs, through a pattern of 'hubs' and 'gateways' that link these regions internally and externally. The linking of hubs and gateways should provide the necessary critical mass for self-sustaining regional development. With respect to the Greater Dublin region, Dublin is expected to continue to grow in population and output terms. However, it is not deemed desirable for the city to continue to spread physically into surrounding counties. In addition, long-distance commuter-based development is deemed unsustainable. The strategy is one of physical consolidation of Dublin and, with respect to the hinterland areas, to concentrate development in strong towns with capacity for growth. Importantly, the role of these towns 'needs to take account, not just of their relationship with Dublin, but also their function in the development and servicing of their own catchment areas' (DELG, 2002, p44). Also at central government level, the idea of polycentric spatial development in Ireland and in the Greater Dublin region is specifically promoted in the National Development Plan (Department of Finance, 1999).

At the regional level, the Regional Planning Guidelines issued by the DRA and the MERA are even more specific about the nature of polycentricity in the Greater Dublin region. One of the goals is to reverse the over-concentration of economic activity in the metropolitan area. Urban centres outside the metropolitan area of Dublin should aim for a high level of employment activity and self-sufficiency, with only limited commuting to the metropolitan area:

The proposed strategy would be the most internationally competitive option, since it would do the most to create an integrated polycentric city region. It would create a basis for marketing the regional city rather than the Metropolitan Area *(DRA and MERA, 2004, p108).*

The Planning Guidelines go on: 'It is further proposed that the [Greater Dublin Area] be marketed as an authentic city-region and a single integrated local market' (DRA and MERA, 2004, p110).

Two aspects of the recent plans appear to deviate somewhat from the polycentric city region 'ideal' that has provided the focus for the POLYNET study. Firstly, the key policy documents generally stress the importance of Dublin as the motor driving the 'Celtic Tiger' and there is no desire to shift high-level service activity out of the metropolitan area to other regional centres. On the contrary, the aim of the infrastructure and land use policies is to further consolidate the success and international competitiveness of Dublin, notably its attractiveness as a location for high-level service activities. Secondly, where the policy documents promote greater economic activity in urban centres outside the metropolitan area, they generally do not specify what types of activity are envisaged. The polycentric 'ideal' involves an outward diffusion of front-office APS activities. It is at least unclear to what extent the recent policy documents envisage the development of this type of activity in the smaller urban centres outside Dublin.

Having said that, recent strategic planning and development policy documents clearly do incorporate the idea of a polycentric city region. The next question is to what extent the policies will actually be implemented. One of the main problems in this regard is the weakness of the administrative structures in Ireland and the Greater Dublin region in particular. Implementation involves a range of government and semi-government authorities and agencies at different levels of administration (from state to local), with different sectoral remits (rail, road, housing, promotion of foreign direct investment (FDI), enterprise support), and with different policy instruments/degrees of power (see Stafford et al, 2005). The actions of these various authorities and agencies tend to be poorly integrated for at least two reasons.

First, most actual decisions regarding the spatial development of an area are made at the local level, with county councils and city councils drawing up their own county development plans, and at the national level where, for example, the main infrastructural investment decisions are made. The regional authorities have only limited statutory power. As mentioned earlier, county councils and city councils are merely required to 'have due regard' for the development strategy advocated by the Regional Planning Guidelines, the NSS and the plans of neighbouring local authorities. It is up to the local authorities to implement the Regional Planning Guidelines as they see fit for the uniqueness of their own constituency. Power is both highly centralized and highly localized.

Second, more specific to the study region, the aim of a greater coordination of spatial planning policy at the regional level as expressed in the *Regional Planning Guidelines for the Greater Dublin Area* (DRA and MERA, 2004) has been hindered by institutional deficits at the regional level. While the Greater Dublin Area is spatially controlled by one set of Planning Guidelines, it falls into two regional authorities, thus exacerbating the challenges with respect to coordination and integration.

Recent actions of government authorities and agencies have been in conflict with the 'ideal' polycentric city region concept and, indeed, with the plans laid out in the NSS and Regional Planning Guidelines. At the central government level, many of the provisions of the NSS have been undermined both by the sectoral curtailment of some funding provisions in the context of general retrenchment and by the recent introduction of the government's Programme for Decentralization. This programme has aimed to move some government agencies and their staff away from central Dublin into smaller towns around the country. The location decisions were clearly in conflict with the NSS – only 20 per cent of the civil servants that will be moved will go to the hubs and gateways identified in the NSS (Morgenroth, 2004).

This development exemplifies another important obstacle for implementing the recent planning policies. It is very difficult in Irish political culture to be seen 'overtly' to favour one town over another. This difficulty in prioritizing spatially is exacerbated by the nature of the proportional representation single transferable vote system, where voters express their rank ordered preferences, and the outcome is a Parliament which yields an elected membership roughly proportionate to votes cast. Governments rarely secure a majority of more than six, and there is constant danger of a disaffected politician running on a local issue – such as the local town being excluded as a hub – and being elected. Hence the 'scatter gun' approach. Drogheda and Dundalk are designated as hubs and gateways respectively in the Dublin region, but this is not reflected in any overt decision to create real nodes in a polycentric Dublin region (Stafford et al, 2005).

The actions of IDA (Industrial Development Agency) Ireland, the agency with responsibility for securing new inward investment, are unlikely to lead to the polycentric city region 'ideal' either. In the case of international financial services for instance, investors are encouraged to set up front-office and head-office type operations in the capital city, while the rest of the country is promoted as being more suitable for back-office functions (Stafford et al, 2005). Although the location of back-office APS functions in the urban centres outside the metropolitan centres would be a development in the direction of a more polycentric city region, it is a long way from the 'ideal' polycentric city region, characterized by an equal distribution of 'front-office' APS activities.

Recently, three local authorities of Mid-East Region (Kildare, Meath and Wicklow) came together to prepare a marketing campaign designed to encourage Dublin-based businesses to relocate in the hinterland urban centres. However, the target here is small and medium size enterprises (SMEs) involved in a range of economic activities, rather than front-office APS activities. At the same time, local authorities in the Dublin metropolitan area do not sit idle. For instance, the Dublin City Development Board, the economic development arm of the Dublin City Council, works actively to foster a favourable business environment in the city. This includes strengthening telecommunications infrastructure and harnessing ICT, obviously enhancing the relative attractiveness of the metropolitan area as a location for APS firms (Sokol and van Egeraat, 2005a).

All this means that, while strategies to support polycentricity do exist, their implementation may prove problematic and a Greater Dublin polycentric city region remains a distant idea.

Conclusion

The main questions addressed in this chapter are whether or not the Greater Dublin region is developing into a more polycentric city region and whether the present planning framework supports such a process. The answer to the first question is clearly negative. With respect to the distribution of APS firms, the Greater Dublin region remains a strongly monocentric region, dominated by Dublin. The extraordinary growth of APS activity during the 'Celtic Tiger' years has largely by-passed the urban centres in Dublin's hinterland. The incipient process of decentralization out of central Dublin tends to have benefited other metropolitan locations or locations outside the Greater Dublin Area.

If anything, the level of polycentricity at the city-regional level has declined. Up to the 'Celtic Tiger' period the region contained a number of self-sustainable towns with a stable population and resident workforce. Since then these towns have been increasingly accommodating the Dublin workforce which is being pushed out of Dublin by the overheated housing market. Many of the urban centres today are little more than dormitory towns, rather than economic nodes in their own right.

For most APS firms, the advantages of a (central) Dublin location appear to weigh stronger than the disadvantages, and recent labour market and infrastructure developments seem only to have reinforced the relative attractiveness of Dublin. Investments in infrastructure are driven by 'needs', i.e. congestion on Dublin's existing access routes, and the solving of this problem further increases

Dublin's centrality. The monocentric structure of the Greater Dublin region has its roots in historical factors and it appears that the structure is presently reinforced by a process of cumulative causation (Myrdal, 1957). It is unlikely that market forces alone will change this process in the direction of a more balanced polycentric development.

If a more balanced polycentric structure is deemed desirable, the realization will require a strong policy intervention. One of the conclusions from the focus group meetings is that polycentricity cannot happen in the Greater Dublin region when development reacts to what is happening rather than controlling it. Development-led policy-making rather than future-led policy-making only reinforces the monocentric structure of Dublin.

Spatial planning policies are an important, although not the only, element of such policy intervention. In this regard, recent strategic planning and development policy documents do promote the idea of a polycentric city region but the implementation of the plans may prove problematic due to institutional deficits. The main problem is the current lack of coordination between the planning bodies operating at different levels of public administration. Notably, there is a need to bridge the gap between national spatial strategy and local planning guidelines. Participants of the focus group meetings identified a need for a regional body with increased powers, which will be able to coordinate planning decisions at the local level and take stronger policy decisions. The authority of this body should cover at least the entire Greater Dublin region. Finally, the spatial planning policies need to be better integrated with other more sectoral policies, most notably in the areas of housing, economic development, labour market, education, transport and telecommunication infrastructure.

Notes

1 'Multi-location' APS firms operate offices in more than one urban centre, either in the region or outside the region.

2 The term 'domestic' refers, somewhat imperfectly, to operations that evolved around (originally) indigenous Irish banks, while the term 'international' is used here to cover operations stemming mostly from foreign direct investment (FDI).

PART 5

Planning Europolis:
The Effectiveness of Policy

From Strategy to Delivery: Policy Responses

Peter Hall and Kathy Pain

The long tour through the eight regions is complete. Its value has been to demonstrate their richness and diversity: not only in terms of their different ways of functioning, but also in the very specific policy responses, nationally and regionally, to the planning challenges they present. In this final chapter, we must return to the attempt to generalize.

It will be useful first, as a refresher, to summarize the key findings of the analysis of the interviews reported in Chapters 6–8.

The interviews: Key conclusions

The most important findings, distilled from the conclusions of Chapter 8, are these:

- *Unique role of 'First Cities'*: just one city in each mega-city region (MCR) constitutes the 'First City' for global advanced producer services (APS), with a degree of sectoral specialization in some cases.
- *Importance of secondary centres too*: offices belonging to regional networks are spread out across secondary centres in each MCR, especially in accountancy; logistics has a distinct – and largely a-spatial – servicing logic; banking/financial services, concentrated in First Cities, play an important role in fostering interrelationships between sectors.
- *Communication flows have different value*: the communication flows occurring within First Cities, and articulated through them, are of a far superior intensity and value to those occurring within firms across the wider MCRs.
- *Cross-linkages probably lacking – except in South East England*: in fact there is limited evidence of functional

linkages within MCRs. South East England is the major exception: here, London's scale of global concentration masks significant functional connections not only between London and secondary centres, but between those secondary centres.
- *Globalization plays a key role*: globalization is an ongoing spur to consolidation, restructuring and specialization; industry regulation and national legislation are key concerns in reducing barriers to cross-border business.
- *Clustering in First Cities still vital*: locational concentration and clustering remain key priorities for most global firms across MCRs; there is no evidence that global functions are deconcentrating from POLYNET First Cities.
- *E-communication increasing, but face-to-face still critical*: in communications, the main change in all First Cities is the massive increase in e-mail and use of intranet systems; but this is not diminishing the absolute need for face-to-face contact, which is particularly associated with high-value exchanges.
- *Intensity and value of communication crucial, but immeasurable*: quantitative measurement of information flows can never present an accurate picture of the volume and value of interactions, many of which are 'invisible': the most intense and important exchanges take place within globally networked First Cities.
- *Travel from central offices essential*: home-working is limited; most skilled front-office staff remain 'locked into' clustered central city locations with an increasing need for travel, especially international travel.
- *Infrastructure confirms First Cities' role*: e-infrastructure mirrors the patterns of inter-city linkages, confirming the role of First Cities as 'information gateways'.

- *Good transport essential, both within and out of MCRs*: mobility is crucial both within, and into and out of, MCRs – car travel via motorway, as well as rail travel, are very important for intra-regional travel and access to airports for international travel, especially from First Cities.
- *Top skills concentrate in First Cities*: First Cities have a unique regional role with respect to high-skill, specialized international labour supplies: competition for labour ties firms to specific central city locations, which depend on the residential preferences of employees.
- *City 'buzz' vital for location*: APS locational decisions are not based solely on rational economic criteria. An attractive 'city environment' proves to be significant, but this is more about 'city processes' – the 'buzz' of the place – than physical infrastructure.
- *Importance of the 'right address'*: mobile talented labour is attracted to specific cities and places; office address and status are critical to the credibility of APS firms, and urban milieux are crucial for fostering innovation.
- *Hub function vital – regionally, sometimes globally*: while the scale of concentration differs from one First City to another, all have a distinctive 'regional hub' function; in addition, London's global concentration gives it a unique role as a central 'meeting place' in the APS 'European region'.
- *First Cities linked internationally*: knowledge produced in – and dispersed through – international networks helps to build complementary functional relations, linking POLYNET First Cities together.
- *Boundaries irrelevant for APS*: geographical or administrative boundaries have little relevance to 'natural' APS markets; national and international functions reside within a space defined by relations between major cities, while regional offices relate to local or sub-regional markets.
- *But MCRs important for policy*: the MCR concept has great policy importance in addressing areas that require non-market interventions – transport infrastructure, education, housing and urban planning.
- *Polycentricity depends on scale*: the concept of polycentricity is scale-dependent and cannot be simply mapped on to fixed MCR configurations, such as the ones used in this study – policy needs to take into account the varying functions and linkages that underlie regional urban geography.
- *Need for integrated policies*: integrated policy approaches are needed to address and promote the cross-cutting processes that help to build complementary (as opposed to competitive) inter-urban relationships.

The policy analysis

Against the background of these findings, in the final research stage of POLYNET the eight teams turned to examine the policy context for their respective MCRs. They did so through two separate but closely-linked exercises. First they examined relevant policy statements – major European Union (EU), national and regional policy documents – in order to establish how well they addressed the key issues identified in the research. Second, in a series of local focus group meetings they presented their findings to government and business stakeholders, and probed the views of their respondents on the key policy issues arising from the study and on the relevance of the empirical findings for planning practice.

The features that proved most important for each of the eight regions have been highlighted in the individual regional chapters. Here, our task is to draw the threads together.

Common policy frameworks for the North West European mega-city regions

First, it is important to keep in mind that planning at national and regional levels in each country increasingly takes account of frameworks set at EU level. The most important such frameworks have all come into being since the late 1990s. These were presented briefly in the UK context in Chapter 9; here they need more attention. There are three:

1 The Lisbon Agenda

The Lisbon Agenda, adopted by the European Council in the year 2000, emphasizes the vital importance of promoting Europe's global competitiveness in the knowledge economy. Major structural challenges – the ageing of European populations and the prospect of demographic decline, the resulting pensions deficit, the rising cost of health provision and enlargement, the rise of the Asian (particularly the Chinese) economies, and the impact of global climate change – make achievement of the Lisbon strategy vitally important. The strategy, adopted at the European Council in Lisbon in 2000, declared that:

The Union has today set itself a new strategic goal for the next decade: to become the most competitive and dynamic knowledge-based economy in the world, capable of sustainable economic growth with more and better jobs and greater social cohesion. *Achieving this goal requires an* overall strategy *aimed at*:

- preparing the transition to a knowledge-based economy and society by better policies for the information society and R&D [*research and development*], as well as by stepping up the process of structural reform for competitiveness and innovation and by completing the internal market;

- modernising the European social model, investing in people and combating social exclusion;
- sustaining the healthy economic outlook and favourable growth prospects by applying an appropriate macro-economic policy mix *(European Council, 2000)*.

Reviewing progress half-way through the decade, in March 2005 the Council had to admit that:

Five years after the launch of the Lisbon Strategy, the results are mixed. Alongside undeniable progress, there are short-comings and obvious delays. Given the challenges to be met, there is a high price to pay for delayed or incomplete reforms, as is borne out by the gulf between Europe's growth potential and that of its economic partners. Urgent action is therefore called for *(European Council, 2005)*.

To that end, the Council affirmed that it was:

essential to relaunch the Lisbon Strategy without delay and re-focus priorities on growth and employment. Europe must renew the basis of its competitiveness, increase its growth potential and its productivity and strengthen social cohesion, placing the main emphasis on knowledge, innovation and the optimization of human capital *(European Council, 2005)*.

That, the Council warned, meant that the budget 'for 2007–2013 will have to provide the Union with adequate funds to carry through the Union's policies in general, including the policies that contribute to the achievement of the Lisbon priorities' (European Council, 2005).

Clearly, as virtually every commentator observed, this was a recognition of the obvious: the performance of the EU economy, in particular the core Eurozone, had been extremely disappointing in relation to that of the United States and the fast-emerging economies of China and India. The 'Community Lisbon Programme', launched in July 2005 as a counterpart to national economic reform programmes, is an attempt to achieve coordinated action at an EU level. It remains to be seen whether negotiations between the Member States, to be continued in Spring 2006, will be successful. POLYNET is centrally relevant for this agenda because its research focuses on core knowledge production activities in the global service economy, which constitute some of the most dynamic sectors in the EU economy. International services are concentrated in London, which plays a key role as European regional centre and 'gateway city' in tripartite global markets. Knowledge-based flows between London, Paris, Frankfurt and other leading North West European business centres are therefore of crucial importance for the achievement of the Lisbon Agenda.

2 The European Spatial Development Perspective

The European Spatial Development Perspective (ESDP) (European Commission, 1999) provides the framework for sustainable development in relation to economic and social cohesion, the conservation of natural resources and natural heritage and the creation of a more balanced and competitive European territory. These objectives are closely linked to the development of a more polycentric European urban system in which there is a concentration of urban functions and improved, sustainable, internal and external accessibility to promote flows between the economically dynamic 'gateway cities' and peripheral regions. In this, a clear aim is to promote a more balanced pattern of urban development across Europe, reducing the weight of the central urban zone of North West Europe (the London–Paris–Milan–Munich–Hamburg 'Pentagon') by promoting the growth of urban clusters as counterweights at Europe's peripheries (see Figure 1.1, p5).

At first sight, this might seem to imply a policy of restricting further growth in the Pentagon. But this is evidently not the case: the shift will be a relative one. The ESDP does not propose to shift activities across Europe, and concentrations in existing global gateway cities will be maintained.

Strategic EU spatial policy in relation to polycentricity does not … appear to threaten the position of the London cluster but rather it seeks to spread the benefits of clustering to other parts of the EU through inter-city co-operation and improved transportation infrastructure *(Taylor et al, 2003, p74)*.

There are issues here of scale: as economic activity redistributes itself Europe-wide in a more polycentric pattern, it may paradoxically concentrate nationally in a highly monocentric fashion, in and around the capital city. This was the pattern in Dublin (and also in Madrid, Lisbon and Athens) in the 1990s; it seems to be the emerging pattern in Warsaw, Prague, Budapest and other eastern European capitals in the 2000s, even in advance of the May 2004 enlargement. With the exception of Dublin, this is not an issue affecting the eight MCRs in this study. But it is of very great significance for other parts of Europe.

What is directly relevant is another matter: the possible enlargement of the Pentagon itself, through simple outward expansion at its borders. London, Paris, Zürich, Frankfurt, Dortmund and Amsterdam are all effectively on these borders; only Brussels is wholly within them, only Dublin outside them. A significant extension of any of these six MCRs might effectively promote further growth of the Pentagon. This is an issue in South East England, where UK government policy deliberately seeks to channel growth into broad growth corridors up to 90 miles (140km) north of London (Chapter 9, pp129). It would promote greater polycentricity within an already polycentric region, but might detract from the goal of a more polycentric Europe: another paradox of scale, to which we return below.

The notion of *territorial cohesion*, embodied in the EU's 1997 Amsterdam Treaty, is inherent in the ESDP (Faludi, 2004a, p161): it seeks to promote spatial equity by maintaining key services even in remote areas (Faludi, 2003b, p133; 2005, pp1–3). The concept stems from French planning traditions, specifically *aménagement du territoire*, reflecting the deep French influence inside DG XVI (DG Regio) (Faludi, 2003, pp130–131; 2004a, p160; 2004c, pp1350–1352); this aims to achieve a harmonious allocation of economic activities (Faludi 2004a, p159, quoting Chicoye, 1992). Territorial cohesion appeared in Article 3 of the abortive 2005 EU Constitution on a par with economic and social cohesion, as a competence shared between the Commission and the Member States through the 'community method' (Faludi, 2004b, p1019; 2005a, p2). There are unresolved issues here in relation to the Lisbon Agenda: territorial cohesion might well suggest promoting growth in lagging regions, even at the expense of the most dynamic and competitive region in each country. This demands further examination.

3 The North West Metropolitan Area Spatial Vision

The NWMA (North West Metropolitan Area) Spatial Vision (NWMA Spatial Vision Group, 2000) effectively seeks to operationalize these ESDP objectives, by developing priorities for national and regional implementation in the European economic core or 'Central Zone' around London, Paris, Brussels, Amsterdam and Cologne: an area similar to (but slightly smaller than) the 'Pentagon', and a smaller version of North West Europe, focus of the POLYNET study. It emphasizes the need to improve internal and external accessibility, to combat congestion and environmental degradation by the containment of urban development and to promote cooperation between cities (NWMA Spatial Vision Group, 2000, p30). Central Belgium, RhineRuhr, the Randstad and Rhine-Main are described as 'strategic polycentric areas' while London and Paris are depicted as (monocentric) 'global cities/gateways' (Figure 9.1, p128); the Randstad and Rhine-Main are included in both categories (NWMA Spatial Vision Group, 2000, pp30–31). The Vision seeks to promote a more balanced distribution of fast-growing high-level urban services (NWMA Spatial Vision Group, 2000, p28). The international competitiveness of the global gateway cities must be maintained while controlling their spatial

development (NWMA Spatial Vision Group, 2000, p30). Transport policy should promote flows from these key cities by sustainable modes, including the high-speed transport network, encouraging more balanced development at the EU scale Spatial Vision Group (NWMA Spatial Vision Group, 2000, pp29, 33). Paradoxically, by regarding both London and Paris as monocentric, the Vision sidesteps the key issue of the spatial expansion of South East England, discussed above.

National/regional policies

How far have these Europe-wide policies been translated down into national and regional policy? To answer this, we need to go back to the specific findings for each MCR in Chapters 9–16, seeking to compare them and to extract from them the most important policy issues, which we set out below in the form of a series of interrogative questions.

Key questions

Is the mega-city region a reality?

In *Greater Dublin* the MCR played no role in planning: the system had been devised in 'a very different environmental climate' and the need was to bridge the gap between national spatial strategy and local planning guidelines (Stafford et al, 2005, p19). Likewise, in *RhineRuhr* the concept of a polynuclear city region hardly existed in the mental map of public and private actors, either within or outside the region: respondents failed to perceive it as a complex, differentiated region offering a set of complementary locations; they recognized some elements of a functional identity, but perceived little strategic and no regional/cultural identity (Knapp and Schmitt, 2005, pp2, 10). Nor did planners or politicians take much notice until the German federal government established 'European Metropolitan Regions' (EMRs) in its Federal Action Plan for National Spatial Development in the 1990s (Knapp and Schmitt, 2005, p3). Consequently, the state lacks any initiative in framing a 'substantial policy discourse' on the future of its biggest agglomeration (Knapp and Schmitt, 2005, p10). Functional interrelations of the MCR *EMR Northern Switzerland* were similarly seen as 'not yet sufficiently anchored in the awareness of most policy makers' (Thierstein et al, 2005, p13).

In the *Paris Region* the MCR is not defined in any policy document. Although it appears implicitly as a concept from time to time, there is no one document focusing on the MCR scale, suggesting that there is insufficient concern to promote a truly metropolitan policy, which crosses administrative boundaries as easily as inhabitants or firms do. An attempt to create a global trans-regional strategy for the metropolitan region in 1994, the *Contrat de Plan Interrégion du Bassin Parisien*, aimed to promote the economic development of the Bassin Parisien by developing functional complementarities with the Île-de-France region. The logic was redistributive: in theory, development in the central part of the region (Île-de-France) should be reduced in order that the rest of the MCR could benefit from stronger economic growth (Halbert, 2005b, p5). But today, it seems that secondary networks in Champagne, Normandy and the Loire Valley have not yet reached sufficient momentum to be ranked as European metropolitan regions, while central Paris concentrates strategic functions and advanced services through a pattern of flows which is centre-periphery rather than polycentric.

In The Netherlands, contrastingly, the *Randstad* is firmly anchored in the mental maps of people and policy-makers alike. Since the introduction of the concept almost 50 years ago it has become one of the mainstays of Dutch spatial planning. True, attitudes towards the 'scattered metropolis' have changed over time (Lambregts and Zonnenveld, 2004), and opinions still vary on whether the region can or should be seen as a coherent urban system. But it is almost impossible to conceive of a Dutch national spatial planning strategy that would fail to take the Randstad as one of its key building blocks, seeking to relate the future development of this region with that of The Netherlands as a whole (Lambregts et al, 2005b, p4).

In *South East England* regional agencies recognized that the concentration of APS in London, and the resulting relationships with the wider MCR, were a vital asset for both the UK and European economies (Hall and Pain, 2005, p11). But in *Central Belgium* respondents generally thought in terms of the particular scale within which they worked, which sometimes led to confusion: the relevant phenomena, questions and solutions considered could be completely different (Aujean et al, 2005c, p7). The 'Flemish Diamond', a well-known territorial planning unit, is seen as a marketing concept rather than as a tangible reality in terms of firms' networks. Firms do not operate within such a predefined urban network; they recognize actors, not territories (Aujean et al, 2005c, p8).

In *Rhine-Main*, the POLYNET functional delimitation actually corresponds well with the perceptions of senior business people – yet this proved irrelevant, since their firms had their own spatial organization. The main problem, here as elsewhere, proved to be political–administrative, but was particularly acute in this case because the region spans three federal states and over 350 municipalities, which in no way correspond to the functional realities of economic organization or their translation into planning policies. A related problem is the

perception that Rhine-Main is strongly associated with the image of Frankfurt as a centre for banking and finance, a place to do business and to work (Hoyler et al, 2005, p13).

In *South East England* information on spatial-economic relationships at the MCR scale was seen to be urgently needed to inform policy and investment. Regions have been identified in the Draft South East Plan that differ from real housing sub-markets and there are important implications for education, skills and major investment in infrastructure (Hall and Pain, 2005, p12). In the *Paris Region* interdependencies between the Île-de-France region and the wider *Bassin Parisien* were thought to be of such importance that participants 'very quickly came to an agreement on the existence of the mega-city region'. However, its perimeter needed careful definition: the geomorphological Bassin Parisien was judged too large (Halbert, 2005b, p10).

Intra-regional functional linkages vary according to the role of First Cities in the global and European city network. London occupies a unique global city role in the EU's North West Europe region, and this appears to spawn complex interdependencies between the city's central business district (CBD) and the South East England regional periphery. As already noted, it is the only MCR to show notable cross-cutting functional relationships based on service network linkages between secondary centres – a true functional polycentricity that reflects knowledge-based interactions.

Other MCRs emerged as more monocentric. In *Greater Dublin* the Greater Dublin Regional Planning Guidelines would:

create the basis for marketing the regional city rather than the metropolitan area … The aim should be to alter the perception that it comprises a metropolis plus a collection of small, scarcely accessible towns. This paradigm or idea is the heart of the strategy *(Stafford et al, 2005, p10, quoting DRA and MERA, 2004, pp108, 110).*

In *EMR Northern Switzerland*, the 'action fields' of agencies responsible for spatial development were largely determined by problems identified at the level of the local, smaller region or, at most, the canton; wider relationships, at the level of the MCR, were 'not yet sufficiently anchored' in policy-makers' perceptions (Thierstein et al, 2005, p13).

In Germany both *RhineRuhr* and *Rhine-Main* form part of a national polycentric functional structure of cities which it is German federal government policy to foster and develop, but at MCR level Rhine-Main appears as a monocentric region. While on global and European scales the Frankfurt functional urban region (FUR) serves as a gateway to the region and sometimes to Germany as a whole, polycentricity at the national scale paradoxically leads to weak functional polycentricity within the MCR (Hoyler et al, 2005, p13).

So a vital lesson emerges: polycentricity can operate at different spatial scales, and polycentricity at one scale can lead to monocentricity at another. Further, all POLYNET First Cities form part of a functional global city network. And all MCRs – even ones that are more monocentric in their built form – show a kind of functional polycentricity in the form of cross-cutting commuting flows.

Generally, then, the MCR is identified by the research teams as a valuable spatial entity for the consideration of policy, but its physical boundaries cannot be rigidly specified. Interrelationships between 'flows' and 'places' are fluid and dynamic; however conceived, nowhere in the eight city regions does the MCR fit generally well either with administrative boundaries or with markets.

Polycentricity: How economically successful, how sustainable?

The objective of sustainable development is widespread in policy frameworks and as an aim of planning practice. It is seen as 'part of the rhetoric' (Thierstein et al, 2005, p13). Similarly, the principle of polycentricity is very widely accepted as a desirable norm to be achieved. But guidance on spatial development lacks the necessary coherence to allow these sustainability objectives to become operational. The possible conflict between more balanced polycentric economic development and environmental sustainability is not identified in policy documents, at either European or national scale. Davoudi (2003) demonstrates that the ESDP uses the concept of polycentricity not objectively, as an existing condition that can be measured, but normatively, as a desirable state to be achieved, well represented by a polycentric city region like the Randstad. But little empirical evidence is presented (Davoudi, 2003, pp991–995; Taylor et al, 2003, p73).

Polycentricity has implications for environmental sustainability. Thus in *Greater Dublin* polycentricity is seen as important in national spatial policy to 'concentrate development in strong towns with capacity for growth on well-served public transport corridors' (Stafford et al, 2005, p12). This is necessary 'to improve access to employment, education, services and amenities' (Stafford et al, 2005, p12). But in South East England, in spite of developments in information and communications technology (ICT), more balanced intra-regional development, especially in a wide arc to the west of London, is leading to increasing cross-commuting and business travel which cannot be effectively supported by public transport (Hall and Pain, 2005, p10). Here, focus groups saw morphological polycentricity as something essentially unsustainable, producing a residentially-driven 'commuting polycentricity' which

should be restricted; but functional polycentricity, constituting a market-driven 'clustering polycentricity', was beneficial to regional development and should be promoted. These policy implications required further consideration (Hall and Pain, 2005, p11).

In *EMR Northern Switzerland*, though 'polycentricity' has proved adequate as a descriptive model, using it as a strategy has proved far more complex. MCR 'polycentric morphology' on the one hand, and functional interrelations on the other, do not automatically lead to sustainable polycentric development. In practice, spatial development has not been sustainable over recent decades. Settlements have grown and spread in response to the building of transportation infrastructure: extending regional and national train services has been the major driving force encouraging urban sprawl, in the form of suburbanization and peri-urbanization. In practice, here, it proves difficult to distinguish between polycentricity and urban sprawl. So difficult questions arise. Does polycentricity lead to sustainable development or instead to non-sustainable dispersion? Where is the distinguishing line between the two? (Thierstein et al, 2005, p14).

In the *Paris Region*, deconcentration during the past 30 years is likewise identified as questionable in terms of environmental sustainability and is 'probably increasing social and spatial fragmentation' (Halbert, 2005b, p11). Urban sprawl cannot easily be channelled; suburbanization is seen as a pervasive process. Polycentricity – conventionally regarded as an environmentally-friendly planning principle to reduce commuting distances – may have the reverse effect, failing to reduce commuter flows and favouring the use of private cars rather than public transport. Most importantly, a spatially more deconcentrated pattern of urban development may not increase the efficiency of the information economy. Recent economic difficulties in the Île-de-France and the role of major metropolitan areas in global competition may suggest a policy change towards greater concentration in Paris.

In *RhineRuhr* and the *Randstad*, too, it is found that morphological polycentricity may generate criss-cross commuting flows, and that such a form of development lacks the benefits associated with strong concentration and intra-regional service-based linkages. A recent comparative study of the Randstad, Rhine-Main and London questions:

whether polycentric patterns of urban development can be successfully superimposed on existing spatial relationships through the policy process... Regional spatial polycentricity is shown to have advantages and disadvantages in relation to three measurement criteria associated with economic, social and environmental sustainability: cross-regional functional interdependencies, distributional patterns of economic growth and development, and environmental impacts *(Taylor et al, 2003, p73)*.

In addition, concentration of global functions in First Cities is identified in all the MCRs as essential to connectivity (both internal and external) within the global city network and to promotion of a 'knowledge gateway' role.

In *Central Belgium*, the Flanders Regional Plan (*Ruimtelijke Structuurplan Vlaanderen* – RSV) develops a polycentric urban concept: through 'concentrated deconcentration', population and activities will be redeployed into existing nodes so as to reinforce the urban fabric, especially in the 'Flemish Diamond' which is seen as an integrated European-level urban network, competing with other major urban networks. The plan also recognizes polycentric networks at a more micro-geographical level in cross-border cooperation between Kortrijk and Lille or between Cologne–Liège–Hasselt–Genk (Aujean et al, 2005c, p6). But in the critical view expressed by Peter Cabus at a Belgian policy workshop, the concept of a polycentric urban network only makes sense if different cities have complementary functions and specializations (as postulated in the theory of polycentric development). Yet empirical studies in Belgium and in the Randstad suggest that their cities show very similar economic structures which are becoming more similar over time (Aujean et al, 2005c, p9).

While the *Randstad* authorities acknowledge the opportunities resulting from a diversified polycentric structure, they observe that their scattered metropolis does not offer the same 'points of excellence' and 'quality of place' as 'real' metropolises such as London, Paris and Frankfurt (Lambregts et al, 2005b, p4). They note that the Randstad's scattered, polycentric layout inhibits the high levels of intra-regional interaction found in those cities, undermines the critical mass necessary for various types of facilities, and limits the spatial scope of markets. Here, therefore, the authorities united in the *Regio Randstad* organization[1] believe that the best way to promote the region's competitive qualities is by strengthening the interactions – hitherto relatively weak – between the centres of the region, in order to unlock its latent 'metropolitan potential' (cf. Chapter 10, p137). Reducing travel times between the main centres by as much as 50 per cent is seen as a key requirement to achieve this (Lambregts et al, 2005b, p7).

Thus concentration is a necessary component in regional economic sustainability as well as less environmentally damaging. In any event, the results for *South East England* show that generation of intense knowledge flows does not necessitate a physical shift of firms and people: paradoxically, concentration spawns new development in patterns of 'concentrated deconcentration' that meet the need for functional specialization across space. Yet here, too, there are difficult problems of environmentally-unfriendly business travel and uneven development in the form of an east–west imbalance in the development of advanced services. Similar imbalances, identified even in morphologically polycentric MCRs such as the Randstad, raise important questions: How do advanced services link to other economic sectors? How can social equity be balanced on different spatial scales – within First Cities and MCRs and also inter-regionally?

Polycentricity thus does not have a direct or axiomatic relevance for sustainable development. It might help achieve greater spatial equality, helping to overcome the general trend to increasing hierarchical division of labour and social polarization. But equally, this might be achieved in a monocentric region, by greater metropolitan integration through improved accessibility. Better links – both physically and in terms of information flows – from the centres of First Cities to secondary cities, and from the latter to other EU metropolitan regions, prove important here.

Is spatial planning useless?

In the *Paris Region* the key planning documents neglect to put any emphasis on APS as a distinct type of high-order activity; they fail to differentiate between research and high-tech activities and advanced services, suggesting a deficiency in the understanding of the regional information economy (Halbert, 2005b, p6).

In *RhineRuhr*, there was awareness of the different and highly specialized sectors of the regional economy, its distinct profiles and areas of competence, but a disappointing lack of understanding of the functional connectivities and 'hidden division of labour' within that economy (Knapp and Schmitt, 2005, p10). Meanwhile in *Rhine-Main*, planners and economic actors 'have different perceptions of polycentricity' (Hoyler et al, 2005, p14). Planners view the issues as relating to territorial space, whereas economic actors focus mostly on trans-boundary relationships which form the reality of their everyday lives.

In the *Randstad* it is felt that planning should be more aware of the strength of market forces. Such forces have put pressure on space in the corridor between Rotterdam and Antwerp; they have also transformed the South-Axis (*Zuidas*) around the new Amsterdam South Station into Amsterdam's major new office location rather than the banks of the IJ (*IJ-oevers*) behind the old Central Station, which the planners wanted to promote. During the focus group meetings it was argued repeatedly that public actors should concentrate their attention on such 'demand-driven' cases (Lambregts et al, 2005b, p18).

In *Greater Dublin* a major issue was that of asymmetry in policy instruments: national government sets financial policy, makes infrastructure decisions (Departments of Transport, National Roads Authority, Department of Communication, Marine, Natural Resources, Rail Procurement Agency), encourages enterprise (Department of Enterprise Trade and Employment) and establishes planning guidelines (Department of Environment, Heritage and Local Government), while local authorities (seven in the Greater Dublin region) make development plans for their areas and administer planning decisions on development proposals in this context. These different functions and instruments have little spatial context, and the result is a lack of joined-up policy (Stafford et al, 2005, p23).

The concept of spatial planning in *South East England* 'has yet to reconcile functional relationships between "economic flows" and "places"'; a more fine-grained strategic vision is needed (Hall and Pain, 2005, p14). 'The complexity of relationships between economic and spatial processes urgently needs to be addressed in policy at all scales and an evidence base built to guide development and investment decisions' (Hall and Pain, 2005, p13).

In *EMR Northern Switzerland*, likewise, virtual and physical connections, and relationships between enterprises, generate spatial patterns outside the framework of spatial planning objectives – a process of 'hidden spatial development'. This helps produce a mismatch between the objectives and strategies for a sustainable spatial development and actual development tendencies (Thierstein et al, 2005, p1). While planning principles rest on a normative, territorial logic, actual spatial development follows a functional logic, largely driven by market forces. So the action fields and strategies of the government departments responsible for spatial planning and the departments responsible for economic development are not coordinated towards a mutual goal (Thierstein et al, 2005, p15).

Are administrative structures failing?

In *South East England* it was noted that the new Regional Spatial Strategies (RSSs) had been produced by bodies that (with the conspicuous exception of London) were not democratically elected. And their boundaries – the so-called UK Standard Regions – do not correspond to the realities of economic and social geography: South East England as defined in POLYNET contains all or part of no less than five of the nine English Standard Regions; regional boundaries bisect two of the major growth corridors in the UK government's Sustainable Communities strategy (Hall and Pain, 2005, p4).

Another question concerns implementation. First, the UK government has proposed – and local authorities have accepted – a great variety of Special Purpose Vehicles (SPVs) for local delivery: Urban Development Corporations, Urban Regeneration Companies, Local Strategic Partnerships, an unspecified 'local delivery vehicle', a commercial consortium (Stratford City) and other arrangements (including a special mechanism for delivery of London's 2012 Olympics). These have varying powers and resources, and some are highly dependent on goodwill and support from the local authorities. Second, though the government has allocated large sums for infrastructure and housing projects, both the South East and East of England Regional Planning Bodies have refused to support higher levels of house building unless considerably more is on offer. There remains a major doubt about whether the strategy can be implemented on the scale and at the speed envisaged (Hall and Pain, 2005, p6). Interviews strongly endorse the need for increased investment in transport, since congestion and delays are considered by business as a major threat, alongside regulation, to the London cluster: an issue further complicated by the fact that rail investment is determined by a combination of public bodies and private companies (Hall and Pain, 2005, p8).

The plans for South East England show a commendable enthusiasm for adopting ESDP-led policies. But, as noticed in Chapter 9, they reflect a traditional land use planning approach; the necessary structures and instruments for implementing a French-style *aménagement du territoire* appear to be lacking, as demonstrated by an apparent lack of integration between land use planning and transport planning, and compounded by a lack of governance at the MCR scale (Hall and Pain, 2005, p13).

Likewise in the *Paris Region*, focus group meetings insisted on the need for more sophisticated structures of horizontal and vertical governance to deal with metropolitan issues. Some new metropolitan strategic project is needed, probably operating at different spatial scales, but with all partners sharing common objectives and priorities. It would be pointless to create yet another administrative layer at the MCR scale; rather, the need is to open up a 'political space' within which different institutions can discuss cross-cutting issues (Halbert, 2005b, p12). Parallel to this, there is a need to fill another gap: to produce a spatial strategy for the Île-de-France CBD, which straddles the *départements* of Paris and the neighbouring Hauts-de-Seine. Despite its major role as the regional and national gateway to the global economy, the dense central area of the first French metropolitan region has no specific planning document, no strategy and no political existence (Halbert, 2005b, p14).

In the *Randstad*, the Dutch administrative structure consists of three different tiers: the national, the provincial and the municipal. For spatial planning, national government provides the overall policy framework (long-term goals, general strategies) while executive planning powers tend to be located at the local level. The Randstad cuts across these layers, encompassing four provinces and about 175 municipalities. It is not represented by a real authority of its own. Yet the need for a form of regional governance in the Randstad is a recurrent issue. Calls for the establishment of a fully fledged Randstad metropolitan authority have been made on several occasions over the past couple of decades, but represent a mission impossible in the current political climate.

Fragmentation is therefore still the key word, although local and regional actors lately have developed different forms of cooperation in order to get things done – or at least discussed (Lambregts et al, 2005b, p15). The best example is the cooperation between the four largest cities, their city regions and the four Randstad provinces in the *Regio Randstad* (see p144). Here the Randstad's key actors develop visions and strategies for the future spatial and economic development of the Randstad and coordinate their interests and position in the Dutch policy arena. Simultaneously, however, there exist several other cooperative arrangements at lower spatial scales.

The national government at present seems more willing to strengthen the role of these lower scale initiatives than that of the *Regio Randstad* at large. Implementation of the latest national spatial strategy (*Nota Ruimte*) for the Randstad will occur not so much at the level of the *Regio Randstad* but will be coordinated and managed predominantly at the level of the so-called Randstad 'wings' – i.e. the North-wing and the South-wing – and the Green Heart (Lambregts et al, 2005b, p16). These three areas will receive a special approach: projects will be jointly weighed and fine-tuned in so-called 'project envelopes' and coordinated between the national government and various coalitions of local and regional authorities and possibly other stakeholders (e.g. Schiphol Airport). It is too early to judge the effectiveness of this decentralized, integrated project- and area-oriented approach (Lambregts et al, 2005b, p16).

In *Central Belgium* each region is responsible for planning its own territory; there is no national structure for consultation, regulation or cooperation at national level, and regions position themselves as rivals rather than as complementary in a win-win strategy (Aujean et al, 2005c, p4). The Walloon and Flemish regions relate strongly to Brussels but not much with each other. One consequence has been intense peri-urban development which has generated commuting movements and cross-subsidization problems between cities and their peripheries, especially in and around Brussels. The first draft of the Walloon territorial plan did not even include Brussels, despite the fact that large numbers of Walloons work in Brussels and spend their income in Wallonia (Aujean et al, 2005c, p5).

In the *Greater Dublin* region greater coordination of spatial planning policy at the regional level has been hindered by institutional deficits. While the region is spatially controlled by one set of Planning Guidelines, which promotes 'self-sufficient' towns in an attempt to curb some of the sprawl of the city, implementation falls to two regional authorities, neither of which is elected or has any legislative or fiscal control. In terms of spatial planning, the local authorities control land use management and have a greater number of policy instruments at their disposal than the regional authorities. It is up to these local authorities to implement the Regional Planning Guidelines as they see fit. Thus, any aspirations in Regional Planning Guidelines to implement polycentric sustainable development are limited (Stafford et al, 2005, p10). Self-sufficiency has declined and many of these towns are little more than dormitory towns (Stafford et al, 2005, p18). Here, it was felt that polycentricity could not be achieved without a more proactive approach. There were very many reports but little implementation. But central government would be reluctant to give spatial policy powers to a Dublin region government. At very least, the crucial section of the 2000 Planning and Development Act should compel local authorities to respect or implement policies set at higher level (Stafford et al, 2005, p20).

The MCR *RhineRuhr* falls under four different district administrations whose territory extends beyond the RhineRuhr boundaries, and each administration thus takes basic responsibility only for its particular part of the region. There has been a welcome development since October 2004: a new Regional Association of the Ruhr Region (*Regionalverband Ruhr*, RVR), with some newly defined tasks (development of master plans, regional landscape management). However, it will still have no real regional planning competence (Knapp and Schmitt, 2005, p5). The autonomous, county-free cities (in particular, the 11 higher-order centres) and the 10 counties and their constituent local government authorities that shape the MCR RhineRuhr usually subscribe to the priority of self-interest (Knapp and Schmitt, 2005, p5). So, due to inadequate institutional structures, 'No one wakes up the "sleeping giant"': the state shows no interest in taking the initiative in framing a major policy discussion on the future of its biggest urban agglomeration (Knapp and Schmitt, 2005, p10).

In *Rhine-Main*, too, functional linkages and administrative demarcations do not correspond. The POLYNET delimitation includes a large area of the federal state of Hessen and also reaches into the federal states of Bavaria and Rhineland-Palatinate. Consequently, Rhine-

Main lacks a central spatial planning authority: every federal state has its own planning body for its respective part of the region and adjacent areas. Three different ministries are responsible for planning at the *Land* level in the functionally defined Rhine-Main region. One level down, five spatial planning regions cover the region. There is a welcome new development in the Frankfurt/Rhine-Main Conurbation Planning Association (*Planungsverband Ballungsraum Frankfurt/Rhein-Main*), established in 2001 to integrate the two levels of regional planning and land use planning for 75 municipalities in the centre of the Hessian part of the Rhine-Main region. The functionally defined Rhine-Main region includes 284 further municipalities, which are responsible for their own land use planning (Hoyler et al, 2005, p3). The *Planungsverband* has yet to complete a combined regional and land use plan, although a Strategic Vision was published in 2005 (Hoyler et al, 2005, p5).

The problem is that the planning authorities do not have the political power to promote integrated regional economic development. Thus the regional plan for *Bayerischer Untermain*, the Bavarian part of the region, puts strong emphasis on the economic autonomy of the Bavarian part of the wider Rhine-Main region (Hoyler et al, 2005, p9). This is compounded by the institutionally guaranteed right of self-government of the municipalities, which are financed through business tax and a share of personal income tax, encouraging competition between municipalities and often running counter to an integrative development perspective (Hoyler et al, 2005, p13). Thus a major policy issue in the Rhine-Main region has to be how to promote effective exchange and cooperation between the multitude of political and economic actors in the region and beyond the region (Hoyler et al, 2005, p15).

In *EMR Northern Switzerland* there are three tiers of government: the Swiss confederation, 26 cantons and about 2800 municipalities, each with its own spatial planning responsibilities. Regional planning associations are non-existent or weak; there is no level of government, or government body, with specific responsibility for agglomerations (which are merely a statistical category), or FURs, let alone the entire EMR Northern Switzerland (Thierstein et al, 2005, p5). The municipalities play a dominant role in administration of planning, and compete for business developments to help strengthen their revenue base (Thierstein et al, 2005, p10). Parish-pump policies likewise prevent cantons from cooperation, with the notable exception of the Association of the 'Greater Zürich area' (Thierstein et al, 2005, p12). Individual cantons have the power to make decisions on issues of nation-wide concern.

Nationally, no fewer than 20 federal agencies have remits which touch upon spatial planning in many areas: agriculture, transportation, communication, energy, security policy and public buildings and installations. The budget for spatial development policies is limited. Further, federal departments do not coordinate spatial development policies: the State Secretariat for Economic Affairs, responsible for regional policies, acts in a contrary way to the planning policies of the Federal Office for Spatial Development. Policy-makers are well aware of these failings but share a feeling of powerlessness (Thierstein et al, 2005, p12).

The national 2005 report on spatial development concludes that spatial development has not been sustainable in terms of critical criteria: urban sprawl, social and functional segregation within agglomerations, disparities between rural and urban regions, increasing numbers of buildings outside the official building zone, and growing mobility. It proposes a polycentric network of urban centres connected to their hinterlands and benefiting from mutual territorial solidarity (Thierstein et al, 2005, pp6–7, quoting Federal Office for Spatial Development, 2005, pp7–58, 87). The problem, as elsewhere, is that spatial planning has a relatively small impact on economic development and on managing the spatial impacts of economic decisions; more influential are sectoral policies concerning agriculture, transportation and a new financial equalization scheme (Thierstein et al, 2005, p9).

There is therefore a pressing need to enhance cooperation between the State Secretariat for Economic Affairs and the Federal Office for Spatial Development, and to develop coordination between spatial development policies, in the narrow sense, and federal responsibilities for sectoral policies such as agriculture, transport and technology and location marketing, which may be critical for spatial development policies in the broader sense (Thierstein et al, 2005, p16).

Is the reality competition – or collaboration?

In *South East England*, London's concentration of APS, coupled with highly specialized skills and supporting services, is recognized as a unique asset that cannot be replicated elsewhere; even if this were possible, constructing similarly extensive transport links in other UK locations would prove unsustainable. London's assets are distinct from those offered by other European cities and cannot be shifted, for example, to Paris or Frankfurt; London's importance must not be underplayed. It is important to keep in mind what might 'turn off the tap marked success' (Hall and Pain, 2005, p11).

In the *Randstad*, coordination between the local and the regional levels has improved considerably in the past five years or so. Many of the new arrangements are proving quite durable and they act as excellent vehicles for building trust and developing a common understanding of a region's spatial development problems and challenges. But this does not mean that all works smoothly or that the cooperating authorities are now achieving one success after another: problems remain. The economic development programmes of the Randstad's individual cities, for example, give little evidence of close coordination and there seems to be scope for improvement in the relationships between the national authorities and the local and regional authorities. After a two-year standstill (a result of the politically turbulent start of the new millennium in The Netherlands), meetings between the two have resumed, but the years of upheaval have produced so many new faces, new views and new ways of communicating that it may take time before routines and trust levels regain their old ways (Lambregts et al, 2005b, p19).

In the highly monocentric *Greater Dublin* region, polycentricity is seen as 'combining the strengths of increasingly contiguous towns in the midlands of Ireland' which lack the critical mass to compete with the larger cities on an economic basis (Stafford et al, 2005, p12, quoting Ireland DELG, 2001, p42). But although *Central Belgium* is more morphologically polycentric, here too problems with inter-city competition are reported. Thus, though it was declared that Liège (with its TGV (*Train à Grand Vitesse*) station) should develop complementary roles with Aachen in Germany and Maastricht in The Netherlands (with its airport), Liège independently developed its airport at Bierset. Paradoxically, then, without a strong central power to organize the complementarity of different urban centres, polycentrism may result in increased powers at lower levels of the urban hierarchy (Aujean et al, 2005c, p12). Nevertheless, alongside inter-urban competition, inter-urban cooperation can exist at another spatial scale: locally Lille competes with Brussels but, in the competition between London and Paris, Lille is eager to collaborate with Brussels (Aujean et al, 2005c, p14).

In *Rhine-Main*, though decentralized concentration and complementary polycentricity feature in planning documents, they remain largely descriptive concepts. The need to act regionally has been clearly identified for a long time. However the intersection of federal structures (three federal states) with strong local government (i.e. relatively autonomous municipalities) has so far prevented the development of effective regional governance structures and institutions, though it has fostered informal and voluntary forms of cooperation (Hoyler et al, 2005, p8).

In *Greater Dublin*, local links between policy-making institutions and development agencies 'would facilitate a more rounded development of county spatial plans'. 'Rather than county competing with neighbouring county

for economic development, regional powers could assist in spreading both the economic and quality of life benefits of a sustained economic growth more fairly' (Stafford et al, 2005, p21). Greater cooperation is needed on issues of planning, economic development and competitiveness (Stafford et al, 2005, p20).

Equally, in morphologically polycentric *RhineRuhr*, 'polycentricity … is seen as an obstacle to more co-operation among stakeholders' (Knapp and Schmitt, 2005, pp10–11). There is a need to move from a focus on a 'designer region' to produce a 'territorial social practice' (Knapp and Schmitt, 2005, p12). Such a policy would start by defining what kinds of complementary functions could be played by each part of the MCR in a regional division of labour.

Generally, the concept of the MCR, as defined by functional relationships – commuting, business travel, flows of information – fits with policy-makers' perceptions: they conceive of the MCR as a unit of territory that will support one or more dense concentrations of core global functions (and also, for Randstad planners, a high quality of interaction), while permitting other activities to deconcentrate and reconcentrate in other centres – thus producing a degree of functional specialization, vital for economic efficiency. That said, however, there is virtually no support in the policy-making structures or in public finance for an integrated MCR administration: in all eight regions, decision-making is fragmented, competition between individual cities is rife (though felt to be counter-productive), and nowhere does a territorial definition of the MCR exist. There is a mismatch between the political pace (short and sometimes medium term) and the tangible results of any decision in the field of spatial planning (medium and especially long term). A determined opposition to local resistances is needed. If every place duplicates functions, this 'produces surpluses and diseconomies of scale … cooperation most of the time has to be induced as it does not come spontaneously' (Aujean et al, 2005c, pp15, 12).

Generally, territorial boundaries do not accord with the reality of economic life. Thus, in *Rhine-Main*, there were 'territory versus network' tensions. 'The economic perspective runs counter to a strictly bounded territorialization' (Hoyler et al, 2005, p14). And in practice, integration and cooperation fall short of the rhetoric found in policy documents. Many regions reported that, in varying degrees, economic strategies were not clearly embedded into spatial planning strategies. There were inconsistencies in different fields of governance; a new relational thinking was needed. Cross-border issues and functional realities required joined-up governance.

In *EMR Northern Switzerland,* there were 'mismatches between different levels and fields of action' (Thierstein et al, 2005, p15). Spatial planning focuses on physical solutions, yet market logic generates functional relations. In *RhineRuhr* no clear shift could be detected away from traditional land use planning, with its limited focus on inter-municipal issues. A more strategic approach is needed to address cross-sectoral issues and the actual functions of the MCR (Knapp and Schmitt, 2005, p11).

A particular problem was how to coordinate different policies within a common spatial framework. Investment, both public and private – but especially public, because this can be directly controlled – proved to be a crucial example for many commentators. One instance is investment in education, research and training. There is a balance to be struck here: what is the role of universities and research, concentrated in a few places, when high-level skills in advanced services are learned 'on the job'? Another issue is the precise role played by key economic 'triggers' in the development of a city and its surrounding FUR. Peripheral areas, it was suggested, would grow not merely through importing multi-national companies (MNCs), but more through the increasing sophistication of the local demands that link one APS sector or firm with another. The image of a place or an area also mattered for inward investment: embedded perceptions and symbolic capital could play an important role (see also Pain, 2005). So there is a need for sectoral policies – in fields like employment, taxation or transport – to be integrated into the spatial planning process: 'Thus, spatial, financial and industrial development could be better combined in the development of Ireland's urban centres' (Stafford et al, 2005, p21).

Polycentricity thus needs to be understood as an active policy objective. Other policy fields might have unintentional consequences for spatial strategies: a goal of achieving 'simple polycentricity' might not address priorities for economic growth, which on the contrary may require economic concentration and functional specialization. Overcoming such problems will require a new form of 'multi-level governance' (Thierstein et al, 2003), inside a new culture of governance and a strengthening of territorial networks: 'political polycentricity', as the Paris team expressed it (Halbert, 2005b, p12), or 'Trans-municipal cooperation and coordination at the level of the MCR' in the words of RhineRuhr (Knapp and Schmitt, 2005, p13).

Distilling the key policy issues

Towards the end of the POLYNET study, the eight teams met to discuss their policy conclusions. Through an intensive process[2] they arrived at a list of common issues.

Key concepts – Key myths?

Certain key concepts have come to dominate policy discussions in Europe, and often beyond its borders. Some indeed have come to assume an almost mythical or spiritual character, to be repeated as some kind of mantra without serious interrogation as to their meaning. But such critical interrogation has been the essence of POLYNET. Here we summarize our conclusions.

- *Polycentricity:* 'morphological polycentricity', which refers to the regional distribution of towns and cities of different sizes, is not the same as 'functional polycentricity', which refers to flows of information and the organization of firms. A balanced spatial distribution of development does not guarantee an even distribution of complementary functions or a more sustainable form of development in the POLYNET MCRs.

- *Balanced development:* indeed, the interview evidence paradoxically suggested that in reality morphological polycentricity is associated with rather weak intra-regional functional linkages. Just as paradoxically, depth of global concentration in London (regarded as a monocentric area in the NWMA Spatial Vision), was found to produce the most concrete evidence of regional functional polycentricity. Yet this too is associated with uneven development, in the form of an east–west economic imbalance in South East England. The growth of MCRs thus has implications for sustainable growth and social equity.

- *Sustainable development:* in spite of advances in ICT, face-to-face contact remains vital to the operation of advanced knowledge-based service functions. Polycentric regional development, whether functional or morphological, is also found to create 'criss-cross' commuting that cannot be effectively supported by public transport. Functional polycentricity in APS is additionally associated with patterns of regional business travel that cross-cut the hub-and-spoke regional transport infrastructure. Hence both types of polycentricity have possible negative implications for environmental sustainability. How to overcome this – for instance, by developing more effective non-radial public transport links – represents a major challenge.

- *Economic competitiveness:* in all MCRs, functional concentration has been found to be essential to the development of international APS agglomeration economies and global business flows. First Cities – Dublin, London, Paris, Brussels, Amsterdam, Frankfurt, Düsseldorf and Zürich – play a vital 'knowledge gateway' role, articulating their MCRs into the worldwide APS economy. Concentration of global functions and specialisms in these primary cities remains essential for high-complexity/high-value knowledge transfer, innovation and production.

- *Spatial scale*: polycentricity was found to be a scale-sensitive phenomenon. For example, Paris appears morphologically monocentric at a *regional* and *national* scale but is functionally polycentric at a *global* scale. Functional polycentricity in APS at a *national* scale in Germany does not transfer across to the MCR *regional* scale: RhineRuhr and Rhine-Main have different spatial and functional configurations and connectivity to *global* APS networks. National contexts are important, but the MCR is identified as a vital spatial scale for spatial development policy and for the Lisbon Agenda of making Europe the world's 'most competitive and dynamic knowledge-based economy' by the year 2010.

- *Sustainable management*: the MCR scale is hard to define, because APS flows are multi-scalar and do not coincide with administrative and political boundaries. Sustainable management of the MCR requires coordinated horizontal and vertical inter-organizational and cross-sector approaches. The concept of 'economic competitiveness' should not be misconstrued as a 'territorial competition' for inward investment. Cooperation is needed between cities and regions to reflect the functional complementarities that result from transnational knowledge-based networks; European policies can help to promote this.

- *Role of spatial planning*: the ESDP addresses problems of social and economic disparity by encouraging polycentric urban development to promote growth in less developed regions outside the 'Pentagon'. The NWMA Spatial Vision aims to spread growth concentrated in London, Paris and the rest of the 'Pentagon' by improving accessibility and development of trans-European networks (TENs). POLYNET policy analyses for the eight MCRs suggest that spatial planning still places a heavy emphasis on physical infrastructure, but policy-makers recognize the need for this to be complemented by new economic development approaches and 'functional thinking'.

- *Territorial cohesion*: the European Commission's (EC) concept of 'territorial cohesion', developed in its Second and Third Reports on Economic and Social Cohesion (European Commission, 2004) focuses on issues of 'spatial equity' and uneven European spatial development, and stresses the need to promote social and economic balance across the EU territory. But POLYNET findings on polycentricity suggest that balanced spatial development does not necessarily result in social equity and quality of life.

- *Spatial governance*: the globalization and liberalization of North West European markets for APS, strongly promoted by the EC, pose a challenge for the governance of flows which requires cross-jurisdictional and cross-sectoral structures. Over and above the specific spatial and functional features of the eight MCRs, the research has revealed important common policy dilemmas. In all cases senior policy-makers have described a serious lack of governance and policy instruments at the level of the MCR.

Sources of confusion

Arising out of this critical examination, we found many points where lack of clarity, and ambiguity, acted as barriers to coherent policy formulation.

- *Unclear interpretations of polycentricity*: the basic issues – is polycentricity more competitive? is it more sustainable? – need to be addressed. The POLYNET results strongly suggest that these propositions are not simply self-evident; indeed, in certain cases the opposite may be true. There is a basic need to distinguish between morphological polycentricity (generally interpreted in terms of commuting) and functional polycentricity (interpreted in terms of business travel and communication, especially face-to-face). The latter is more significant, and it is not axiomatic that it yields either more competitive or more sustainable outcomes than its opposite, monocentricity (or primacy). There is scope for a major new research programme on this topic as an essential part of the revision of the ESDP.

- *Lack of understanding* of functional as opposed to morphological issues, especially in regard to polycentricity, leads to thinking solely in terms of physical infrastructure instead of 'thinking functionally'. Of course, infrastructure is relevant to functional polycentricity: accessibility within MCRs is important for face-to-face contact, vital for APS, so all regions need adequate investment in infrastructure and better management of transport networks to support major gateway cities and to strengthen external and internal flows. But this is only part of the story.

- *The emphasis on self-containment and minimal travel* does not always accord with regional economic development priorities, particularly with the needs of knowledge-based business service suppliers and their workers; it therefore acts as an obstacle to regional economic development. Urban containment is assumed to be a realistic goal alongside polycentricity, but the reality is far more complex and even contradictory. Physical or morphological containment may in fact increase long-distance commuting because it causes people to live farther away from their jobs than they would otherwise do.

- *There is a need for better understanding of the impacts of functional polycentricity* on a number of key issues, including social equity and environmental sustainability. There are tensions and choices and tradeoffs here, as well as a basic policy paradox: that an even distribution of functions may conflict with environmental sustainability objectives. Equally, a failure to support regional development could inhibit economic growth. Thus, sustainable development may prove to be an oxymoron (Blowers and Pain, 1999). The focus should be on addressing uneven economic and social equity as opposed to balancing the spatial distribution of development. Polycentric regional development does not necessarily enhance quality of life.

- *MCRs have common features, but are also diverse*: the ESDP therefore needs to be more scale-sensitive to Europe-wide, national, regional and urban levels. There may be contradictions between policies at one scale and those at another: thus, promoting polycentricity at the European scale (out of the central 'Pentagon' to favour peripheral regions) may promote monocentricity at a national scale, as has been evident in Ireland and Southern Europe and is becoming evident in Eastern Europe. Further, contrasts between national contexts may make one overriding European set of priorities inapplicable. The application of polycentricity to different spatial scales must be addressed, especially the national scale, not currently prioritized in the ESDP. This may have major implications for investment and the management of infrastructure.

- *There is also a need to understand functional specialization* across North West Europe's MCRs, in particular how this relates to the completion of the Single Market and the opening up of the EU to global flows through World Trade Organization and G8 agreements. Morphological polycentricity appears to be associated with sectoral specialization between centres of a similar size, whereas a greater concentration of services and sectors in one city improves agglomeration economies and boosts regional functional polycentricity.

- *Contradictions between policy agendas*: there are implicit contradictions between the Lisbon Agenda and the ESDP on key issues, particularly on encouraging spatial competition versus spreading growth to lagging regions. Changes to the ESDP are required to incorporate Lisbon priorities for EU economic growth, regional equity and sustainable development.

Implications for policy

- *Role of the ESDP*: in spite of the doubts expressed about its applicability to diverse national and regional circumstances, and possible contradictions with the Lisbon Agenda, the findings suggest that *the ESDP in fact requires more prominence* as a network for Member States and regional cooperation. It currently has little visibility or recognition. It needs to be better understood because of its influence on national and regional planning in Member States – and, insofar as it is felt to have limitations and deficiencies, these need to be fully and expertly debated.

- *Policy coordination: how and where?* There is a diversity of policy frameworks and development perspectives for the MCR beneath the EU-wide level; but *is coordination either necessary or desirable at the level of the nation state?* When it is actually taken into account by policy-makers, the ESDP is perceived as too abstract, dealing with a macro-level that does not relate to the diversity of circumstances at the MCR scale. Yet this scale has great importance for the Lisbon Agenda and requires specific attention.

- *There is a need to involve the business community* to gain a better understanding of market drivers and conditions, inter-firm and inter-sectoral relationships, economic and spatial relationships. Otherwise policies may be based on a misunderstanding of the ways in which firms, especially but not exclusively in APS, may react. This is likely to represent a major challenge.

- *There is serious lack of governance almost everywhere at the scale of the MCR*, including a lack of policy instruments. Within existing administrative structures, some policy-makers think they have powers but in fact lack them. Some have powers but do not realize it, and thus there are direct and indirect influences that can have unintentional consequences.

- *There is a need to think both strategically and locally.* To do this it will be necessary to promote cooperative relations in MCR governance so as to reflect the network connections between cities across policy and sectoral fields at all geographical scales. There is likewise a need for cooperative MCR management networks – both vertical and horizontal.

- *Inter-regional competition for inward investment – and its converse in prosperous regions, local 'nimbyism' – need to be countered*, but this is hampered by the lack of governance structures for the MCR. Thus there is a need to upgrade the entire MCR concept, including injection of a democratic input at this scale.

- *The POLYNET MCRs are strongly interconnected through the global city network.* Support for transnational cooperation through INTERREG (EC community initiative promoting cross-border, transnational and inter-regional cooperation) is necessary because the MCRs are functionally interconnected and impact on each other. EU funding must continue to reflect this.

In conclusion: A continuing research agenda

In concluding the POLYNET study and this book, it is useful to review these research findings once more, to answer one final question: what questions remain at least partially unanswered, and so open for further research? Some suggest themselves.

Territorial disparities and territorial cohesion

In the 2005 Draft Constitutional Treaty, territorial cohesion was placed on a par with economic and social cohesion (Faludi, 2005b; Zonnenveld and Waterhout, 2005). Research by the European Spatial Planning Observation Network (ESPON) has identified important indicators of territorial disparity, based on official population and demographic statistics, accessibility and economic forecasting. The European Territorial Cohesion Index (ETCI), developed in ESPON 3.2, has been devised to assist policies that promote balanced spatial development and the allocation of Structural and Cohesion funds. POLYNET's findings on transnational flows (Chapter 5) highlight the need for a deeper understanding of solutions to economic and social inequity across the EU territory, which may paradoxically require increased investment in areas of concentration.

Spatial and functional complementarities

POLYNET has shown that morphologically polycentric MCRs display sectoral specialization between centres, whereas morphologically monocentric MCRs, with greater service concentration in one city, show multi-sector clustering and the co-location of synergistic financial and creative milieux. But how exactly do highly clustered MCR global functions support different functions in different centres – locally, regionally and in distant places? There is a need to extend and deepen POLYNET's quantitative and qualitative analyses in order to inform policies on functional specialization and spatial complementarities within, between and beyond the POLYNET MCRs.

Accessibility and knowledge

The NWMA Spatial Vision advocates the diversion of flows from London, Paris and the Pentagon to other regions through the investment in TENs projects. Major investment in infrastructure is being supported through the INTERREG programme, but little is known about the role of accessibility in promoting sustainable regional development. How important is investment in transport and e-infrastructure, as well as directly into centres of excellence within the knowledge economy, for development of that economy? What will be the effect of EU expansion on demand for specialized business services? What level of regional investment and financial support is needed, in what places and with what objectives? Who should decide, and in particular what should be the role of regional and national governments?

Territorial capital

In all the POLYNET MCRs, the functional geographies of the APS proved to be uneven. It appears that polycentricity, whether morphological or functional, fails to provide a sustainable solution to issues of territorial social and economic inequity: a deeper understanding is needed of the forces that underlie prevailing geographies of uneven development. What part does the historical evolution of cities and regions play in contemporary development patterns? What is the relevance of national and regional contexts? What is the role of 'city capital' and is a new scale of 'MCR capital' emerging? How can policy interventions support this and what are the implications for regional powers and governance and wider 'EU territorial capital'?

Inter-sector flows

In more morphologically polycentric MCRs, some scepticism emerged in the policy analysis about the value of polycentricity as a regional development objective. Key questions were raised: is it correct to plan for polycentricity? What form of polycentricity? And, if so, how to achieve it? Would social and economic equality be better encouraged through sectoral policy? How do POLYNET APS interrelate with other economic sectors, and what are the implications for polycentricity, sustainable development and policy?

These questions represent a continuing research agenda, of central importance for policy at European, national and regional scales. They deserve to be addressed in a successor programme to both ESPON and POLYNET, and in other parallel EU Interreg-funded research projects. The mysteries of the polycentric metropolis have been partially unravelled, but there is much work still to do.

Notes

1 The four largest cities, their city regions and the four Randstad provinces.
2 An intense process of brainstorming, dividing into two groups and then recombining to consider each others' recommendations.

Appendix 1
The Web Survey

Page 1 is a greeting page on entry to the site, explaining that the survey, which is strictly confidential, will take only about 15 minutes to complete and will produce results of great value for policy formulation both Europe-wide and at a nation state level. The respondent is asked to click a button to proceed on.

Page 2 then explains that there are two ways of completing the survey and gives guidance about doing so. It then asks for an access code (already e-mailed to the respondent) in order to enter the confidential area of the website.

Page 3 asks for information about the respondent: the firm's main area of business, the respondent's position in the firm, and the location of his/her office and the firm's head office (for small firms, invariably the same).

Page 4 asks for business travel data. It covers a five-day working week. Respondents are asked to start at home or other location (e.g. hotel) and to list each location visited, including the journey to and from work, ending at home or other location. Details of travel mode for each stage are also requested. Finally the respondent is asked for the total number of meetings inside and outside the firm or organization each day.

Page 5 covers telephone calls. Respondents are asked to list the top five locations for calls made and calls received during the working week, with an estimate of the number of calls in each category. They are also asked for the total number of calls made inside and outside the firm or organization.

Page 6 similarly requests details of conference calls (phone or video). The categories are the same as for phone calls.

Page 7 similarly asks for details of e-mail and web-based communications. Again the categories are the same as for telephone and conference calls.

Page 8 introduces a new theme: business location factors. Respondents are asked to check 13 possible location factors, all relating to accessibility to communications either for face-to-face contact or telephone/electronic contact, and to rate them first as to their level of relative importance, and second as to their own level of satisfaction/dissatisfaction at their present location.

Page 9 continues this inquiry, but now extending it to cover a wider range of factors ranging from economic (taxation, cost and flexibility of labour) to social and environmental (quality of life, local schools), but then returning to accessibility by different transport modes, and concluding with a general overall assessment of the location.

Finally, *page 10* thanks the respondent and closes the session.

Appendix 2
The Interview Questionnaires

General introduction: Research purpose/focus

The research has been funded by North West Europe European Regional Development Fund (NWE/ERDF), to inform public and private sector decision-making on the changing geography of information and transport flows associated with service business networks in NWE global city regions.

The research covers eight regions across seven NWE countries: UK, *South East England*; Ireland, *Greater Dublin*; France, *Paris Region*; Germany, *Rhine-Main* and *RhineRuhr*; The Netherlands, the *Randstad*; Belgium, *Central Belgium*; Switzerland, *European Metropolitan Region (EMR) Northern Switzerland*.

It covers eight service business sectors: banking, insurance, law, accountancy, management consulting, advertising, logistics, design consulting.

Interview questionnaire A: Firms

1a Why did your firm originally choose this office location? What are the current advantages of this location for your business? Which, if any, of these advantages is associated with proximity to [hub city]?

1b Where are the sources for new ideas, products and innovation in your business?
Function of office/nature of business activities conducted (complexity, skills, risk, profitability, front-/back-office) – macro and micro, including proximity to global hub city critical mass; access to: staff (depth and breadth of skills and languages, cost of labour); business services; clients and markets; finance capital and infrastructure; other firms and institutions;
intelligence and knowledge transfer; flexibility of labour market (ease of recruitment and release of staff); regulatory/tax environment; transport and communications; availability/cost of suitable business accommodation; significance of address, creative milieux.[1]

2 What is the nature of your labour market: local, regional, national, European, global? In what ways are living and travel to work patterns changing in this firm/line of business/vicinity?
Spatial reach of labour market commuting (daily/weekly) at different spatial scales (local, hub city, region, national, international). Changing lifestyle preferences/career ambitions of staff/two-earner households. Typical housing location preferences/housing and commuting cost/children's education. Changing modes/distances of travel to work. Extent of home-working, hot-desking, travel to other offices (within same network, to customers etc.).

3 What changes have occurred in the firm's organizational strategy and functional relations between this and other office locations? What have been the consequences of these changes?
Core activities in different locations; division of labour; turnover/profitability; location of chief executives/partners and headquarters functions; level of work complexity/risk; level of financial integration; size and functions of staff/number of revenue-earners; personnel movement; number of assignments per year; percentage of non-national employees; relationship with head office/other offices; status of offices; level of communication between offices including in global hub city, other key cities in country, Europe, globally.

4 How typical would you say your firm is for the sector? How is the sector as a whole changing? How

are relations between service business sectors changing and with what consequences? Who are the leading firms in your sector in this region, country, Europe, globally?

5   How do you communicate with other offices within your organization? How do you communicate with people and offices located at a distance? How important are spatial proximity and face-to-face contact?

Travel and means of travel (air, road, train); phone/IT/video-conferencing, frequency. Increase/ decrease in different communication modes, risk control, team-building. At this point ask if they would be willing to join in a (strictly confidential) diary study.

6   What is the nature of your business relationships with other firms (in your own or other business sectors) and institutions in: this area; hub city; region; country; Europe; globally? How are these relationships changing?

Connections within sub-sector; with firms in other sub-sectors; with institutions/government. Need for access to project teams; knowledge transfer; markets/ international clients and business/other clients and types of business; outsourcing relationships; social/business opportunities – clubs/professional/trade associations – significance of trust.

7   How do you communicate with people and offices in other organizations? How do you communicate with people and firms located at a distance? How important are spatial proximity and face-to-face contact?

Significance of relationship building, knowledge transfer. Methods/regularity/ease of travel/other forms of communication/where hub city etc. E-mail/phone/fax/ video-conferencing; restaurants, clubs and bars.

8   What are the implications of these changes for the future of your business location? Has your firm recently considered moving to a different location, if so where? If you were free to move to another location anywhere, where would that be?

9   What factors are likely to enhance or threaten business activity in this vicinity? What action is required and by whom?

Industrial and market changes; buildings/infrastructure; cost of office space; telecommunications facilities; transport facilities; lifestyle preferences; environmental issues/crime; policy issues: regulation/finance capital/taxation/skills availability/immigration and employment policy.

10   Are there any other key issues I have not covered?

Interview questionnaire B: Institutions

Show interview questionnaire, which is the same as that for firms, and go through each question in turn asking what understanding the respondent has of the issues from their experience working in that institution.

Note

1   The text in italic beneath some questions provided an aide mémoire of topics to be raised by interviewers.

References

Note: POLYNET reports cited here can be accessed on the POLYNET website: www.polynet.org.uk/. So that they can be easily identified each report citation is preceded by an asterisk.

Anon (2002) 'Grans Aglomeracions Metropolitanes Europees', Institut d'Estudis Regionals I Metropolitans, Paper 37. Barcelona: Institut d'Estudis Regionals I Metropolitans de Barcelona

Anon (2005) 'Regionalpolitik rückt wieder zum Rand'. *Neue Zürcher Zeitung*, 1 July, p13

Association of London Government (1997) *The London Study: A Socio-Economic Assessment of London.* London: ALG

*Aujean, L., Castiau, E., Roelandts, M. and Vandermotten, C. (2005a) *POLYNET Action 1.1: Commuting & the Definition of Functional Urban Regions: Central Belgium.* London: Institute of Community Studies/The Young Foundation & Polynet Partners

*Aujean, L., Castiau, E., Roelandts, M. and Vandermotten, C. (2005b) *POLYNET Action 2.1: Qualitative Analysis of Service Business Connections: Central Belgium.* London: Institute of Community Studies/The Young Foundation & Polynet Partners

*Aujean, L., Castiau, E., Roelandts, M. and Vandermotten, C. (2005c) *POLYNET Action 3.1: Analysis of Policy Documents & Policy Focus Groups: Central Belgium.* London: Institute of Community Studies/The Young Foundation & Polynet Partners

Axhausen, K. W. (1995) *Travel Diaries: An Annotated Catalogue*, 2nd edition. Working Paper, Institut für Straßenbau und Verkehrsplanung. Innsbruck: Leopold-Franzes-Universität

Beaverstock, J. V., Hoyler, M., Pain, K. and Taylor, P. J. (2001) *Comparing London and Frankfurt as World Cities: A Relational Study of Contemporary Urban Change.* London: Anglo-German Foundation

Beaverstock, J. V., Hoyler, M., Pain, K. and Taylor, P. J. (2003a) 'London and Frankfurt: Competition or Synergy?', in Shearlock, P. (ed) *International Investor.* London: Sovereign Publications, pp225–229

Beaverstock, J. V., Hoyler, M., Pain, K. and Taylor, P. J. (2003b) *In London's Long Shadow: Frankfurt in the European Space of Flows.* GaWC Research Bulletin 120 http://www.lboro.ac.uk/gawc/publicat.html#bulletin accessed in December 2005

Beaverstock, J. V., Hoyler, M., Pain, K. and Taylor, P. J. (2005) 'Demystifying the Euro in European financial centre relations: London and Frankfurt 2000–2001'. *Journal of Contemporary European Studies*, vol 13, pp143–157

Beaverstock, J. V., Smith, R. G., Taylor, P. J., Walker, D. R. F. and Lorimer, H. (2000a) 'Globalization and world cities: Some measurement methodologies'. *Applied Geography*, vol 20, pp43–63

Beaverstock, J. V., Smith, R. G. and Taylor, P. J. (2000b) 'World-city network: A new metageography?'. *Annals of the Association of American Geographers*, vol 90, pp123–134

Beaverstock, J. V., Taylor, P. and Smith, R. G. (1999a) 'A roster of world cities'. *Cities*, vol 16, pp445–458

Beaverstock, J. V., Taylor, P. and Smith, R. G. (1999b) 'The long arm of the law: London's law firms in a globalising world economy'. *Environment and Planning* A, vol 31, pp1857–1876

Beckouche, P. (1999) 'Marché du travail, espace social et enjeu scolaire en Île-de-France'. *Pouvoirs Locaux*, no 40–41, pp38–47

Berry, B. J. L. (1961) 'City size distributions and economic development'. *Economic Development and Cultural Change*, vol 9, pp573–588

Berry, B. J. L. (1964) 'Cities as systems within systems of cities'. *Papers, Regional Science Association*, vol 13, pp147–163

Berry, B. J. L. and Horton, F. (1970) *Geographic Perspectives on Urban Systems, with Integrated Readings.* Englewood Cliffs, NJ: Prentice-Hall

Blöchliger, H. (ed) (2005) *Baustelle Föderalismus. Avenir Suisse.* Zürich: Buchverlag der Neuen Zürcher Zeitung

Blotevogel, H. H. (2002) 'Städtesystem und Metropolregionen', in Institut für Länderkunde (ed) *Nationalatlas Bundesrepublik Deutschland. Bd. 5: Dörfer und Städte.* Heidelberg: Spektrum Akademischer Verlag, pp40–43

Blotevogel, H. H. and Schmitt, P. (2005) 'The "European Metropolitan Region Rhine-Ruhr" in the context of the gradual paradigm shift in strategic spatial planning in Germany', in Feldhoff, T. and Flüchter, W. (eds) *Proceedings of the Japanese-German Geographical Conference. No.1: Shaping the Future of Metropolitan Regions in Japan and Germany: Governance, Institutions and Place in New Context.* Duisburg: Duisburg-Essen University

Blowers, A. and Pain, K. (1999) 'The Unsustainable City?', in Pile, S. Brook, C. and Mooney, G. (eds) *Unruly Cities? Order/Disorder.* London: Routledge, pp247–298

Boiteux-Orain, C. and Huriot, J. (2002) 'Modéliser la suburbanisation, succès et limites de la micro-économie urbaine'. *Revue d'Economie Régionale et Urbaine*, vol 1, pp73–104

Bontje, M. and Burdack, J. (2005) 'Edge cities, European-style: Examples from Paris and the Randstad'. *Cities*, vol 22, pp317–330

Bördlein, R. (1999) '"Region Rhein-Main": Rahmenbedingungen und Konzepte im Institutional isierungsprozess einer Region'. *DISP*, nos 136/137, pp63–69

Bördlein, R. and Schickhoff, I. (1998) 'Der Rhein-Main-Raum', in Kulke, E. (ed) *Wirtschaftsgeographie Deutschlands*. Gotha, Stuttgart: Klett-Perthes, pp465–495

Breheny, M. (1990) 'Strategic Planning and Urban Sustainability', in *Proceedings of TCPA Annual Conference, Planning for Sustainable Development*. London: Town and Country Planning Association, pp9.1–9.28

Breheny, M. (ed.) (1999) *The People: Where Will They Work?* Report of TCPA Research into the Changing Geography of Employment. London: Town and Country Planning Association

Brunet, R. (1989) *Les Villes 'Européennes'. Rapport pour la DATAR*. Paris: La Documentation Française (RECLUS/DATAR)

Bundesamt für Statistik (2004) *Statistisches Jahrbuch der Schweiz 2004*. Zürich: Verlag Neue Zürcher Zeitung

Cairncross, F. (1995) 'Telecommunications: The death of distance'. *The Economist*, 30 September

Cairncross, F. (1997) *The Death of Distance: How the Communications Revolution Will Change Our Lives*. New York: McGraw-Hill

Camagni, R. and Salone, C. (1993) 'Network urban structures in Northern Italy: Elements for a theoretical framework'. *Urban Studies*, vol 30, pp1053–1064

Capello, R. (2000) 'The city network paradigm: Measuring urban network externalities'. *Urban Studies*, vol 37, pp1925–1945

Carlstein, T., Parkes, D. and Thrift, N. (1978) *Human Activity and Time Geography. (Timing Space and Spacing Time*, Vol. 2). London: Edward Arnold

Castells, M. (1989) *The Informational City: Information Technology, Economic Restructuring and the Urban-Regional Process*. Oxford: Basil Blackwell

Castells, M. (1996) *The Information Age: Economy, Society and Culture. Vol. I: The Rise of the Network Society*. Oxford: Blackwell

Castells, M. (2000) *The Information Age: Economy, Society, and Culture. Vol. I, The Rise of the Network Society*, 2nd edition. Oxford: Blackwell

CBS (Centraal Bureau voor de Statistiek) (2005) Population and employment statistics for selected years. www.statline.cbs.nl/ accessed in December 2005

Cheshire, P. C. (1995) 'A new phase of urban development in Western Europe? The evidence for the 1980s'. *Urban Studies*, vol 32, pp1045–1063

Cheshire, P. C. (1999) 'Cities in competition: Articulating the gains from integration'. *Urban Studies*, vol 36, pp843–864

Cheshire, P.C. and Carbonaro, G. (1996) 'Urban economic growth in Europe: Testing theory and policy prescriptions'. *Urban Studies*, vol 33, pp1111–1128

Cheshire, P. C. and Hay, D. G. (1989) *Urban Problems in Western Europe: An Economic Analysis*. London: Unwin Hyman

Chicoye, C. (1992) 'Regional impact of the Single European Market in France'. *Regional Studies*, vol 26, pp407–411

Chorley, R. J. and Haggett, P. (1967) *Models in Geography*. London: Methuen

Christaller, W. (1966 (1933)) *Central Places in Southern Germany*. Translated by C. W. Baskin. Englewood Cliffs, NJ: PrenticeHall

Clark, C. (1940) *The Conditions of Economic Progress*. London: Macmillan

Coakley, J. (1992) 'London as an International Financial Centre', in Budd, L. and Whimster, S. (eds) *Global Finance and Urban Living: A Study of Metropolitan Change*. London: Routledge, pp52–72

Cochrane, A. and Pain, K. (2000) 'A Globalising Society?', in Held, D. (ed) *A Globalising World*. London: Routledge, pp5–45

Cohen, S. and Zysman, J. (1987) *Manufacturing Matters: The Myth of the Post-Industrial Economy*. New York: Basic Books

Corpataux J., Crevoisier O. and Thierstein A. (2002) 'Exchange rate and regional divergence: The Swiss case'. *Regional Studies*, vol 36, pp611–626

Davezies, L. (1999) 'Le mythe d'une région spoliatrice'. *Pouvoirs Locaux*, no 40, pp38–46

Davoudi, S. (2003) 'Polycentricity in European spatial planning: From an analytical tool to a normative agenda'. *European Planning Studies*, vol 11, pp 979–999

DELG (Department of Environment, Heritage and Local Government) (2002) *National Spatial Strategy 2002–2020 for Ireland: People, Places and Potential*. Dublin: The Stationery Office

Department of Finance (1999) *Ireland: National Development Plan*. Dublin: The Stationery Office.

Derudder, B. and Taylor, P. J. (2003) 'The global capacity of Belgium's major cities: Antwerp and Brussels compared'. *Belgeo*, vol 4, pp459–476

Derudder, B., Vereecken, L. and Witlox, F. (2004) *An Appraisal of the Use of Airline Data in Assessments of the World City Network*. GaWC Research Bulletin 152. www.lboro.ac.uk/ gawc/publicat.html#bulletin accessed in December 2005

DETR (Department of the Environment, Transport and the Regions) (2000) *Our Towns and Cities: The Future* (Cm 4911). London: The Stationery Office

Dickinson, R. E. (1967) *The City Region in Western Europe*. London: Routledge & Kegan Paul

Diener, R., Herzog, J., Meili, M., Meuron, P. de and Schmid, C. (2005) *Die Schweiz. Ein Städtebauliches Porträt*. Basel: Birkhauser

DRA (Dublin Regional Authority) and MERA (Mid-East Regional Authority) (2004) *Regional Planning Guidelines: Greater Dublin Area*. Dublin: DRA and MERA

Dümmler, P. (2006) *Wissensbasierte Cluster in der Schweiz: Realität oder Fiktion? Das Beispiel der Medizinaltechnikbranche*. Bern: Haupt Verlag

Dümmler, P., Abegg, C., Kruse, C., Thierstein, A. (2004) *Standorte der innovativen Schweiz. Räumliche Veränderungsprozesse von High-Tech und Finanzdienstleistungen. Statistik der Schweiz, Analysen zur Betriebszählung 2001*. Neuchâtel: Bundesamt für Statistik

EERA (East of England Regional Assembly) (2004) *East of England Plan: Draft Revision to the Regional Spatial Strategy (RSS) for the East of England*. Bury St Edmunds: East of England Regional Assembly

*Egeraat, C. van, Sokol, M. and Yarwood, J. (2005) *POLYNET Action 1.2: Quantitative Analysis of Service Business Connections: Greater Dublin*. London: Institute of Community Studies/The Young Foundation & Polynet Partners

Eisinger, A. and Schneider, M. (eds) (2003) *Urbanscape Switzerland. Investigations and Case Studies on Development in Switzerland*. Basel: Birkhäuser

ESPON (2003) *ESPON Project 1.1.1: The Role, Specific Situation and Potentials of Urban Areas as Nodes in a Polycentric Development*. 3rd Interim Report, Part 3. Luxembourg: ESPON. www.espon.lu/online/documentation/projects/ thematic/0/3-ir.1.1.1_part_3.pdf accessed in January 2006

ESPON (2005) *ESPON Project 1.1.1: The Role, Specific Situation and Potentials of Urban Areas as Nodes in a Polycentric*

Development. Final Report; Final Version, 31 March. Luxembourg: ESPON. www.espon.lu/online/documentation/projects/thematic/1873/fr-1.1.1_revised.pdf accessed in January 2006

European Commission (1999) *ESDP: European Spatial Development Perspective: Towards Balanced and Sustainable Development of the Territory of the European Union*. Brussels: European Commission

European Council (2000) *Presidency Conclusions – Lisbon European Council, 23 and 24 March*. http://ue.eu.int/ueDocs/cms_Data/docs/pressData/en/ec/00100-r1.en0.htm accessed in December 2005

European Council (2005) *Presidency Conclusions – Brussels European Council 22 and 23 March 2005*. http://ue.eu.int/ueDocs/cms_Data/docs/pressData/en/ec/84335.pdf accessed in December 2005

Faludi, A. (2003) 'Unfinished business: European spatial planning in the 1990s'. *Town Planning Review*, vol 74, pp121–140

Faludi, A. (2004a) 'Spatial planning traditions in Europe: Their role in the ESDP process'. *International Planning Studies*, vol 9, pp155–172

Faludi, A. (2004b) 'The open method of co-ordination and "post-regulatory" territorial cohesion policy'. *European Planning Studies*, vol 12, pp1019–1033

Faludi, A. (2004c) 'Territorial cohesion: Old (French) wine in new bottles?' *Urban Studies*, vol 41, pp1349–1365

Faludi, A. (2005a) 'Territorial cohesion: An unidentified political objective'. *Town Planning Review*, vol 76, pp1–13

Faludi, A. (2005b) 'Polycentric territorial cohesion policy'. *Town Planning Review*, vol 76, pp107–118

Federal Council (Bundesrat) (2001) *Agglomerationspolitik des Bundes*. Bern: Swiss Federal Council

Federal Council (Bundesrat) (2002) *Nachhaltige Entwicklung 2002*. Bern: Swiss Federal Council

Federal Department of Economic Affairs (DEA) (Eidgenössisches Volkswirtschaftsdepartement) (2004) *Neue Regionalpolitik. Erläuternder Bericht für die Vernehmlassung*. Bern: Switzerland Federal Department of Economic Affairs

Federal Office for Spatial Development (Bundesamt für Raumentwicklung, ARE) (2005) *Raumentwicklungs-bericht*. Bern: Switzerland Federal Office for Spatial Development

Federal Office for Spatial Planning (1996) *Grundzüge der Raumordnung Schweiz*. Bern: Switzerland Federal Office for Spatial Planning

*Fischer, C., Freytag, T., Hoyler, M. and Mager, C. (2005a) *POLYNET Action 1.1: Commuting and the Definition of Functional Urban Regions: Rhine-Main*. London: Institute of Community Studies/The Young Foundation & Polynet Partners

*Fischer, C., Freytag, T., Hoyler, M. and Mager, C. (2005b) *POLYNET Action 1.2: Quantitative Analysis of Service Business Connections: Rhine-Main*. London: Institute of Community Studies/The Young Foundation & Polynet Partners

*Fischer, C., Freytag, T., Hoyler, M. and Mager, C. (2005c) *POLYNET Action 2.1: Qualitative Analysis of Service Business Connections: Rhine-Main*. London: Institute of Community Studies/The Young Foundation & Polynet Partners

Fischer, C., Freytag, T., Hoyler, M. and Mager, C. (2005d) 'Rhein-Main als polyzentrische Metropolregion: zur Geographie der Standortnetze von wissensintensiven Dienstleistungsunternehmen'. *Informationen zur Raument-wicklung*, no 7, pp439–446

Freund, B. (2002) *Hessen*. Gotha: Perthes

Friedmann, J. (1986) 'The world city hypothesis'. *Development and Change*, vol 17, pp69–83

Friedmann, J. (1995) 'Where We Stand: A Decade of World City Research', in Knox, P. L. and Taylor, P. J. (eds) *World Cities in a World System*. Cambridge: Cambridge University Press

Friedmann, J. and Wolff, G. (1982) 'World city formation: An agenda for research and action'. *International Journal of Urban and Regional Research*, vol 6, pp309–344

Garrison, W. L. and Marble, D. F. (1962) 'The structure of transportation networks'. *U.S. Army Transportation Command, Technical Report*, vol 62–II, pp62–88

Geddes, P. (1915) *Cities in Evolution*. London: Williams and Norgate. Reprinted (1998) in LeGates, R. and Stout, F. (eds) *Early Urban Planning 1870–1940*, vol 4. London: Routledge

Gershuny, J. and Miles, I. (1983) *The New Service Economy: The Transformation of Employment in Industrial Societies*. London: Frances Pinter

Gilli, F. (2005) 'La Bassin parisien, une région métropolitaine'. *Revue Européenne de Géographie*, no 305, pp1–20

*Glanzmann, L., Grillon, R., Kruse, C. and Thierstein, A. (2005) *POLYNET Action 2.1: Qualitative Analysis of Service Business Connections: Northern Switzerland*. London: Institute of Community Studies/The Young Foundation & Polynet Partners

Goddard, J. B. (1973) 'Office linkages and location'. *Progress in Planning*, vol 1, pp109–232

GOEM (Government Office for the East Midlands) (2005) *Regional Spatial Strategy for the East Midlands* (RSS8). Nottingham: GOEM

GOSE/GOEM/GOEE (Government Offices for the South East, East Midlands, East of England) (2005) *Milton Keynes & South Midlands Sub-Regional Strategy: Alterations to Regional Spatial Strategies covering the East of England, East Midlands and South East of England*. March 2005. London: The Stationery Office for ODPM

Gottmann, J. (1961) *Megalopolis: The Urbanized Northeastern Seaboard of the United States*. New York: Twentieth Century Fund

Graham, S. and Marvin, S. (1996) *Telecommunications and the City: Electronic Spaces, Urban Places*. London: Routledge

Gravier, J.-F. (1947) *Paris et le Désert français*. Paris: Le Portulan

*Green, N. (2004) *General Functional Polycentricity: A Definition*. POLYNET Working Papers. London: Institute of Community Studies/The Young Foundation & Polynet Partners

Haggett, P. (1965) *Locational Analysis in Human Geography*. London: Edward Arnold

Haig, R. M. (1926) 'Toward an understanding of the metropolis'. *Quarterly Journal of Economics*, vol 40, pp179–208, 402–434

Halbert, L. (2002) Les emplois supérieurs en Île-de-France. Vers de nouvelles polarités? Note Rapide de l'IAURIF, no 12 Bilan Stratégique du S.D.R.I.F. Paris: IAURIF

Halbert, L. (2004a) *Densité, deserrement, polycentrisme et transformation économique des aires métropolitaines*. Thèse pour Obtention du Grade de Docteur en Géographie de l'Université Paris-I

Halbert, L. (2004b) *La spécialisation économique des villes françaises*. Paris: DATAR.

Halbert, L. (2005a) 'Les limites du Polycentrisme Économique ou la Persistance de la Concentration en Région Francilienne', in DATAR (ed) *Territoires 2030*. Paris: DATAR, pp119–134

*Halbert, L. (2005b) *POLYNET Action 2.1: Qualitative Analysis of Service Business Connections: Bassin Parisien*. London: Institute of Community Studies/The Young Foundation & Polynet Partners

*Halbert, L. (2005c) *POLYNET Action 3.1: Analysis of Policy Documents & Policy Focus Groups: Bassin Parisien*. London: Institute of Community Studies/The Young Foundation & Polynet Partners

Hall, P. (1966) *The World Cities*. London: Weidenfeld and Nicolson

Hall, P. (1984) *The World Cities*, 3rd edition. London: Weidenfeld and Nicolson

Hall, P. (1988) 'Regions in the Transition to the Information Economy', in Sternlieb, G. (ed.) *America's New Market Geography*. Piscataway, NJ: Rutgers University, Center for Urban Policy Research, pp137–159

Hall, P. (1991) 'Moving Information: A Tale of Four Technologies', in Brotchie, J., Batty, M., Hall, P. and Newton, P. (ed.) *Cities of the 21st Century: New Technologies and Spatial Systems*. Melbourne: Longman Cheshire, pp1–21

Hall, P. (1993) 'Forces shaping urban Europe'. *Urban Studies*, vol 30, pp883–898

Hall, P. (1995a) 'The future of cities in Western Europe'. *European Review*, vol 3, pp161–169

Hall, P. (1995b) 'Towards a General Urban Theory', in Brotchie, J., Batty, M., Blakely, E., Hall, P. and Newton, P. (eds) *Cities in Competition: Productive and Sustainable Cities for the 21st Century*. Melbourne: Longman Australia, pp3–31

Hall, P. (1996) 'The global city'. *International Social Science Journal*, vol 147, pp15–23

Hall, P. (1998) *Cities in Civilization*. London: Weidenfeld and Nicolson

Hall, P. (1999) 'Planning for the Mega-City: A New Eastern Asian Urban Form?', in Brotchie, J., Newton, P., Hall, P. and Dickey, J. (eds) *East West Perspectives on 21st Century Urban Development: Sustainable Eastern and Western Cities in the New Millennium*. Aldershot: Ashgate, pp3–36

Hall, P. (2001) 'Global City-Regions in the Twenty-first Century', in Scott, A.J. (ed) *Global City-Regions: Trends, Theory, Policy*. Oxford: Oxford University Press, pp59–77

Hall, P. (2002) 'Christaller for a Global Age: Redrawing the Urban Hierarchy', in Mayr, A., Meurer, M. and Vogt, J. (eds) *Stadt und Region: Dynamik von Lebenswelten*. Leipzig: Deutsche Gesellschaft für Geographie, pp110–128

Hall, P. (2003) Growing the European Urban System. *ICS Working Paper WP3*. London: Institute of Community Studies

*Hall, P. (2004) *Polycentricity: Concept and Measurement. POLYNET Discussion Paper*. London: Institute of Community Studies/The Young Foundation.

Hall, P. (2005) 'Back to China – with no apologies'. *Town and Country Planning*, vol 74, pp220–221

Hall, P. and Hay, D. (1980) *Growth Centres in the European Urban System*. London: Heinemann

*Hall, P. and Pain, K. (2005) *POLYNET Action 3.1: Analysis of Policy Documents & Policy Focus Groups: South East England*. London: Institute of Community Studies/The Young Foundation & Polynet Partners

Hall, P., Thomas, R., Gracey, H. and Drewett, R. (1973) *The Containment of Urban England*. 2 volumes. London: George Allen and Unwin

Hart, M. 't (1994) 'Intercity Rivalries and the Making of the Dutch State', in Tilly, C. and Blockmans, W. P. (eds) *Cities and the Rise of States in Europe, A.D. 1000 to 1800*. Boulder, CO: Westview Press, pp196–217

Holtfrerich, C.-L. (1999) *Frankfurt as a Financial Centre: From Medieval Trade Fair to European Banking Centre*. München: C. H. Beck.

Ho-Shin, K. and Timberlake, M. (2000) 'World cities in Asia:

Cliques, centrality and connectedness'. *Urban Studies*, vol 37, pp2257–2285

Houtum, H. van and Lagendijk, A. (2001) 'Contextualising regional identity and imagination in the construction of polycentric urban regions: the cases of the Ruhr area and the Basque country'. *Urban Studies*, vol 38, pp747–767

*Hoyler, M., Mager, C., Freytag, T. and Berwing, S. (2005) *POLYNET Action 3.1: Analysis of Policy Documents & Policy Focus Groups: Rhine-Main*. London: Institute of Community Studies/The Young Foundation & Polynet Partners

Hoyler, M. and Pain, K. (2002) 'London and Frankfurt as World Cities: Changing Local-Global Relations', in Mayr, A., Meurer, M. and Vogt, J. (eds) *Stadt und Region: Dynamik von Lebenswelten. Tagungsbericht und Wissenschaftliche Abhandlungen*. Leipzig: Deutsche Gesellschaft für Geographie (DGfG), pp76–87

IAURIF (Institut d'Aménagement et d'Urbanisme de la Région Île de France) (1996) *North-West European Metropolitan Regions: Geographical Boundaries and Economic Structures*. Paris: IAURIF

Institut für Kulturgeographie, Stadt- und Regionalforschung (ed) (2000) *Regionalatlas Rhein-Main: Natur – Gesellschaft – Wirtschaft*. Frankfurt am Main: Selbstverlag des Instituts für Kulturgeographie, Stadt- und Regionalforschung der Johann-Wolfgang-Goethe Universität zu Frankfurt am Main

Ipenburg, D. and Lambregts, B. (2001) *Polynuclear Urban Regions in North West Europe: A Survey of Key Actor Views*. EURBANET Report 1, Housing and Urban Policy Studies 18. Delft: DUP Science

Ipenburg, D., Romein, A., Trip, J. J., de Vries, J. and Zonnenveld, W. (2001) *Transnational Perspectives on Megacorridors in North West Europe*. Corridesign Action 18, Project No. 0042. Delft: Delft Institute of Technology, OTB Research Institute for Housing, Urban and Mobility Studies

Jones, P. M., Dix, M. C., Clarke, M. I. and Heggie, I. G. (1983) *Understanding Travel Behaviour*. Aldershot: Gower

Keil, R. and Ronneberger, K. (1994) 'Going up the country: Internationalization and urbanization on Frankfurt's northern fringe'. *Environment and Planning* D, vol 12, pp137–166

King, A. D. (1990) *Global Cities: Post Imperialism and the Internationalization of London*. London: Routledge

Kloosterman, R. C. (2004) 'Recent employment trends in the cultural industries in Amsterdam, Rotterdam, The Hague and Utrecht: A first exploration'. *Tijdschrift voor Economische en Sociale Geografie*, vol 95, pp243–252

Kloosterman, R. C. and Lambregts, B. (2001) 'Clustering of economic activities in polycentric urban regions: The case of the Randstad'. *Urban Studies*, vol 38, pp717–732

Kloosterman, R. C. and Musterd, S. (2001) 'The polycentric urban region: Towards a research agenda'. *Urban Studies*, vol 38, pp623–633

Knapp, W., Kunzmann, K. R. and Schmitt, P. (2004) 'A co-operative spatial future for RheinRuhr'. *European Planning Studies*, vol 12, pp323–349

*Knapp, W., Scherhag, D. and Schmitt, P. (2005) *POLYNET Action 2.1: Qualitative Analysis of Service Business Connections: RhineRuhr*. London: Institute of Community Studies/The Young Foundation & Polynet Partners

Knapp, W. and Schmitt, P. (2002) 'The socio-economic profile of RheinRuhr'. (Economic Performance of the European Regions – GEMAC). *Les Cahiers de l'Institut d'Aménagement et d'Urbanisme de la Région d'Île-de-France (IAURIF)*, no 135, pp66–72

Knapp, W. and Schmitt, P. (2003) 'Re-structuring competitive metropolitan regions: On territory and governance. *European*

Journal of Spatial Development, Refereed Articles Oct 2003, no. 6. www.nordregio.se accessed in December 2005

*Knapp, W. and Schmitt, P. (2005) *POLYNET Action 3.1: Analysis of Policy Documents & Policy Focus Groups: RhineRuhr.* London: Institute of Community Studies/The Young Foundation & Polynet Partners

Knox, P. L. and Taylor, P. J (eds) (1995) *World Cities in a World System.* Cambridge: Cambridge University Press

Knox, P. L. and Taylor, P. J. (2004) *Globalisation of Architectural Practice.* GaWC Research Bulletin 128. www.lboro.ac.uk/gawc/publicat.html#bulletin accessed in December 2005

Kunzmann, K. R. (2004) 'An agenda for creative governance in city regions'. *DISP*, no 158, pp5–10

Kynaston, D. (1994) *The City of London.* Vol. I. *A World of Its Own 1815–1890.* London: Chatto & Windus

Kynaston, D. (1995) *The City of London.* Vol. II. *Golden Years 1890–1914.* London: Chatto & Windus

*Lambregts, B., Röling, R., Werff, M. van der, Kapoen, L., Kloosterman, R. and Korteweg, A. (2005a) *POLYNET Action 2.1: Qualitative Analysis of Service Business Connections: The Randstad.* London: Institute of Community Studies/The Young Foundation & Polynet Partners

*Lambregts, B., Röling, R., and Kloosterman, R. (2005b) *POLYNET Action 3.1: Analysis of Policy Documents & Policy Focus Groups: The Randstad.* London: Institute of Community Studies/The Young Foundation & Polynet Partners

*Lambregts, B., Werff, M. van der, and Kloosterman, R. (2005c) *POLYNET Action 1.2: Quantitative Analysis of Service Business Connections: The Randstad.* London: Institute of Community Studies/The Young Foundation & Polynet Partners

Lambregts, B. and Werff, M. van der (2004) 'International profiel van de Randstad in perspectief'. *Rooilijn*, vol 37, pp 270–276

Lambregts, B. and Zonneveld, W. (2004) 'From Randstad to Deltametropolis: Changing attitudes towards the scattered metropolis'. *European Planning Studies*, vol 12, pp299–321

Lang, R. E. and Dhavale, D. (2005) 'America's megalopolitan areas'. *Land Lines: Newsletter of the Lincoln Institute of Land Policy*, vol 17, no 3, pp1–4

Langhagen-Rohrbach, C. and Fischer, R. (2005) 'Region als Prozeß? Regionalwerkstatt FrankfurtRheinMain'. *Standort – Zeitschrift für Angewandte Geographie*, no 2, pp76–80

Llewelyn-Davies (1996) *Four World Cities: A Comparative Study of London, Paris, New York and Tokyo.* London: Comedia

Lösch, A. (1954) *The Economics of Location.* Translated by W. H. Woglom and W. F. Stolper. New Haven, CT: Yale University Press

MacLaran, A. and Killen, J. (2002) 'The suburbanisation of office development in Dublin and its transport implications'. *Journal of Irish Urban Studies*, vol 1, pp21–35

Magrini, S. (1999) 'The evolution of income disparities among the regions of the European Union'. *Regional Science and Urban Economics*, vol 29, pp257–281

Marchand, B. (1989) *Paris, Histoire d'une Ville, 19–20ᵉᵐᵉ Siècles.* Paris: Seuil

Marlet, G. and Woerkens, C. van (2003) *Atlas voor Gemeenten 2003.* Breukelen: NYFER Research Institute

Marshall, A. (1890) *Principles of Economics.* London: Macmillan

Mayor of London (2004) *The London Plan: Spatial Development Strategy for Greater London.* London: Greater London Authority.

McGee, T. G. (1995) 'Metrofitting the Emerging Mega-Urban Regions of ASEAN', in McGee, T. G. and Robinson, I. (eds) *The Mega-Urban Regions of Southeast Asia.* Vancouver: University of British Columbia Press

Meijers, E. (2005) 'Polycentric urban regions and the quest for synergy: Is a network of cities more than the sum of the parts?' *Urban Studies*, vol 42, pp765–781

Ministerie van Volkshuisvesting, Ruimtelijke Ordening en Milieu (VROM) (2004) *Nota Ruimte: Ruimte voor Ontwikkeling. Deel 3: Kabinetsstandpunt.* The Hague: Ministry of Housing, Spatial Planning and the Environment

Mitchell, W. J. (1995) *City of Bits: Space, Place and the Infobahn.* Cambridge, MA: MIT Press

Mitchell, W. J. (1999) *E-topia: Urban Life, Jim – But Not As We Know It.* Cambridge, MA: MIT Press

Mogridge, M. J. H. and Parr, J. B. (1997) 'Metropolis or region: On the development and structure of London'. *Regional Studies*, vol 31, pp97–115

Mokhtarian, P. L. and Meenakshisundaram, R. (1999) 'Beyond tele-substitution: disaggregate longitudinal structural equations modeling of communication impacts'. *Transportation Research* C, vol 7, pp33–52

Moran, M. (1991) *The Politics of the Financial Services Revolution: The USA, UK and Japan.* Basingstoke: Macmillan

Morgenroth, E. (2004) 'Decentralisation: High cost for little return'. *Irish Independent*, 4 February

MURL (Ministerium für Umwelt, Raumordnung und Landwirtschaft des Landes NRW) (ed.) (1995) *LEP NRW. Landesentwicklungsplan Nordrhein-Westfalen. Landesentwicklungsprogramm – Landesplanungsgesetz.* Düsseldorf: MURL

Myrdal, G. (1957) *Economic Theory and Under-Developed Regions.* London: Gerald Duckworth

Nadin, V. and Duhr, S. (2005) 'Some help with Euro-planning jargon'. *Town and Country Planning*, vol 74, p82

NWMA Spatial Vision Group (2000) *Spatial Vision for the North Western Metropolitan Area (NWMA).* Bristol: University of the West of England

OECD (Organisation for Economic Co-operation and Development) (2002) *Territorial Reviews: Switzerland.* Paris: OECD

ODPM (Office of the Deputy Prime Minister) (2003a) *Sustainable Communities: Building for the Future.* London: ODPM

ODPM (Office of the Deputy Prime Minister) (2003b) *Creating Sustainable Communities: Making it Happen: Thames Gateway and the Growth Areas.* London: ODPM

Pain, K. (2005) *Spaces of Practice in Advanced Business services: The Case of London and Frankfurt.* GaWC Research Bulletin 84(B). www.lboro.ac.uk/gawc/publicat.html#bulletin accessed in December 2005

Parr, J. B. (2004) 'The polycentric urban region: A closer inspection'. *Regional Studies*, vol 38, pp231–240

Planungsverband Ballungsraum Frankfurt/Rhein-Main and Regierungspräsidium Darmstadt (2005) *Frankfurt/Rhein-Main 2020 – the European Metropolitan Region. Strategic Vision for the Regional Land Use Plan and for the Regionalplan Südhessen.* Frankfurt, Darmstadt: Planungsverband

Porter, M. E. (1998) 'Clusters and the new economics of competition'. *Harvard Business Review*, vol 76, pp77–90

*Potts, G. and Pain, K. (2005) *POLYNET Action 2.1: Qualititative Analysis of Service Business Connections: South East England.* London: Institute of Community Studies/The Young Foundation & Polynet Partners

Pred, A. R. (1973) *Urban Growth and the Circulation of Information: The United States System of Cities 1790–1840.* Cambridge, MA: Harvard University Press

Pred, A. R. (1977) *City Systems in Advanced Economies: Past Growth, Present Processes and Future Development Options.* London: Hutchinson

Préfecture de la Région Île-de-France, Direction Régional de l'Equipment (1994) *Schémadirecteur de la Région d'Île-de-France*. Paris: La Préfecture

Putnam, R. D. (2000) *Bowling Alone: The Collapse and Revival of American Community*. New York: Simon and Schuster

Rellstab, U. (2004) *Die Schweiz muss neu eingeteilt werden*. Zürich: Verein Metropole Schweiz

Roger Tym & Partners (2005) *South East Counties: The Cost and Funding of Growth in South East England*. London: Roger Tym & Partners

Saey P. (1981) 'De evolutie van het stedennet in Oost- en West-Vlaanderen'. *De Aardrijkskunde*, nos 1–2, pp223–232

Sassen, S. (1991) *The Global City*. Princeton, NJ Princeton University Press

Sassen, S. (1994) 'La ville globale. Eléments pour une lecture de Paris'. *Le Débat*, no 80, pp146–164

Sassen, S. (2001) *The Global City*, 2nd edition. Princeton, NJ: Princeton University Press

Sassen, S. (ed) (2002) *Global Networks, Linked Cities*. New York: Routledge

Schamp, E. W. (2002) 'From Industry to Services: The Changing Basis of the Frankfurt/Rhein-Main Metropolitan Economy', in Felsenstein, D., Schamp, E. W. and Shachar, A. (eds) *Emerging Nodes in the Global Economy: Frankfurt and Tel Aviv Compared*. Dordrecht: Kluwer, pp11–34

Scheller, J. P. (1998) *Rhein-Main: eine Region auf dem Weg zur politischen Existenz*. Frankfurt: Institut für Kulturgeographie, Stadt- und Regionalforschung der Johann-Wolfgang-Goethe-Universität Frankfurt am Main.

Schmitt, P. and Knapp, W. (2001) 'The RheinRuhr Area', in Ipenburg, D. and Lambregts, B. (eds) *Polynuclear Urban Regions in North West Europe. A Survey of Key Actors' Views*. Delft: Delft University Press, pp78–100

Schmitt, P., Knapp, W. and Kunzmann, K. R. (2003) 'RhineRuhr', in Meijers, E., Romein, A. and Lambregts, B. (eds) *Planning Polycentric Urban Regions in North West Europe: Value, Feasibility and Design*. Delft: Delft University Press, pp154–195

Scott, A. J. (ed) (2001) *Global City-Regions: Trends, Theory, Policy*. Oxford: Oxford University Press

SEERA (South East England Regional Assembly) (2005) *Clear Vision for the South East: Draft South East Plan*: Part 1: *Core Regional Policies*. Guildford: SEERA

Sieverts, T. (1999) *Zwischenstadt: zwischen Ort und Welt, Raum und Zeit, Stadt und Land*, 3rd edition. Braunschweig, Wiesbaden: Vieweg

Sit, V. F. S. and Yang, C. (1997) 'Foreign-investment-induced exo-urbanisation in the Pearl River Delta, China'. *Urban Studies*, vol 34, pp647–677

Smith, D. A. and Timberlake, M. (1995) 'Cities in Global Matrices: Toward Mapping the World-System's City System', in Knox, P. L. and Taylor, P. J. (eds) *World Cities in a World System*. Cambridge: Cambridge University Press, pp79–97

Sokol, M. and Egeraat, C. van (2005a) Locational Strategies of Advanced Producer Services in Dublin: Towards a Polycentric Mega-city Region? Paper presented to the *Regional Studies Association (RSA) Annual International Conference 'Regional Growth Agendas'* (Gateway 4: Strategic Spatial Planning), University of Aalborg, Aalborg, Denmark, 28–31 May

*Sokol, M. and Egeraat, C. van (2005b) *POLYNET Action 2.1: Qualitative Analysis of Service Business Connections: Greater Dublin*. London: Institute of Community Studies/The Young Foundation & Polynet Partners

*Stafford, P., Sokol, M. and Convery, F. (2005) *POLYNET Action 3.1: Analysis of Policy Documents & Policy Focus Groups: Greater Dublin*. London: Institute of Community Studies/The Young Foundation & Polynet Partners

Stewart, J. Q. (1959) 'Physics of population distribution'. *Journal of Regional Science*, vol 1, pp99–123

Stiftung Greater Zürich Area Standortmarketing (2003) *Standortmonitoring Wirtschaftsraum Zürich 2003*. Zürich: No publisher

Taylor, P. J. (2001) 'Specification of the world city network'. *Geographical Analysis*, vol 33, pp181–94

Taylor, P. J. (2003) 'European Cities in the World Network', in Dijk, H. van (ed) *The European Metropolis 1920–2000*. Rotterdam: Erasmus Universiteit. http://hdl.handle.net/1765/1021 accessed in January 2006

Taylor, P. J. (2004a) *World City Network: A Global Urban Analysis*. London: Routledge

Taylor, P. J. (2004b) *Leading World Cities: Empirical Evaluations of Urban Nodes in Multiple Networks*. GaWC Research Bulletin 146. www.lboro.ac.uk/gawc/publicat.html#bulletin accessed in December 2005

Taylor, P., Beaverstock, J., Cook, G., Pandit, N., Pain, K. and Greenwood, H. (2003) *Financial Services Clustering and its Significance for London*. London: Corporation of London

Taylor, P., Catalano, G. and Gane, N. (2002a) 'A geography of global change: Cities and services 2000–01'. *Urban Geography*, vol 24, pp431–441

Taylor, P. J., Catalano, G. and Walker, D. R. F. (2002b) 'Measurement of the world city network'. *Urban Studies*, vol 39, pp2367–2376

Taylor, P. J., Walker, D. R. F., Beaverstock, J.V. (2002c) 'Firms and Their Global Service Networks', in Sassen, S. (ed) *Global Networks, Linked Cities*. London: Routledge, pp93–115

Thierstein, A., Held, T. and Gabi, S. (2003) 'City of Regions. Glattal-Stadt as an Area of Complex Institutional Levels Needs Reforms', in Schneider, M. and Eisinger, A. (eds) *Urbanscape Switzerland. Investigations and Case Studies on Development in Switzerland*. Basel: Birkhäuser, pp273–306

*Thierstein, A., Kruse, C., Gabi, S., and Glanzmann, L. (2005) *POLYNET Action 3.1: Analysis of Policy Documents & Policy Focus Groups: Northern Switzerland*. London: Institute of Community Studies/The Young Foundation & Polynet Partners

Thomas, R. (1969) *London's New Towns: A Study of Self-contained and Balanced Communities*. London: PEP

Tinkler, K. J. (1977) *An Introduction to Graph Theoretical Methods in Geography*. Norwich: Geo Abstracts

Thrift, N. (1987) 'The Fixers: The Urban Geography of International Commercial Capital', in Henderson, J. and Castells, M. (eds) *Global Restructuring and Territorial Development*. London: Sage, pp203–233

Tripartite Agglomerationskonferenz (TAK) (ed) (2004) *Horizontale und vertikale Zusammenarbeit in der Agglomeration*. Bern: TAK

Turok, I. and Bailey, N. (2004) 'The theory of polynuclear urban regions and its application to central Scotland'. *European Planning Studies*, vol 12, pp371–389

UNCTAD (United Nations Conference on Trade and Development) (2004) *World Investment Report 2004, The Shift Towards Services*. New York and Geneva: United Nations

Urban Task Force (1999) *Towards an Urban Renaissance*. London: Spon

Vandermotten, C. and Vandewattyne, P. (1985) 'Les étapes de la croissance et de la formation des armatures urbaines en Belgique'. *Bulletin du Crédit Communal*, no 154, pp41–62

Wenglenski, S. (2004) *Une mesure des disparités sociales d'accessibilité au marché de l'emploi en Île-de-France*. Créteil: Thèse Université Paris-12

*Werff, M. van der, Lambregts, B., Kapoen, L. and Kloosterman, R. (2005) *POLYNET Action 1.1: Commuting & the Definition of Functional Urban Regions: The Randstad*. London: Institute of Community Studies/The Young Foundation & Polynet Partners

Williams, B. and MacLaran, A. (1996) 'Incentive Areas for Urban Renewal', in Drudy, P and Maclaran, A. (eds), *Dublin Economic and Social Trends*, vol 2. Dublin: Centre for Urban & Regional Studies, Trinity College Dublin, pp43–46

Wolf, J., Guensler, R. and Bachman, W. (2001) 'Elimination of the travel diary: An experiment to derive trip purpose from GPS travel data'. *Transportation Research Record*, no 1768, pp125–134

Wood, P. (2002) *Consultancy and Innovation: The Business Service Revolution in Europe*. London: Routledge

Xu, X.-Q. and Li, S.-M. (1990) 'China open door policy and urbanization in the Pearl River Delta region'. *International Journal of Urban and Regional Research*, vol 14, pp49–69

*Yarwood, J., Sokol, M. and Egeraat, C. van (2004) *POLYNET Action 1.1: Commuting & the Definition of Functional Urban Regions: Greater Dublin*. London: Institute of Community Studies/The Young Foundation & Polynet Partners

Yeh, A. G. O. (2001) 'Hong Kong and the Pearl River Delta: Competition or cooperation?'. *Built Environment*, vol 27, pp129–145

Yeung, Y. M. (1996) 'An Asian perspective on the global city'. *International Social Science Journal*, vol 147, pp25–31

Zonnenveld W. and Waterhout, B. (2005) 'Visions on territorial cohesion'. *Town Planning Review*, vol 76, pp15–28

Index